# TERROR AND PERFORMANCE

# TERROR AND PERFORMANCE

RUSTOM BHARUCHA

Tulika Books

Published in 2014 by
**Tulika Books**
35 A/1 Shahpur Jat, New Delhi 110 049, India
tulikabooks.wordpress.com



ISBN: 978-93-82381-37-2

*For sale in India and South Asia only*

Printed at Chaman Offset, Delhi 110 002

*In memory of*

JAN KOTT *and*

DRAGAN KLAIĆ

# CONTENTS

*America is afraid.*

– Jean Genet

*[D]oes terrorism have to work only through death? Can't one terrorize without killing? And does killing necessarily mean putting to death? Isn't it also 'letting die'? Can't 'letting die', 'not wanting to know that one is letting others die' . . . also be part of a 'more or less' conscious and deliberate terrorist strategy?*

– Jacques Derrida

*What difference does it make to the dead, the orphans, and the homeless, whether the mad destruction is wrought under the name of totalitarianism, or the holy name of liberty and democracy?*

– Mahatma Gandhi

# PREFACE

> [In the state of nature], men live without a common Power to keep them all in awe, they are in that condition which is called Warre; and such a warre as is of every man against every man . . . In such condition, there is no place for Industry . . . no account of Time; no Arts, no Letters; no Society; and, which is worst of all, continuall feare, and danger of violent death; And the life of man, solitary, poore, nasty, brutish, and short.
>
> Thomas Hobbes, *Leviathan*

Rethinking Hobbes's 'warre' of 'every man against every man' in the context of the global war on terror in the twenty-first century, the critical reflections on terror in this book, envisioned through the lens of performance, have proved to be 'nasty', 'brutish', but not 'short'. If anything, writing about terror, as I have discovered in trying to bring this book to an end, is a seemingly infinite process, as it brings one in touch with a ceaselessly deferred future which resonates in the turbulent immediacies of the here and now. Inevitably, this writing demands stamina as it faces an onslaught of uncertainties and cruelties at a global level that challenges the basic assumptions of what it means to be human. Leaving aside the fundamental impulse as to why one would want to subject one's self to unease by living with terror one more time through the act of writing – it is hard enough living with it in everyday life – I will leave you to read in the introduction to this book the uncanny accident that compelled me to write about terror in the first place. Suffice it to say that once one starts writing about terror, there are at least two predicaments that one faces as a writer.

The first is a no-exit condition, not in an existential Sartrean sense, but in what I would regard as a more mythic predicament of not being able to free one's self from the closure of violence, in which one is more likely to come out dead than alive. I have in mind here the formidable, labyrinthine military formation of the *chakravyuha* in the *Mahabharata* where the young warrior, Abhimanyu, valiantly counters the multi-directional attack of the Kauravas, whom he slaughters only to realize that there is no exit from this battleground. In one of the many versions of the epic, we learn in a flashback that Abhimanyu, while secreted in his mother's womb, had eavesdropped on his father Arjuna telling his mother Subhadra the secret of infiltrating the *chakravyuha*. But, unaccountably, Subhadra falls asleep and Arjuna is not able to tell her how to exit the military formation. Consequently, with half-knowledge of battle and survival, Abhimanyu himself is slaughtered within the *chakravyuha*, reminding us that he could be regarded, for all his heroic demeanour, as an adolescent child-soldier, one among thousands in the world today who get indoctrinated by the ethos of righteous violence only to find that they cannot leave the ranks of the living dead.[1]

If Abhimanyu's predicament may seem too mediated by myth and destiny, let us consider the second predicament faced in writing about terror, where one has no other choice but to accept a state of suspension. Here one recalls that dour Scotsman who, with unabashed Elizabethan flamboyance, voices what has been for me a deeply unsettling, yet familiar state of unease. Haunted by the fact that he is not able to reverse the tide of terror, Macbeth reflects with deep metaphorical density: 'I am in blood / Stepp'd in so far that, should I wade no more, / Returning were as tedious as go o'er.' Trust Shakespeare to come up with the unpredictable word that resonates with startling pertinence – not 'blood', which is the most obvious sign of terror, but the fact that returning through the sea of blood is a massively *tedious* exercise. Once one enters the narrative of terror, one has no other choice but to keep wading through the blood even as the possibility of reaching the other side cannot be readily assumed.

Not a warrior, but a writer struggling to make sense of the terror of our times, I draw some solace from the predicaments of both Abhimanyu and Macbeth. In a less metaphorical register, however, I would emphasize that getting to the end of a book on terror does not make me a 'terror expert'. In other words, I have no allegiance to or any particular interest in aligning my research to anti-terror political think-tanks, whose manipulations of defence, security and surveillance need to be strongly questioned rather than endorsed. I write out of my affinities to the humanities, and, more specifically, out of my immersion in the field of theatre and performance studies, which enables me to 'see' terror in specific ways – not with any omniscience, but through a glass darkly.

In the beginning of the end that the preface to any book signifies, I would acknowledge that I did not quite know what would evolve – and mutate – in the course of writing this book. When I started writing it three years ago at the International Research Centre/Interweaving Performance Cultures in Berlin, rewriting some key passages from earlier essays on 'Muslims and Others' (2003a) and 'Genet in Manila: Reclaiming the Chaos of our Times' (2003b), terror seemed so tangible that I failed to reckon with its multitudinous discourse, almost hydra-like, with one text almost killing the other in a ceaseless cycle of never-ending verbiage. Terror, I soon discovered, has an unsettling capacity to proliferate through words.

And yet it is necessary to point out that this surfeit of discourses on terror is of relatively recent origin. Reviewing Benjamin Netanyahu's *Terrorism: How the West Can Win* (1986) at a time when Netanyahu was the Israeli ambassador to the United Nations, Edward Said had questioned the absence of an object in the title of Netanyahu's book: 'Win what?' Contextualizing his review within the vacuity of the larger discourse of terrorism, Said had commented with critical insight:

> Today's discourse on terrorism is an altogether . . . streamlined thing. Its scholarship is yesterday's newspaper or today's CNN bulletin. Its gurus . . . are journalists with obscure, even ambiguous backgrounds. Most writing about terrorism is brief, pithy, totally devoid of the scholarly armature of evidence, proof, argument. Its paradigm is the television interview, the spot news announcement, the instant gratification one associates with the Reagan White House's 'reality time,' the evening news.[2]

This was first published in *The Nation* on 14 June 1986, long before 'September 11' and the 'war on terror' had catalysed the war of words on terrorism, and even before the Gulf War and Operation Desert Storm of 1990–91 had prefigured the terror lying ahead.

Today, in the aftermath of these deadly events, the literature around terrorism has grown substantially, with extraordinary inputs by some of the leading thinkers of our times, some of whom are addressed in this book, such as Jacques Derrida (2003), Tzvetan Todorov (2009), Paul Virilio (2003), Susan Buck-Morss (2003), Talal Asad (2007), Gayatri Chakravorty Spivak (2004), Mahmood Mamdani (2004), and experts on visual studies, international relations and anthropology, such as W.J.T. Mitchell (2011), James Der Derian (2009a) and E. Valentine Daniel (1996), respectively, to name just a few of the writers whose work has enabled me to think through terror in this book. Clearly, there is no dearth of complexity in the academic discourse on terrorism and extreme states of violence today.

However, if one had to position these relatively few scholarly interventions against the mind-numbing fact that 'since 9/11 a new book on terrorism has been published in English every six hours' (*The Guardian*, 3 July 2007),[3] perhaps one can begin to realize that some of Said's reservations on the mainstream discourse of terrorism still hold true. Much of this writing is not so much a product of critical thinking as it is an 'aid to political decision-making' by intelligence services, public sector organizations, security think-tanks and international commissions, whose self-appointed task is to provide pragmatic analyses and solutions to the war on terror 'in the face of a threat presented as imminent'.[4] Even as this threat seems to have ebbed, if we are to believe recent media reports in the United States, and grander narratives like Steven Pinker's (2011) tome on 'the decline of violence in history and its causes', I would be far more circumspect about linking the alleged quantitative decline in the number of terrorist attacks and mass genocides to the disappearance of terror in our times.[5] Rather, I would call attention to the disturbing fact that terror has the capacity to lurk and go underground within the inner recesses of human consciousness, which are elusive and hard to measure.

To complicate the scenario, I discovered in the course of researching the book that if the discourse on terror has proliferated, the same can be said for performance, which has received an exponential degree of attention in academic writing, with only some 127 dissertations on performance written between 1861–1944 and over 100,000 written since then.[6] As the category of 'performance' expands into new areas of investigation like performance management and techno-performance, whose interdependent genealogies have been brilliantly mapped by Jon McKenzie (2001), the older associations of 'performance' in performance studies, drawn from the practices and techniques of theatre and ritual anthropology, have come under considerable stress.

In addition, as James Der Derian has elaborated in *Virtuous War* (2009a), the innovation of virtual weapons and missiles has resulted in new assessments of 'performance', which are controlled by technocrats and military experts, in collusion with the hard-sell marketing strategies of the war industry. Weapons and missiles, not least in relation to the recent spate of drone attacks, have become the most deadly performers of our times. Not a Luddite, but nonetheless technically challenged, I must acknowledge that my reading of performance in this book is not high-tech. Later, in the introduction, I will elaborate on how I use the word 'performance' within the more familiar discourses and embodied practices of theatre and performance studies, cultural studies, visual studies and critical theory, but also stretched by the new imaginaries and technologies of our times.

Without underestimating the demands involved in bringing terror and performance together through a spectrum of relationships, one of the most rewarding aspects of writing this book has been its dialogical process. For some curious reason, which is unprecedented in my experience as a writer, I found myself turning relentlessly to individuals, friends and strangers, scattered in different parts of the world, trained in different disciplines and creative practices, to clarify specific questions relating to terror. Despite the numerous books that I could turn to for reference, these questions demanded a more personal interrogation and verification, some of which fuel critical junctures of thought in the book.

Let me thank, in this regard, the victims of my numerous e-mails and Skype conversations: Ananda Breed for the generous sharing of her formative research on *gacaca* in Rwanda, to which I am deeply indebted; Ajay Skaria and Tridip Suhrud for their close readings of Gandhi; Christina Zück for alerting me to the virtual archives of terror; Joseph Pugliese for sharing his deeply compassionate essays on refugees and asylum seekers in Australia; Judy Freya Sibayan and Rody Vera for their contributions to my production of *The Maids* in Manila, produced by PETA (Philippine Educational Theater Association); Khalid Amine for arranging a special trip to Larache, Morocco, where I could pay homage to one of the key spirits of this book, Jean Genet; Lawrence Liang, bibliophile, for his prompt responses to my ceaseless requests for books; Paul Rae and Frederick Hertz for their perceptive comments on 'passing' and 'covering'; Pepita Seth for her visionary perspective of Theyyam; Premesh Lalu for his valuable references on key texts relating to the Truth and Reconciliation Commission (TRC) in South Africa, notably Adam Sitze's reading of the TRC as an 'impossible machine'; Ray Langenbach for his unfailingly rigorous guidance on performative matters with laser-sharp critical insights; Teesta Setalvad for her courage and stamina in sustaining the struggle for justice in relation to the genocide in Gujarat; and Veenapani Chawla for her precise inputs on Sri Aurobindo's views on 'just war'. From this spectrum of inputs I would acknowledge that one is not alone in thinking about terror, and that, oddly enough, terror has the capacity not only to kill, but to bring friends and strangers together in new alliances and solidarities.

In a more formal register, I wish to thank Erika Fischer-Lichte, Christel Weiler, Holger Hartung and Claudia Daseking, among other staff members of the International Research Centre/Interweaving Performance Cultures in Berlin, for their care and generosity which made my sporadic, three-year residency as a Fellow in the Centre so productive. I am particularly grateful to the research associates and student assistants for their support on technical matters and library facilities, and to Katrin Wächter in particular for re-formatting my manuscript. To the Fellows of the Centre between 2010–12 I owe my thanks for their collegial support and intellectual inputs. Likewise, I would like to thank my colleagues at the School of Arts and Aesthetics at the Jawaharlal Nehru University in New Delhi for their warmth and convivial support.

I am particularly indebted to four readers of my book – Sundar Sarukkai, Ray Langenbach, Janelle Reinelt, Rowena Hill – whose exacting and honest comments proved to be challenging and productive. Manas Ray and Gene Ray also provided useful perspectives on sections in the book. Five readers of the

Routledge edition of the book, including Stephen Barber, Jennifer Hughes and Alan Read, in addition to two anonymous readers, also provided constructive criticism. To Stephen, in particular, I owe a special debt for his quiet professional and fraternal advice in suggesting valuable cuts when my book was threatening to get out of control, and for his long-distance consultation on publishing matters. I owe a special debt of thanks to Indu Chandrasekhar of Tulika Books for her editorial care and down-to-earth advice. I am also grateful to Shad Naved for his painstaking and highly informed copy-edit of my manuscript. It has been a pleasure to work with them.

Finally, I would like to dedicate this book to Jan Kott, former mentor at the Yale School of Drama, not only for the performativity that he read into states of terror, but for the grit, wit and survival tactics by which he not merely evaded terror during the worst years of the Second World War, but even got a kick out of doing so. Dragan Klaić was a different kind of survivor during the disintegration of the former Yugoslavia, as he chose a life of exile with cosmopolitan civility and a droll sense of humour. Both these mentors and friends have passed on, but I would like to believe that their capacity to think critically through the worst of times serves as an inspiration for the struggle that has gone into writing this book.

# INTRODUCTION
## Mapping Terror in the War of Words

### PROVOCATION

On 1 October 2001 I am in Manila beginning to direct a production of Jean Genet's *The Maids*, barely three weeks after a critical event hit the world and got identified in the media as 'September 11'.[1] In the weeks that follow I direct the play haunted by the explosive power of terror, if not by the imminence of another attack. However, there is not enough time to actually *process* the unfolding of 'September 11' through the virulence of its mediatization, not least because its narrative is mutating and metamorphosing in disturbing ways even as the production acquires a life of its own. Only in critical hindsight do I realize how terror entered the political unconscious of the production even as it was not consciously inscribed in the *mise-en-scène*.

When the short run of the play ends in Manila on 24 November 2001 and I am back in my home-city of Kolkata, seeking refuge in the habitual chaos that animates the daily life of the city, something happens: nothing of magnitude, not another terrorist attack, just a minor event that does not get represented in the international news even though it receives some reportage in the newspapers of Manila. The Republic of Malate, the funky bar and dance club in which *The Maids* had staged their rage against Madame, burned down on 27 November 2001, just three days after the last show of the production. Nothing remained of the Republic: it was burned to ashes.

Was this an accident or an act of arson? An attack or sabotage? Following Paul Virilio's instruction that the elements of destruction are already factored into the technology of any apparatus, the theatre, both as an institution and as an actual site of production, cannot claim any immunity from the imminence of accidents.[2] We will elaborate on this axiomatic condition later in the book, but for the moment let us hold on to Virilio's prescient reminder that 'the accident is inseparable from its velocity of unexpected emergence' – a velocity whose invisibility is perhaps more lethal than its material manifestation.[3]

Fortunately, there were no casualties at the Republic of Malate, but given the fact that the only entrance to this 'theatre' was also its exit, there could have been many charred bodies if the fire had broken out during the dress rehearsals or the actual run of the production. Without sounding unduly alarmist, I might not have been alive to be writing this narrative in the first place. More will be said in the first chapter of this book about Genet in Manila, 'September 11' and the burning of the theatre. However I might as well acknowledge these juxtapositions at the start of the narrative as a *provocation*, the spark that catalyses the agenda of this book, through the short-circuits of diverse performances disrupted by the actualities of terror.

Not having witnessed the actual burning of the Republic of Malate, I could afford to interpret it, in the aftermath of the production, through the comfort of metaphor – the ashes of the theatre providing a central trope for the perilous evanescence of performance. A short critical essay emerged, entitled 'Genet in Manila: Reclaiming the Chaos of Our Times' (2003b), in which 'September 11' provided an arresting backdrop for a reflection on theatre in the context of 'chaos' rather than 'terror'. In retrospect, I would acknowledge that the thesis of this essay was somewhat too buoyant in its uncomplicated radicality: it is better, I had argued, to live with chaos and to resist 'chaos management', just as it is necessary to fight terrorism by countering counter-terrorism. The essay had some circulation in postcolonial and Genet studies, and I could have allowed it to pass, had the political unconscious of its unwritten text not continued to haunt me.

Some years later, while attempting to rework the essay through an integration of several insights generated around the discourse of 'September 11', not least Jacques Derrida's subversive reading of 'autoimmunity' in the larger context of the 'war on terror',[4] I faced a crisis. Challenging my naive assumption that the rewrite of the essay would not pose any particular problem, something uncanny happened: almost like a letter-bomb or some minuscule weapon hidden in the recesses of my computer, the unformulated content of the essay exploded as it were in my face. I found myself confronting the hard truth that it was no longer possible to circumvent terror through a fictionalization of a somewhat bizarre theatrical accident; I had to *think through it*. Therefore, from providing the mere background of an essay, terror is now foregrounded in this book, doubling as both its catalyst and subject in and through its relationship to performance.

## IMPULSE

While the burning of the theatre can be regarded as the provocation of the book, its actual creative impulse is somewhat more idealistic, as I have been driven by one pivotal question: How can one free terror from the hegemonic discourse of terrorism? This disentangling of terror from terrorism can be seen as a dilution of the political, even as a capitulation to a form of philosophical thinking that risks anaesthetizing the 'real'. However, I would argue that the only way of breathing life into the vocabulary of terror is to insist that it should not be conflated with what has come to be hegemonized as 'terrorism', even as Talal Asad reminds us that, in terms of actual usage and discursive practice, terror has become a 'shorthand' for terrorism.[5]

I could be challenged: Why this impulse, this somewhat anarchist desire to 'free' terror? Today's language of terrorism, I would respond, is inseparable from the larger discourse that has emerged around 'September 11', which has been primarily authored, produced and performed by the Security and Defense Departments of the United States, buttressed by a plethora of warmongering think-tanks and advisory committees, information and disinformation services. If one wishes to counter this discourse and emphasize the obvious fact that Americans are not the exclusive victims of terror, then one needs to acknowledge that terror is experienced in multitudinous, palpable and infinitesimal ways across the world, where ordinary people live *with* terror on a daily basis.

In this scenario, which is more truly global than the essentially American war on terror, there needs to be some way of calling attention to these other manifestations of terror which are not determined by 'September 11' even though they may be affected by its fall-out. Far from being exceptional, terror can be regarded as the new banality of evil in our times, functioning in a diversity of ways, open to a spectrum of causes, manipulations, rumours, fears, tensions and resentments, ranging from the most global and national of political interventions to the most quotidian intimacies of everyday life. Terror can strike when one least expects it, not just in cyberspace or the anonymity of the global city, but in the most familiar of neighbourhoods and streets.

Having acknowledged my impulse to free terror from terrorism, I should also acknowledge that it is fraught with methodological and theoretical problems. To spell out a bitter home truth which emerged in the actual writing of this book: even as the impulse to free terror from terrorism is desirable and necessary, it is not exactly *viable* given the sheer dominance of the discourse on terrorism today, which may be engineered by the United States but which has proliferated worldwide, both among its allies and adversaries. Indeed, as much as one needs to resist the conflation of terror with the so-called 'war on terror' precipitated by 'September 11', it is not easy to dis-imbricate the diverse epistemologies and affects of terror from the larger rhetorical and political apparatus of terrorism in which it is subsumed.

In effect, all we can do is to keep the tensions alive between 'terror' and 'terrorism' by calling attention to different contexts, modalities and histories of terror, which, in this book, extend to an examination of communal violence in the Indian subcontinent, the genocide in Rwanda, and the intensified racial divides following the Truth and Reconciliation process in South Africa, among other insurrections and failed experiments in peace-building and secular coexistence. As will become apparent in the course of the book, these widespread manifestations of terror demand their own articulations of local, regional and national contexts, whcih tend to be flattened, if not erased, within the terrorist imperatives of the 'September 11' narrative. In close engagement with these diverse contexts, therefore, this book is an attempt to open the multiple languages of terror, not merely to inflect the global discourse of terrorism, but to suggest other ways in which it can be understood and resisted at more concrete levels of lived history and experience.

## DOUBLESPEAK OF 'TERRORISM'

Enough has been said for the discerning reader to demand some clarity on the terms being used, not least 'terrorism' and 'terror'. What follows is a brief exposition of these terms at discursive and disciplinary levels. Even as there is no consensus on the official definitions of terrorism, we have no other option but to engage with them, not least because they could be the most powerful legitimizing devices for the perpetration of terror in our times. The absence or lack of consensus around adequate official definitions does not stop them from being used in insidious ways.

If we turn to the prevailing definition of 'terrorism' provided by the US State Department – a definition which preceded and framed the 'war on terror' – we learn that it is identified as '[p]remeditated, politically motivated violence perpetrated against noncombatant* targets by subnational groups or clandestine agents, usually intended to influence an audience'.[6] The asterisk following 'noncombatant' indicates that, for the State Department, the word refers not only to 'civilians' (the target of most terrorist attacks, also identified as 'innocent people'), but to 'military personnel' as well, who are 'unarmed or off duty at the time'.[7] This obvious stretching of the word 'noncombatant' was evidently inadequate for the US State Department, because, as the 'war on terror' intensified, it proceeded to invent an entirely new 'legal' category – 'illegal enemy combatant' – which confounds legal experts to this day. In this regard it would not be an exaggeration to say that the language of the law has been radically altered since 'September 11', and liberal lawmakers in the US are as puzzled and provoked by these changes as legal experts and activists in the rest of the world.

Exposing the chicanery of the State Department's use of 'illegal enemy combatant', Tzvetan Todorov (2009) calls attention to the well-established distinction between those perpetrators of violence in peacetime who are generally designated as 'criminals', and those 'enemy soldiers' in war time who must be treated according to the protocols of international conventions.[8] Since the Al-Qaeda terrorists are not 'regular army members of a country that signed the Geneva Conventions', they cannot 'benefit from these protections' (32–33). At the same time, they cannot be designated as 'ordinary criminals', because then the police would be a more appropriate institution to deal with their crimes. This is where it becomes expedient to designate a '*war* on terror' – the first of its kind in the world where a war is being waged on nothing less than an abstraction with no end in sight, thereby enabling the United States to set itself above all national and international laws for an indefinite period of time. In a state of 'war' the State Department is under no obligation to adhere to 'laws applicable in times of peace' (33). Yet, as Todorov points out the obvious irony: '[S]ince the war is not directed against another country, the international conventions do not apply either!' (33) So, within the logic of this doublespeak, the State Department creates its own legitimacy to invent a conundrum like 'illegal enemy combatant', which effectively 'allows the US government to place apprehended individuals outside the reach of laws and norms, and hence to practice torture' (33).

Inevitably, 'torture' in turn gets re-defined. Detainees at detention centres like Guantánamo and the former Abu Ghraib prison can no longer be considered 'tortured' if they are 'regularly raped, hung from hooks, immersed in water, burned, attached to electrodes, deprived of food, water or medicine, attacked by dogs and beaten until their bones are broken' (34–37). None of these violent and sadistic acts, and no amount of 'sensory deprivation' involving hearing, smelling, seeing, breathing and sleeping, can qualify as torture.[9] All these 'deprivations' are better designated as 'abuse', not 'torture', as the former Secretary of Defense, Donald Rumsfeld, confirmed in his equivocal response to the atrocities at the Abu Ghraib prison. For 'torture' to be *truly torture*, as Todorov emphasizes, it is necessary for the detainee to lose at least 'one vital organ' – it could be 'a leg, or an arm, or a burst liver, or incontinence for life' (34). Even the *death* of a detainee following 'abuse' can qualify as 'torture': the grotesquerie could not be more extreme.

In contrast, 'abusive' actions are more cogently linked by the Central Intelligence Agency (CIA) to the necessary task of extracting 'actionable intelligence' from detainees – an 'intelligence' which was endorsed by President Bush in his paternalistic assumption that the American people expected the government to do their job.[10] Exposing the absurdity of '[pretending] . . . to act on things by changing their name', Todorov articulates a sober truth: 'It is not because we say that the systematic destruction of a person will not be *called* torture that it ceases to *be* torture . . . [R]eality is not altered in any way by this new designation' (39–40).

Predictably, there is no dearth of deadly euphemisms in the larger discourse around terrorism and torture which attempts to camouflage blatant crimes against humanity. Alex Danchev, a particularly fine reader of such euphemisms, points out the absurdity of an official report on abuses at Guantánamo whose 'treatment [of detainees] did not rise to the level of prohibited inhumane treatment'.[11] There is almost a parodic quality to such official niceties. More blatantly, a familiar category like 'prisoner of war' (POW), subject to the laws of the Geneva Convention, has been replaced – first in Afghanistan and then in Iraq – by the more malleable 'person under control' (PUC), which is 'literally pronounced puck', as in 'fuck a puck', which literally means to 'administer a beating'.[12] A Human Rights Watch report confirms that PUCs held during the war in Iraq in Fallujah were 'fucked' routinely; they were also 'smoked' (subjected to 'forced physical exertion').[13]

If I somewhat overemphasize a discursive thrust in this war on words, it is to highlight their performative energy, whereby words are not just descriptions but the embodiments of action. Later in this introduction I will emphasize why the concept of 'performativity', whereby words are actual manifestations of *doing*, is so integral to the critical analysis of this book. For the moment let us recall that in the 'Holy War of Error', to use Sami al-Haj's felicitous phrase,[14] the nomenclature of entire missions has been subjected to linguistic alteration and distortion. Operation INFINITE JUSTICE, for instance, was replaced by ENDURING FREEDOM following the reminder that the former category is more readily associated with the prerogatives of deities and divine forces than governments.[15] Likewise, the notorious word 'crusade', mouthed by born-again Christian President George W. Bush, was promptly censored for its association with specifically Christian forms of violence against Muslim 'infidels'.

It could be argued that these political blunders and semantic shifts in the language of war are not new: prior to 'September 11' the American branding of 'rogue states', for instance, used aggressively during the Clinton administration between 1997 and 2000, was abruptly replaced by the impossibly bland 'states of concern'.[16] However the figure of the 'rogue' (a wild animal capable of running amok at any moment) continued to mutate in its demonization of targets like Saddam Hussein, arguably the 'beast of Baghdad'. As Derrida reminds us, 'The beast is not simply an animal but the very incarnation of evil, of the satanic, the diabolical, the demonic – a beast of the Apocalypse.'[17] Primordial associations die hard even as beasts are tamed or effectively culled, and the language of violence and torture 'cleaned up'. The old names lurk like palimpsests that refuse to be erased, not unlike the 'global war on terror', which continues to resonate long after it has been renamed 'Overseas Contingency Operation'.

Beyond the manipulation of categories by the US Defense and Security

Departments, one needs to acknowledge that the global discourse of terrorism, as James Der Derian (2009b) reminds us, rejects any attempt to be subsumed under rigid official definitions. Disdaining the dominant tendency to simplify terrorism under the weight of a 'corrosive mix of official opportunism, media hype, and public hysteria', Derian emphasizes the need to highlight the 'differences and contradictions' of terrorism, which constitute 'a heavily conflicted field' in terms of ideology, philosophy and practice.[18] Even as all terrorism may be said to converge around 'strategies of intimidation and violence', these strategies get consolidated through vastly different mechanisms, agencies and targets encompassing a wide series of formations, including mythoterrorism, anarchoterrorism, socioterrorism, ethnoterrorism, narcoterrorism, state terrorism, antiterrorism and pure terrorism.[19] What concerns me in this book is not this spectrum of terrorism(s) as mapped so virtuosically by Derian across histories, cultures and times, but the ways in which words in the 'war on terror' get secreted within the most normal – and lethal – of categories.

One such category is the almost territorial regard that Americans have expressed for 'Ground Zero', a category which emerged with an uncanny complicity at the very start of the 'war on terror' in the United States, out of a consensus between the print and electronic media, and public sentiments in the American population at large. With an eerie swiftness, as the cultural critic Gene Ray (2005) has pointed out, *The New York Times* used 'Ground Zero' on 16 September 2001 to describe the smouldering ground of the ruins of the World Trade Center. By this time the category had already caught on and spread widely across different sectors of civil society, without any significant debate or discomfort relating to its use in everyday life. Countering this proliferation of an essentially deadly category, Ray reminds us that 'Ground Zero' was first used to designate the ground of the nuclear site of Hiroshima where all traces of life had been annihilated.[20] Tellingly, to this day, all photographic and visual evidence of the atrocities on Hiroshima and Nagasaki still continues to be censored in the United States, thereby reducing the most formidable demonstration of 'terror bombing' on civilians to a dark secret, internalized yet unacknowledged in the public domain.[21] With 'September 11', however, it could be argued that this secret has been finally 'outed' by the strange appropriation of Americans claiming their victimhood through an implicit, yet unacknowledged comparison to those Japanese people on whom their own government had used the first nuclear bomb in the world.

With such appropriations of categories, whereby Ground Zero of Hiroshima becomes Ground Zero of the World Trade Center, one begins to realize the layers of deception by which the terror inflicted on a particular population in one part of the world continues to be denied, even as a very different kind of terror is claimed through the same description in another part. Is this historical amnesia, or political delusion? How may we develop a closer understanding of how people suffer in different contexts of violence and intimidation without conflating their suffering under the sign of a common victimhood?

## RISKS OF MISUNDERSTANDING

In any scenario of terrorism, it could be argued, there is an acute, almost hypertense paranoia in relation to the use of words. What makes the language surrounding the 'global war on terror' particularly paranoid has to do with its emphatically unilateral and monochromatic discursive thrust, which is further enhanced through the intensification of surveillance. Against this scenario, any writer reflecting on terror today faces the fear or the very real possibility of being misunderstood. In my own experience, I am compelled to return to my tract on *The Question of Faith* (1993), which was published shortly after the demolition of the Babri Masjid in Ayodhya, India, on 6 December 1992, precipitating communal riots across the country.[22] In my attempt to free 'faith' from the demons of 'fundamentalism', which is somewhat similar to my impulse to free 'terror' from 'terrorism' in this book, I am reminded of the prescience of the rather grand opening sentence in my tract on faith: 'In the best of all possible worlds, writing can be misunderstood.' Why is misunderstanding more fraught with risks today? Is it because we are living in the worst of times? This could be a hopeful conjecture.

On a more pragmatic note, I would say that we are living in an environment where technologies of surveillance have intensified, particularly in liberal democracies where the myth of free speech has been placed under severe duress. There are new legal mechanisms which place enormous curbs on critical thinking or dissent – the Freedom Act in the United States, and internal surveillance mechanisms monitoring telephone conversations, websites, e-mail correspondence and academic writing border on an almost 'unreal' surveillance, resulting in intimidation and a climate of unease at unconscious levels. While this cannot stop us from writing critically, any more so than it can stop WikiLeaks from countering state surveillance through its own subversive, information-busting practices, it does demand a new vigilance that should not degenerate into paranoia or self-censorship.

Looking back on my attempt to question the inner complexities of faith, I remember indicating in my tract that there is a sinister side to faith, as the Epistle of James (2:19) in the Bible recognizes: 'Thou believest that there is one God; thou doest well: the devils also believe and tremble.' Even devils have faith. This is a chastening thought in the context of the global scenario on terror, except that the identification of devils may not correspond to what the likes of Fox News and CNN would have us believe. The crusaders of 'just' wars could be devils in their own right. Nonetheless, juxtaposing *The Question of Faith* with what I am writing now, there is something to be said about speaking *for* faith in opposition to different kinds of fundamentalism and intolerance. It is much harder to make any such claim in speaking *for* terror. The obligatory assumption is that one needs to speak *against* terror. To speak for terror, or even to address it in a non-judgemental context, is to risk being branded either as a terrorist or a terrorist sympathizer. Will this narrative escape being branded in this manner and identified as 'anti-American', if not 'pro-terrorist'? Without sounding unduly pessimistic, an honest response to these knee-jerk reactions, which, in my view, restrict the possibilities and risks of critical thinking, would be: I'm not sure.

Another, more pragmatic reason for being misunderstood is that my use of 'terror' in this book *sprawls*. I draw the word 'sprawls' from a fine reflection by the sociologist Charles Tilly on 'Terror, Terrorism, Terrorists' (2004) which refuses to get locked in the purism of heuristic categories. Adopting a sceptical position, Tilly emphasizes that '[s]ocial scientists who attempt to explain sudden attacks on civilian targets [like the World Trade Center] should *doubt* the existence of a distinct, coherent class of actors (terrorists) who specialize in a unitary form of political action (terror) and thus should establish a separate variety of politics (terrorism)'.[23] Refusing to make a virtue out of coherence even while enunciating his position with scrupulous clarity, Tilly opens himself to a spectrum of extreme forms of violence like genocide and ethnic cleansing, which 'sprawl across a wide range of human cruelties'.[24]

This 'sprawl' of 'human cruelties' is only too evident in my own reading of terror in this book, which I refuse to confine within any one location or modality of violence, playing into the narrative of American exceptionalism that the 'war on terror' seems to demand. Not only does my narrative encompass different locations and practices of terror in the Philippines, the United States, India, Rwanda and South Africa, it also engages with different modalities of violence including genocide, war, ethnic and communal violence, in addition to acts of terrorism. Needless to say, there is a risk here in diffusing the grammar of terror, which is further complicated by the interdisciplinary methodology adopted in this book.

Interdisciplinarity becomes almost mandatory in exposing the scattered locations, cultural contexts, disjunctive temporalities and multiple agencies of terrorism, which, as Tilly emphasizes, is not 'a single causally coherent phenomenon'.[25] Rather, it is increasingly a mutant and technological hybrid of intersecting networks, driven less by any clear-cut ideology or religious belief than by a multitude of discontents and resentments. To pin terror down to any particular discipline, within the strictures of any one vocabulary or institutional framing, is to miss out on its deadly elusiveness. If, in this book, I find myself intersecting the languages of theatre and performance studies with cultural studies and the social sciences, this is not so much a strategy on my part but rather a methodology, in attempting to make sense of violence in all its multitudinous, enigmatic and yet intransigent circumstances.

## AMBIVALENCES OF TERROR

Moving outside the domain of sociology, one needs to acknowledge that terror could be more ambivalent than terrorism. Turning to the *Oxford English Dictionary* (*OED*), one is struck by the gamut of enigmas surrounding the word, as opposed to the more technical and instrumentalist definitions of 'terrorism'. The very agency underlying 'terror' in the *OED* is complicated in its two most dominant senses: 'terror' is at once 'the state of *being terrified* or extremely frightened', as well as 'the state or quality of *being terrible* or causing intense fear or dread'. Terror can be felt, experienced, embodied, but it can also be inflicted and imposed, as in the Reign of Terror during the French Revolution between September 1793 and July 1794. During this time revolutionary tribunals conducted arbitrary trials and executed 'enemies of the people', legitimizing their actions on the grounds that terror is 'an emanation of virtue', a necessary 'government by intimidation'.[26]

According to Terry Eagleton (2005), this 'modern invention' of terror operating as terrorism is 'twinned at birth' with the 'modern democratic state'.[27] Contrary to its political legitimacy, it is the state which provides one of the most deadly grounds for the relentless spate of riots, killings, massacres and ethnic cleansings that take place within its borders. Even while states across the world would like to claim some kind of immunity against the charge of terrorism by virtue of their legality sanctified by constitutions, law courts and the rule of governance, the reality is that 'state terrorism' intensifies in almost direct proportion to its capacities for being camouflaged or euphemized. The usual pretexts of maintaining 'law and order' against insurgents and anti-social elements, along with the grander mission of protecting civilian rights against foreign aggression, are often used as legitimizations of terror in their own right.

In its adjectival uses, 'terror' is indeed linked to 'terrorism', as in the familiar associations of 'terror alert', 'terror attack', 'terror plot', 'terror suspect', 'terror tactics' and 'terror act'.[28] More formidably, there is the phenomenon of 'terror-bombing', inflicted, for instance, on Germany during the Second World War by the Allied forces, resulting in the deaths of 600,000 civilians. This deliberate targeting of civilians has been justified by Michael Walzer (2000), the foremost proponent of the 'just war' theory, on grounds of 'supreme emergency' where it becomes necessary to 'wager' the crime of terrorism in order to avert 'moral disaster' – in this particular case, the evil of fascism.[29] However, there would appear to be a time-frame for the dubious ethics of such terror bombing: in early 1942 it was necessary, according to Walzer, because Britain was vulnerable to being defeated by Germany; however, by 1943, when it was evident that Germany was not going to win the war, terror-bombing became a morally unacceptable strategy to end the war.[30]

From this example it becomes clear that 'terror' cannot be freed from 'terrorism' even as it gets justified through strategically evasive advocacies of 'just wars', which I will elaborate on towards the end of this book in the difficult context of seeking justice outside the law. Countering the equivocal ethics underlying a 'moral' understanding of war – after all, from whose implicitly superior, reasonable and non-relativist sense of morality can 'terror-bombing' be justified? – we have more sublime incarnations of 'terror' provided by the *OED*. Here we encounter surreal images like the 'terror bird', which refers to a species of 'large, extinct and typically flightless birds of prey'; the 'terror-gleam' or 'dark mist that hovers over the river Thund in Scandinavian mythology'; and, at a deeply visceral and corporeal level, a 'terror-drop', which refers both to a 'terrifying parachute drop' as well as to a 'drop of sweat produced in a state of terror'.

I have deliberately inserted these startling associations of terror to work against the dominant assumption that 'terror' is best regarded as an abstract and external condition or state. Indeed, in the early stages of writing this book, I was advised by at least two philosopher-friends that it was prudent to keep terror at a distance, and, at all costs, to avoid the emotional and psychological dimensions of terror. At a linguistic level, I realized that my interlocutors were keen on pinning terror down to a noun – an abstract noun – without acknowledging its adjectival and verbal implications. I also realized that they were not entirely ready to implicate themselves *in* terror. Therefore, the simple expression, 'I am terrified', had at least one of them struggling for an adequate translation in German.

In addition to regarding terror as 'extra-state collective action' involving 'physical force', we have no other choice, I believe, but to regard terror, in Gayatri Spivak's words, as 'the name of an affect'.[31] In chapter 2 of this book, which focuses on the demonization of Muslims in the larger context of communalism in India, I will discuss the insidious ways by which minorities are marked through specific aspects of their physiognomy or dress – a beard or a turban can *affect* all kinds of terrorist identifications or mis-identifications. 'Where "terror" is an affect,' as Spivak emphasizes, 'the line between agent and object wavers.'[32] While the consequence of this 'wavering' results in the volatility of fear and uncertainty in the public sphere, it also affects the way in which terrorists are perceived by those who are threatened by their menace.

Spivak complicates the affect of terror: '[T]here is also a sense in which the terrorist is taken to be numbed to terror, does not feel the terror of terror, and has become unlike the rest of us by virtue of this transformation.'[33] This notion of terrorists being numbed to the terror they inflict on others is one way by which they are demonized, reduced to 'machines', or unthinking, unfeeling brutes or 'beasts', as opposed to those whom they terrify, who remain only too human and vulnerable. For terrorists, it is assumed, human life is cheap, if not dispensable. This leads to all kinds of hypocritical associations: 'When the soldier is not afraid to die, s/he is brave. When the terrorist is not afraid to die, s/he is a coward. The soldier kills, or is supposed to kill, designated persons. The terrorist kills, or may kill, just persons.'[34] Through her precise analysis Spivak makes us see how the 'affect' of terror leads to questionable moral judgments. Far from being locked within a vortex of incomprehensible emotions, it compels us to be more reflexive about our own complicities in the production of 'common sense' around terror.

If the dominant imperative suggested by the 'war on terror' assumes that terror is an adversary, an Enemy, necessarily outside one's self, destined to be fought and killed if necessary over and over again, terror as affect challenges this false Manichaeism. Dismantling the objectification of terror, it demands some kind of recognition of how we are implicated in terror, disturbing any false illusions of an implicit, 'non-terrorist' goodness or innocence. Terror can be imposed from outside, but it is also secreted from within, and affected by our own fears and prejudices. No one can escape terror quite so easily, and certainly not with the pyrrhic assumption that in a war on terror one will necessarily come out alive or victorious, and with one's sense of moral judgement intact.

## HOLY TERROR

Let me push the drift of associations here by invoking that most seemingly innocent of constructions – 'holy terror' – a phrase that involuntarily makes one smile because it calls to mind a troublesome child. In this most popular of associations represented in comics and cartoons, one could say that Dennis the Menace is a holy terror: he is the detonator of all kinds of household appliances and norms, and the very scourge of Mr Wilson's life. How does 'terror' get linked to a child through the mediation of the 'holy'? What happens when a holy terror becomes Holy Terror?

Here, with the incursions of the noumenal, the sacred and the metaphysical, I am reminded of the most divine of child manifestations in Hindu mythology and religion, Lord Krishna, who as a child is the absolute bane of his mother's life. Krishna's pranks are lovingly reiterated in the repertoire of classical and folk Indian dance and performance traditions where he is shown breaking milk pots, stealing butter and eating dirt from the ground.

At one point his infuriated mother orders him to open his mouth so that he can spit out the mud. In a wondrous moment of illumination, she sees the cosmos whirling in her child's mouth. This is a moment of awe, not Shock and Awe, which is what the US war machine wished to engineer through its bombardment of Iraq during the Gulf War, but another kind of awe coming out of celestial wonder. Later, in the *Bhagavad Gita*, another, more militant manifestation of Krishna in the Mahabharata battlefield reveals his universal form (*vishvarupa*) to Arjuna, through which he instructs the reluctant warrior how to detach himself from the delusions of 'false consciousness' which prevent him from fighting his own kin. Exposed to the terrifying manifestation of Time in Krishna's omnipresence, Arjuna responds to the call of war and submits to the task of performing his duty determined by the warrior caste (*kshatriya dharma*).

Arguably, in these examples, we encounter different epistemologies of terror from other times which cannot be yoked to contemporary readings of terrorism. Without engaging with these differences, Terry Eagleton, in his book *Holy Terror* (2005), outlines a metaphysics of terrorism by conceptualizing the relationship between terror and the sacred.[35] Without quite separating the mythical residues and dimensions of 'terror' in the ancient world from the contemporary phenomenon of 'terrorism', and without differentiating metaphysics adequately from either theology or religion, Eagleton articulates the complex ambivalences underlying concepts of 'evil', 'the sublime', 'sacrifice', 'God' and 'death' in order to disrupt deeply embedded secular pieties, particularly on the Left, in relation to the violence of our times. While the categories of 'sacrifice', 'forgiveness' and 'evil' also enter my narrative in the larger context of truth and reconciliation, and the ambivalent ethics of suicide-bombing, they have very different significances, as will become evident in chapters 3 and 4 of this book. Any reading of terror today demands a context-sensitive engagement with these terms, which do not merely have a moral or spiritual significance, but a performative value in terms of how they are actually enforced in political culture: how, after all, are 'sacrifice', 'forgiveness' and 'evil' activated today within different scenarios of war, genocide and ethnic violence?

Against the performative force of these concepts Eagleton adopts a somewhat too fuzzy methodology, his 'metaphysical' categories almost tripping over each other, drawing their affinities through an over-hasty analogical thought process. The epistemological fact that the Latin word *sacer* can mean either 'blessed or cursed, holy or reviled' is given the same conceptual weight by Eagleton as the more generalized observation that 'there are kinds of terror in ancient civilization which are both creative and destructive, life-giving and death-dealing' (2). Without providing historical evidence for this vast claim, Eagleton builds his argument on the false premise that '[t]error begins as a religious idea, as indeed, much terrorism still is today; and religion is all about deeply ambivalent powers, which both enrapture and annihilate' (2). In such conceptual slippages there are obvious problems relating to temporality and causality: even if one accepts that terror 'begins' as a religious idea (though, perhaps, it would be more accurate to say that terror is one of the many manifestations of religion), it is wrong to equate terrorism in our times with this 'religious idea' (in so far as it has remained constant). Indeed, one of the fundamental misinterpretations of contemporary terrorism is to read it as a 'religious' phenomenon in the first place.

Contradicting Eagleton's tendency to illuminate terror through an excavation of past religious, metaphysical and literary imaginaries, I will argue that these illuminations are potentially useful only to the extent that they can help us to discriminate what is specifically *different* about the mindsets of terrorism today. Instead of a continuum between manifestations of terror in the past and present, I would highlight their disjunctions. Therefore, in elaborating on the concept of 'sacrifice' (which originally meant 'to make sacred'), Eagleton makes the important point that not every act of self-destruction in our times – for instance, suicide-bombing – is necessarily sacrificial or transformative (100). This is precisely the kind of discrimination that is needed in thinking about terror today. The myths and concepts of the past, I would emphasize, help us to see the present, not because they are being re-lived in an 'eternal present', but because they acquire new significances and altered meanings in a simulacrum of what has already passed. It is only by puncturing the counterfeit of similitude that the reality of dissimilitude becomes visible.

An additional problem with Eagleton's attempt to meld different trajectories of time and culture in reflecting on terror could be the non-reflexive Eurocentric context of his analysis, in accounting for 'the otherness at the core of the self' (13). This attempt fails, not least because Eagleton has no engagement with Islam or Hinduism, or, for that matter, any 'non-Western' religion, philosophy or aesthetics. For all his cosmopolitanism, his reading of terror is, in the final analysis, very English. I would argue that if one wishes to present a counter-cultural political imaginary of terror for our times through a reading of, say, Dionysus's sensual and spiritual force – Eagleton regards Euripides's charismatic protagonist as one of the 'earliest terrorist ringleaders' (3) – it is necessary to invoke other eschatologies and metaphysical frameworks of the divine force. If, for example, I wished to highlight the relationship of terror to the 'sacred' as it lives in India today, through diverse material, social, religious and ritual practices, I would necessarily have to reckon with the fact that these practices are not merely textual (as in Eagleton's literary and philosophical examples presented in *Holy Terror*), but embodied and fleshed out in actual performances.

To provide just one example from my own home-city of Kolkata, I would invoke, for instance, the complexity and enduring contemporaneity of the goddess Kali, at once terrifying and maternal, who exists in a multitude of figures and forms. Unlike Dionysus who is, at best, a mythical figure invoked in the Euro–American canon of classical art and literature, Kali is actively worshipped in India today as diverse manifestations of the Divine Mother. Earlier, during the Swadeshi movement in Bengal at the turn of the last century, she was invoked as the patron deity of numerous revolutionaries and terrorists, and to this day, her divine force carries a political legacy from the ancient period through the colonial struggle via the ambivalent articulations of modernity. To invoke Kali as a destructive manifestation of 'terror' necessitates an engagement with her power in an affective dimension.

To experience something akin to the force and danger of Kali's power, one possible site of transformative energy would be the ritual performances of Theyyam in Kerala where low-caste actors incarnate multiple manifestations of the Divine Mother in the form of ferocious local deities. In spectacular all-night performances involving spirit-possession, trance and worship, these embodiments of energy in raw, yet highly charged ritual contexts are not readily appropriated for academic political purposes. In contrast to the subaltern sacred power of Theyyam, Eagleton's idea of the 'sacred' comes across like an ideologically driven, post-Marxist trope, ultimately yoked to the wish-fulfilment that moribund leftwing politics can be re-animated through 'metaphysics'. The terror of the sacred as it is lived and experienced in performances like Theyyam is made of sterner stuff, and I don't see Eagleton surviving it.[36]

If I have dwelt at some length on Eagleton's attempt to force a relationship between terror and the sacred within the contemporary context of terrorism, it is to highlight why I do not deal with the sacred in this book. Not only does it demand a different conceptual and discursive framework, but, more critically, it cannot be used to explicate the terror of our times. Terrorist global agencies like the Al-Qaeda may invoke the language of Holy War, but this is less about the sacred, or even religion, than it is about a particularly perverted form of megalomaniacal violence and anti-Western hatred. Even as the misappropriation of the sacred by the contemporary phenomenon of terrorism is not part of this book, I have found it necessary to inscribe it in this introduction in order to clarify what this book is *not* trying to do.

## TERROR THROUGH A LITERARY LENS

*Neti neti* ('not this, not this', or 'neither this nor that'), the philosophical premise found in the Upanishads, among other ancient Sanskrit texts, would seem to be mirrored in my own attempt to understand 'terror' through the path of *via negativa*. While '*neti neti*' has been used at metaphysical levels to account for the *Brahman* or the divine force, which cannot be adequately described through its positive attributes but only in terms of *what it is not*, it has also been used by Buddhist philosophers to work against any notion of grounding the meaning of words in a particular essence.[37] Deploying this rhetorical strategy for my own purposes, I find it useful to strategize how this book begins to enter the conceptual orbit of terror by outlining what is *not* an integral part of its discussion. The exclusions do not amount to a denial of what is less important to the larger discourse of terror; they simply contribute to highlighting what is integral to the argument of this particular book.

With this premise in mind I feel somewhat more at ease in acknowledging that I am not attempting, for instance, a detailed reading of the aesthetics of terror in this book. Certainly, 'aesthetics' figure and resonate in the narrative at several points – for instance, in the debate around the composer Karlheinz Stockhausen's controversial claim that the destruction of the Twin Towers can be regarded as a magnificent 'work of art' (chapter 1), or in the rhetoric of the 'beautiful terrorist' in the Urdu popular press (chapter 2). These insertions, however, are best read as *fragments* that punctuate the larger political analysis of terror presented in this book; they cannot be said to constitute a larger reading of the aesthetics of terror replete with a theory of the sublime, which demands the writing of another book.[38]

Nor am I concerned with the literary imaginaries of terror on the lines indicated by Terry Eagleton, even as their tropes are suggestive and even provocative in pushing the limits of terror beyond the sequestered confines of the social sciences. Keeping this qualification in mind, it is nonetheless useful within the strategic framing of this introduction to address the Indian poet and literary critic Rukmini Bhaya Nair's book on *Poetry in a Time of Terror* (2009), which draws heavily on the concept of 'ambivalence' from Eagleton. Nair affirms that 'terror in the literary or poetic mode destabilizes the unitariness of terror as we understand it, via the real world events such as 9/11 – terror as an inexplicable bolt from the blue – by infusing it with ambivalence or interpretability that is the defining character of a literary text.'[39]

Countering this position, one could argue against the presumed 'unitariness' of events like 'September 11' by calling attention to the torrent of contradictory emotions that it has elicited from almost the very moment it struck consciousness at a global level. Indeed, can it be said to exist in the same way across political locations and constituencies? Questioning the privilege of the global cosmopolis in which the discourse of terrorism is most eloquently read and explicated, outside the actual killing fields of Taliban-controlled Afghanistan or drug-infested cities like Juárez, Mexico, we need to ask: Are events like 'September 11' as omnipresent as they are made out to be? Can one assume their translation and political intelligibility across all cultural contexts? Arguably, even if they do exist for rural and indigenous communities in the cultures of the South, as Bhaskar Mukhopadhyay has suggested through his description of a '9/11'-inspired *pat*, a folk-painting performance practice in rural West Bengal, the task would be to question *how* global states of emergency get transformed within the struggles of everyday life on the margins of the rural South.[40] If there is a 'global village', then how do local languages and forms of cultural expression incorporate and talk back to the Empire, or appropriate its state of emergency, for their own material purposes?

This is a large question that extends beyond Nair's scrupulously honed argument, which centres around the premise that 'terror becomes emotionally available via the literary'.[41] How, then, one could argue, is terror perceived in (non-literary/non-literate) everyday life? Is it a spectre drained dry, divested of any emotion, or is its reality simply too horrifying to be processed and transformed into poetry in the first place? Inflecting her own valorization of poetry, which 'offers an ambiguous verbal space in which terror flowers without physical danger but disturbing verisimilitude', Nair offers an insight into the actual psychophysical immediacy of terror as she imagines its corporeal affect: not through the deadening impact of its lightning-like 'bolt from the blue', but through a more tense conflict of sensations.[42]

Unlike the state of horror which encounters terror in the present – beholding it 'face to face', eyes bulging, transfixed – terror, in Nair's imaginary, has an opposite effect: the terrorized victim's eyes tend to remain 'willfully and staunchly shut'.[43] This compels Nair to question what such a 'deliberate voiding of vision' could suggest:

> To open her eyes would be to behold what is too awful to bear. This is what makes the emotion of terror temporally as well as emotionally ambivalent – the victim at once anticipates the dreaded event, by placing it in the future tense, and knows that it has 'already happened,' but were she to 'open her eyes,' her reason tells her that she would see right before her the very thing that she so fears. This is the essential paradox of terror.[44]

Questioning this paradox, I would argue that the problem does not lie in the vacillation between 'seeing' and 'not seeing' terror; the reality is that we have *no other choice but to see and re-see the same images of terror over and over again* through their relentless circulation in the media, which does not figure in Nair's reading at all.[45] Instead of 'to see or not to see', the dilemma of our times is *compulsive seeing, repetitive seeing* with a vengeance.

With the rampant mediatization of terror on television, cable networks, YouTube and other electronic sites, we have no other option but to see what the media wants us to see, strategically sanctified by the powerbrokers of terror through an almost infinite referral to 'the same images', which begin to acquire an archetypal power. Along with the usual charge of the 'deadening impact' of images, can one totally deny the voyeuristic pleasure derived in the compulsive act of 'seeing' terror *ad nauseam*? A pleasure that is indeed terribly ambivalent, in so far as it is both oppressive and yet irresistible. While, arguably, there is no specific visual code or apparatus which enables one to *see* the terror of our times with global uniformity, our eyes themselves have been subjected to a new phenomenology of reception in which we are more participatory and complicit than ever before in the actual reproduction, interpretation and circulation of images of terror.

## VISUAL OVERKILL

Precisely because images of terror can no longer be assumed to terrify, the task of theorizing the larger visual culture of terror is a complex undertaking best approached by specialists like W.J.T. Mitchell, whose book on *Cloning Terror* (2011) is a masterful analysis of image production relating the 'war on terror' to the simultaneous incursions of biotechnology in the public sphere. If I am sparing in my use of images in this book, it is because I resist the valorization of the 'visual turn' in cultural studies, which has been overdetermined and consolidated over the years. Even so it would be disingenuous to deny that images hit the eye, capture the imagination, circulate and serve as reference points for conversations, discussions, gossip, rumour and propaganda, more readily than words. How many people, after all, have *read* the detailed investigative reports on Abu Ghraib? On the other hand, millions have *seen* the sadistic and torturous acts inflicted on the Iraqi prisoners at Abu Ghraib. While the random access of the Abu Ghraib images at a global level cannot be denied, it is much harder to assess *how* they are being read and endorsed in the 'war on terror.' Indeed, how do images of terror get produced in the first place, and does their distribution have any tangible effect on the larger quest for justice and the exposition of truth?

Part of the seduction of images of terror could lie in the fact that once exposed in our electronic and digital visual culture, they spread like a virus, stimulating a torrent of interpretations which, in the final analysis, would seem to take us farther and farther away from the actual political content of the images. Almost with an adrenaline rush, one can get high on visualizing terror. I was witness to one such experiment at the Hebbel Theater in Berlin, where W.J.T. Mitchell ended his lecture on terror by soliciting responses from the audience to the widely circulated image of all the key members of the Obama team in the White House watching Osama bin Laden killed in 'real time.'[46] I will not go into the many possibilities of reading this image, with Obama sitting in a corner in shirtsleeves, Hillary Clinton covering her mouth with her hand, the White House staff sitting with solemn expressions, others standing with concentrated attention, everyone's gaze fixed on *what cannot be seen*.

What stunned me at the Hebbel Theater event was the virtuosity with which this image was interpreted by members of the audience in an unconscious spirit of hermeneutic one-upmanship, each interpretation outdoing the other in its brilliant, surely-I'm-right reading. While one spectator claimed that the image called to mind the arrival of the Messenger in Greek tragedy, another saw a hydra of heads in the White House office, and a photographer-friend sitting alongside me had no difficulty in claiming that the White House team was 're-living' the moment of the destruction of the Twin Towers. Without undermining the creative intensity of any of these intuitive readings, I would question to what extent these interpretations had any relevance to the actual killing of Osama bin Laden and its virtual witnessing within the sanctum of the White House. Perhaps what needed to be inserted in the discussion was not just the *mise-en-scène* of the image itself, but the very deliberate process of its framing, shooting and ultimate selection by the White House. Indeed, without the green signal from the White House this particular image could not have been seen in the first place, indicating the monitoring and backstage politics of image-production that demands much closer analysis. Such analysis could open up unfashionable questions relating to the *propaganda* of state departments in projecting images of power, control and civility in managing the 'war on terror', in an ostensibly democratic, freethinking public domain.

Instead of what gets seen – or 'cloned', as Mitchell would argue, in endless variations of the same image – it is what gets *invisibilized* that should be an equally urgent source of critical concern. The erasure of images in the 'war on terror' is as much a part of its deadly visual culture as the bombardment of specific images in global mediaspace. Following the surfeit of images by which Osama bin Laden was demonized on television and the media, it is telling indeed that he has ultimately been whitewashed. Ostensibly for 'security' reasons and on the dubious grounds of honouring basic human 'decency', we have almost no images of the dead Osama, his brain shattered, even as Obama watches the operation leading to his death intently and with a look of determined, quiet, controlled concentration, rather like a coach watching the final moments of a ball game. The job is done, the demon allegedly 'buried' in the sea with strict observation of religious rituals (for which there is no evidence), and life goes on at the White House.

## PERFORMANCE/PERFORMATIVITY/THEATRE

At this point the reader of this introduction might justifiably express deep impatience, because all I have done in this chapter is to indicate what my book is *not* focusing on. To recapitulate: I cannot claim to be a 'terror expert' by assuming any expertise in military studies, or war studies, or 'torture studies'. Neither does my book offer a religious studies perspective on issues of the sacred in relation to terror, nor does it provide an elaborate reading on the aesthetics of terror or a media studies approach to terror. While I have been inspired by the different languages and conceptual approaches of these various disciplines, in the final analysis, I have to tell my story on terror through my own affinities to the language of performance, accessed through the fields of theatre and performance studies, which enable me to *see* and *engage* with terror in the first place. More precisely, it is through the rhetoric of performativity that I am able to *read* terror in relation to its dominant discourses. Let us turn now to these discriminations of 'theatre', 'performance' and 'performativity' by emphasizing that they all play a role in this narrative, at once independently and through strange collusions.

Against the larger spectrum of performances in everyday life, to which the examination of terror in this book is inextricably linked, there is a more focused, yet familiar understanding of performance in the theatrical sense, as 'a tangible, bounded event that involves the presentation of rehearsed artistic action' for a specific audience in a particular time-and-space-bound continuum, as in '*a* performance of a play, a dance, or a symphony'.[47] In such a reading of 'performance', which is inextricably linked to aspects of 'acting', 'directing', 'dancing', 'playing', and all the elements that go into the shaping of a *mise-en-scène* or choreography or the conducting of a concert, there is a symbiotic linkage of 'performance' to the artistic practice of theatre and the performing arts. This understanding of 'performance' necessitates a critical engagement with the constituents of training and rehearsal, skill and virtuosity, trained reception and spectatorship.

Tellingly, this book does not focus on theatre through 'cutting-edge', masterpiece, 'out-of-the-box' productions by tracing the theme of terror through Aeschylus's *Persians*, Shakespeare's *Macbeth*, Büchner's *Danton's Death*, Brecht's *The Measures Taken* and Dorfman's *Death and the Maiden*, to mention just a handful of warhorses representing the theatre of terror. Nor am I attempting to inventory avant-garde performance art or visual installations of 'September 11' or 'Abu Ghraib' or 'Guantánamo', to name a few of the notable tropes that exemplify the 'war on terror', even though they enter my narrative *as performative events* in their own right. Far from addressing terror at a purely dramaturgical level of theatrical representation or through the immediacies of the *mise-en-scène*, this book prioritizes those instances of terror which are unscripted, unplanned, undetermined and which are nonetheless *performed*, at times explosively or, at other times, so unobtrusively that one may not even be aware that terror has already been unleashed.

My reading of 'performance' in this book, therefore, is less conditioned by the 'artistic' orchestration of a corporeal, 'live', rehearsed, time-and-space-bound event framed within the cultural norms of civic institutions like state theatres, than by a much wider understanding of 'performance' inextricably linked to social interactions, behaviours, strategies, deceptions, manipulations and negotiations of terror in the public sphere. The epistemological thrust of this wide understanding of 'performance' is well captured in the primary definition offered in the *OED*, where 'performance' is defined not, as one would expect, in the context of theatrical enactment, but rather as '*the accomplishment or carrying out of something commanded or undertaken; the doing of an action or operation*.' With keywords like 'commanded' and 'doing', it becomes clear that there is nothing nebulous about this 'performance': it is inextricably linked to social action on a specific order and set of instructions.

In this context, there is a close theoretical linkage with the axiomatic assumption made by J.L. Austin in his seminal text on *How to Do Things with Words* (1975), where he challenges the notion that 'language simply "constates" or reports on reality'; rather, 'performatives' (Austin's neologism, a noun rather than an adjective) are 'not informational reports, but actions, events, doings. Today, performative utterances are understood to be crucial to the construction of reality, a construction that is sociotechnically *ordered*.'[48] It is this 'sociotechnical' understanding of 'performance', and its relationship with 'performativity', that enables me to structure and make sense of the evidence on terror presented in this book, particularly in dealing with the political and juridical processes relating to post-genocide Rwanda and post-apartheid South Africa, addressed at length in chapter 3. Even as the 'post' in 'post-genocide' and 'post-apartheid' is used more as shorthand for a description of events following the 'official' ends of genocide and apartheid in Rwanda and South Africa, respectively, the performative analysis of these processes will reveal that the residues and crimes of genocide and apartheid continue to persist and mutate in diverse ways.

Given the predominantly discursive nature of my critical inquiry in dealing with states of transitional justice where words are catalysts which make acts of terror tangible and significant, I draw on Judith Butler's eminently succinct understanding of 'performativity' as 'the power of discourse to produce what it names.'[49] The discourses *of* terror and *against* terror, which are represented in a wide range of registers in this book through the rhetorics of American exceptionalism, Islamophobia, communalism, torture, genocide, truth and reconciliation, and non-violence, are what *make* terror. Instead of merely describing or reporting on the excesses of terror at a purely descriptive level, capitalizing on first-person narratives of excruciating pain and suffering,

I am more concerned to understand how terror actually gets implemented through the speech-acts of the state, among other authoritarian and terrorist agencies.

In this regard, one of the most chilling demonstrations of performativity comes from Khalid Sheikh Mohammed, the alleged mastermind of the 'September 11' attack, who, in response to George Bush's declaration – and activation – of the 'war on terror', declares in his own right: '*we are doing the same language*'.[50] The fact that performative statements, in their very 'uttering', also 'perform a certain action and exercise a binding power',[51] in Butler's exacting words, is evident on both sides of the terror divide. Bush and Mohammed are both users of 'war as a language' – arguably, a 'common language' that enemies share with each other.[52] In a testimonial, which has been transcribed verbatim without any grammatical or stylistic corrections, Mohammed says:

> I don't like to kill people. I feel very sorry they been killed kids in 9/11. What will I do? *This is the language* . . . I know American people are torturing us from seventies . . . I know they talking about human rights. And I know it is against American constitution, against American laws. But they said, every law, they have exceptions, this is your bad luck you been part of the exception of our laws. They got have something to convince me but *we are doing the same language*.[53]

A chilling exposition of How to Do Terror with Words, regardless of which side you're on: language is not just 'speaking'; it is 'doing', 'torturing', 'killing'.

Needless to say, despite the force of performativity, performance does not disappear, even as it becomes necessary to maintain some theoretical distinctions as Butler so rigorously delineates in her exposition of these terms:

> [P]erformance as a bounded 'act' is distinguished from performativity insofar as the latter consists in a reiteration of norms which precede, constrain, and exceed the performer and in that sense cannot be taken as the fabrication of the performer's 'will' or 'choice'; further, what is 'performed' works to conceal, if not to disavow, what remains opaque, unconscious, unperformable. The reduction of performativity to performance would be a mistake.[54]

If 'performance', for Butler, is something akin to 'an act in the here-and-now', implying 'a presence . . . bounded in the will of the performer', performativity is fundamentally discursive, and always already anticipated and succeeded by the regulatory norms of socially established meaning. And yet, despite Butler's caution against 'the reduction of performativity to performance', she does attempt to suggest a possible permeability of these terms, in so far as she makes space for the 'promising deregulation' of performance to resist being fully subsumed in 'the compulsory character of certain social imperatives'.[55] This permeability could be read as a 'convergence', as Jon

McKenzie suggests, drawing on Butler's ever so slight hint in this direction.[56] However, I would argue that it is more productively viewed as a *tension* in the larger context of a queer refusal to submit to norms that define and constrain attempts to trouble regulation through acts of dissidence.

Balancing his role as performance analyst with a mischievous 'take' on his own colleagues in performance studies, McKenzie imagines them responding to Butler's 'misuse' of language with consternation – a misuse that he correctly chooses to read as a 'tactic of resignification, of queering'.[57] In the process, he performs some of the fictional responses of his colleagues: '[Performativity] is linguistic rather than embodied!'; 'it means normativity as much as subversion!'; 'couldn't she use another term?'[58] Joining the chorus, I cannot deny the temptation on the part of any theatre or performance practitioner to reclaim 'performativity' in favour of a more sensuous embrace of the body's infinitesimal secrets and enigmas, against Butler's arguably non-corporeal, if not anti-visceral, reading of 'the body', which is far too socially constructed. Indeed, I should prepare the reader of this book for a very perceptible tension in my use of the word 'performative', which is, on the one hand, read as a *noun*, following the linguistic and discursive models set by Austin and Butler; but, on the other hand, I also use 'performative' as an *adjective* in a non-discursive, expressive, histrionic sense, as in 'performative energy' or 'performative dynamics', in describing the actual process and somatic impact of a particular performance.

Is it 'too late to reclaim *performativity* for the nondiscursive realm of performance', as Diana Taylor (2007) suggests in her scarcely concealed impatience with the 'false cognates' of 'performative' and 'performativity' for 'performance'?[59] My own view is that we may have no other choice at this point in time but to embrace the tensions of 'performance', 'performative' and 'performativity', not least because these categories are so deeply imbricated both within and beyond performance practice. To seek clear distinctions across the larger terrains of 'performativity' and 'performance' on Butler's terms is theoretically useful, but only to the extent that the ambivalences, enigmas and secrets of corporeal performance are not undermined or eliminated.

Against all these theoretically challenging considerations relating to 'performance' and 'performativity', what happens to theatre? Is it of no relevance in explicating the discourses and massive events surrounding terror? If one assumes that theatre appears somewhat archaic in an age of 'virtual war', where weapons designed to kill long-distance with minimal deaths (and unaccounted collateral damage) have become the most deadly 'performers' of our times, it is worth keeping in mind Giorgio Agamben's (2009) deeply insightful reminder on what constitutes the 'contemporary'. For Agamben the twist in the argument is that only those who perceive 'the indices and signature of the archaic in the most modern and recent can be contemporary.'[60] If there is a 'secret affinity' between 'the archaic and the modern', it is not because 'archaic forms' like theatre continue to exercise a 'particular charm' on the present; rather, 'the key to the modern is hidden in the immemorial and the prehistoric'.[61] Contemporariness cannot be reduced to a singular relationship 'with one's own time'; on the contrary, the contemporary is more meaningfully grasped through a 'relationship with time that adheres to it *through a disjunction and an anachronism*.'[62]

Theatre, I would argue, should be regarded as precisely this kind of 'disjunction' and 'anachronism' that challenges the hegemonic common sense which assumes that only the language of 'performance' (as defined by performance studies) can legitimately address the terror of our times. This bias is only too evident in John Bell's pitch for 'Performance Studies in an Age of Terror' (2007), which asserts that 'the idea of performance offers concepts, means of analysis and methods of action which can help us figure out where we are and what we ought to do – certainly better than concepts of "art" or "drama" or "theatre".'[63] While fully accepting that 'performance' is the broadest and most flexible category available to encompass the multiple acts, actions, reactions, movements and after-effects of terror recorded in this book, I would not rule out the lurking presence and interruptive power of the languages and concepts of theatre in making sense of the diverse 'performances' of terror.

Circumventing the assumptions of which discipline or field is 'better' than the other, W.B. Worthen has argued against the unproductive dichotomy between 'performance' and 'theatre': '[T]o define this "new paradigm" [of performance studies] in opposition to theatre studies . . . is, finally, to reinscribe performance studies with at least some of the analytical hierarchies its practitioners would contest.'[64] Focusing more minutely on Richard Schechner's opposition between 'reading' and 'doing' – the former associated with dramatic literature and a rather narrow understanding of 'the text' as opposed to 'textuality', the latter connected with the contingencies and hands-on practices of engaging with other cultures in all their corporeality and density – Worthen points out that to sustain 'a simple opposition between text and performance is to remain captive to the spectral disciplines of the past.'[65]

What emerges from Worthen's rigorous, yet subtle position is that reading is an act, a performance in its own right, involving a critical engagement with multiple textualities in all their worldliness. The text is not just a passive or virtual appendage to the 'real' of performance; textuality is even more fluid a category in so far as it can exist only in the state of a text being textured – or, more precisely, performed – in specific ways. Far from upholding the purism of immutable categories stuck in the past, Worthen seizes '*this moment* of undisciplined, interdisciplinary flux' to offer the eminently sensible view that 'no simple opposition between text and performance', or the 'paradigms' constituting them, will be sufficient to capture 'the rich, contradictory, incommensurable ways that they engage one another'.[66] If anything would qualify as 'archaic' in my view, it would be the rather tired and redundant disciplinary war between 'theatre' and 'performance' as affirmed by their respective academic constituencies in theatre studies and performance studies. Fortunately, through the formative research of many scholars crossing the divide, it is now somewhat more axiomatic to assume that the 'genealogies' of these 'disciplines', as Shannon Jackson has indicated, may be more interwoven and hybridized than their die-hard supporters would care to admit.[67]

Countering academic wars, let us also acknowledge that there are more serious 'wars' deserving our critical attention, like 'the war on terror', and that it is time to forge closer alliances across and within each other's disciplines and practices in order to strategize *which* language is most appropriate for a particular inquiry in a particular context. If the language of 'performativity', for example, tends to be prioritized at particular junctures in this book, it is because of its pertinence in deconstructing the discursivity of official policies and rhetoric relating to, say, 'forgiveness' in post-genocide Rwanda, or 'truth and reconciliation' in post-apartheid South Africa. However, for other sections in my narrative, which are more linked to body behaviours and the *habitus* underlying particular gestures and improvisations, I have found the language of 'performance' as articulated by Richard Schechner, in his much-cited formulation of 'restored' or 'twice-behaved' behaviour, to be useful in dealing with the repetition of particular performances both within the confines of theatre institutions and in the public domain at large.[68]

On the one hand, a concept like 'restoration of behaviour' is particularly effective in dealing with a spectrum of ritual, artistic and cultural performances across time which get altered through new technologies and inventions of tradition. But, at the same time, the epistemology of categories like 'restoration' and 'behaviour' can run up against huge ethical and political problems when the 'performance' in question is linked to specific contexts of genocide, and the annihilation of basic human resources and lives. The point is not to undermine the vitality of the concept, but to indicate *where* and *how* it resonates with greater intensity in specific contexts as opposed to others. In a broader register, and as a leitmotif that runs through the entire book, I indicate *the limits of performance* in dealing with the aftermaths of terror, notably the actual deaths resulting from suicide-bombing, or the killing of religious minorities in a communal atrocity or genocide. Likewise, there are limits to the performativity of social transformative processes built around Truth and Reconciliation in post-apartheid South Africa and post-genocide Rwanda. Inevitably, this articulation of the limits of any discourse compels one to acknowledge one's own unease in finding adequate words or conceptual tools to analyse *all* aspects of the terror of our times within the same epistemology and methodology of understanding performance.

Along with the capacities of 'performance' as a language, and a set of tools and practices, to illuminate the terror of our times, the practice of 'theatre', I would reiterate, continues to be a valuable resource despite its seeming marginality. Theatre's vocabulary of 'entrances', 'exits', 'presence', 'energy', 'conflict', 'transformation' and 'repetition' continues to haunt and catalyse new manifestations of these words. The paradox is that when one least expects it, theatre is always already there. Let me provide a small example here, drawn from the formidable fieldwork of international studies scholar James Der Derian, who, without engaging directly with the language of theatre or performance, assumes the role of a virtuoso theorist–performer in his *tour de force* of a book, *Virtuous War: Mapping the Military–Industrial–Media–Entertainment Network* (2009a).

Presenting himself as something of a Lone Ranger, Derian infiltrates high-level conferences on security and war, in addition to simulated military war zones within the United States, where the 'war on terror', among other earlier wars, is staged and rehearsed in preparation of 'real' wars by US army personnel and military specialists. The chilling ethnography on the 'theatre of war' resulting from Derian's infiltration is nothing short of a bravura performance. Adopting the mode of thick description, he grabs the attention of his readers by exposing the musculature and kinetics of US soldiers re-enacting Rambo, dressed in high-tech, laser-sensitive outfits, accoutred with digital weapons. Their 'performance' is symptomatic of a capitulation to a larger 'military–industrial–media–entertainment network', as Derian describes it, where the idea of a 'virtuous war' is actively rehearsed to test out virtual weaponry and ground-fighting tactics in the here and now of make-believe 'Iraqs' and 'Afghanistans'.

In one such experiment where two groups of marines enact a 'force-on-force operation', in which one group's mission involves the recapturing of an abandoned naval hospital, Derian describes a somewhat 'eccentric' scenario which is worth quoting at length:

> The sound of gunfire from the stairway ahead dropped the Bravo company into firing positions, M-16s ready. Just then, a young African–American woman descended the staircase, stepped over the prone marines, and walked out the door. She was dressed in the refugee-slacker look of enemy 'Country Orange,' but her red jacket and the freeze-frame quality of the movement evoked the girl walking through the grayness of the Jewish ghetto in *Schindler's List*. After a long pause and an exchange of befuddled looks, an order was shouted out, and

> three marines scrambled to their feet to grab her as she left the building. Was she a terrorist, a hostage, or just lost? Adding to the tension – and absurdity – two observers/controllers in colonial pith helmets kept a careful watch from a short distance away. The marines couldn't tell who or what the young woman was: using some kind of sign language, she appeared to be either deaf, or foreign. Literally dumb-founded, the marines finally let her go. Later, when the battle was over, I spotted her chatting among a group of fellow refugees in the hospital parking lot. I asked her what had happened in the hospital. She laughed, and said that she had been bored and decided on the spot to do some improv.[69]

For me, this moment of 'improv' is pure theatre – it is impulsive, irreverent, funny, working against the rules of a choreographed 'battle' and totally oblivious to the threat of simulated weaponry. Unlike other high-tech experiments described by Derian where there are 'technical fuck-ups', this impulse to 'do some improv' is driven by human agency and creative instinct. The savvy African–American actor counters the possibility of being marked as a 'terrorist' or 'hostage' by resorting to sign-language, leaving her aggressors 'dumbfounded'.

I will resist the temptation to share more such stories from Derian's thoroughly gripping and entertaining journey into 'the war machine', but the point to be made is that even in the most futurist of performative experiments, where one cannot quite figure out the 'real' from the 'simulated' or the 'human' from the 'machinic', there is the subterranean 'archaic' presence of theatre, in Agamben's formulation. It is precisely this 'archaism' which makes the contemporaneity of war games all the more deadly. With this qualification in mind, I would argue that instead of regarding 'theatre', 'performance' and 'performativity' as heuristic and exclusive categories, it is more useful to place them in an interactive context where there is a certain elasticity in their dynamics, moving in and out, between the personal and the political, the corporeal and the discursive, almost converging at times only to stretch apart at breaking point.

If this book is about terror, it is also about theatre, performance and performativity, which are the categories, conceptual modalities and practices that enable me to see, think and write about terror in the first place. There is no Archimedean perspective on terror which can be examined from any one modality of performance. At a methodological level, therefore, it is necessary to prepare the reader for a certain volatility in my methodology of analysing terror. Chapter 1, which bounces off a production of Jean Genet's *The Maids* in Manila, within and against the political moment of 'September 11', is almost inevitably coloured by the volatile practice of *theatre* and its spill-over into the critical and philosophical discourses of 'September 11'. In chapter 2, I widen my understanding of *performances in everyday life* within the larger global immediacies of Islamophobia, which impact at local levels in the acts of 'passing' and 'covering' as a Muslim, and of 'queering' the Muslim as 'terrorist'. As I have mentioned earlier, chapter 3, on the Truth and Reconciliaton process in Rwanda and South Africa, focuses more sharply on the concept of *performativity* animating political discourse, which draws its analytical logic from Judith Butler's enunciation of 'the power of discourse to produce what it names'. And chapter 4, on the possibilities of rethinking non-violence in the age of terror, melds together different readings of Gandhi's *activist performances* and the actual *video performances* of suicide bombers presenting their testimonials in front of the camera, among other extremist acts performed by refugees and asylum seekers.

Even within this far too cryptic encapsulation of the entire book, it becomes obvious that the categories of theatre, performance and performativity cannot be placed in watertight compartments. If, for instance, in chapter 3, the discourse of Truth and Reconciliation lends itself to being read almost exclusively within the theory of performativity, I have found it unavoidable to juxtapose *performativity* with the *theatricality* of the victims' hearings, drawn from my close reading of the rigorous research on Rwanda and South Africa provided by Ananda Breed (2007, 2008, 2009, 2014) and Catherine Cole (2010), respectively. Indeed, a lot of my 'evidence' on terror in this book is not first-hand but drawn from important secondary critical sources, like Arjun Appadurai's provocative essay on 'Dead Certainty: Ethnic Violence in an Era of Globalization' (1998), which I found necessary to insert in chapter 2 *vis-à-vis* my larger reading of the 2002 genocide in Gujarat where Muslims were marked – and killed – with 'dead certainty'. Likewise, in chapter 4, the discourse on 'just war' could not have been possible without critical readings of key texts provided by Michael Walzer (2000, 2004) and Talal Asad (2007), which I juxtapose tangentially against Sri Aurobindo's (1970, 2006) views on anti-fascist resistance in the state of war.

While many of these critical readings of both primary and secondary textual resources can be said to counter the practice-inspired research of chapter 1, I would emphasize that this is how 'terror' has registered for me as a writer: not as one phenomenon demanding a singular approach and methodology, but as a cluster of discourses, affects, sensations and critical moments of emergency and crisis. While I have responded to these stimulations within my cognitive and hermeneutic capacities – and limitations – as a writer, I do not rule out many other ways in which terror can be performed in the life of the mind.

## DANGEROUS LIAISONS: TERROR AND PERFORMANCE

Having outlined some of the key theoretical aspects of terror and performance as they impact on the formulation of this book, the actual dynamics and interpenetration of these categories are what constitute the actual content of the book. Without attempting to spell out how terror and performance interrelate, which I would prefer you to read and interrogate in the course of reading the book, suffice it to say for the purpose of this introduction that it is the interrelationships between terror and performance that matter to me, and not any illumination of the ontology of terror through a singularized understanding of performance.

My book is specifically entitled *Terror and Performance*, and not *Terror as Performance*, for the simple reason that terror itself, to spell out a critical point as bluntly as possible, is not a performance. In my understanding, the performative understanding of terror begins only when one *responds* to an act of extreme violence, however vulnerably and in a state of acute fear, either through spectatorship or an act of witnessing. Terror can also be performed as one *re-lives* the act, either through an immersion in its representation on the media, or, even more precisely, through a critical response to the media and the discourses that have accumulated around the event. The performance of terror, I would emphasize, is built through the accretion of these responses and not through the act of terror itself, such as the actual demolition of the Twin Towers in Manhattan, or the genocide of ethnic communities or minorities in Rwanda and Gujarat. To regard the involuntary deaths of victims *as performances in their own right* raises troubling issues around the agency, if not the privilege, to name 'performance' in the first place. As I will demonstrate at different points in the book, there are complex *ethical* issues relating to the equation of death with performance which compel one to be wary about reducing acts of terror to spectacles and images, decontextualized from those who are killed or liquidated in the activation of terror.

Even as I question the ethics of naming acts of extreme violence *as* performance, I could be justifiably asked: Why do I engage with performance at all? As one of my most astute readers, the philosopher Sundar Sarukkai, has asked me, 'What work does "performance" do? What does it reveal about terror that other analyses – such as the psychological, social, political and economic – cannot do?' To this robust and pertinent question I would say, first of all, that 'performance' does not have to work independently of the psychological, the social, the political and the economic dimensions of any analysis of terror. Performance has a capacity to synthesize these different domains of inquiry within its specific synaesthetic capacities of incorporating ideas and realities. Second, if I had to specify some key concepts and modalities of analysis that are distinctive to performance, I would say that its capacities of 'embodiment', 'affect', 'corporeality', 'kinesthetics' and 'reflexivity' are more palpable than what is found in the social sciences, enabling a different kind of analysis of terror from what is available in political or economic theory.

Having made this qualification, I would be reluctant to claim that this difference amounts to being somehow more 'enlightened' or 'perceptive' or 'creative' about terror. Rather, as my own dependence on the social sciences in engaging with the realities of communalism, genocide, truth and reconciliation, and the law will become only too evident in the course of reading this book, it is perhaps more productive to ask not what one discipline can do at the expense of the others, but, rather, what kind of discourse can be arrived at through a dialogic process of interweaving disciplines at their very limits. Therefore, in response to Sarukkai's question, 'What work does "performance" do?', I would reiterate one of Brecht's favourite maxims by affirming that 'the proof of the pudding is in the eating'. I can only hope that the readers of this book will find at least some insights into the phenomenon of terror through the language of performance that they might not have realized from other disciplines.

Narrative plays a key role here. It is not just the elaboration of concepts that facilitates a performative reading of terror, but the ways in which these concepts are juxtaposed and embodied within a counterpoint of autobiography, testimony and anecdote which constitute a 'performance' in its own right. In the narrative of this book, terror and performance share an intimate spectrum of relationships which are not fully determined until their specific circuits of energy are brought into contact. These points of 'contact' have the potential to ignite suddenly and abruptly, without any adequate cognizance or preparation on our part as readers. In this volatile state, terror and performance share what could be described as dangerous liaisons – not one tryst with the unknown and the diabolical, but a series of compulsive relationships which disintegrate only to re-ignite in even more devious ways.

Within the dark and secret intimacies of dangerous liaisons, it would be disingenuous to regard terror and performance as oppositional categories. In other words, I do not assume that performance provides some kind of *intrinsic* wholesomeness or liberatory potentiality that can serve as a counter to the demons of terror and terrorism in our times. I cannot claim to have written a 'feel-good' narrative which provides the false hope that by doing theatre and engaging with performance, the world at large will be a somewhat safer and saner place. Rather, in response to the increasingly deviant ways by which terror gets performed, not only by human agencies but through cyber warfare or bioterrorism, it becomes hard to keep up with the ways in which the performance of terror outwits the existing surveillance systems, which are manifestations of terror in their own right.

Even as I may acknowledge that almost all the practitioners of theatre and performance represented in this book, both voluntary and involuntary, are well-intentioned, in so far as they would like to find ways of resisting violence, or healing wounds, or getting on with life beyond the trauma of terror or genocide, the reality is that these intentions cannot be assumed to result in positive actions or consequences. More often than not they can backfire, or, worse, they can be attacked or implode from within. While it would be hard to affirm at an axiomatic level that there is a terrorist potentiality within *all* performances – one would need to specify *which* performances are under consideration, and by *whom* and *how* they are performed *in specific circumstances* – I would not close the possibility of some performances by governments or prison authorities or the judiciary from feeding the narratives of terror, or cashing in on its destructive power in opportunistic and parasitic ways.

At times these performances can backfire, as for instance when anti-terror rescue missions by state agencies become terrorist operations in their own right. One of the most chilling examples of this volte-face can be detected in the raid of the Dubrovska Theatre in Moscow in October 2002 by the Russian state police, following the disruption of a high-tech Broadway-like musical when the entire audience was taken hostage by Chechen rebels. Tellingly, it was not the Chechens who killed the spectators, thereby affirming their status as 'terrorists'; rather, it was a poisonous gas pumped into the theatre by the Russian militia that resulted in the deaths of a majority of the hostages, many of whom choked to death on their own vomit. Worse, the police and its benefactors in the upper echelons of the state refused to divulge the identity of the gas, thereby preventing doctors from using the appropriate antidote to counter its pernicious effects on the survivors. At all costs state secrets needed to remain secret even as people died in agony, compelling the philosopher Roberto Esposito to acknowledge that faced with 'the question of the survival of human beings suspended between life and death', the state inevitably resorts to a brutal final solution: 'To keep [citizens] alive at all costs, one can even decide to hasten their death.'[70]

By not elaborating at length on such events as the terrorist attack on the Dubrovska Theatre and reducing it in the process to a mere 'example', however illuminating, of terror, I am only too aware that my book has some glaring elisions and omissions. All that I can say in defence is that I am not attempting to provide an exhaustive or synoptic perspective on global terror through the lens of performance; rather, all I have tried to do is to open up some of the enigmatic and troubling relationships between terror and performance through specific case studies, experiments and improvisations in everyday life. Tellingly, when I started the book, fired by the radical politics of Jean Genet, I had no idea that Gandhi would figure so forcefully in the last chapter, but such are the unexpected surprises in reflecting on terror, which is the task that I have set myself to do. Far from surrendering to the dictates of a manifesto or a polemic against terrorism, I have attempted to *reflect* on terror, which is not just a difficult task, but also one that risks coming across as an indulgent intellectual exercise. Besides, does terror lend itself to reflection?

A necessary clarification: If my narrative engages with terror in diverse geographical locations, it is not because I had any particular desire to be 'comprehensive', but because the specific instances of terror in relation to theatre, performance and performativity addressed in this book through 'minor' and 'major' events in the United States, Philippines, India, Rwanda, South Africa, Palestine and Australia have compelled me to think through terror in specific ways. The focus on these critical instances is not meant to imply that terror does not exist in other parts of the world. Nor should my concentration on these specific manifestations of terror indicate that they are somehow more lethal or tragic in their implications than their counterparts elsewhere. Such comparative assessments of terror are in poor taste, not unlike the politics that are played around grief and loss whereby hierarchies are set up in which the grief and loss of some people are somehow worth more (or less) than the grief and loss of others. Avoiding the pitfalls of comparativism, which is best negotiated by 'terror experts' committed to a regular stocktaking of terror in different parts of the world, I prefer to think from the ground up through local densities which provoke a concatenation of thoughts – disjunctive, processual, and, at times, deliberately left unprocessed and unfinished. To provide an 'ending' to the terror of our times would be a hopelessly optimistic gesture.

Finally, I would acknowledge that writing on terror is a hazardous exercise not only because it is always on the verge of breaking down under the sheer pressure of conflicting discourses; rather, it also has the potentiality of blowing up in your face. Therefore, the statutory warning accompanying any such narrative should be, 'Handle with Care'. Like the task of assembling the components of a bomb, all the wires deftly and neatly interwoven without touching, the writing of terror requires as much vigilance and subtlety as the reading of its narrative. With these preliminary comments, let me hand over the book to you for your critical attention, hoping that your collaboration in the act of reading will enable us to think through terror together.

# 1

# GENET IN MANILA

## 'September 11' in Retrospect

## PRE-TERROR

Oh what a beautiful mornin',
Oh what a beautiful day,
I've got a beautiful feelin',
Everything's goin' my way.
– *Oklahoma*, Rodgers and Hammerstein

### DEADLY INNOCENCE

Returning to the initial provocation of this book, let us revisit Manila in the first week of October 2001 when I was ready to start a rehearsal process culminating in a long-desired production of Genet's *The Maids* in Tagalog translation.[1] The production was six weeks away and everything seemed to be 'goin' my way', as the opening song of *Oklahoma* declares, and which, indeed, was very much the sentiment of most people on that bright and crisp morning on 11 September 2001 in Manhattan before two planes crashed into the Twin Towers of the World Trade Center, precipitating an event that has come to be memorialized as 'September 11'. Since there is no way in which we can 'reverse the video of 9/11, [and] watch the two towers climb back out of the rubble, two planes emerge intact from the buildings, nineteen terrorists return to Hamburg, Saudi Arabia, Yemen', as James Der Derian reminds us caustically,[2] we have no other option but to exhume the terrifying effects of 'September 11' from its overstated, yet unresolved discourse. Before we focus on a critique of this discourse in the second part of this chapter, let me reconstruct the deadly innocence underlying my dramaturgical preparation for *The Maids*, which had begun on a previous trip to the Philippines between January and March 2001. Perhaps it was during this period, in that buoyant pre-rehearsal stage of dreaming *The Maids*, that I imagined, in a state of no-terror whatsoever, that everything was not just 'goin' my way' but surpassing my expectations.

In critical hindsight, I should have been a lot more alert to the fact that directing Genet – and, more specifically, the task of performing Genet – is a form of terror in its own right. Mocking the protocols of security which determine public culture, of which theatre is the most established of 'civic' institutions, *The Maids* can be regarded as a masterpiece of multiple deceptions which compels its practitioners to submit to the most unsettling of insecurities. On the surface it comes across like a seemingly staid one-act play which deals with two maids, Solange and Claire (Soledad and Clara in their Filipina adaptations), who are constantly interrupted in their role-switching performative rituals as they attempt to kill their beloved, yet insidious Madame. However, this is the mere plot around which Genet improvises a devious meta-performative exercise in which the most basic tropes of theatre – time, illusion, identity – are deconstructed with a combination of intense decorum and manic energy.

While the action of the play takes place ostensibly in linear time in the illusory present, the actual performance of the play embraces and slips through a multitude, a labyrinth, a kaleidoscope of several conflicting times. Indeed, such is the treachery involved in performing *The Maids* that even within the span of a sentence, time shifts at vertiginous levels. In this groundbreaking dramaturgy – groundbreaking in quite a literal sense because there is no firm epistemological ground on which Genet's 'characters' stand – the actors are compelled to work outside the realistic demands of psychological acting to explore a gamut of performance styles: playacting, mimicry, dissemblance, lying, melodrama, burlesque, farce, bad acting, no-acting. In such a virtuosity of styles, blatantly fake and emphatically framed within the deadly artifice of repetition, one is reminded – yet again, in critical hindsight – that the maids could be exemplars of all those border-crossers, including terrorists, criminals, refugees, undocumented non-citizens and ordinary people on the run, whose only 'identity' remains constantly re-invented, in ceaseless flux.

Recalling his early production of *The Maids* in 1963, long before performance studies was on the horizon, Richard Schechner focuses accurately on the 'identity slippage' that animates Genet's dramaturgy, which makes it 'impossible to pin down the characters'.[3] In this sense, the Pirandellian distinctions between 'actors' and 'characters' in search of an 'author' are made far more complicated by the fact that Genet's characters are not just more fluid; they are molten energies, processual animations, always becoming something else more often than not through the compulsions of desire, only to break down almost instantaneously. To perform Genet, therefore, is to subject one's self to 'a great sense of insecurity',[4] as the director Jean-Baptiste Sastre has correctly emphasized. Not only is 'character' always on the verge of dissolution and de-formation, the problem has to do with 'meaning' itself, which shifts even after it has been determined and analysed in rehearsal, consolidating for a moment in performance only to 'evaporate'.[5]

To elaborate on Genet's dramaturgy is tempting, but that is not the purpose of this chapter which focuses on more elliptical, yet resonant connections between performance and terror in the larger discursive context of 'September 11'. Genet is at once the stimulus and the *pretext* for the commentary on 'September 11' that follows. In this regard I will not be offering an analysis of the *mise-en-scène* of the Manila production, which can be accessed in Marian Pastor Roces's 'thick description' of the maids' performative bodies, 'meta-women' played by 'men' cross-dressed in all-black push-up bras, girdles, torn fishnet stockings and unlaced army boots.[6] These hybrid creatures (who could be regarded as queer terrorists in at least some of their manifestations), 'repulsed, embraced and un-manned reality', as Roces enunciates in her laser-sharp reading of how the actors deconstructed themselves as 'men', 'women', 'gays', 'actors' and 'maids'. An even more quirky deconstruction of the mythology of 'the maid' was provided by Judy Freya Sibayan in an installation on 'The Rights of Passage', which was staged in the lobby of the Republic of Malate, the impressively named but gritty dance club and bar where *The Maids* was staged in Manila.[7]

If I resist the temptation to elaborate on the sexual corporealities and masquerades of both the *mise-en-scène* and the installation, it is because this chapter is not *about* the representation of *The Maids* in Manila; rather it is more enigmatically linked to the 'political unconscious' of the production, to those dimensions of terror which never got expressed in the *mise-en-scène*. It is these dimensions of terror-in-waiting, terror suspended and terror deferred that are of concern to me. What follows, therefore, is a post-mortem not of my production, but of the larger historical moment and the time of 'September 11' that unconsciously pervaded the rehearsal process of *The Maids*, and which continues to haunt the writing of this chapter today.

## INTENTIONALITY

Looking back on the euphoric moment of beginning to rehearse *The Maids* in Manila, I would acknowledge that the intentionality underlying my concept of the production had much to do with the illusion that 'everything's goin' my way'. Even as one may be aware that intentionality is invariably subverted in the actual practice of *doing* theatre, the point is that it always exists in some inchoate form, as much as one may deny it. Therefore, in addition to my directorial choice to highlight an explicitly gay sexuality in *The Maids* against Genet's aversion to identity politics – Leo Bersani has famously identified

Genet as 'the least gay affirmative of gay writers'[8] – another reason to do the play was irrevocably linked to the political and economic fact that 'the maid' is one of the biggest export items of the Philippines. She earns more foreign exchange than almost any other commodity produced in the Philippines, and contributes to 12 per cent of the Philippines' GDP through remittances made by around 8.5 million Filipino workers, mostly women, who constitute slightly less than 10 per cent of the population.[9]

Even as these facts can lend themselves to a dramaturgy of social realism or documentary theatre, which Genet specifically shunned, how can one ignore the brutal fact that thousands of Filipina maids live and work in varied conditions of neo-slavery, separated from their homes and families, in countries as far-flung as Hong Kong, Saudi Arabia, Singapore and Japan? Social outcasts, neither residents in their own homes nor citizens in their places of work, they are humiliated, beaten, abused, raped, terrorized and even, in one chilling event masterminded by the state of Singapore, executed.

I refer to the tragic fate of the working-class Filipina maid Flor Contemplacion (literally, 'Flower Contemplation', a very Genet-like name reminiscent of *Our Lady of the Flowers*) who was hanged in Singapore on 17 March 1995 for allegedly strangling another Filipina domestic worker and drowning a four-year-old child on 4 May 1991.[10] No amount of high-level governmental intervention on the part of the former President of the Philippines, Fidel Ramos, was adequate to waive her death sentence in Singapore. When Flor's body was brought home to the Philippines following massive public outrage against the Singapore government, she had already become a 'people's saint'. The conclusive evidence provided by the Singapore government substantiating her crime was not sufficient to convince the people of the Philippines that she had not been grievously wronged and exploited. Instead, she was transformed into an icon representing thousands of her sisters who continue to be dehumanized, and occasionally raped and killed, as 'overseas foreign workers' or 'domestic helpers', the politically correct euphemisms for 'maids' today.

Can I deny that Flor Contemplacion provided the fundamental political stimulus for the concept of my production? Inspired by her numerous fictional avatars in soap opera, pop music and, above all, her eerie alter ego in Nora Aunor, the brown-skinned, diminutive 'superstar' of the Philippines cinema, I had already strategized a key sequence in the production before the rehearsals started. Almost compulsively – such is the hubris of any concept prior to the performance process – it was clear to me that I had to use the film footage of Flor Contemplacion's body brought back to the Philippines after her execution in Singapore, which I had wanted to intersect with Soledad's orgasmic funereal dirge at the end of *The Maids*. In this dirge, Soledad envisions a procession of maids and other menials accompanying Clara to her final resting place. What had seemed to me in prior readings of Genet's play as a virtuoso delirium of a maid caught up in her own hallucinations now began to resonate like a requiem for Flor Contemplacion, with all the contradictory signs of performing this moment in Manila within Genet's complex mythology.

In this mythology, the criminal is a saint. Hard as it may be to accept, Flor Contemplacion was branded – and proved – a criminal in the eyes of the law. Even so, her execution exemplifies precisely the brutality that Genet associates with the self-righteous, moralistic state, as opposed to the violence of so-called criminals. In his seminal essay on 'Violence and Brutality' (1977), Genet expresses his allegiance to terrorists through his support for the Red Army Faction (later stigmatized by the media as the Baader-Meinhof gang), who 'have made us understand', as he puts it, 'not only by words but by actions, both in and out of prison, that violence alone can bring an end to the brutality of men'.[11] The timing of this essay, which was first published in *Le Monde* on 2 September 1977, was particularly provocative because, three days later, the president of the German Employers Federation, Hans-Martin Schleyer, was kidnapped in Cologne by the RAF. This high-profile media event only contributed towards the outrage against Genet's alleged defence of 'terrorism'. Nonetheless his position, as outlined in *Violence and Brutality*, remained unequivocal: if violence is associated with the necessary and just actions of revolutionaries, rebels and terrorists, brutality is the anaesthetizing prerogative of the state and its agencies, notably the armed forces and the police, in upholding the law against violence.

Significantly, even as Genet prioritizes his critique of brutality in relation to massacres in war, torture in prison and the intimidation of immigrants, he has a more intimate envisioning of brutality embedded in the cultures, topographies and gestures of everyday life. Focusing on the unacknowledged dimensions of brutality, Genet calls our attention to the fact that,

> Brutality takes the most unexpected forms, often not immediately discernible as brutality: the architecture of public housing projects; bureaucracy; the substitution of a word – proper or familiar – by a number; the priority, in traffic, given to speed over the slow rhythm of the pedestrian; the authority of the machine over the man who serves it; the codification of laws that override custom; the numerical progression of prison sentences; the use of secrets that prevent the public from knowing what concerns it; the useless slaps and blows in police stations; the condescending speech of police addressing anyone with brown skin . . . [12]

This gamut of manifestations relating brutality to the most ordinary and banal levels of social interaction reveals how people live with terror in everyday life, which gets routinized and accepted. However, from the perspective of the outcast and the criminal, and his affinities to the underworld, Genet is able to question the hegemonization of brutality through his deep awareness of its actual performances at sensory and somatic levels. Thus, a common gesture, like a policeman's hand clutching on to the scruff of a criminal's neck, epitomized for him the 'brutal gesture' that 'halts and suppresses a free act'.[13]

It is precisely this corporeality that complicates Genet's envisioning of the police from more philosophical readings of their power. In Walter Benjamin's prescient analysis, we learn how the 'law' assumed by the police is '*independent* of the rest of the law', residing in a 'no-man's land' that exists outside of the state's control and is yet 'indispensable to the maintenance of the law'.[14] Calling attention to this lethal indeterminacy by which the police are 'paid to be free of the law so as to be able to get on with their job', Michael Taussig (2006) directly links this condition to the New York City Police Department, whose licence to interpret the law has increased terrifyingly in accordance with the larger laws of Homeland Security in the United States and the extra-legal jurisdiction of prisons like Guantánamo. The violation of the law in the name of protecting it is no longer the exception but the rule.

For Genet, this practice of the police extending the larger brutalizing mechanisms of the state would come as no surprise, habituated as he was to the blackmailing, extortionist and double tactics of the police, in collusion with the immigration authorities and the legal system. However, what he brought to the complex relationship between the criminal and the police, far surpassing anything Benjamin could have envisioned, was a profoundly troubling dimension of *desire*. More specifically, it was homosexual desire which enabled him, for instance, to rail against the brutal practices of the US police in an anti-establishment political rally organized by the Black Panthers, even while admiring their muscles and thighs. There are many such instances in Genet's oeuvre where the very signs of power, like the policeman's badge, elicit a charge in which the police and the criminal are 'erotically intertwined', as Taussig puts it pithily.[15] At the same time, for all the paradoxical ambivalence that can be read into the figure of sexually desirable 'cops' – a more intimate identification of the 'police' – the point is that they are repositories of brutality, and no amount of liberal persuasion to discriminate between the 'tough' cop doing his job under harrowing conditions, and the 'brutal' cop killing prisoners indiscriminately, is sustainable.[16]

Returning to the task of producing Genet in Manila at a time when 'September 11' had not yet disrupted my directorial fantasies, I cannot deny that Genet's critical discrimination between violence and brutality was confirmed for me by the Singapore state's summary execution of Flor Contemplacion. At the risk of sounding perverse, I was *excited* by the possibilities of inserting this 'real' event – extravagantly mediatized and mythologized in Filipino public culture – into my *mise-en-scène* of Genet's text. I was convinced that the mediatization of the maid's mythology through the death of Flor Contemplacion offered a chilling counterpoint to what remains one of the most poignant lines in Genet's play, when one of the maids asserts through her colliding fantasies and persistent disillusionment: 'I want to be a *real* maid'. What is a 'real' maid within the extreme artifice of Genet's dramaturgy? Indeed, how does one posit 'the real' in relation to the dominant illusion of theatre and the performativity of politics?

## POLITICS OF THE 'REAL'

This brings us to a more direct confrontation of the 'real' in my dramaturgical preparation for *The Maids*: even as the concept of the production was in the process of crystallizing, political demonstrations had erupted on the streets of Manila between 30 April and 1 May 2001, mocking the civic and democratic people's protests of EDSAs 1 and 2 that had raged against the administrations of former Presidents Marcos and Estrada, respectively. EDSA is the popular acronym of the Epifanio de los Santos Avenue in Metropolitan Manila, where around two million Filipino civilians had congregated between 22–25 February 1986, along with religious and activist groups, to protest against the authoritarian regime of Ferdinand Marcos. Building on this archetypal memory and the actual success of EDSA 1 in getting rid of dictatorship – a triumphant vindication of people's power – EDSA 2 was directed against the corrupt leadership of President Joseph Estrada, who, between 17–20 January 2001, was impeached and eventually charged with plundering the nation. Most histories of Filipino 'people's power' in the last two decades are likely to stop here, celebrating the efficacy of peaceful, non-violent, civilian protest as exemplified in EDSA 1 and EDSA 2.

*But* there is an EDSA 3, which is almost never mentioned by most historians and civil society activists in the Philippines, not least because it is something of an embarrassment rather like a badly timed sequel to Hollywood blockbusters like *Rocky* and *Jaws*. This EDSA was anything but civil: unruly, violent, crude, frenetic, abusive and blatantly partisan, without any pretensions of social networking and the inclusive rhetoric of civil society, EDSA 3 was spearheaded by the outcasts of society, not dignified enough to be called citizens but closer to Frantz Fanon's 'wretched of the earth' – the down-and-out scum scavenging in garbage and living off refuse in the jungle-city of Manila. In retrospect, I would invoke EDSA 3 as the time of *The Maids*, an uprising of the most marginalized sections of society brutalized by poverty and neglect.

Ironically yet significantly, the outcasts of EDSA 3 had taken to the streets not against the state, but in support of their hero, Joseph 'Erap' Estrada, who spoke their language and appeared to protect their rights: ex-action hero in B-grade Filipino movies, womanizer, gambler and master crook. Much to the horror of the civil society activists of EDSA 2, this personification of corruption metamorphosed into the people's saint, thereby compelling the activists to confront the bitter truth that their progressive politics 'in the name of the people' was being rejected and abused by the people themselves.

In a self-reflexive analysis, the well-known social activist Walden Bello has provided a chastening perspective on EDSA 3.[17] He does acknowledge some truth in many of the accusations that have been brought against this movement – for instance, the allegation that the street-fighters of EDSA 3 were 'paid' to fight, instigated by the pro-Erap forces of the Iglesia ni Kristo (Church of Christ) and the charismatic El Shaddai movement, in opposition to the establishment of the Catholic Church represented by venerable civil society heroes like Cardinal Sin (surely a name that Genet would relish). Another accusation brought against the street-fighters of EDSA 3 is that they were high on *shabu* and other drugs. However, none of these possible stimulants can undermine the rage and class dimensions of the movement, which compelled the most disorganized and impoverished sections of society to take to the streets in defence of their superstar rags-to-riches hero, and in opposition to the rich and privileged who would include those very activists upholding democracy and constitutionalism in EDSA 2.

In language clearly inspired by Genet, Rody Vera, translator of *The Maids* in Manila, describes the moment of EDSA 3 seductively, focusing on the May Day riot in Mendiola on 1 May 2001, just four months before rehearsals started:

> I saw the darkened, sweating faces of the very same despised outcasts [as Genet's thieves] in the streets of Mendiola, armed only with rocks and sticks, their brute faces pocked by smut and dried spit, their urine-scented legs standing firm ground, fuelled by an uncontrollable rage, padded by money bills they got from their instigators. . . . Could anyone like Genet depict them as angels blaring their trumpets and floating above these phalanxes of police truncheons and shields?[18]

These subaltern outcast-activists of EDSA 3 broke all norms of civic protest: they threw rocks, burned cars, destroyed police stations, attacked reporters, and even tried to break the barricades of Malacañang Palace. One of their many crude violations of 'decency', reported by an outraged bourgeois media and an even more outraged Cardinal Sin, was their deposits of urine and shit in front of the hallowed EDSA Shrine of the Virgin Mary, prototype of Genet's Our Lady of the Flowers. While this biological waste can be attributed to a 'call of nature' and the absence of adequate public sanitation, it ironically counterpoints Genet's mythologizing in *The Thief's Journal* of a discarded public urinal marked and cordoned off by the police force, which becomes a shrine for gay outcasts.[19] Within this mythopoeic world affirming the rituals of the oppressed, the biological has the potential to be transformed into an ethereal ized fantasy through a libidinal investment in bodily fluids and waste: blood, semen, urine, shit and tears. If, in Genet, a public urinal can become a shrine, in EDSA 3, one of the most hallowed shrines in metropolitan public space, endowed with the blessings of Roman Catholicism and democratic civic protest, degenerated into an improvised public toilet. The stench of urine could not be a more visceral reminder of how EDSA 3 asserted its politics in 'real' space and time.

Needless to say, when I learned about EDSA 3 from Rody Vera, who has the uncanny knack of combining robust translation with street-smart local knowledge and the Tagalog–English gay lingo of *swardspeak*, I was thrilled, because this evidence of struggle on the streets was not so much an *interruption* of my concept of *The Maids*, but an *infusion* of energies reinforcing my interpretation of the play. The imminent 'now' of the play and the 'real' of Filipino politics seemed to be melding into each other's situations. *Then*, as with all such tumultuous immediacies, there was a rupture – 'September 11' – and with its insertion the theme of terror can at long last be introduced in this chapter, even as it lurked with deadly innocence in the preparations leading to the production.

## EVENT AND BETRAYAL: RETHINKING THE POLITICAL

For the interruptive power of the historical present one turns inevitably to Bertolt Brecht, whose *Verfremdungseffekt* introduced, in the words of Walter Benjamin, a 'consciousness of the present' which has the potentiality to 'explode' the 'continuum of history' itself.[20] But, one is tempted to say, 'this is only theoretically so', because the actual execution of the *Verfremdungseffekt* in its numerous derivations and manifestations in different theatre cultures has become predominantly emotive, histrionic and, indeed, a testament to the habitual repetition of theatre. What was intended to be a thought-event in disjunctive terms has become a stylistic convention through its very reiteration. If we seek the interruptive power of the historical present in theatre, not as a metaphor or a normative idea or political ideal, then we will have to agree with Alain Badiou that 'theatre's interruption cannot be intentionally manufactured by stylistic devices or manipulated by politically motivated dramatic agendas'.[21] Badiou introduces the provocative notion of 'event', which is 'something that happens' through a 'breach in time', producing a temporary 'rupture' within the narrative that normally sustains itself through repetition.[22] The event is unconditioned, unpredictable, unprecedented and unexpected, and, in this crucial sense, it cannot be programmed. In a sense, it cannot even be imagined. At best one could say that one has no other option but to anticipate the suddenness of its blow, the eruption of its volcanic force, but this can be acknowledged only in retrospect of 'something' that has already 'happened'. This recognition demands a radically different relationship to the world through the articulation of a new subjectivity.[23]

In the burning necessity to re-imagine the political against its cooptation within agendas of neo-liberalism and corporate humanitarianism, and also in opposition to the cult of difference which has been promoted through instrumentalist readings of multicultural diversity, Badiou has become something of a guru for those performance theorists determined to work against the commodification and infinite compromises of the political. Maura Wickstrom (2012), for instance, has read Badiou's 'event' painstakingly in her attempt to conceptualize a new framework of the political for performance practices in battlegrounds like Palestine. Following her close reading of key passages from Badiou which illuminate his envisioning of the 'event', we learn that the very 'essence' of the event is 'not to be preceded by any sign', as it 'catch[es] us unawares, regardless of our vigilance'.[24] Significantly, once it manifests itself, the event 'disappears' quickly, leaving behind its 'consequences' (16). What remains of the event is a Truth or the Idea which is 'always a universal, applicable to everyone' and 'eternal', in so far as it can be 'resurrected' in another part of the world at any point in time (16–17).

In this regard, the Idea unleashed to the world through the rebellion of Spartacus or the French Revolution or the Paris Commune can be 'relived' over and over again, in and through diverse concrete manifestations. Affirming the implacable power of political universals, Badiou nonetheless suggests something like a 'truth procedure' that is 'inaugurated' by the event, but carried through by the 'subject', who 'declares it to be true, without debate or consensus as to its veracity or any democratic procedure' (17). Tellingly, it is not the event itself that produces Truth, because it is a 'void'; nor is there a 'hero' underlying or spearheading the event, because Badiou negates the possibility of any protagonistic agency emerging from the event itself. Rather, the only agency comes from the political subject's *reaction* to the event, which is cast within the ethics of 'fidelity'. Significantly, in asserting that it is the subject that declares the Truth of the event, one has no other option but to see Badiou's 'truth-procedure' *as a performative*, in so far as it manifests itself through *declaration* and not through negotiation or interpretation.

Peter Hallward, one of Badiou's most persuasive readers, strikes the right note of clarity as he compels one to see Badiou's absolutist discourse grounded in the immediacies of political action:

> When the enslaved call for freedom, for instance, or the colonized for liberation, or women for equality, the declaration of freedom or liberation or equality is itself primary or unconditioned, and not a matter of investigation or confirma-

> tion. *Equality is not something to be researched or verified but a principle to be upheld.*[25]

While it could be argued that a similar idea of equality fuels Genet's belief in the emancipation of the oppressed and dispossessed, this realization of equality, or 'the equal worth of human beings', is far more sensory and grounded *in the flesh* than Badiou's more prescriptive affirmation of equality.[26] Unlike Badiou's schematic division of events into the domains of love, science, art and politics, there is more of a slippage, if not an imbrication, of these categories in Genet's universe, particularly in the tense intimacies of love and politics. More critically, love and politics are upheld only to the extent that they can be *betrayed.*

Arguably, betrayal is the dominant leitmotif in Genet's writings that runs through his reflections on language,[27] theft[28] and friendship.[29] This apparent perversity permeating Genet's affinities to betrayal, which constitutes an ethics in its own right, is completely at odds with Badiou's more objectified allegiance to 'fidelity', a radical devotion to Truth. Arguably, both thinkers follow an anti-communitarian and anti-identitarian politics, but Genet's profound distrust of the discourses of community and identity is more visceral and irreverent. Family, marriage, nationality and citizenship lie outside his framework of reference, except in the context of derision, suspicion and hostility bordering on hatred. As Edward Said has pointed out, it is not just French national identity that Genet insists on dismantling, it is the 'very notion of identity itself' that is subject to his corrosive critique. In the process, his anti-communitarianism cannot be separated, as Said puts it, from the 'extreme radicality of [his] anti-identitarian logic'.[30]

This anti-identitarian logic extended even to his ambivalent assertion of homosexual identity. As much as he was a 'lover of Arabs', as Said puts it in a forthright register, drawn to the 'actuality and *presence*' of men of colour, in whose company he felt entirely at ease without feeling any need to 'go native' or to Orientalize the relationship, the point is that 'he was, and remained, different'.[31] Despite his tacit acknowledgement that 'perhaps if I had not made love with Algerians, I might not have been in favor of the NLF [National Liberation Front]',[32] this did not stop him from almost flaunting the necessity of betraying his affiliation to a political movement. Therein lies the very crux of his difference from Badiou who, for all his reservations about the identitarian claims underlying Palestine's quest for an independent nation-state, is ultimately loyal to the universal imperative of the endeavour. Genet's position is a lot more deviant and troubling, even as his allegiance to the Palestinian cause is never in question.

No one has understood this more deeply than Edward Said, who is drawn to Genet's disarming acknowledgement that 'much more important than commitment to a cause' is the act of betraying it, which makes it 'more beautiful and true'.[33] Said reads in this betrayal not just Genet's assertion of 'exceptionalism', but, more rigorously, 'his power to elude any attempts to rehabilitate or reclaim him'.[34] Embracing what Said has succinctly formulated as a 'fierce antinomianism', Genet was prepared to love the Other, affiliating himself to the Palestinian revolution with an almost metaphysical sense of affinity – 'my heart was in it, my body was in it, my spirit was in it' – but, in the final analysis, he was not prepared to fully give himself to the movement. Neither his 'total belief' nor his entire being could be surrendered.[35] As he put it bluntly: 'The day the Palestinians become an institution, I will no longer be on their side. The day the Palestinians become a nation like other nations, I won't be there anymore.'[36]

In Genet's audacious desire to betray the Palestinians if and when they succeed in creating a state, Michael Hardt sees a readiness to sustain 'the utopian openness of "revolutionary time"'.[37] As he explicates this 'time':

> Genet may betray a constituted State but he will never deny the revolutionary force of things. He may betray an identity (in fact, he would happily betray all identities), but he will continuously, without fail, abandon himself to the constituent time, the ceremonial time, the revolutionary time that always remains open and exposed. This revolutionary time is the time of love.[38]

Countering the formation of the Palestine state advocated by Badiou, among other supporters of the Palestinian struggle, Genet's affinities are more closely linked to the mutations of revolutionary struggle, to the *movement* itself. For Genet, there can be no eternal loyalties, still less any acceptance of the state providing ultimate legitimacy for a struggle. In this sense, his politics is embedded in the contingency and temporality of struggle, neither yoked to the Past that needs to be reclaimed, nor suspended in the endless deferral of the Future in which much contemporary politics finds refuge these days. Genet, I would argue, lives in the turbulent Present driven by 'revolutionary time', which manifests itself through 'the force of things' in the NOW. This time is relentless, ongoing, palpable, metabolized by contradictory impulses. Once it 'stops' and gets congealed in the form of a state or a liberated nation, the revolution regresses into a political formation, which is what Genet specifically rejects.

If the underlying ethic of Badiou is to insist on a 'fidelity' to the Truth of any event, Genet's ethic lies in sustaining his passionate struggle for the oppressed without allowing it to congeal into Truth. To some extent this political principle has already been prefigured dramaturgically in plays like *The Maids*, where 'truths' are always mutating and metamorphosing into lies within the playful and performative registers of meta-theatricality. Within the deconstructive ironies of such a compulsive theatricality, there is a categorical rejection of the existence or primacy of any one Truth, most notably the overthrow of the oppressors by the oppressed in an affirmation of a fully realized revolution. Genet's 'revolutions' need to be seen for what they are: parodied, botched and compromised acts of betrayal and failure, which are even subjected to blasphemous irreverence.[39] In my reading, it is precisely Genet's rejection of any moral or political absolute or solution that should alert us to the risk of converting his ethic of betrayal into another moral absolute. Indeed, if we have to be 'true' to him, then, tentatively yet inexorably, we have to be prepared to 'betray' him in our turn.

## 'SEPTEMBER 11': FIRST EXPOSURE

If I have dwelt at length on the critical motif of betrayal, it is because it contributes at a subterranean level towards providing an epistemological ground for the articulation of my own politics in this book *vis-à-vis* the larger narrative of terror. Returning to the megalopolis of Manila where I witnessed 'September 11' on CNN on hot, muggy nights in an over-chilled, anonymous hotel room, let me attempt a more subjective response to the event as a torrent of contradictory emotions. Even as one may agree with Jacques Derrida, in his exacting reflections on *Philosophy in a Time of Terror* (2003), that 'September 11' is not so much a 'major event' but the '*impression* of a major event',[40] the reality is that it impacted on public consciousness with an unprecedented ferocity. Perhaps no one could have quite predicted the actual execution of this event, with the exception of its audacious, deadly, suicidal perpetrators who carefully timed the bombings of the Twin Towers for maximum media coverage, and possibly George Bush and his cronies in the FBI and CIA who chose not to pay heed to its calamitous potentiality.

In Manila, watching 'September 11' unfold on CNN and get increasingly more complicated in its global implications, I remember experiencing a cluster of sensations. This was a visceral experience, triggered by a split-second of jubilation synchronized with disbelief, followed instantly by horror, grief, and then, at a later stage, solidarity with the victims and fire-fighters, and anger against the demonization of all possible suspects including Osama lookalikes and turbanned Sikhs passing as Muslims. Recalling the act of seeing 'September 11' unfold on the television screen with no ethnography to fall back on beyond the current thoughts in my mind, I cannot deny that I was hit. More specifically, my somewhat overconfident conceptualization of *The Maids* was attacked.

Let us pause for a moment here and try to complicate that 'split-second of jubilation', which I have inserted into the torrent of emotions that followed my first contact with 'September 11'. In a politically correct mode, one could argue that it is reasonable to feel 'solidarity' (for the victims) and 'anger' (against those xenophobes targeting minorities, and Muslims in particular). 'Horror' and 'grief' are even more acceptable as valid emotions in the repertoire of affects sanctioned by the critical event of 'September 11'. However, in our self-censoring times when accusations of sympathizing with terrorists are fraught with serious risks and misunderstandings, it is clearly not quite so acceptable to acknowledge 'jubilation', even for a split-second. I am trying to problematize here the difficult aporia in acknowledging that there is a *jouissance* linked to the moment of terror, which then gets overwhelmed by and subsumed in other emotions. It is not as if in the moment of terror that one relishes what one is seeing; the jubilation is almost inseparable from 'disbelief', and even as it is being registered it is getting *transformed* into something else. And yet, if one has to be brutally honest, there *is* a split-second of jubilation, which one is compelled to cover up or deny at a later stage in a desperate act of self-censorship.

Sharing a similar kind of ambiguity, an activist American friend acknowledged feeling a peculiar sense of envy on hearing about the attack on the Pentagon on 'September 11'. Only partially successful as it was, this attempt reminded my friend of the vain rhetoric that he and other activists had indulged in during the 1960s when 'Bomb the Pentagon' was one popular slogan, perhaps more of a symbolic wish-fulfilment than a rhetoric with any possibility of destroying the ultimate icon of the US military establishment. Somewhat sheepishly, in the aftermath of 'September 11', my friend was compelled to admit that the Al-Qaeda had actually got around to doing what he and his friends were merely fantasizing. This acknowledgement compels one to ask a more difficult question: Is the radical unrealized utopianism of the 1960s against militarism and capital now being appropriated by terrorists in their own militant imaginary of social transformation?

Returning to the actual moment of 'September 11' in Manila and its impact on my emergent concept of *The Maids*, I would reiterate that I was hit. More precisely, I was made aware of how terror *strikes*. Terror gives one no time to think. Critical thinking comes later only as one works through and against the hydra of counterterror discourses unleashed by the media, attempting to control *how one should think about terror*. And yet, watching 'September 11' unfold on CNN in Manila, I began to question my dramaturgical impulse to take refuge in the reassurances of 'the real' drawn voyeuristically from the execution of Flor Contemplacion and the disruptions of civic life in EDSA 3. Now I realized, however unconsciously, that I had to test my political affinities to Genet within the global terror of our times. Given his passionate commitment to the Palestinian struggle, his love for the *fedayeen*, supplemented by his notorious defence of the Baader-Meinhof terrorists and deeply provocative charge that 'America is afraid' (1971) following the murder of Black Panther leader George Jackson in San Quentin Prison, can there be any doubt of Genet's allegiance in the post-'September 11' scenario? Would his loyalties be with the 'civilized' world headed by the likes of Bush and Blair? Or would they not lie unstintingly, passionately, with the so-called terrorists?

These post-production questions only begin to be fully articulated *now*, in *this* moment of writing, separated more than ten years from my tryst with Genet in Manila. While glimmers of these very questions probably existed while I was rehearsing the production, I must reiterate that it was not possible in Manila to fully assimilate 'September 11', which, ironically, has become more real for me now, as the proliferation of its images and multiple discourses compels me to think about what I did not actually witness. Let us now turn to one such discourse around terror within the constituency of theatre and performance studies, which I would like to read against the background of Genet and 'September 11' presented so far in this chapter.

## DISCOURSE

### GENRES OF TERROR

#### *Tragedy*

Instead of attempting a critical retrospective on how 'September 11' has registered in the world at large – a hopelessly ambitious undertaking – let me narrow my focus to a few symptomatic responses which were published in the *Theatre Journal* (hereafter *TJ*), whose editor had invited leading scholars in the field to 'respond to the concept of tragedy in the context of these world-changing events'.[41] Two assumptions are evident in this editorial statement. First of all, it becomes clear that 'September 11' can be meaningfully addressed through 'the concept of tragedy', which is specifically singularized and privileged over other genres. Second, 'September 11' is a part of 'world-changing events', which remain unnamed. 'World-changing' could be a synonym for the more normative category of a 'major event', which Jacques Derrida subjects to rigorous questioning. Like many other activists and thinkers, he is sceptical that 'September 11' is 'without precedent' or that it was entirely 'unforeseeable'.[42] This 'unforeseeability' is exaggerated if we remind ourselves that the World Trade Center was indeed attacked on 26 February 1993, provoking a number of warnings from the official media on the imagined immunity of the United States.[43] In retrospect, one could regard the less deadly attack on the World Trade Center in 1993 as a dress rehearsal or, more precisely, a botched technical rehearsal for the more devastating demolition of the Twin Towers in

2001; or else, invoking Richard Schechner's concept of 'restoration of behavior', in which all actions are repetitions of what has already been performed, we could see both attacks of 1993 and 2001 as part of a larger script, which might be 'restored' through yet another attack in the future.

Without playing into the mean-spirited tendency to compare the tragedies of the world or to subject them to a mere quantification of detail, the reality, as Derrida puts it tacitly, is that the overwhelming casualties of genocides and bloodbaths in Cambodia, Rwanda, Palestine and Iraq never quite assume 'major' proportions in the eyes of the world. Derrida makes this point carefully, having already differentiated between the 'heart of the event', which demands *unconditional* 'compassion for the victims [of 'September 11'] and indignation over the killings', and 'the interpreted, interpretative, informed impression, the conditional evaluation that makes us *believe* that this is a major event'.[44] There is a loaded discrimination at work here, which is elided in *TJ*'s sincere editorial decision to equate 'September 11' with tragedy in all its density and depth of suffering.

Inevitably, 'tragedy' in the *TJ* forum is equated with Aristotle, and with no other modality or formation of the tragic in other performance cultures. Even so, at least some of the contributors express their discomfort with the sanitized Aristotelian framing in which they are compelled to think. While Diana Taylor sees tragedy as an exercise in 'containment' which cuts 'catastrophe down to size', ordering 'events into comprehensible scenarios' with the assurance that the 'crisis will be resolved and balance restored' (95), Elin Diamond frames tragedy in terms of a management of chaos, 'to make sure that we see the right things' (136). In both readings, tragedy has a propensity to censor other, more dangerous ways of engaging with crisis. Countering the critical tenor of these readings, there are more normative endorsements of the humanist ethos underlying Greek tragedy, which is captured in Marvin Carlson's dirge-like lament on the hubris of fellow Americans: 'Like the proud, prosperous, and apparently blessed Oedipus, we [Americans] were men [*sic*] most mighty, on whose fortunes what citizen of the world did not gaze with envy' (134). Countering this bombast, Carlson ends on a humbler note: 'Let us now pray that, as the Greek tragedians hoped, we can find the wisdom that comes through suffering' (134).

'Whose suffering?' I am compelled to ask. The humanist bias in Greek tragedy rests on the protagonist's capacity to have his or her crimes redeemed through an 'opening of the eyes' (*anagnorisis*), which facilitates his or her reintegration into society. Not only can this singular focus on the tragic protagonist blind one to the suffering and social exclusion of others, it can also pre-empt the actual possibilities of radical transformation in society at large. Following this argument, one may not necessarily agree with the strident anti-Aristotelianism of political theatre activists like Augusto Boal, who, in his seminal book on *The Theatre of the Oppressed* (1979), specifically sees in the Aristotelian model a means of numbing the possibilities of liberation and preserving the status quo. However, the conflation of 'September 11' with Aristotelian tragedy does carry a risk in so far as it can work against the possibility of rethinking the political in the larger context of Empire, where the hubris of capitalist greed and global corporate power far surpasses the misguided pride and anger of flawed individuals like Oedipus.

In her thought-provoking intervention in the *TJ* forum, Sue-Ellen Case highlights this dimension of Empire in her contextualization of Aristotelian tragedy within the hegemonic 'cultural apparatus' of the state (107–09). Arguing that the supra-national position of 'moral empires' is consolidated by the mediatization of official culture, Case draws on Aeschylus's *The Persians* (472 BCE), the first tragedy in the Western canon which legitimized the victory of the Greeks over the Persians at the battle of Salamis. As is well known in theatre studies, there is a deeply complex emotional layering in Aeschylus's representation of the defeat of the Persians, who are at once Orientalized as the malevolent, untrustworthy and effeminate Other, but also projected as tragic protagonists whose loss of Empire is rendered with searing pain and choric lamentation. As Case argues, Aeschylus's opening of 'state violence to moral scrutiny' for the specific gaze and aesthetic pleasure of the Athenian audience can be read as a strategic way of upholding Greek sovereignty – a sovereignty, as she emphasizes pithily, that is 'based not so much on military right as moral right' (107).

Likewise, in our world today, as Case builds her argument, the United States also upholds the intrinsic morality of its 'supra-national sovereignty' through its control over the global media, which targets 'a unified virtual audience' (108). This audience is assumed to *judge* events like 'September 11' from 'a collectively unitary perspective of pity, horror and moral approbation' (108). In a slight twist to Case's construction of the 'unified audience', Una Chaudhuri, in her contribution to the *TJ* forum, reads a 'reverse panopticon' in the mass media, where instead of 'the one surveying the many, the many are mesmerized by the one' (98). Countering these interpretations, I would argue that the 'unitary perspective' articulated by Case and Chaudhuri, in the interrelated contexts of global audience and media, is far too framed within an American mediascape. From my location in India and with the benefit of critical hindsight, the attempt to consolidate a global consensus on the 'war on terror' via the US media not only failed; arguably, the blatant propaganda and bullying of the US state to accept its line on the 'war on terror' only produced more resentment. Moreover, while the media may be ubiquitous, parasitic, repetitive and seemingly 'unified' through its global mechanisms, the news and images manufactured in the United States do not necessarily travel at the same pace to all destinations. There are mediations, interventions, alterations, modifications and glitches along the way. Besides, if there is CNN, there is also Al-Jazeera, among any number of alternative networks and social media which challenge the views of the US State Department. The panopticon of the mass media, both in its singular and reverse manifestations, as expressed by Case and Chaudhuri, may be more refracted than we imagine.

Against her perspective on the media, Case inserts the trope of the 'terrorist' through the figure of Medea, a 'foreign woman' who is both a 'victim of imperialism (Jason)' and a 'perpetrator of terrorist acts' (108). Case associates these 'terrorist acts' with Medea's 'secret recipes for poison', which are in turn linked to the anthrax scare following 'September 11'. While this analogy with the threat of bioterrorism is dramaturgically provocative, Case shifts her argument too swiftly from the individual persona of Medea as 'terrorist' to the US media's representation of Afghanistan's persecuted women as contemporary Medeas who are seen as 'Jason's victims . . . oppressed by both a colonialist past and a Taliban present' (108). This opportunistic representation of Muslim women's victimhood is ruptured by Case's timely reminder that the Revolutionary Association of the Women of Afghanistan (RAWA) had blamed the United States for supporting terrorism in the region – an accusation that followed their earlier plea for international solidarity in their fight against the Taliban.

Significantly, RAWA is also a point of reference in Elin Diamond's intervention in the *TJ* forum, except that she reads the figure of Cassandra rather than Medea in the politics of revolutionary Afghan women. For Diamond, there is a 'performative' which can be read in the 'hopeful prediction' made by the Afghan women-activists, namely, that 'the peace and justice-loving people of the world will be on the side of the Afghan people' (138). Affiliating herself far too unproblematically to this 'peace and justice-loving' caucus, Diamond adds: '*We* can become Cassandras and join with *other* Cassandras to see the world as it needs to become' (138; my emphasis). Clearly, Diamond's confidence in empathizing with radical Afghan women dominates over the differences that need to be negotiated in any such search for global feminist solidarity, which is more easily invoked than put into practice. RAWA's disillusionment, after all, was not just with the US state but with the larger patronization of mainstream North American feminism, which Case and Diamond fail to address.[45]

If Diamond affiliates herself to RAWA in a gesture of global feminist solidarity, Case offers a far more troubling and ambiguous position in relation to revolutionary Afghan women: 'We pity them for wearing the *burqa*, and we are terrified at what it might conceal' (108). In a reiteration of the most obligatory components of catharsis, the emotions of pity and fear are yoked together through a very clearly defined positionality of 'us' and 'them' ('We pity them'). Even as Case is only too aware of the predicament of minorities in her own culture ('people of color, women, immigrants, and homosexuals'), for whom the terror of facing racism and abuse in everyday life is not new, there has to be an inevitable *pity* for the RAWA women's prison-like incarceration in the *burqa*. Arguably, this position might justifiably enrage many women in the Arab world and elsewhere, for whom the *burqa* could have a different epistemology and religio-cultural significance. At the same time, there is fear – indeed, terror – in the possibility that these 'sisters' could be suicide bombers.

What is striking about Case's dense and cryptic position, in addition to many others contained in the *TJ* forum, is their highly subjective embeddedness within specific histories of American cultural identity, which are taken for granted and normalized. This normalization, I would argue, is consolidated rather than questioned through the nomenclature of Aristotelian tragedy, and its constructs of hubris, catharsis, pity and fear, which provide the fundamental tropes by which 'September 11' is commemorated without being deconstructed in a critical register. Perhaps there is something about the very discourse of tragedy which numbs the kind of self-criticism that is so urgently needed in confronting any catastrophe.

Reflecting on tragedy in the larger context of 'September 11' *vis-à-vis* other atrocities in Rwanda and South Africa, the political theorist Mahmood Mamdani provides the right note of critical disillusionment when he acknowledges:

> Before 9/11, I thought that tragedy had the potential to connect us with humanity in ways that prosperity does not. I thought that if prosperity tends to isolate, tragedy must connect. Now I realize this is not always the case. One unfortunate response to tragedy is a self-righteousness about one's own condition, a seeking proof of one's own special place in the world, even in victimhood.[46]

Even as it could be argued that the contributors of the *TJ* forum do not succumb to the language of victimhood, there is something about their engagement with tragedy that elicits a form of unconscious self-righteousness. To examine the deconstructive possibilities of 'September 11' rather than its commemoration through tragedy, let us turn to the Theatre of Cruelty by which the liberal tenor of the *TJ* forum is more likely to be ruptured and problematized.

*Theatre of Cruelty*

At least three of the contributors in the *TJ* forum seize the very same lines from Artaud's essay 'No More Masterpieces' (1958), to encapsulate the idea of terror: 'We are not free. The sky can still fall on our heads. And the theatre has been created to teach us that first of all.' While Una Chaudhuri reads in Artaud's words the possibilities of encountering 'the unknown and the unimaginable' in theatre, 'a place that teaches the necessary humility of not knowing' (98), Marvin Carlson intensifies the humanist register of this reading by lamenting that the Artaudian knowledge derived from 'terrible and necessary cruelty' is smothered by America's propensity for melodrama (134).[47] Perhaps it is Richard Schechner who captures most bluntly the terror of Artaud's visionary statement, but even he seems to dilute this terror through the mandatory inscription of tragedy. After emphasizing that the 'metaphysical and the tragic in the classical sense will elude us', he ends his piece with a rhetorical question which he answers somewhat too categorically: 'But is this situation of not knowing from whence the next terror will come and what it will be a situation befitting of tragedy? Artaud thought so' (132).

To my mind, it is not tragedy that concerns Artaud in his metaphysical surrender to the terrifying unknown of the future, which can be more accurately read as an imperative in his vision, a force of energy that has the potentiality to demolish anomie and complacency. When Artaud invokes the sky falling on our heads in his essay 'No More Masterpieces', he is not addressing a monumental natural disaster like an earthquake or the tsunami, or political atrocities relating to war and genocide; he is attacking something a lot more lethal, a state of emergency which has become habitual – nothing less calamitous than the logocentricity which determines the cult of 'masterpieces' in the theatre, marked, in his words, by 'boredom', 'inertia' and 'stupidity'. Even while acknowledging that Artaud's inflammatory rhetoric can leap off the page, contradicting linearity and straightforward logic, it still needs to be read in context, or else, we risk confusing his metaphors for reality.

Therefore, to place Artaud's rhetoric in context at both discursive and political levels, one could argue that the 'sky falling on our heads' has, at best, an elliptical relationship to terror, despite its apocalyptic tone. The scholar–archivist Stephen Barber points out that its echo of the 'volatile firmament', which was included in a collaborative libretto project entitled *The Astronomer* (1932) with the composer Edgar Varèse, needs to be linked to a much wider range of textual correspondences in Artaud's oeuvre in order to be accurately understood.[48] At a more empirical level, it should also be emphasized that Artaud, for all his extremity and iconoclastic non-conformity, had no engagement with 'terrorist' groups as such, quite unlike Genet's close affiliations to the Red Army Faction, the Black Panthers and the Palestinian liberation fighters. Following his expulsion from the Surrealist movement in the 1920s after the temporary rapprochement of the Surrealists with the Communist Party, Artaud had a specific loathing for the institutionalization of politics. Genet, in contrast, retained close ties with Left political constituencies even as he teased and provoked their pieties.

Ironically, for contemporaries like Genet and Artaud, both extremists in their own right, united through their hatred of French national sovereignty and passion for the French language, it is telling that they never seem to have met, as Stephen Barber has pointed out to me, even as they frequented the same cafés in Boulevard Saint-Germain and shared a common confidant in the editor Paule Thévenin. The reality is that Artaud had died by 1948 following nine years of internment in the asylums of Ville-Évrard and Rodez, where he had been subjected to as many as fifty-one electric shock treatments. Given this assault on his body through the torture of rehabilitation and detoxification, it would not be inaccurate to acknowledge Artaud as a victim of medical terror whose life was destroyed by the regulatory mechanisms of clinical psychiatry. Genet, in contrast, continued to live until 1986, surviving the wars in Algeria, Vietnam, the Arab world, the massacre in Shatila, and the last years of the Cold War just on the cusp of the Soviet Union's disintegration. This witnessing of critical political events in the last decades of the twentieth century makes him very much a contemporary of 'our times'.

Shifting the critical inquiry from this biographical perspective on terror, let us return to Artaud's statement on 'the sky falling on our heads' and try to read it in a different register. At one level it could be argued that the apocalyptic imaginary of the statement does lend itself to being envisioned as 'terror', so long as one acknowledges that this terror is linked to the lucidity of a disintegrating consciousness. Even as it burns with intensity and inspirational force, Artaud's incandescent and self-destructing vision cannot be translated into critical theory or political practice. At no point can one 'use' Artaud to 'explain' the terror of our times. With this qualification in mind, Stephen Barber acknowledges that even as Artaud had 'no specific engagement with terror' at a political level, '[his] apocalyptic manifesto, *The New Revelations of Being* (1937), in which entire populations are to be decimated, reads in some ways like a terror manifesto'.[49]

Circumspect in his acknowledgement that Artaud's apocalyptic statements read 'in some ways' like a terror manifesto, Barber provides more volatile material from Artaud's letter written to André Breton in 1947 following his visceral performance at the Vieux-Colombier theatre, where the 'ideal performer' would be one 'who would bring bombs out of his pockets and throw them in the audience's face with a blatant gesture of aggression'.[50] Here, the ideal actor (Artaud himself) would seem to be no different from a terrorist hurling bombs at pedestrians in a public space: a very different performativity from that of Genet, the ironic observer and critic of actors, who could watch student activists from the ramparts of the Théâtre de l'Odéon during his production of *The Screens*, whom he later dismissed as 'pseudo-revolutionaries' who needed to read some Lenin.

Enough of a context has been provided to suggest that Artaud's statement, 'we are not free and the sky can still fall on our heads', can be read as revelatory of the terror in our times only at the cost of a closer reading of his oeuvre. This is not to fault *TJ*'s contributors for bouncing off these lines which have a talismanic quality, to which I cannot deny responding myself. However, to push the pertinence of these lines in the context of 'September 11', one needs to shift the argument into a different modality by raising the crucial issue of temporality. When Artaud posits the possibility that 'the sky can still fall on our heads', and there is the quick assumption among *TJ*'s commentators that with 'September 11' the sky has indeed fallen on our heads, one would have to add *not yet*. The sky *can* still fall on our heads. What has fallen are the Twin Towers. The sky has yet to fall. And it is in this interim of the 'not yet' that terror resides and mutates. There is no reason to see in this interim a 'tragedy'. Artaud would look upon it as *necessity*.

## THE TERROR OF REPETITION

Theatre is proverbially regarded as the domain of the Now, not the 'not yet'. To complicate the temporalities of performance, more specifically in the context of the actual destruction of the World Trade Center, how does one rethink 'once' in performance in terms of an irretrievable moment, as opposed to 'now', which connotes a mixing of times in an unspecifiable duration? Following the axiomatic assumption of performance studies, theatre can never occur once; it can only occur twice, or many times, in its ceaseless repetition. As Schechner puts it, performance is 'twice-behaved behavior'; it gets to be called 'behavior' in the first place because 'it is performed much more than twice'.[51] In the enunciation of performance as 'restored behavior', *how* repetition actually alters performance, and what *happens* to repetition itself in the process of its seemingly infinite deferral, are issues which tend to be marginalized, prompting Peggy Phelan to ask a valid question: 'If we accept that performance is "twice-behaved behavior," we must then ask, what is the force of that repetition?'[52] To 'force', we could also add 'nuance', 'inflection', 'alteration', 'distortion', 'dilution', 'diffusion', 'depoliticization'. The fact that performance repeats itself, it seems to me, is far less significant than what happens *to* it in the process of its repetition.

Against the axiomatic formula of 'twice-behaved behavior', let us insert into the discussion the problematic of a 'one-time' performance. I draw the concept of 'one time' from Artaud, who, in one of his most memorable and lucid passages from *The Theatre and Its Double*, enunciates his own set of radical axioms relating to the temporality of 'cruelty' in performance. We need to recognize, as he puts it, that

> an expression does not have the same value twice; does not live two lives; that all words, once spoken, are dead and function only at the moment when they are uttered, that a form, once it has served, cannot be used again and asks only to be replaced by another, and that the theatre is the only place in the world where a gesture, once made, can never be made the same way twice.[53]

These uncompromising axioms relating to 'one time' work totally against the idea of representation. In addition, they complicate the notion that any gesture, expression or word can be 'restored' in the first place.

Explicating this complex philosophical conundrum, Derrida says, '*Artaud wanted to erase repetition in general.* For him repetition was evil . . . Repetition separates force, presence, and life from themselves . . . This power of repetition governed everything that Artaud wished to destroy, and it has several names: God, Being, Dialectics.'[54] In theatre, where 'the menace of repetition is nowhere else as well organized' – the French word for 'rehearsal' is *répétition* – the entire thrust of Artaud's theatre of cruelty was to push representation to the limits of impossibility. For him, 'there can be theatre only from the moment when the impossible really begins',[55] which, in essence, means that theatre can never really begin. As he was compelled to acknowledge towards the end of his life, 'theatre has *not yet* begun to exist'[56] – a total rejection of the celebratory fervour embodied in the valorization of 'now' in much political theatre.

At one level, this non-existence of Artaud's theatre can be regarded as a 'failure' of his practice, which Susan Sontag (1976) highlights in her memorable reading of Artaud's 'phenomenology of suffering'. But, perhaps, at another level, the fact that theatre does not exist (which could make Artaud appear in his own self-estimate as an 'enemy of theatre')[57] is also the premise that enables him to affirm the non-representation of theatre. Following Derrida, we are alerted to at least three levels of non-representation: (1) 'the inaccessible limit of a representation which is not repetition'; (2) 'a *re*-presentation which is full presence'; and (3) 'a present which does not repeat itself', in other words, a 'present outside time, a nonpresent'.[58]

If there is a 'tragic' dimension in Artaud's 'impossible' vision, it has little to do with the imminence of terror which is suspended into the future, as Schechner had indicated in his brief response to Artaud's apocalyptic vision that the 'sky can still fall on our heads'. Rather, the 'tragedy' in Artaud's universe is linked to the fact that as much as he would like to reject the idea of representation, he is also aware of the necessity of repetition from which there is no escape. As Derrida highlights this metaphysical impasse: 'Artaud knew that the theatre of cruelty neither begins nor is completed within the purity of simple presence, but rather is already within representation, in the "second time of Creation," in the conflict of forces which could not be that of a simple origin.'[59] Therefore, as much as Artaud 'cannot resign himself to theatre as repetition', at the same time, he 'cannot renounce theatre as non-repetition'.[60]

It seems to me that we lose out imaginatively and creatively when we streamline the aporias underlying Artaud's vision by settling for an axiomatic reading of repetition in the theatre. Instead, we need to ask: What are the different modalities in which repetition can be understood, and what are the exceptions to the rule? Particularly in the context of terror, there is some validity in inscribing the explosive power of *once* both in theatre and life, which, for Artaud, were almost indistinguishable realities. At the risk of pushing this proposition into a somewhat extreme register, I would suggest that the phenomenological complement of 'once' in performance can be detected in the act of terrorism, which *strikes* with deadly precision in a split-second of irretrievable destruction. Even while acknowledging that the devastation of the Twin Towers had been 'preceded' by an earlier attempt to destroy the World Trade Center, it could be argued that for those witnesses (including many of the contributors to the *TJ* forum) who actually saw the Towers crumble to dust, it was a once-in-a-lifetime experience with no precedent in sight. The 'once' of the experience is inextricably linked to the irreversible process of destruction.

Translating this 'once' within the dynamics of a theatrical experience, what needs to be highlighted here is the incalculable *speed* with which a theatrical moment is capable of striking its spectators with immediacy. This speed directly affects/afflicts the senses with a phenomenological intensity that is different from the more philosophical 'logic' of speed articulated by Paul Virilio, which he links to the imminence of catastrophe. For him, 'the major accident is indeed, the consequence of the speed of the acceleration of the phenomena engendered by progress'[61] – and, one could add, globalization in all its cumulative fetishizing and compulsive need to break temporal barriers. However, returning to the speed with which a theatrical moment is capable of striking consciousness, one needs to trouble its terrorist assumptions because, even at the level of metaphor, theatre's capacity to hit or strike consciousness is surely not 'death-like' or 'catastrophic'. Rather it is *processual*, operating on the unconscious in unprecedented ways, and extending way beyond the duration of a performance in totally undetermined spaces and discourses.

Even as the 'once' of any performance is not absolute, Artaud's provocation that 'the same gesture can never be repeated the same way twice' continues to lend itself to a volatile reading of 'terror' which strikes in an instant. While it is tempting to regard Artaud as a visionary terrorist in his own right, who craved nothing less than the extinction of the Occidental theatre and the values consecrated in it, one should keep in mind that this was an extinction more imagined than real. Expressed in an apocalyptic language, it can be linked to states of emergency like the plague, which, despite Artaud's obsessive immersion in researching actual plagues documented in European archives, remains a *metaphor* for re-imagining and revitalizing the theatre.[62] To literalize Artaud's metaphors is to risk succumbing to the worst kind of avant-garde fundamentalism. Indeed, if we have to be 'true' to Artaud, we have to consciously make the effort not to reduce the impossibility of his vision to the techniques of a revolutionary or terroristic agenda.

## DECONSTRUCTING TERROR

### *Trauma*

Against the theatrical discourse of 'September 11', to which we will return later in the chapter, let us insert at this stage two interrelated concepts from Jacques Derrida's memorable intervention in *Philosophy in a Time of Terror* (2003) – 'trauma' and 'autoimmunity' – which could help us to engage with the unknown of terror in a different theoretical register. Derrida's point of departure in relating trauma to terror is located within a 'new temporalization', as he describes it:

> We are talking about a trauma, and thus an event, whose temporality proceeds neither from the now that is present nor from the present that is past but from an impresentable to come (*à venir*). A weapon wounds and leaves forever open an unconscious scar; but this weapon is terrifying because it comes from the to-come, from the future, a future so radically to come that it resists even the grammar of the future anterior.[63]

The reading of '*this* weapon', as opposed to the weapon that 'wounds' (from which the word 'trauma' is derived), is thrust into the future-to-come. This temporality is different from the unresolved dynamics of past and present in which most conventional readings of trauma are framed. In these readings, an 'overwhelming experience of sudden or catastrophic events' resists being incorporated into a clearly worked out past; instead, in a ghost-like manner, it continues to haunt the present through the 'often delayed, uncontrolled repetitive appearance of hallucinations and other intrusive phenomena'.[64] Unable to live in either a clearly defined past or present, but caught within an interstitial space–time, the traumatized victim, or 'survivor–sufferer', is unable to bring closure to his or her life-narrative, whose continuum is severely disrupted.

Without reiterating these familiar assumptions of trauma relating to the 'unconscious scar' from an open wound – a scar which refuses to heal – Derrida is more concerned with outlining a different temporality for the understanding of the 'wound' itself. The trauma of our times, post-'September 11', as he puts it, is 'terrifying' precisely because 'it comes from the to-come, from the future'.[65] In this reading, the suffering and pain of the present are linked not to an *event* that has already passed but which remains unassimilated without the closure of a fully resolved narrative; rather they are connected to the *premonition* of a 'weapon' that has yet to strike in the future. Not only is the worst not over, it may never be over.

Shifting his rhetorical register in a more direct address to 'Americans', Derrida adds:

> Imagine that the Americans and, through them, the entire world had been told . . . it's all over, it won't happen again . . . I assume that mourning would have been possible in a relatively short period of time . . . One would have spoken of the work of mourning and turned the page, as is so often done, and done so much more easily when it comes to things that happen elsewhere, far from Europe and the Americas. But this is not at all what happened. There is traumatism with no possible work of mourning when the evil comes from the possibility to come of the worst, from the repetition to come – though worse. Traumatism is produced by the *future*, by the *to come*, by the threat of the worst *to come*, rather than by an aggression that is 'over and done with'.[66]

I have quoted this passage at length, not least to trouble the illusory reassurance that has been constructed around the multitude of performative acts that spilled on to the streets, parks and public spaces of New York City in the immediate aftermath of 'September 11'. While these performances of grief and solidarity by ordinary people were enormously moving and beneficial in their attempt to heal wounds, Derrida complicates any possibility of long-term healing derived from such acts by questioning the reconciliatory process of mourning 'September 11'.

Clearly, this is not the perspective that one receives from more local readings provided by 'native' New Yorkers, whose ethnography of grief acquired somatic and interactive dimensions as they engaged with the multitudinous narratives of loss that marked their beloved city. As a professional anthropologist and performance theorist, Barbara Kirshenblatt-Gimblett missed no opportunity in providing an inventory of this moment at a panoramic level. 'Every surface of the city', as she informs us, ranging from 'sidewalks, lampposts, fences, telephone booths, barricades, garbage dumpsters, and walls – was blanketed with candles, flowers, flags, and missing persons posters'.[67] The photographs of the missing (not yet claimed to be dead) became the 'votive objects' around which roadside shrines were improvised, with all the obligatory accessories of 'flowers and candles, teddy bears, and items of clothing'[68] – highly personalized and grief-embedded installations suspended between 'a call for information and a death notice'.[69] And yet, for all the fervour of these citizen-initiatives, which would seem to have contributed towards the dual process of memorializing the dead and suspending the act of mourning

In the absence of any definitive confirmation of 'the living dead', there was another set of initiatives instituted by the civic authorities of New York City. These initiatives exemplified a matter-of-fact 'brutality', to use Genet's sense of the word.

Just as the state had prevented New Yorkers from 'witnessing' the remains of 'Ground Zero' in the immediate aftermath of 'September 11', accusing them of 'gawking', the civic authorities ruthlessly affirmed that there are 'temporal limits to public grief'.[70] In this regard, the Department of Parks and Recreation prohibited the creation of memorials in parks just three weeks after 'September 11', and by June 2002, the Department of Transportation declared that all memorabilia at Ground Zero would be trashed on a daily basis. Along with this no-nonsense, let's-get-on-with-life reaffirmation of civic hygiene and law and order, it was business as usual for the larger creative economy, notably the video-games industry. As Kirschenblatt-Gimblett points out, this industry lost no time in inventing new war games featuring the Twin Towers and the killing of Osama bin Laden in bizarre, interactive and sadistic visual narratives.[71]

Today, as tragedy has given way to museumization, it remains to be seen how the National September 11 Memorial and Museum, which is scheduled to open in the spring of 2014, will either contribute to the healing process or aggravate old wounds. Will it bring diverse ethnic communities together, or create new divisions between those who are worthy of being museumized and those who have been summarily left out of America's most intensely patriotic national commemoration of grief? Already publicized and sold in advance as the biggest tourist attraction of the Big Apple, the Museum stands as a testament to the positive, never-say-die triumphalism of the American spirit. But, in the empty skyline of Manhattan – 'nothing in the sky indicates that the towers ever existed', as Kirshenblatt-Gimblett puts it in an unsentimental register[72] – the substitution of the National September 11 Memorial and Museum to fill the void in the sky could further circumvent the act of mourning as Derrida envisions it.

Perhaps, rather than a Memorial Museum intent on forgetting the trauma of the past and incorporating its wounds into an illusory pyrrhic victory in the 'war on terror', it would have been more courageous for the New York City authorities to have allowed the Freedom Museum to be built, instead of censoring and eliminating it almost overnight with no adequate public discussion.[73] Virilio's Museum of the Accident would probably be far too sinister to consider as a museological proposition, still less his Museum of the Accident of the Future, even as these hypothetical schemes reflect deeply on catastrophes produced by the logic of globalization and the valorization of the techno-scientific spirit.[74] Not only would all these 'mad' schemes be rejected on patriotic grounds, they would also be maligned on the basis of protecting the 'right to grief' of those suffering families who have lost their loved ones in the demolition of the Twin Towers. A more disingenuous argument would be hard to find: if indeed the grief of the families has to be honoured, as I believe it should, it might have been more appropriate to accept 'Ground Zero' as an empty space, a graveyard, defying its astronomical real-estate value in favour of a non-commercial, public, ecumenical site of reflection and prayer. Not a viable option, I realize, for America's undying commitment to the spirit of capitalism, which outlasts the demolition of the World Trade Center, testifying to the hubris of corporate power, targeted but not eliminated by terrorist violence.

*Autoimmunity*

By reflecting on the museumization of grief, this discussion has somewhat deflected attention from Derrida's tacit refusal to dwell on 'mourning' in favour of relating trauma to an *autoimmunitary* process. This process, as he describes it with his characteristic complexity, is one in which 'a living being, in a quasi-*suicidal* fashion, "itself" works to destroy its own protection, to immunize itself *against* its "own" immunity'.[75] This bizarre logic clearly works against the familiar (and ostensibly comforting) protection provided by more readymade examples of immunity – at once biological (a mother's capacity to immunize her child through breast-feeding) and political (the state's 'protection' of its citizens through the mechanisms of security and surveillance). Significantly, Derrida does not deal with the truism that we need immunity in order to survive, or that, as Roberto Esposito spells it out, 'life, be it single or common, would die without an immunitary apparatus'.[76]

In order to grasp the 'dialectic character of immunity', we need to grasp, in Esposito's framework, both the 'protection and the negation of life', although, as he puts it, one could more easily say that 'protection is the negation of life'.[77] At one level, this dialectic raises issues of measure and risk in assessing the dynamics of both protection and negation. For example, Esposito uses the example of vaccination, where the injection of a tolerable amount of disease into the patient's body is precisely what is needed in order to safeguard the patient from that very disease. Yet, an overdose of the poison can land up destroying the life one wants to protect. This reading, as Esposito acknowledges, merely echoes Derrida's famous study of the Greek *pharmakon*, which operates through 'the double meaning of "cure" and "poison," poison as cure, the cure that takes place through a poisoning'.[78]

Esposito's more distinctive contribution lies in his understanding of the oppositional relationship of *immunitas* to *communitas*, in which he brings together biomedical and juridical languages:

> In biomedical language immunity is understood as a form of exemption or protection in relation to a disease. In juridical language immunity represents a sort of safeguard that places the one who holds it in a condition of untouchability *vis-à-vis* common law. In both cases, therefore, immunity or immunization alludes to a particular situation that protects someone from a risk, a risk to which an entire community is exposed. You can already see the opposition between community and immunity. Immunity – or, using its Latin formulation, *immunitas* – emerges as the contrary or the reverse of *communitas*.[79]

This *immunitas/communitas* opposition does not enter Derrida's concept of autoimmunity, not least because he elides the concept of 'community' altogether in favour of 'friendship'. Neither does he engage with the biomedical considerations of immunity, which would compel him to engage with the potentially beneficial possibilities of, say, organ transplants, which may or not work in their transference from one body to another, depending on a particular body's 'immunological tolerance'. While Esposito would claim that it is precisely such a life-enhancing possibility that needs to be seen as a 'gamble',[80] Derrida does not engage with such paradoxes, and focuses almost exclusively on the more perceptibly destructive and specifically self-destructive propensities of immunity, which he renames 'autoimmunity'.

While the concept first appeared somewhat sketchily in his reflections on religion at the limits of reason,[81] it is fully developed in the context of 'September 11', where he rejects the idea of the terrorist threat as an external force destroying the protective devices of the world's allegedly most 'secure' and powerful state. Instead, Derrida highlights the inner mechanisms of terror that disrupt the apparatus of immunity itself. With violent irony, therefore, we are compelled to engage with the phenomenon of a 'living organism' *protecting* itself 'against its self-protection by destroying its own immune system'.[82] Protection, in other words, becomes a lethal form of destruction that can no longer be ascribed to the machinations of the state alone. Rather, there are invisible elements at work *within* the existing apparatus of a cultural system that operate with their own suicidal logic. The agencies of autoimmunity are not just camouflaged enemies, but perfectly at home in their site of destruction, 'domesticated', to use Derrida's precise word, by the very system they plan to destroy. Therein lies the difficulty of marking the 'enemy', or of locating its origins or habitat in a clearly marked geographical location *outside* the cataclysm of terror.

Inevitably, within such a topography of terror, there are new aporias at work in the conventional vocabulary surrounding 'terrorists', who were more easily marked at one point in time as 'national' or 'foreign', as 'militants' or 'insurgents'. Today, there are more profound blurrings of terrorist identity. And yet the tired, yet tenacious relativism by which one country's 'terrorist' can be another's 'freedom fighter' is an axiom that is still to be accepted by most governments in the world, who would prefer to reduce 'terrorists' to 'evil people'. In contrast, a tougher appraisal of the realities on the ground would demand the need for more fluid discriminations in the nomenclature describing the agencies of militant struggle. A 'militant' is not an 'insurgent'; an 'insurgent' is not a 'terrorist' – but a 'terrorist' could have been a 'militant' at one point in time as indeed an 'insurgent' could metamorphose into a 'terrorist', if not a rehabilitated minister of state. The realities of struggle are never static and demand recognition of the *temporality* involved in identifying the volatile phenomena of armed resistance. Along with temporality, it is also necessary to recognize the *authorization* of power that sanctions the making of definitions around terror: who defines what, and under whose jurisdiction.

Returning to the logic of autoimmunity, the epistemology of terror for Derrida has been considerably complicated by the virtual networks wherein assailants are invisibilized within the high-tech apparatus of technoscience. The irony is that terrorists have been trained to operate these systems by their own enemies. Without mincing words, Derrida elaborates on this irony succinctly: 'Immigrated, trained, prepared for their act in the United States by the United States, these *hijackers* incorporate, so to speak, two suicides in one: their own . . . but also the suicide of those who welcomed, armed and trained them.'[83] In this construction, it would seem that the United States has contributed to the execution of its own 'suicide' through its complicity in the autoimmunitary process. Or, to appropriate the title of one of Artaud's essays on Vincent van Gogh, America can be said to have 'suicided itself'.

While elaborating on these elusive dimensions of self-destruction, Derrida's comments are not to be read, I would emphasize, in the strident register of a New European anti-Americanism. Rather, he makes his case through a scrupulous distinction between the execution of actual events and brutal killings. Thereby he differentiates between victims and assailants, even while compelling us to confront the predicament of living in a world of terror in which we are unconsciously complicit as good citizens and patriotic subjects. Working against the easy assumption that all terrorism is 'voluntary, conscious, organized, deliberate, intentionally calculated', from which 'we' can conveniently distance ourselves, and uphold our moral standards and economies, Derrida throws out some troubling questions:

> [D]oes terrorism have to work only through death? Can't one terrorize without killing? And does killing necessarily mean putting to death? Isn't it also 'letting die'? Can't 'letting die', 'not wanting to know that one is letting others die' – hundreds of millions of human beings, from hunger, AIDS, lack of medical

treatment, and so on – also be part of a 'more or less' conscious and deliberate terrorist strategy?[84]

These questions provoke – indeed detonate – any convenient amnesia that we as socially concerned citizens are not responsible for 'letting others die'. And perhaps, this indifference or apathy in allowing others to die is not just a humanist lapse on our part, but an actual submission to the legitimization of terrorism from which scholars, critics and practitioners in the world of theatre and performance are not free.

## CONTROVERSIES

### *Stockhausen's Blunder*

Let us consider some of the controversies surrounding 'September 11' to which artists and scholars cannot claim any immunity, even as their liberal, if not radical credentials, almost exempt their representations of terror from being questioned on grounds of insensitivity or cultural imperialism. I will focus my attention on one massive public controversy that raged around the German avant-garde composer Karlheinz Stockhausen's notorious comment, that the attack on the Twin Towers on 11 September 2001 could be described as '*das grosse Kunstwerk, das es je gegeben hat*' (the greatest work of art there has ever been). Since this remark is frequently misread, it would be useful to contextualize it within John Bell's summary of the background leading to the controversy, where we learn that Stockhausen's remark was made in a conference following a twenty-eight-hour-long performance cycle entitled *Licht* (Light), which featured contemporary archetypal forces like Saint Michael, Eve ('the mother of life') and Lucifer (the prince of light).[85] While Lucifer would appear to be one of the presiding deities of terror in our times, for Stockhausen, he appears to have represented 'the cosmic spirit of rebellion, of anarchy', who 'uses his high degree of intelligence to destroy creativity'.[86] Clearly, this apparent critique of anarchy was lost on Stockhausen's critics, who lambasted him for his arrogance and insensitivity in daring to compare 'September 11' to a monumental work of art.

Undermining the capacity of composers (including himself) to meet the impossible standards of this 'art', Stockhausen elaborated on his audacious point of view:

> That minds [*Geister*] should carry out something like that in an act that we in music could never dream of doing: that people could rehearse like crazy for ten years, totally fanatically, for a concert and then die. Just try and imagine what happened there. Those are people who are so concentrated on the one performance and then 5000 people are blown to resurrection in one moment. I couldn't do that. In comparison to that we composers are nothing.[87]

As Christopher Balme, a contributor to the *TJ* forum, has pointed out, there are explicit comparisons being made by Stockhausen between the terrorist attack and a performance, not least through the metaphor of rehearsal. More chillingly, Stockhausen highlights the singularity of the event that is concentrated around 'one performance', with the final 'resurrection' of the spectators being accomplished in 'one moment'. There are disturbing echoes here of Artaud's valorization of 'one time', which we had discussed earlier in this chapter, although the notion of a ten-year rehearsal period leading to 'one performance' indicates that the terrorist attack was always already in the process of being repeated, even as it was building towards a performance that was simultaneously climactic and apocalyptic.

As Stockhausen was compelled to qualify his statement later, after his concerts were cancelled and his comments were condemned in the media, these 5,000 ostensibly liberated souls did not *agree* to being blown up by their perpetrators. Therefore, their alleged 'resurrection' can more meaningfully be described as mass murder – a 'crime', as Stockhausen acknowledged at a later stage. And yet, as Balme emphasizes, Stockhausen's original statement comparing 'September 11' to a work of art cannot be let off the hook: quite clearly, he 'said and no doubt meant what he said at that time' (116). Later he emphasized that all great art has to make the necessary and perilous 'leap into uncertainty', or else, it is 'nothing' (116). The obvious extremity of this belief led Stockhausen into affirming that 'only terrorist acts of this dimension can attain to what art in modernist terms sets itself as a task' (116).

At this point, one needs to voice a cautionary note on the apparent affinities of this artistic extremity to the theatre of cruelty, which, as Artaud took pains to point out, has nothing to do with 'blood' or actual violence. Stockhausen's position, in contrast, would appear to be far less nuanced and even unethical in so far as he totally fails to problematize – or even regret – the actual mortality underlying 'the greatest work of art', the deaths of 5,000 people reduced to a rhetorical flourish, almost as if they needed to die in order to make the artwork possible. There is also no perspective in his viewpoint on the role of the artist as suicidal perpetrator–victim, in so far as the terrorists of 'September 11' perished along with the victims, thereby raising critical issues concerning the legitimacy of their own 'resurrection' in an Islamic context.

As I see it, Stockhausen's hyperbolic focus on 'Art', or, more specifically, the 'greatest work of art', plays into the worst kind of 'masterpiece' syndrome, albeit not of the Artaudian variety, steeped in antagonistic dismissals of authorial control and verbalism. Rather, today's masterpieces in the global avant-garde of late modernity are assertively media-driven, and centred around charismatic personalities whose promotion on the festival circuit is not free of the outmoded yet tenacious cult of genius which merely flirts with the promise of 'impossibility'. Here, again, one needs to probe carefully the Artaudian echoes of the 'impossible': whereas for Artaud, 'there can be theatre only from the moment when the impossible really begins',[88] for Stockhausen, it would seem that the impossible has already been realized as a staggering, once-in-a-millennium experience. Therein lies the horror of Stockhausen's statement: it is not just the absence of ethics in his reading of aesthetics; rather it is the self-illusory bombast that ordinary spectators can be 'blown to resurrection' for the realization of an Impossible Idea of Art. One way of deflating this valorization of a *realized* 'impossibility' is by reminding ourselves, in the valuable perspective offered by the Indian cultural theorist Ashis Nandy, that a 'realized utopia' could be 'another name for terror'.[89]

Returning to Stockhausen's comment, it is significant how one of the contributors (Ann Pellegrini) in the *TJ* forum, while expressing her obligatory unease with Stockhausen's position, nonetheless acknowledges that it 'works' for her, in a way that 'comparisons to historical events, film, and reality TV do not' (114). She adds that this affinity may have 'something to do with [her] academic location in performance studies' and 'physical location in New York City' – a city in which she could actually *smell* the after-effects of 'September 11' (114). Indeed, as she puts it in a strong olfactory register, 'I still smell that smell – a pungent commingling of all that remains uncounted, unaccountable for' (114). Working against the grain of the valorization in performance studies of 'rich world-making capacities', Pellegrini puts forward the radical possibilities of 'performance's power to rupture the social and inspire a range of affective responses – not just joy and delight and insight, but also (sometimes alongside them, sometimes not) terror and rage and horror' (114). This position stretches the widest spectrum of performance's affective capacities beyond what is normalized in performance studies or valorized in utopian readings of theatre. Here, one needs to mention Jill Dolan's (2005) widely circulated missives of hope through 'utopian performatives', in which she calls attention to 'small but profound moments in performance' which 'lift everyone slightly above the present, into a hopeful feeling of what the world might be like if every moment of our lives were as emotionally voluminous, generous, aesthetically striking, and intersubjectively intense'.[90] In contrast, Pellegrini's vision is far more circumspect in its openness to the possible commingling of 'terror and rage and horror' with (or without) 'joy and delight and insight' (114).

I respond strongly to Pellegrini's affective politics, not least because she does not deny the dystopic in her engagement with performance and terror. However, the problem with her position could lie not in positing daring new affects of performance, nor in questioning that ultimate trope of performance as always on 'the verge of loss', which she justifiably questions (114). Rather the difficulty lies in her somewhat too hasty affirmation that 'September 11th was . . . performance unto death', to which she adds more emphatically that 'there was nothing metaphorical about the disappearances and deaths that day' (115). Very true, but do these disappearances and deaths have to be seen as 'performances' in the first place? In whose authorial framework, and from which disciplinary set of protocols and expertise, can death be proclaimed as performative? Who determines performance for others, including the dead in whose name we speak? One could argue that there is an automatic reflex in interpreting death as performance through the spectacular effect of its visuality for a particular audience. One could deepen the argument by suggesting that this effect is integrally linked to how performance *affects* us in a moment of extremity. What are the political limits of affect? Indeed, what are the limits of empathy which make affect possible in the first place?

*The Politics of Empathy*

These questions compel us to explore the complex dynamics of 'empathy', which are inadvertently triggered by Jill Dolan's passionate contribution to the *TJ* forum where she performs her own grief in the aftermath of 'September 11'. Placing her subjectivity at the centre of her response, using the first personal singular with a totally uninhibited and repetitive force, Dolan 'shares' her experience with us:

> As I watched television, listened to radio, or read news reports, I felt myself a passenger on those planes . . . I felt myself in the World Trade Center, walking down 80 flights of stairs . . . I felt myself an office worker, turning on my computer, hearing a thunderous noise behind me and looking up one last time to see the nose of a plane inexplicably crash through the wall. I felt myself standing in a burning office . . . I felt myself the woman leaping from one of the towers with, unfathomably, her purse clutched to her chest. (106)

When one reads this 'sharing' of deeply empathetic responses, in which Dolan enters the minds and bodies and psyches of the 'passenger', 'the office worker', the 'woman clutching her purse to her chest', one can begin to understand the risks of empathy in confronting human tragedy.

Empathy, as explicated by Susan Foster (2011), is a term that suggests 'a strong and vital component of kinesthetic sensation' as 'one's entire subjectivity' gets immersed in 'another object, or person, or image'.[91] This is not so much the 'casting' of 'one's self into the position of the other', but a more psychophysical projection of 'one's three-dimensional structure into the energy and action of the other'.[92] At one level it could be argued that empathy trains one's aesthetic sensibility, and indeed, Dolan affirms nothing less in her *TJ* response: 'If our imaginations can lead us to profound, performative empathy,

I believe ever more strongly that the space of performance must be harnessed to imagine love instead of hatred, to create hopeful fictions of meaningful lives instead of senseless deaths' (106). Leaving aside the illusory quality and optimism of this faith in 'love' and 'hope' and 'meaningful lives', the obvious point to be made is that the persons catalysing Dolan's emotions are dead. She is not unduly perturbed in this regard: 'I know that performance couldn't stop the woman with the purse from jumping, but I hope it can memorialize and make sense of her actions' (107). 'Making sense' of people's extreme actions leading to their deaths is surely a worthwhile response, so long as this process is subjected to a lot more political reflection and contradiction than 'painful empathy' (106).

Even as Dolan's text needs to be contextualized as a 'first response' to the horror of 'September 11', it is necessary to keep in mind, in focusing on the ostensibly all-American victims of this tragedy, that 372 casualties were foreign nationals, excluding the 19 perpetrators; Wikipedia clearly separates the 'perpetrators' from the rest of the 'victims' and 'casualties'. It is almost as if they belong to a different category of 'the dead', thereby challenging the utopian assumption that all human beings are equal in death. It was Noam Chomsky who, in his 'quick reaction' to the tragedy on 12 September 2001, pointed out the salient fact that most of the casualties were 'working people', including janitors and technical staff doing the morning shift in the Twin Towers.

Moving beyond the social statistics of the tragedy, one is compelled to ask in a more speculative register: What space is there in the concept of empathy for 'feeling' the emotions of those terrorists who perpetrated their own deaths in the process of destroying the World Trade Center? In a more performative register, if we had to shift Dolan's gaze from the office worker looking out of the window to see the airplane crashing into the wall and focus, instead, on Mohammed Atta or any of his colleagues flying the airplane into the wall, would it be possible to feel any empathy for them? Can these 'terrorists' be denied courage (as Susan Sontag was among the first Americans to acknowledge), or are they always going to be demonized as worthless 'cowards'? Can one *feel* for them, or is the very posing of the question an involuntary revelation of one's own diabolical affinities to terrorism?

It is at this point that we need to acknowledge that an unproblematized empathy, on the lines of Jill Dolan's position as articulated in the *TJ* forum, can be unconsciously exclusionary. We can feel empathy for a few individuals only at the expense of others; for every immersion in another body, we implicitly (or explicitly) avoid the touch of others. And yet, in acknowledging that the somatic, kinaesthetic, tactile and emotional *limits* of empathy are hard to fully accept, we may need to differentiate 'empathy' from 'sympathy', which can be more directly linked to 'a capacity for fellow-feeling' and compassion for those who are 'suffering and less fortunate'.[93] At one level sympathy, like empathy, does involve a transference of feelings for the other, but unlike empathy, it does not have to manifest itself through a physical and visceral state of embodiment and movement. This tricky differentiation between 'empathy' and 'sympathy' inevitably inflects the well-meaning liberal assumption that all human beings are *equally* deserving of our most intense feelings. But *how* does one feel for them? The complexities of this question intensify when we position ourselves in relation to 'the dead'. Can we empathize for *all* the dead in a particular disaster across race, class and nation?

Here, the politics of location matters. In Dolan's case, it would seem that, at a totally unselfconscious level, she empathizes entirely with the victims entrapped within the Twin Towers, who are unequivocally 'American'. But, perhaps, from the perspective of a theatre scholar living in an Arab country, or from some other part of the so-called Third World, it is possible that this person could feel enormous sympathy for those killed in the attack, but his or her empathy could be reserved specifically for the suicide bombers, who could be perceived as martyrs. Yet another possibility is for some individuals, across national divides, to categorically reject feeling either sympathy or empathy for the terrorists. Their deaths, it could be argued, are inevitable and not worth thinking about; the self-destruction of terrorists is an expendable factor inextricably linked to the larger extinction of 'innocent lives'. In such a response, it is sufficient to mourn for the victims, but not for the perpetrators, whose suicidal attack could be condemned as *haram* (forbidden) within the tenets of Islam. However, a harder question to ask would be that even if one chooses not to mourn for the perpetrators, how can one not acknowledge them as *human*?

It is a chilling fact that the dead bodies of terrorists, such as the corpses of those terrorists who were shot dead following the attacks in Mumbai on 26 November 2011, remain *unclaimed*. Not one citizen or social organization in India offered to bury the dead. At one level this is understandable, given the fact that even the most perfunctory gesture of respecting the dead terrorists with the barest civic rituals would be inextricably associated with anti-patriotism, if not traitorous behaviour. Poignantly, we are made to confront a situation which is radically different from that of Antigone, whose 'claim' to burying her brother Polyneices, branded a traitor by the state, is deeply embedded in subversive reinterpretations of kinship, authority and the law, as Judith Butler (2000) has argued so powerfully. For most terrorists, however, unnamed for the most part in the moment of death, there can be no such claim on their bodies; even as some of them may be remembered as martyrs in absentia, for the most part, at the moment of death, they remain the unclaimed non-citizens of the world.

To engage with these positions necessitates thinking through a cluster of national, political and religious beliefs that we internalize in our responses to terror, even as we may consciously resist all jingoist forms of nationalism and fundamentalist manifestations of religion. To what extent are we prepared to accept that terrorists are human? In recognizing the limits of empathy, I would emphasize that we do not have to stop feeling for the Other or for ourselves, or for ourselves in the Other. Rather we need to be more vigilant about how our emotions, seemingly self-contained, present and real, have already been embedded in narratives and discourses of patriotism and citizenship that operate with their own hegemonic devices and value systems. Against our will, we are complicit in these statist narratives and discourses of social well-being that we attempt to deconstruct and condemn, only to be inscribed in them at subterranean levels.

Later in the book, in chapter 3, it will become clear that there can be no universal framework of values in which to 'feel' for the victims and to 'judge' the perpetrators of terror. This does not mean that terrorism and other extreme acts of violence should be condoned, but in their condemnation, we would do well to question our own assumptions of what is right and good.

## EXIT THE THEATRE

Returning to Manila and my production of *The Maids*, which has triggered a torrent of thoughts relating to terror and performance in this chapter, I should reiterate that they have taken a long time to crystallize, a period of ten years. At one level, these thoughts expose the submerged dimensions of the 'political unconscious' of my production of *The Maids*, which, as I have emphasized earlier, did not directly reflect the terror of 'September 11'. When I look back on the production, there is little that was explicitly related to 'terror', even though I had inserted a sequence on surveillance where the maids are watched by cameras as they plot their subterfuge against Madame. For all their threat, there were no attempts to inscribe the 'Muslim' persona of the maids as terrorists. Nonetheless, even as I acknowledge this fact, there is one chilling moment which continues to haunt me today, reminding me that the spectres of 'September 11' were very much present even through their erasure in the *mise-en-scène*.

During the final rehearsals of the production, I remember my stage manager having a problem with one of Madame's lines, when she fantasizes about following her lover to Siberia. 'Oh, that's just a flamboyant line,' I tried to explain, 'Siberia is so far away.' 'But it's jarring,' my stage manager countered, 'it sounds so foreign in Tagalog.' 'Well, what would you replace Siberia with?' I asked. He thought for a moment and then said, 'Mindanao.' So near and yet so far, not unlike Kashmir in India, the site of dissident, unpatriotic, terrorist-sympathizing Muslims resembling the supporters of the bandit outfit of the Abu Sayyaf in Mindanao, allegedly linked to the Al-Qaeda. From this moment I was alerted to the fact that what we are witnessing today in postcolonial states like India and the Philippines is a deterritorialization of the national imaginary, which does not involve any surrender of territory as such, but which rests on the wish-fulfilment that the aliens ('Muslims') living in this territory should relocate elsewhere, or simply disappear.

In the next chapter, I will address at length the Islamophobic backlash to 'September 11', but what I have to say now is hard to fully register even as I put it down in writing. Three days following the last show of our production, I received an e-mail from my translator Rody Vera, informing me that the Republic of Malate had burned down on 27 November 2001. Literally, to ashes. Nothing remained of it. Rody reminded me of an eerie correspondence: the maids' fantasy as 'arsonists' and the actual razing of the theatre to the ground by unknown forces. 'Arsonist' was the Tagalog equivalent for the more eloquent 'incendiary' of the original text: a word that is almost caressed by one of the maids as a 'splendid title'. For me, while directing *The Maids* during the aftermath of 'September 11', this word functioned unconsciously as a synonym for 'terrorist', but I never made any attempt to spell this out in the *mise-en-scène*. Such one-to-one equations need to be rejected in directing Genet's deeply metaphoric and deconstructive text, where words become objects, which in turn become fantasies, and then return as echoes of previously uttered words in whirligigs of shifting meanings. To 'fix' Genet's imaginary with politically relevant equivalences is to reduce its anarchic possibilities.

The reasons for the fire at the Republic are, as yet, unclear. If it was 'accidental', the result of an electrical short-circuit, then the threat of fire was imminent during our occupation of the space. This threat has some affinities to Virilio's seminal suggestion that 'technologies and their accidents are immanent to one another. The invention or production of any technology is simultaneously also the production of its accident.'[94] This position subverts the more normative definition of 'accident' provided by the *Oxford English Dictionary* as 'an unusual event, which proceeds from some unknown cause, or an unusual effect of a known cause.'[95] Disturbing the Aristotelian premise that accidents can only be conceived in terms of their peripheral, contingent and unexpected relationships with essential substances, Virilio reverses the stability of this position to indicate that the 'unknown quality' of accidents has always already been factored into substances.

And yet, one needs to question the pertinence of this position in relation to the durability of theatre institutions – and, of theatre buildings in particular – which have been specifically created to resist accidents of all kinds. There is a long history here which takes us back to the apparatus of protection embedded in the first articulations of performance as described in the ancient Indian encyclopaedia of the *Natyashastra* (*c.* second century BCE–second century CE). Indeed, it could be argued that *natya* – an assemblage of acting, song, dance, music, costume, make-up – is made possible through the *immunity* provided to performers and spectators within the protocols of a protected space. This immunity, however, is not a metaphysical given; it has been strategized and constructed in response to the imminence of disturbance and destruction.

In the religio-mythic opening chapter of the *Natyashastra*, which I choose to interpret as a political allegory, we are told that the first performance in the celestial realm featuring the defeat of *asuras* by gods, performed in the presence of *asuras* and gods, was decisively disrupted. *Asuras* are often mistaken as demons, even though they can be more accurately described as arrogant, quasi-celestial beings who question and disrupt the divine order: Lucifers of another kind, one could say. Enraged by their humiliating portraiture on stage, the *asuras* in the *Natyashastra* invade the stage and promptly 'paralyse the speech, movement, and memory' of the actors. Nothing, as any actor would be prepared to confirm, is more terrifying than to lose one's lines on stage. To 'dry' is to 'die' a performative death. After being subjected to this humiliation, the actors consisting of Bharata's one hundred sons turn to the god Brahma for advice. In total affirmation of the power of immunity, the Celestial Censor advises the actors to build a playhouse that needs to be blessed and sanctified in every corner, thereby preventing *asuras* and other demonic forces from interrupting or disrupting the world of performance ever again. Accidents are clearly ruled out in the divine ordinance of *natya*.

Countering this fable-like solution, we know only too well that the history of theatre has never been free of accidents or acts of violence, despite the civic regimen of laws, rules, regulations, licences and all kinds of official clearances by local governments, fire departments, insurance companies, tax authorities and other state agencies like the censorship board, which legitimize and sanction the practice of theatre. These mechanisms of protection could be regarded as the new 'gods' of our times, which tend to dominate more strongly in technologically driven 'First World' theatre economies than in the more chaotic and disorganized conditions of theatre cultures in the South. The more 'developed' the theatre economy, the stronger the laws, which are ostensibly meant to ward off any disturbance including terror attacks; theatres in battlegrounds like Ramallah, however, continue to be attacked – and destroyed – by the *asuras* of our times.

Working against the premise that theatres in metropolitan cities operate within their own security zones, the destruction of the Republic of Malate by fire offers a disturbing corrective. There is an epic inventory of theatres burned through fires, one of the most legendary examples being The Globe in Elizabethan England, which burned down in 1613 during a performance of *Henry VIII*, when a spark from a cannon-shot set the thatched roof aflame. This historical 'fact' is inevitably accompanied by the anecdotal detail of a spectator whose burning breeches were doused with a bottle of ale. Such is the humour and odd sense of reassurance that one derives from this historiography that even more sinister details of nineteenth-century ballerinas being burned alive as their tutus brushed against oil and gas fires contribute towards the Grand Guignol of Theatre.[96] The overall effect is not essentially different from the sensation provided by 'the cabinet of curiosities' dominating the earliest museological imaginaries.

Tellingly, in our engagement with this historiography, it is not the threat or danger or the deaths of artists and spectators that ultimately register, but the enigmatic 'causes' that are surreptitiously linked to the larger event – 'a lantern left alight during a rehearsal' of a ballet performed at the Royal Theatre of San Carlo, Naples, on 12 February 1816; the 'spontaneous combustion' of wood-shavings in a carpenter's store at Covent Garden on 5 March 1856; and, in a more sinister register, the clandestine planting of bombs in the seating area of the Teatro del Picadero in Buenos Aires on 6 August 1981.[97] Such are the ruptures between event and fact, discourse and the body, rumour and fiction, that fire in the theatre succeeds in separating 'the past from the present so efficiently', as Alan Read puts it, 'as to have been the invention of historiography itself'.[98] Refusing to play into the 'reality' of the historiography surrounding fire as unquestioned factuality, Read compels us to be more sceptical as to what we are capable of learning about historiography through fire.

Returning to the Republic of Malate, and other such performance venues in the cultures of the South, one cannot emphasize enough that a historiography of fire in such contexts does not exist, not least because the technologies of 'safety' and 'prevention' through fire laws have yet to be integrated within the jurisdiction of most theatres in countries like India and the Philippines. There is no canonical date like 1881 in the histories of these theatres, the 'watershed year for fire prevention measure in [European] theatre' when electricity replaced gas lighting in a significant way.[99] To this day, the idea of a 'safety-curtain', the iron curtain which descends like a guillotine during intermissions in Euro–American metropolitan theatres, would be considered an oddity, if not an aberration, in 'Third World' theatrical contexts. In the absence, if not summary denial of 'safety measures', therefore, one could say that theatre workers in countries like India and the Philippines 'play with fire' at levels which would be considered *illegal* in Western contexts.

Let us face it: the Republic of Malate in Manila flouted almost all fire laws. I remember my lighting designer (Shoko Matsumoto) complaining constantly during the technical rehearsals, that the wiring of the performance space was not reliable for her special light effects. The fact that the only exit of the Republic was also the only entrance could have resulted in serious casualties if the fire had broken out during one of the performances or rehearsals. If, however, the fire was an act of 'arson' – this has been suggested in one of the few newspaper reports on the subject, which mentions that the fire broke out in several places at the same time – then its motives become even more sinister. Everything from a homophobic attack to deliberate sabotage for the lucrative benefits of real estate would need to be taken into account. The fact that the owner of the Republic was a fervent born-again Christian adds to the hermeneutic dilemma, not least because she appears to have railed against the Devil in one of her interviews. The Devil, as Genet would remind us, is one of the accomplices of the maids in their sexual fantasies and desire to kill Madame.

Resisting the populist tendency in the Philippines to convert every possible disaster into soap opera, I would question the enduring metaphor of the death-in-life in theatre, which reminds us with due sobriety that the ashes of last night's performance nurture the ground for future performances. This rhetoric of theatre, I would argue, is far too suffused with myths relating to the transformative power of performance: the phoenix rising from the ashes, and Artaud's invocation of the fire-like energy of actors who are 'burnt at the stake, signaling through the flames'.[100] In the case of the Republic of Malate, however, the burning of the theatre is not metaphoric, but real. Even as I have no option but to grieve for its loss, in its kitschy combination of baroque nostalgia, the Wild West, gay erotica and decadence – all these elements paying architectural tribute to the principle of chaos – I also choose to read in the Republic's ashes not just the lessons of renewal, but of radical hope.

Instead of the phoenix, I see a void, not unlike Alain Badiou's envisioning of the Event which 'disappears' leaving behind a vast emptiness. As nostalgia gives way to critical reflexivity, I am provoked into confronting an elemental truth: when the theatre burns down, there is something to be learned from this unprecedented event. To return to the practice of theatre with the metaphoric reassurance drawn from its habitual phoenix-like, death-in-life process is to risk lapsing into a kind of regression, if not a time warp. From the void of the Republic of Malate, therefore, I get two kinds of provocation: (1) 'You're lucky, you got away with it'; and (2) 'Your theatre is so safe'. I regard the second remark as a taunt, a self-accusation, which compels me to draw more critical ballast from Badiou, when he says that the event produces subjects out of individuals whose 'fidelity to the event' compels them 'to *invent* a new way of being and acting in the situation'.[101] Perhaps not just in the situation, but through the processes that sustain it and which extend into the act of living in the world. 'Keep going! Never forget what you have encountered': these are useful reminders, not least because 'not-forgetting is not a memory', as Badiou emphasizes, but rather 'following through on the consequences and implications of the event' in which one is reconstituted as a subject.[102]

I would like to believe that what follows in the rest of the book provides evidence of my reconstituted subjectivity, as I continue to pursue the consequences and implications of 'September 11' in different scenarios and contexts. From the world of theatre I turn now to the performativity of everyday life, in which my subjectivity is annexed, against my will, to the spectre of the 'Muslim as terrorist', which registers in the aftermath of 'September 11' with a peculiar resonance and threat.

# 2

# 'MUSLIMS' IN A TIME OF TERROR

## Deceptions, Demonization and Uncertainties of Evidence

## PHANTOMS OF THE MUSLIM AS TERRORIST

### PASSING AS A MUSLIM

In this chapter, I will shift the exploration of terror in relation to theatre and performance practice by reflecting more broadly on how the spectre of 'Muslims' has haunted and infiltrated the language of terrorism in our times. Focusing on Islamophobia in the cultures of everyday life, I will begin somewhat elliptically with my own predicament of passing as a Muslim in a growing scenario of global terror in which Muslims are stigmatized and demonized. The tropes of 'passing' and 'covering' will be explored as performative subterfuges whereby the gestures, expressions and appearances of 'minorities' can lend themselves to being incorporated into the affective registers of demonization. In a different theoretical register, the second part of the chapter highlights the discourse of communalism in contemporary India, which documents how Muslims have been targeted, othered and killed. The focus here is on the discursivity of genocide and the extent to which the killing of the Other can be interpreted as a performative action: an interpretation fraught with ethical questions, dilemmas and risks.

Let me begin with my own predicament of being marked as a Muslim, which I will not attempt to inventory but simply indicate through the seemingly trivial evidence of an anecdote. I have in mind Walter Benjamin's prescient statement that

> [a]necdote brings things closer to us in space, allows them to enter into our lives. Anecdote represents the extreme opposite of history – which demands an 'empathy' that renders everything abstract. Empathy amounts to the same thing as reading newspapers. The true method of making things present is: to imagine

> them in our space (and not to imagine ourselves in their space). Only anecdote can move us in this direction.[1]

With Benjamin in mind, let me share the following anecdote:

*In the aftermath of the demolition of the Babri Masjid in Ayodhya on 6 December 1992, which precipitated the worst riots since the Partition, I remember having a conversation with an Indian publisher that was sparked, unexpectedly, by my beard.*

*The publisher looked at my beard, sniggered and then remarked, somewhat derisively: 'You must be an intellectual.' I didn't quite know how to respond to his sarcasm, so I said the first thing that came to my mind: 'Actually I've been mistaken for a terrorist.'*

*To which the publisher responded without batting an eyelid: 'It's a good thing you haven't been mistaken for a Muslim.'*

What this anecdote reveals is a deadly slippage of categories by which an 'intellectual' metamorphoses into a 'Muslim' via the mediation of a 'terrorist'. Would it be any less deadly if we had to juggle the categories around – intellectual Muslim terrorist, terrorist intellectual Muslim, Muslim terrorist intellectual? These combinations are deadly in their own right, and need to be studied in relation to the communal unconscious of the Indian subcontinent, which mutates in states of secretion even as riots subside and things appear to return to normal. In actuality, nothing is normal these days. Indeed, would I be in a position today to acknowledge my resemblance to a terrorist, which is what I am made to feel every time I stand in front of an immigration counter? Perhaps not. Today, in the aftermath of 'September 11', when surveillance in public spaces and the censorship of electronic and critical discourse have intensified, I would be a lot more wary about making this equation, even in jest, not least because the possibilities of my actually being mistaken for a terrorist have increased. It is dangerous passing as a Muslim these days; it is even more dangerous to flaunt one's affinities to a terrorist.

At a performative level, then, how does one read the situation of an intellectual 'passing' as a terrorist/Muslim? First of all, one needs to differentiate the act of 'passing' from the more conscious subterfuge involved in 'enacting' the roles of an impostor or an infiltrator. These roles are consciously plotted even as their functions are rigorously concealed. After all, what kind of an impostor/infiltrator would one be if one allowed one's 'true' identity to be revealed through the camouflage of pretence?[2] Terrorists are effective precisely because they infiltrate security zones with all the performative accoutrements of 'normal' behaviour, circumventing the protocols of surveillance. They are, for the most part, highly skilled performers who accomplish their roles through rigorous training, supplemented by improvisatory audacity, and a readiness to kill and die.

Unlike the dynamics of 'infiltrating', the phenomenon of 'passing' is perhaps most closely related to 'covering', but with significant differences. There is a growing literature around the interstices of 'passing' and 'covering', which are prefigured in Erving Goffman's pragmatic discriminations in relation to stigma. The genealogy of this concept can be traced to the Greek interpretation of the word as referring to 'bodily signs designed to expose something unusual and bad about the moral status of the signifier'.[3] These signs were not infinitesimal, but actually 'cut or burnt into the body' and 'advertised' so that individuals could be marked as 'slaves or criminals or traitors, blemished persons, ritually polluted, to be avoided, especially in public places'.[4] Almost eerily, this reading of stigma remains palpably alive in the Indian public sphere, particularly in relation to the stigmatization of low-caste communities and so-called untouchables who suffer the potentiality of caste violence on a daily basis. This is another kind of terror that gets normalized and hegemonized in the cultures of everyday life in the Indian subcontinent.

In an earlier essay, 'Phantoms of the Other: Fragments of the Communal Unconscious' (2000), I have elaborated on the caste violence underlying my conceptualization of a Kannada adaptation of Büchner's *Woyzeck*, which was at one level sparked by an image in a local newspaper: a dalit ('low'-caste) labourer tied to a stake with a shit-smeared *chappal* (slipper) rammed into his mouth. So intense is the stigmatization of caste that it is not just the equation of low-caste untouchables with dirt that leads to taboos relating to the pollution of touch, or of sharing food or water with a 'low'-caste person; the very *shadow* of an untouchable or his/her passing *presence* on the street can be viewed as sources of contamination. Stigma in these contexts has subterranean, almost invisible ways of manifesting itself, which would lack the overt physicality by which Goffman defines the term in relation to the disabled, the elderly, the infirm and the obese.

Extending the parameters of Goffman's argument, the legal scholar Kenji Yoshino (2006) has elaborated on the discriminations between the modalities of 'passing' and 'covering'. For Goffman, those persons who are 'ready to admit possession of a stigma . . . [but who] may nonetheless make a great effort to keep the stigma from looming large', may be considered to 'cover' their behaviour.[5] Passing, in contrast, occurs when a person from an ethnic or racial minority, for instance, performs his or her 'real self' in private, while attempting to blend into the majoritarian signs of the dominant culture: persons of colour of African–American ancestry passing as 'white' to improve their social status, or Jews in Nazi Germany passing as 'Aryans' to survive and escape deportation to concentration camps are among some of the historical examples representing the risks and compulsions underlying the act of passing. If passing works through a process of 'invisibilizing' one's 'real' identity in the public domain, covering is a more dodgy and covert form of playing hide-and-seek with the dominant norms of a particular situation or context in so far as one engages with public culture by strategically concealing those signs that would be considered offensive. In other words, as Yoshino elaborates, blacks in professional work spaces could avoid styling their hair in cornrows, gays could avoid 'flaunting' their sexuality and so on. Such minorities are accepted *as minorities* in 'mainstream' culture only by 'covering' their differences.

At this point Yoshino emphasizes the crucial legal distinction made between those 'immutable' traits which cannot be changed in any human being and which 'mainstream' society has no other option but to tolerate – for instance, skin colour or ethnicity. In contrast, 'mutable' traits are those which are capable of being modified or suppressed altogether by minorities with due deference to institutional norms. Drawing on a number of legal cases, Yoshino points out the paradoxes of 'immutable' and 'mutable' discrimination: 'African–Americans cannot be fired for their skin colour, but they could be fired for wearing cornrows. Potential jurors cannot be struck for their ethnicity but can be struck for speaking (or even for admitting proficiency) in a foreign language.'[6] In this coercive demand for assimilation whereby minorities are expected to behave 'normally' without exhibiting their racial, sexual, linguistic or behavioural preferences, the 'pressure to cover', according to Yoshino, is nothing less than a violation of personal liberties, which he strongly defends in favour of an 'inclusive' register of 'new civil rights'.[7]

Arguing against the divisiveness of identity politics and multiculturalism, which has been aggravated by debates around the exclusive rights of minority groups, Yoshino opts, in my view, for a somewhat too liberal, if not unrealistic reading of 'universal rights'. These rights are based on the axiom that 'everyone covers' in human society including those in the so-called mainstream, which, as Yoshino emphasizes uncritically, is something of a 'myth' in so far as it is in a constantly mutant state.[8] It would be more accurate to acknowledge that the mainstream always already exists even in the process of mutating. Affirming that it is 'not normal to be completely normal', Yoshino speaks out, surprisingly, in favour of those anti-minority baiters like 'straight white men' whose 'right to self-expression' is not given the same importance as the rights of racial minorities, women or gays.[9] In this pitch for inclusiveness, Yoshino does not deny the rights of minorities; rather, with an excess of urbane reasonableness and inclusivity, he demands that these rights need to be affirmed in the context of 'liberty' to which 'we are all entitled', rather than as a 'remedial concession' granted to a particular group.[10] In this reading, the rights to gay marriage would need to be framed on the basis that 'we' all have the right 'to marry the person we love', rather than defending gay marriage as a 'separate institution'.[11] Likewise, the right to speak one's mother tongue needs to be affirmed not on nativist grounds, but as part of a general freedom of speech.

From my location in India, I would argue that the liberal inclusiveness of this position does not engage with the virulence of economic disparities, cultural and educational differences, and the sheer scale of social injustices, which cannot be wished away through 'conversations' across sectors of the population. Instead of advocating any form of affirmative action or reservations, which is the official Indian way of engaging with social injustice for marginalized and underprivileged 'low'-caste communities, or recommending any solution-facilitating authority of the law, Yoshino advocates freewheeling 'conversations' in the public domain for the production of a renewed civility. But, where and how are these conversations likely to take place in a society normalized through discrimination, and increasingly built around gated communities and ghettos, refugee camps and no-go zones?

Moving outside the privileged sectors of the United States, the struggle for equality in caste-bound and communally charged societies like India, for instance, cannot be written off quite so easily in favour of liberty, which ultimately gets equated with Yoshino's self-affirmation of 'the freedom to be who I am'.[12] Such liberal individualism is totally at odds with a political culture formed on the basis of community identities and 'personal laws' which are structured essentially around the norms and codes of specific religions. The 'personal', it could be argued, is 'religious' within some readings of the 'secular' law in India, where communities have the option, in specific contexts, to turn to the civil courts to seek justice and to switch back to 'personal law' for yet another negotiation of grievances. There is a flexibility, therefore, written into 'secular' law in the Indian context, at least at a normative level, in so far as religion is not treated as an absolute in the tradition of a theocratic state, but neither are the manifestations of religious practice or behaviour summarily excluded from public life.[13]

It is in this context that any attempt to read 'Muslims' on a purely individual basis, divested of religious or communitarian associations, poses challenges in the Indian subcontinental context. Even if the category of 'Muslim' is totally rejected on religious grounds by atheists or cosmopolitan elites, and even as it may be theoretically expedient at a postmodern level to explicate 'when is a Muslim *not* a Muslim' and to question 'to what extent is a Muslim *more* than a Muslim',[14] if only to counter the homogenization of statist categories and the intensification of religious bigotry, the ethos of radical or liberal individualism cannot be valorized and made into an absolute in its own right. At a more empirical level one has no other option but to placc on the agenda the far more pervasive non-liberal or orthodox option: 'when is a Muslim *only* a Muslim'. In what circumstances and contexts does such a mentality and self-identification prevail? And to what extent is its assertion a matter of choice rather than coercion?

## CONSTRUCTING 'MUSLIMS'

Far from being a primordial identitarian category going back centuries, the 'Muslim' is a relatively recent invention. In this regard, it is no different from other such 'labels', as Arjun Appadurai puts it, as 'Sikh' and 'Kurd', which are 'transformations of existing names and terms to serve substantially new frameworks of identity, entitlement, and spatial sovereignty'.[15] For many historians, the religio-political associations of Muslims in the Indian subcontinent, if not the very marking of the 'Muslim' as a category, can be traced back to the census reports of the late nineteenth century in colonial India. Within the mechanisms, statistics and nomenclature of such reports, the monolithic figure of the 'Muslim' (with regional variations) was constructed and disseminated according to fixed criteria of origins, customs and laws. Admittedly, the earliest tropes revolving around Muslims were not unequivocal; they were 'split', as early ethnographers and census officials vacillated between tracing the Arabic origins of hereditary Muslims who were subsequently indigenized in India, and the conversion of native Hindus to Islam.[16]

With technologies like cephalic indexing, early colonial ethnographers such as Herbert Risley measured the heads and noses of Muslims to prove that these individuals were not of Semitic origin, but of native stock from the poorer tribal communities.[17] Through such manufactured and 'scientific' evidence, it was accepted that the vast majority of Muslims were the descendants of low-caste Hindu communities who had converted to Islam in order to free themselves from the tyrannies of the caste system. Were these converts 'lesser' Muslims, or could they be regarded as more 'authentically' Hindu? While politicizing such questions, the thrust of the census reports between 1872 to 1901 was to prove, as Gauri Viswanathan has pointed out, that the Indian Muslim was not an 'autonomous other', but a 'version of the Hindu'.[18] In other words, Muslims were *covering* their Hindu origins even while *passing* as Indian.

Apart from being regarded as 'versions' of Hindus, Muslims can also be regarded as 'copies', not unlike the Ahmadiyya community in Pakistan who have, since 1974, faced severe legal penalties for ostensibly passing as 'Muslims', an identity that is denied to them in the public sphere through legislation and social prejudice, if not overt hostility. It is useful to dwell here briefly on the predicament faced by the Ahmadiyyas in order to puncture the global homogenization of 'Muslim' identity. In a succinct essay by Naveeda Khan (2005), which attempts to locate the 'trespassing' identity of the Ahmadiyya in relation to the Pakistan state, we learn that Mirza Ghulam Ahmad, the founder of this Muslim sect of nineteenth-century origin, identified himself first as a *mujaddid* (renewer) of the faith and then as a *muhadith*, which implied that he was 'in conversation with the angels, if not with the Prophet and with God'.[19] Later, from representing himself as a shadow (*zil*) of the Prophet, he went on to claim his own prophetic powers.

Significantly, even after the 1974 constitutional amendment in Pakistan, which relegated the Ahmadiyya from the mainstream of Islam to the 'non-Muslim' minority category, the Ahmadiyyas were marked as *kafir* (infidels), *murtadd* (apostates), *taghut* (devils, sorcerers) and *munafiqun* (hypocrites).[20] Today, as minorities they have also been labelled, in a more contemporary idiom, as *copies* – and not just 'bad' copies, but 'dangerous' ones as well.[21] Inevitably, this word 'copy' lends itself to being read in the larger contemporary context of copyright violations, even as it is being set against some kind of authentic religiosity which is essentially 'unrepresentable'. It is through such epistemological and theological complications that Euro–American tropes of 'copying' at secular and symbolic levels get deeply problematized.

Of particular interest here is not just the scepticism and suspicion with which copies are regarded in the context of designating Ahmadiyya identity, but also the ways in which, on very rare occasions, they can be defended. One piece of evidence provided by Naveeda Khan is particularly striking: as an exception to the Supreme Court judgment against the Ahmadiyyas, one dissenting judge made 'an argument for dissimulation (pretence under fire) as opposed to deliberate deception'.[22] In the context of minorities being hounded by the majority community, this learned judge argued that it made sense for minorities to 'dissimulate' their identities as they 'trespass' the norms of the state, because this could be their only way to survive. 'Covering', therefore, has a pragmatic ethical dimension linked to the basic right to protect one's life, and should not be summarily reduced to hypocritical and duplicitous behaviour.

Returning to the colonial construction of 'Muslims' in the Indian context, and elsewhere in formerly colonized nations, one needs to push the borderlines by which identities are officially manufactured against the dissimulations of 'passing' and 'covering'. Official identities are state-determined, legally sanctioned *political identities*, as Mahmood Mamdani has argued, in contradistinction to *cultural identities*, which are 'consensual', 'voluntary' and 'multiple'.[23] Admittedly, without contextual clarification there would seem to be a reductionism both in Mamdani's separation of the 'cultural' and the 'political', as well as in the constituents of their independent domains. While 'cultural' in his reading would appear to be arbitrarily annexed to the voluntarist assumptions of cultures of choice, seemingly divested of ideological and hegemonic framing, the 'political' is far too embedded within a juridical conception of community inscribed within the larger regulatory codes of governance. Mamdani is well aware of these reductions and qualifies that, in his reading of 'cultural identity', he does not wish to 'romanticize the domain of consent or to detract from the existence of power relations'. [24] It could also be argued that not every 'political' identity needs legal verification or sanction, but may indeed materialize through an opposition to or denial of legality in the first place.

Keeping these caveats in mind, I would argue that the fundamental thrust of most research in theatre and performance studies has been in the area of 'cultural' as opposed to 'political' identities, to adopt Mamdani's strategically over-emphatic distinction. Our basic exploration (I would include myself among these theatre and performance researchers) has been in the area of blurring and hybridizing identities, and, at all costs, in 'transgressing' official norms, as if this were the only decent, responsible and, above all, creative thing to do. In the process, we have played into the fetishization of the 'liminal-norm',[25] as articulated by Jon McKenzie, by which performance studies has projected and valorized its liberal, if not radical credentials. Even while liminality does not – and, indeed, should not – disappear in our deconstruction of political identity, it is chastening to be reminded by Mamdani that non-liminal (i.e. normative, 'fixed') identities are not easily disregarded: 'A legal identity is neither voluntary nor multiple. The law recognizes you as one and none other.'[26]

Instead of dismissing the singularity of legally sanctioned political identity as mere dogma and an irritant to cultural research, perhaps we need to find ways of engaging critically with its norms because they could be more ambivalent than we assume. Besides, on a more pragmatic note, why should we assume that all political, legally sanctioned identities are intrinsically undesirable and anti-liberal? Perhaps, for a refugee or stateless person, nothing could be more coveted than a legally sanctioned identity or passport. It is only when such an identity can be safely assumed, possessed and mobilized that it becomes possible to reject or subvert it, thereby revealing the privilege that is inherent in critical dissent and the cavalier dismissal of all officially determined identities.

## PHENOMENOLOGY OF PASSING

Having elaborated at some length on what goes into the political construction of 'Muslims' in the Indian context, let us now approach the predicament of 'passing as a Muslim' at a more phenomenological level. 'Passing', one could argue, is best understood as a process, a movement, which opposes the tendency in identity politics to 'fix' identities within a grid of signs and stereotypes. As Paul Rae puts it perceptively,

> [P]assing suggests that you need to stay on the move in order to avoid being found out. Put your head down and just keep walking: otherwise, the seams will show – the places where the disguise doesn't quite cover the actuality; where the improvised props, the too-studied speech and the over-mannered gesture are brought to light. Just passing through, one blurs the borders.[27]

At one level, this business about 'putting your head down and continuing to walk' could also lend itself to the subterfuge of 'covering'. Immigrants, after all, can be legally allowed and even encouraged to 'keep walking', affirming their 'multicultural' identities, but without creating trouble or flaunting their minority status. In this sense, they are encouraged to cover as they pass, playing into the norms of difference that have been legislated by the state through strategies of assimilation. The important thing is not to disturb the script that has been worked out in advance even as any act of passing, as Rae astutely points out, is 'a process of co-creation'.[28] Never fully located in any one participant, and relational to the extent that it feeds on the Other's gaze and perception, the act of passing breaks down only when the assumptions of appearance and dissimulation are challenged, when one party refuses to play the game and calls the bluff of the person passing as the Other.

Perhaps there is another problem as well, which is not always recognized in the discourse surrounding 'passing'. When one 'passes' for somebody else from another community, I would emphasize that the pretence may not be entirely voluntary. Indeed, to return to my own predicament, I may not necessarily want to pass as a 'Muslim' (or, by implication, as a 'terrorist'), but that is how I will be read within the larger codes and technologies of identification manufactured by governmental regimes and surveillance systems. While the more conventional reading of 'passing' would assume a certain degree of transitivity – in other words, an agency and intentionality embodied in the act of passing as the Other – the situation is different when *one is passed, irreversibly, against one's will*. 'I pass as a Muslim' opens a different set of performative registers from 'I look like a Muslim' and, therefore, 'I am passed as a Muslim.' In this scenario it is harder to read a process of co-creation, although at some point in time one may have no other option but to enter the narrative of 'being passed'.

The options here are tricky. If, for example, an immigration officer 'passes' me as a Muslim, a great deal of tact is needed before my 'real' identity (as a non-Muslim) can be affirmed – or, more precisely, proved through official forms of evidence. In outing oneself, one may have no other option but to work against the logic of predetermined passing, where one runs the risk of offending the immigration officer, who would like his surveillance expertise to be confirmed rather than disproved. If one is lucky to have one's passport returned in such a scenario, one still has no other option but to accept one's 'passed identity' as some kind of alter ego, a palimpsest that will forever shadow one's future encounters with immigration officers: a shadow that sticks to one's skin as it were.

'Passing', therefore, operates like an unconscious reflex in the unscripted narratives of everyday life. It can be disrupted when the sheer repetition of being mistaken for the Other has the potentiality to compel a self-confrontation of specific signs in one's physiognomy and behaviour that are inadvertently responsible for connoting another identity. At this moment of self-confrontation one may, of course, either choose to continue 'passing' for what one is not, or one could work against the signs of being mistaken for another. While the temptation to perpetuate a counterfeit identity has subversive potentiality, the imperative to survive on one's own terms demands certain risk-free alterations in behaviour and appearance – for instance, one way of *not* passing as a Muslim could be to shave one's beard, or else, to trim it in a different, less 'Muslim' fashion. Needless to say, this altered physiognomy could amount to a form of self-censorship, which can be interpreted as yet another suppression of one's personal freedom and state of being.

But can one be so sure that in shaving one's beard, 'Muslimness' can be elided? Can it not, inadvertently, reinforce the 'Muslim' identity? The lighter skin over the shaved bearded area in relation to the dark epidermis of the top part of the face could arouse suspicions.[29] In this avatar, one could be marked as a terrorist in disguise, and thereby subjected to even more suspicion and abuse. Damned with a beard or damned without, the Muslim/terrorist is always already marked. In his incisive catalogue of 'biotypologies of terrorism', Joseph Pugliese addresses the lethal suspicions surrounding 'the freshly shaved "Muslim zealot"', in addition to give-away signs of smell: 'Is the individual wearing too much cologne or perfume, or does he or she smell of talcum powder or scented water (for ritual purification)?'[30]

In addition, there are new biometric technologies like VEW (Video Early Warning) and HID (Human Identification at a Distance) whereby anti-terrorist surveillance is linked to the subtleties of 'gait research' – in other words, 'detecting how strangers walk'.[31] 'You could be charged as a terrorist if you walk in a funny way', as Pugliese warns us – and the 'funny walk' need not be Michael Jackson's 'moonwalking', which the radar has in all probability assimilated as a legitimate form of kinky performative behaviour. Alongside these technologies relating to walks, which can detect the most minute of kinetic discrepancies or shifts in energy, in addition to iris scans, facial scans and finger scans – technologies of terror in their own right – surveillance agencies can go overboard in 'imagining' terrorists like Osama bin Laden in all kinds of ingenious costumes. In a number of widely circulated mug-shots on the internet, Osama looks positively bohemian and natty, if not the kind of guy one could encounter in a country club or golf course. So, bearded or beardless, there can be diverse terrorist subterfuges of the 'Muslim', which are not merely the invention of terrorists but of counterterrorist agencies as well, who outdo each other in attempting to 'perform' their own fantasies of terrorists.

## QUEERING THE MUSLIM TERRORIST: BEARDS AND PENISES

The dynamics of 'passing' can be most easily read within the narrative of mistaken identity, which is perhaps one of the most ancient tropes of world theatre, as represented in Roman comedy, Shakespeare, Parsi theatre, *The Importance of Being Earnest* and so on. Once provocative, these tropes have assumed the reassurance of archaisms: an object (a perambulator) or a sign (a mole on a cheek) can facilitate the clarification of a lost heritage or genealogy or relationship, leading to a denouement. In contrast, returning to the dominant sign of the beard to designate 'Muslim' identity, this sign is not about marking an individual identity *per se*, but of annexing this identity to that of an entire community, if not a species. Once marked, 'the Muslim' assumes a hyperreal significance, regardless of whether or not it is linked to a mistaken or real identity. A political signifier with global implications, it assumes omnipresence, ruthlessly indifferent to the multitudinous and differentiated realities of the signified.

As Osama bin Laden has been ruthlessly invisibilized even as his spectre is barely kept alive in the aftermath of his killing (which is officially designated as a 'military operation' or 'assassination'), how many of us remember the process of his demonization which has now been almost entirely erased? For me, this demonization was linked, at physical and visceral levels, to the marking of his beard. Most chillingly, I was made to confront this beard in an early David Levine cartoon in the *New York Review of Books*, where it was rendered with liberal insouciance and wit as bin Laden was blithely defaced. All that remained of him was a long, bushy, greying, unkempt beard cut around the lips. A brutal framing, which brought to mind other such framings of minorities – notably, the black man as represented in Robert Mapplethorpe's widely circulated image of the 'Man in a Polyester Suit'. Here, too, the man is defaced, cut above the shoulders, but with his penis exposed, firmly intact.

While there have been many responses to this image, ranging from critiques of racism to fantasies of homosexual desire, it exemplifies, to my mind, Frantz Fanon's uninflected injunction: 'One is no longer aware of the Negro but only of a penis; the Negro is eclipsed. He is turned into a penis. He *is* a penis.'[32] Likewise, the 'Muslim', in the hate literature of the Indian subcontinent circulating around his unclean body, polygamy and lasciviousness, is often equated with a circumcised penis; indeed, in actual acts of terrorism inflicted on minorities, it provides the ultimate physical evidence of 'Muslim' identity. '*Laandya*', the Marathi word for an animal with its tail cut off, is one of the abusive epithets that have been hurled at Muslims in the post-Ayodhya communal crisis in India.

Drawing on the evidence of such communal abuse, a report by the International Initiative for Justice states that 'Muslim men, in the Hindu Right discourse [in India] are not seen as "men" at all: they are either "oversexed" to the extent of being bestial (they can satisfy four wives!) or they are effeminate and not masculine enough to satisfy their women'.[33] In other words, their sexuality vacillates between hypermasculinity, and the abject femininity associated with homosexuals and *hijras* (eunuchs). As these deviant psychophysical attributes of 'Muslims' get solidified at global levels, they get 'queered' in the larger context of terrorism, as Jasbir Puar (2007) has elaborated in her politically incisive reflections on 'terrorist assemblages'. For Puar, it is not simply a matter of recognizing 'what is terrorist about the queer' or, conversely, 'what is queer about the terrorist'; the point is that, at a performative level, queerness has always already been 'installed' in the 'naming' of the terrorist.[34]

And yet, one needs to question to what extent 'queer politics' can be annexed to the naming of terrorists outside the grassroots realities of community and sexual politics in the United States, which provides the primary evidence for Puar's dense research. In a synoptic perspective, Puar draws on a generalized sweep of popular and cultural associations by which the terrorist is 'concurrently an unfathomable, unknowable, and hysterical monstrosity', which only 'the exceptional capacities of US intelligence and security systems can quell'.[35] 'Unfathomable' and 'unknowable' resonate as valid descriptors of the terrorist's elusive personality and action, but 'hysterical monstrosity' strikes me as being something of a rhetorical overkill which undermines the deadly violence of the 'real' terrorists of our times, who can be only too real, ordinary and straight.

If we follow the evidence provided by Faisal Devji of the London terror attacks of 7 July 1995, for instance, the majority of the terrorists come across like regular 'lads', with jobs, hobbies, regular visits to the gym and girlfriends.[36] They were not rabid Islamists or particularly devout Muslims; nor had they been indoctrinated over a long period of time, one of the quirks of their terrorism being the astonishing speed of their training and their relatively low-tech expertise in engaging with information technology and weaponry. Without engaging with the heteronormative 'ordinariness' of such terrorist personae, even at the level of masquerade, Puar builds her argument incrementally on the trope of 'monstrosity'. The prime exemplar of this trope is Osama bin Laden who, in the immediate aftermath of 'September 11', was both racialized and sexualized with 'negative connotations of homosexuality': 'feminized, stateless, dark, perverse, pedophilic, disowned by family (i.e. fag)'.[37]

Contradicting these overly cryptic markers of bin Laden's image and aura, one would have to emphasize that this is *not* how he registered to vast sections of the population in the Indian subcontinent and the Arab world. Even as he may have been condemned as 'evil' or, indeed, disparaged as a 'bad Muslim', or, worse still, a 'bad terrorist', he was not demonized in Indian public culture on grounds of his sexual perversity, femininity or paedophilic affinities. Even his most intense critics would dismiss these charges as absurd. Instead, Osama bin Laden came across on television to millions of viewers in the Indian subcontinent as a Muslim patriarchal figure – menacing, dangerous, but not undignified. It was Bush and his cronies who appeared to be 'monstrous'.

The obvious theoretical point that needs to be emphasized here is that the queering of the terrorist is perhaps most convincingly read within the tropes of US popular culture. Here, Puar's evidence is positively virtuoso as she zeroes in on all kinds of cultural artefacts, ranging from toilet paper with Osama bin Laden's image imprinted on it to posters which appeared in midtown Manhattan showing a caricature of a turbanned bin Laden being anally penetrated by the Empire State Building: '*The Empire Strikes Back . . . So you like skyscrapers, huh, bitch?*' is the blatantly homophobic inscription.[38] Puar also calls attention to a website where 'weapons are provided to sodomize Osama bin Laden to death'.[39] While anal penetration is not foreign to the anti-Muslim hate literature that circulates in the pamphlet culture of the Hindu Right,[40] it is invariably linked to making Muslims into *hijras* (eunuchs), one of the most traditional associations of abject femininity in the Indian subcontinent with a long and complex history of both empowerment and debasement. This history provides a different identitarian context from the populist irreverence and abuse by which Osama bin Laden's body was forcibly queered in the United States in the immediate aftermath of 'September 11'.

## THE BEAUTIFUL TERRORIST

To call attention to yet another conceptual framework in which the body of the 'Muslim terrorist' has been rhapsodized rather than queered, it is necessary to address different iconographies surrounding the 'beauty' of the terrorist. This is a discursive realm that lies beyond Puar's reading of the terrorist in terms of 'hysterical monstrosity' and 'perversity'. To complicate the demonization of terror, I offer an example drawn from a panegyric report in the popular Urdu press which extols the beauty of Omar Saeed Sheikh, the killer of the American journalist Daniel Pearl. Countering the humanist idiom in which Pearl's brutal murder has been widely condemned, not only in the international press but among the national dailies of the Indian subcontinent as well, the Urdu report in question provides a totally different perspective – and language – from which to *relish* the proponent of the crime. The focus is not so much on the validity of terrorist action as on the beauty of the terrorist himself.

I quote this report at some length, as much for its seductive rhetoric as for the obvious provocation it poses in working against the aura of a marked 'terrorist' in his globally demonized persona:

> Sheikh is not only Pakistan's but the entire Islamic world's most *vajeeh*, most *haseen*, most *jameel*, most *sohna*, most *mohna*, (all meaning beautiful) young man. The real beauty is of character. He has become the ideal and *adarsh*. His beauty is not dependent on beauty of face and years. His beauty has been born of his steadfastness, courage and bravery. This is his internal beauty. His external beauty is like that of Prophet Yusuf. His stature is that of the cypress tree, his forehead is shining. His face carries the impression of a lion on which a dark beard is like a precious decoration. Shining from behind his gold-frame glasses, his eyes are intelligent and reflective, while his proportionate aquiline nose and white rosy complexion can be likened to a crystalline bowl (*biloreen sabu*) filled with crimson pomegranate juice (*anar ka ahmareen sharbat*). He is the beautiful son (*sohna sapoot*) of a beautiful land (*sohni dharti*) who said welcome to death in a beautiful way![41]

Whose death, it could be asked: Omar Sheikh is still alive, allegedly imprisoned in Pakistan, while Daniel Pearl is dead following one of the most brutal and sadistic murders which has been disseminated on the electronic media.

From the homosocial/homoerotic rhetoric of the Urdu panegyric quoted above, it becomes clear that the rapture of its tone contrasts sharply with the 'perversity' emphasized by Puar in the demonization of terrorists in the US media and popular culture. In the Urdu panegyric, the rhetoric is built at several levels through the opposition between 'inner' and 'outer' beauty; the ultra-patriotism, if not pan-nationalism surrounding the 'son of the land'; the time-tested conventionality of the rhetorical epithets ('cypress tree', 'pomegranate juice', deflected ever so slightly by the 'gold-rimmed glasses'). Through such an assemblage of details, the rhetoric compels one to stretch the existing imaginaries of 'Muslim terrorists' available in Euro-American studies of terror. Against the malevolence of their portraiture, we need to acknowledge that these very terrorists can be objects of beauty in the eyes of their compatriots.

Ironically, yet significantly, one can also trace registers of 'beauty' in Islamophobic accounts of terrorists, which testify to the ambivalences of how terror can be perceived on diametrically opposite sides of the political divide. Arguably, both the supporters and denigrators of individual terrorists can share some elements of a common language evoking a terrifying beauty. This is not the language of poetry, of Yeats evoking 'a terrible beauty', which is born in the massacre of Irish nationalists fighting against British colonizers in the Easter Rising of 1916; nor is it the beauty invoked by Rilke in the *Duino Elegies*, which he envisions as 'the beginning of terror / which we are barely able to endure' because 'it serenely disdains to destroy us'. Complicating the extreme romanticism read into Rilke's illuminations of beauty and terror – 'every angel is terrifying', as he puts it – the 'beautiful terrorist' who concerns me here is more likely to be found in pulp fiction and sensational reportage.

Alongside the Urdu panegyric of Omar Saeed Sheikh analysed earlier, therefore, let us examine what happens to the figure – and, more precisely, the body – of this terrorist in Bernard-Henri Lévy's racy narrative entitled *Who Killed Daniel Pearl?* (2004). Written with the flair of a seasoned investigative journalist, Lévy's narrative reveals layers of barely concealed fascination for Omar Sheikh in his reconstruction of Daniel Pearl's death. At one level, for Lévy, Omar comes across in a forthright idiom as a 'handsome' terrorist, his masculinity emphatically marked:

> . . . his face well-constructed, high forehead, a look without vice or malice though somewhat veiled. His physiognomy appears intelligent and rather frank, tortoise-shell glasses, a strong chin under a well-trimmed beard, a good man it would seem, slightly tart smile, an intellectual demeanor, very Westernized – nothing, in any case, that signals the obtuse Islamist, the fanatic.[42]

In contrast to this demeanour of a 'good' terrorist, Lévy reads other photographs and videos of Omar Sheikh in which the refined, educated persona of Omar begins to acquire more sinister overtones, approximating the 'monstrosity' that Jasbir Puar invokes in her queering of the figure of Osama bin Laden.

Most vividly, Lévy captures Omar's menace in a rough video documentation of an arm-wrestling match in a noisy London pub. Apart from chess, Omar was an arm-wrestler of some repute, a somewhat incongruous association for a reticent, well-behaved, middle-class South Asian student at the London School of Economics. Capturing the 'rough and good-humored' atmosphere of the arm-wrestling match ('very 1960s Teddy Boys'), Lévy depicts Omar as the very picture of concentration and indifference to the cacophony surrounding him – 'the crowd yelling and applauding', with 'young people with close-cropped hair and tattoos, muscle-bound torsos, sitting on the floor with pints of beer'.[43]

Pitted against a formidable competitor, 'a colossus with a shaved head . . . a mountain of muscle and fat', who is twice his weight and almost twice his size, Omar is undeterred. Lévy describes the warm-up in graphic detail:

> [Omar] stamps, taps his foot and nods his head as though he were searching for the beat. He takes his opponent's hand, does it again several times to get the right grip, and when he has, he paws it, shakes it, still chewing his gum, and always rhythmically, as though he were jacking himself off, shakes it gently. Finally he presses up against the table, rubs against it. With his chest projected, his stomach glued to the wood of the table, nostrils flaring, fixed stare, he's the one who looks like he's having a wank now.[44]

In contrast to this overt sexualization, Lévy juxtaposes Omar's strategic determination as a fighter who, on the point of losing the match, suddenly 'marshals his muscles' and takes advantage of his over-confident opponent's slight ease of pressure to 'reverse the movement and, with one thrust, just one, plasters the wrestler's arm on the table to the cheer of the crowd'.[45] In Omar's subsequent 'air of indescribable pride', Lévy reads 'his secret face of a brute'.[46]

Playing on the mixed signs of Omar's appearance, Lévy sees a 'brute' in the trim, physically fit, handsome terrorist. At another point in his narrative he invokes a 'monster', but not a hysterical one on the lines of Puar's description. Rather this monster is 'also a man like any other'; he is a 'killer' in whose face Lévy fails to 'find any stigmata that, in the common imagination, signals the presence of absolute Evil'.[47] Drawing on a more minute reading of Omar provided by one of his hostages – Omar, it should be remembered, had built his terrorist credentials by kidnapping tourists and seasoned journalists like Daniel Pearl, luring them with his charm – Lévy reveals a man seemingly 'English', but who is driven by 'a thorough and radical hatred of England'.[48] Invoking Omar's arm-wrestling matches in London pubs, Lévy's hostage informant has a 'theory' that

> deep down inside, [Omar] hated [the English]. He had only contempt for those fat Englishmen bursting with beer, tattooed, obscene, propping up the bar. Just that – he learned to know them and to hate them. He was like a double agent in contact with the enemy. That's what arm wrestling did for him.[49]

Given his links with both Pakistan's Inter-Services Intelligence (ISI) and the Al-Qaeda, Omar was perhaps more than a double agent. Along with his compulsive, chimerical and deceptive persona, concealing both 'the perfect Englishman and the ultimate enemy',[50] as Lévy puts it somewhat too dichotomously, what also needs to be put on the agenda are the sensual ways by which 'terrorists' are perceived in the first place. Along with his neoconservative politics, flamboyant personality, diplomatic connections and anti-Pakistani biases, it would seem that Lévy also has an unacknowledged voyeuristic interest in 'other' (non-European) masculinities. Indeed, in the absence of any systematic study of how the figure of 'the terrorist' has registered across the world in diverse political imaginaries, one has to be cautious in homogenizing the language of demonization by which figures like Osama bin Laden (and, more ambivalently, 'beautiful terrorists' like Omar Sheikh) have been vilified in 'the West'. My point is that this language may be more diverse than we imagine and a lot more revealing about the fascination for terror by individual writers rather than an objectification of the 'terrorists' themselves.

This fascination is not just evident in the polemical writings of right-wing Islamophobes like Lévy, but in the more urbane commentary of non-specialists on terror like the celebrated spy novelist John le Carré. Barely concealing his abhorrence of the Islamist onslaught on liberal values, he somewhat overstretches his interpretive capacities as a fiction writer by reading a demonstration of 'narcissistic homoeroticism'[51] in Osama bin Laden's video performances. It would be useful to question in whose gaze homoeroticism gets read so easily in the first place. Totally failing to read himself in the picture of bin Laden that he so confidently paints, le Carré goes on to provide some 'hope' to Americans by reassuring them that '[bin Laden's] barely containable male vanity, his appetite for self-drama and his closet passion for the limelight . . . will be his downfall, seducing him into a final dramatic act of self-destruction, produced, directed, scripted and acted to death by Osama bin Laden himself.'[52]

Aspersions of vanity to the contrary, I would say that it is le Carré's predictions which have backfired: Osama bin Laden did not self-destruct in the manner of some malignant evil spirit; he was clinically killed by the American security forces in a script that had the full approval of the President of the United States and his colleagues, who even ensured that they had the opportunity to see the 'killing' being performed in 'real time'. Even while official images relating to the killing itself have been resolutely erased from the eyes of the world, what is fully on display in the much-replicated photograph of Obama and his staff watching the killing is the White House's vanity in demonstrating to the rest of the world that Operation Geronimo was a success. Arguably, the reference to the Native American Apache leader Geronimo, hounded by the American forces in the last years of his life, was more of a racist political blunder on the part of the American security forces than an obligatory pseudonym for Osama bin Laden. Or perhaps it was not a blunder but a carefully calculated reaffirmation of American national sovereignty, reasserting its imperial power through the 'discursive resignification and double death' of Geronimo.[53] Once killed as a renegade Native American troublemaker, the United States had no other option but to kill him one more time as Geronimo EKIA (Enemy

Killed In Action), in and through the body of the most wanted man on earth: Osama bin Laden. Wanted dead or alive, bin Laden ultimately landed up, like Geronimo, dead.

## THE SIKH AS MUSLIM

Returning to the trope of 'mistaken identity', it is necessary to trouble the identity of 'terrorists', instead of marking them over-emphatically with lurid signs. The terror of terrorism lies in the fact that its signs are often opaque and lend themselves to be misread. At times this 'misreading' is made by terror experts themselves, who may switch the identities of terrorists either strategically or by falling prey to information glitches. Other misreadings take place in the public domain, as, for instance, during the xenophobic backlash to 'September 11' when turbanned Sikhs were misidentified as Muslims and targeted as Osama clones. Here, Jasbir Puar's evidence is particularly valuable in the grassroots historiography that she provides of ordinary people killed in American suburbia for no particular reason apart from the fact that they happened to resemble 'the enemy'.

Foremost among the victims, one needs to remember Balbir Singh Sodhi, a 52-year-old turbanned Sikh who was the first victim of a hate crime following 'September 11': he was shot five times in the back at a gas station in Mesa, Arizona, on 15 September 2001.[54] Despite the valiant efforts made by the US Sikh community groups to highlight the obvious fact that *their* turbans were different from the headgear of Muslims, and that they were good American immigrants, not terrorists, their self-proselytizing had to counter the colossal cultural insularity and visual illiteracy of the US public at large. Puar provides a meticulous documentation of the random, yet calculated violence inflicted on Sikhs, which encompassed a spectrum of crimes:

> Verbal harassment . . . hate mail; defecating and urinating on Sikh gurdwaras, Islamic mosques and Hindu temples, leading in some cases to arson; blocking the entrance of a Sikh temple in Sacramento with a tractor and truck and jumping into the sacred holy water at the temple; throwing bricks, gasoline bombs, garbage and other projectiles into homes of Sikhs and Arabs and slashing car tires; death threats and bomb threats; fatal shootings of taxi drivers, the majority of whom have been turbaned Sikhs; . . . and attacks with baseball bats, paintball guns, lit cigarettes and pigs' blood.[55]

This is a chilling testimony of how terror can be 'communalized' in the American context, not significantly different from other such ethnically driven violence in the Indian subcontinent.

Focusing on the actual somatic dimensions of violence, Puar describes the diverse ways in which the Sikh turban, which is sacrosanct for the commu-

Photograph: Zahid Hussein; courtesy, Reuters Picture Archives

**A case of mistaken identity?**

On 11 September 2002, exactly a year after the attack on the Twin Towers in New York City, an image circulated in the global media showing a terrorist captured in Karachi, surrounded by rifle-wielding members of the Sindh Police. The terrorist was identified as Ramzi bin al-Shibh, Al-Qaeda compatriot and roommate of Mohammed Atta in Hamburg, who is seen blindfolded with a cloth tied around his forehead and eyes, his body arched and mouth protesting in what appears to be a defiant cry. The soldiers stare into the camera claiming possession of their captured prey.

Jump cut to April 2011: Wikileaks begins to publish its files on 779 Guantánamo inmates (including Ramzi bin al-Shibh). The Detainee Assessment Briefs (DABs) confirm that he had been captured the previous night in Karachi in a different location, leaving open many unanswered questions: Was he taken to the second site in Karachi after being arrested and then paraded on the streets? Was there another terrorist arrested in his place and 'passed' as Ramzi bin al-Shibh? Was this simply an information glitch on the part of the secret services? Or, was the scene deliberately staged to show that counterterror action was being taken by the Pakistani authorities on the anniversary of 'September 11', when President Musharraf was addressing the United Nations in New York City?

The missing pieces of this jigsaw puzzle have been deftly put together by independent photographer Christina Zück, whose article on 'The Captured Image' (*frieze* magazine, issue 3, Winter 2011–2012) provides a fuller context of the dissimulations at work in the visual propaganda around terror. Her practice of reading images with forensic intensity testifies to Walter Benjamin's famous statement that, 'In times of terror, when everyone is something of a conspirator, everybody will be in a situation where he has to play detective.'

nity at large, and a sign of self-respect and masculinity, was subjected to abuse. At one level it was the butt of abusive verbal commands ('Hey, you fucking terrorist, take that turban off!'), but it was also the target of actual violence as turbans were 'clawed at viciously', with the 'unshorn hair' pulled and, occasionally, 'cut off'.[56] Any reader with a perfunctory knowledge of the 1984 anti-Sikh riots in Delhi, following the assassination of Indira Gandhi by her Sikh security guards, will recognize at least some of these acts of violence by which the turban was attacked. This subcontinental violence, however, needs to be differentiated from the post-'September 11' scenario in so far it was fuelled not by acts of *misrecognition*, but rather by the formidable and non-negotiable *equation* of Indian Sikh men with the turban itself. In the immediate aftermath of the anti-Sikh riots in Delhi, it was not uncommon for at least some Sikh men to cut their hair and stop wearing turbans, which can be regarded both as an act of humiliation as well as of strategic dissimulation, by which these men had no other choice but to 'pass' as non-Sikhs, like regular 'Hindu' men.

Puar's analysis of the turban takes on a dynamic performative force when she moves away from the *signification* of the turban to its actual *affectivity* in the public sphere. Emphasizing that it is 'fear' that 'materializes the turban',[57] she maps a volatile trajectory of associations as she shifts our critical attention away from visibility to affect. In this shift, misrecognition gives way to a form of resemblance, which operates through different stages of perception:

> The move from visibility to affect takes us from a frame of misrecognition, contingent upon the visual to discern the mistake (I thought you were one of them), to the notion of resemblance, a broader affective frame where the reason for the alikeness may be vague or repressed (You remind me of one of them). As distinct from the 'looks like', relegated to the optical restrictions of visibility, the 'seems like' is mired in loaded tactile economies, an affective space that pushes the 'seems like' towards 'feels like' and even, to explain the conviction of radical difference, 'feels like nothing I could ever feel like' or 'nothing I have ever felt before'.[58]

In this lethal movement towards affect, Puar attempts to push the limits of how signs get deployed in a realm of signification, emphasizing the need to work beyond semiotics towards a more visceral, corporeal and kinetic sensibility of the body – a 'body', as Brian Massumi puts it, that 'knows before it cognates'.[59]

In a more phenomenological register, Puar deploys the notion of how bodies are not 'fixed', but are perpetually in the state of 'becoming' and melding into other transformations of bodies. In this reading, the turban cannot be relegated to a sign, unlike 'the beard', which is what I had called attention to in my earlier reading of the 'Muslim'. For Puar, 'the turban is always in the state of becoming, the becoming of a turbaned body, the turban becoming part of the body'.[60] In this state of ceaseless mutation, the turban ceases to be a referent for the 'Sikh' and lends itself to both misrecognition and false resemblance. Inevitably, this interpretation calls into question the politics of identity surrounding not just the 'Sikh', but the 'terrorist' as well. Without quite betraying her queer activist identity by affirming an anti-identitarian position, Puar claims that '[t]here is no entity, no identity, no queer subject or subject to queer, rather than queerness coming forth at us from all directions, screaming its defiance, suggesting a movement from intersectionality to assemblage'.[61]

Once again, there is a *movement* at work in Puar's thinking which compels her to work against the distinct components of 'race, class, gender, sexuality, nation, age, religion', which form 'an intersectional model of identity'[62] – indeed, the model that has been implicitly upheld earlier in this chapter in my designation of the ways by which 'Muslims' have been marked in specific ethnographic, racial, colonial and postcolonial contexts. Puar would regard such an intersectional model, relying on 'the knowing, naming, and thus stabilizing of identity', to be overly dependent on the 'logic of equivalence and analogy', which generates 'narratives of progress that deny the fictive and performative aspects of identification'.[63] In contrast, 'assemblages' are more tuned to 'interwoven forces that merge and dissipate time, space, and body against linearity, coherency, and permanency'.[64] If intersectionality 'privileges naming, visuality, representation, and meaning', assemblage 'underscores feeling, tactility, ontology, affect, and information'.[65]

In this far too emphatically determined dichotomy of assemblage and intersectionality, which would seem to deny any possibility of a dialectical relationship between the categories, Puar over-privileges the dynamics of assemblage, which would seem to lend itself to the ceaseless subversions of queerness. In contrast, the strictures of intersectionality would seem to have no other option but to 'collude with the disciplinary apparatus of the state', through the modalities of 'census, demography, racial profiling, surveillance'.[66] Strategically, Puar punctures, however perfunctorily, the limits of flow and multiplicity in her advocacy of 'assemblage' by acknowledging 'the enduring capacities of intersectionality', which can never be entirely 'left behind'.[67] Far from seeing a permanent state of freedom in the temporal and spatial possibilities of the assemblage, Puar is compelled to highlight its fragility: 'The assemblage is momentary, fleeting even, and gives way to *normative identity markers even in the midst of its newly becoming state*.'[68]

This volatile, contradictory temporality captures very finely, to my mind, the complexity of any politics orchestrated around the principle of 'assemblage': even as it opens itself to the 'as yet unknown, perhaps even forever unknowable', it is also in the process of producing 'new normativities'.[69] If our cultural theory today could capture this double bind, instead of highlighting the 'unknowable' over the production of 'new normativities', it would be more accurate in analysing the multivalent dynamics and tensions of terror in our times. In the process, even as our politics would be somewhat less utopian, it could also become more sceptical and questioning. Let us acknowledge that even as terror can be evoked as the Great Unknown, it is also fast becoming the Norm, a terrifying point of reference by which to measure and designate diverse forms of violence and brutality in the banalities of everyday life.

## THE TERROR OF THE REAL

### RECAPITULATION

To recapitulate: In the last section, I attempted to raise some performative questions relating to the politics of passing and covering, dissimulation and mistaken identity within the larger context of the 'Muslim' as constructed in the political discourse of the Indian subcontinent, and as 'queered' in the post-'September 11' discourse of US popular culture. In this section, I shift gears into a more empirical and historical register, to address the terrifying realities faced by Muslims in the Indian subcontinent within the larger context of communalism – more specifically, in the context of the genocide in Gujarat in 2002. Needless to say, this shift in context from the first section of this chapter demands a different critical language, which is sceptical of the very discourse of performance in engaging with the actual eruptions and lingering legacies of terror in everyday life.

Indeed, at a broader level, one needs to ask: To what extent does the language of performance studies and queer cultural theory make sense in understanding terror outside the Euro–American context? Does it divert attention away from a more historically grounded political analysis of terror? By upholding a Euro–American epistemic framework of minorities as terrorists, what are the risks of translating such theory into other cultural and political contexts where the histories of minorities are structured around significantly different epistemologies and mythologies of danger and threat? More substantially, moving beyond the specificities of queer theory, what are the limits of performance analysis in understanding terror?

I spell out this last question at the very start of this section in order to be critically vigilant about interpreting the performativity of killing in contexts of genocide. Deploying the language of performativity in the context of death is challenging and fraught with all kinds of possible traps – hermeneutic, political, ethical. Building towards my critique of representing *death as performance*, I work against the predilection to theorize acts of terror independently of their history and factuality. In this regard, one should acknowledge that while historical evidence may not 'explain' terror in all its virulence and madness, it can help to contextualize its moment of ignition, actuality and consequence. With these provisions in mind, let us focus now on a brief history of what 'communalism' signifies in the Indian context, which may be all too familiar to some of my readers, but without which it becomes impossible to address the genocide in Gujarat with any clarity or critical responsibility.

## OTHERING INDIAN MUSLIMS

While 'communalism' is often used synonymously with 'communitarianism' in Euro–American contexts, the 'communal' being assumed to embody a common core of beliefs, values, customs and practices, the words need to be more sharply discriminated. Contrary to the innate wholesomeness associated with the 'communal', communalism in the Indian context is a form of sectarianism by which *other* communities are marked by acts of hostility, violence, hate speech, lynching and genocide. In short, communalism can manifest itself as a form of terror; there is blood in the word.

Since communities in the Indian secular-constitutional context are identified primarily on religious grounds, with 'majority' and 'minority' communities being determined in the process, it is not surprising that religion should be the dominant marker of communalism in the Indian context, with 'Muslims' (or 'the minority community', as it is often euphemized) being pitted against 'Hindus' or the national mainstream of undifferentiated 'Indians'. While there are other markers of sectarian difference, like region, language and profession, the political misuse of religion has been the most virulent provocation of communal violence, with Muslims in particular being targeted as the very source of the problem. Therefore, in a statement that has now acquired an almost axiomatic tenor, the Chief Minister of Gujarat, Narendra Modi, charged by many activist and social action groups for masterminding the genocide in Gujarat, has been associated with the widely circulated belief that 'All Muslims are not terrorists, but all terrorists are Muslim.' Sadly, this formidable generalization has begun to acquire the force of a performative which has been hegemonized in many different parts of the world, contributing towards the homogenization of Muslims and the legitimization of Islamophobia at global, national and local levels.

Keeping the normativity of political identities in mind, let us return to the slippery logic of the British colonial imperative which attempted to prove that Muslims were different, but not *essentially* different from Hindus. The hermeneutic twist in this argument was further complicated by the assumption that even as the vast majority of Muslims were identified as local converts, the entire community ('Muslims') was implicitly blamed for othering itself. Within the logic of the colonial administration, it was assumed, as Gauri Viswanathan points out, that 'the idea of Muslims as "outsiders" . . . was propagated by Indian Muslims themselves'.[70] In other words, they were responsible for othering themselves.

Beyond the boundaries of the Indian colonial state, this accusation levelled against the self-othering of minorities can be regarded as a familiar trope in the contemporary rhetoric of racism. Minorities worldwide are frequently blamed for othering themselves, as if 'racial consciousness' were 'the *cause* of social division, rather than the *product* of preexisting patterns of discrimination'.[71] A familiar accusation could run along these lines: 'They have themselves to blame; if they didn't mark themselves as different, there wouldn't be a problem in the first place.' But who marks 'them' in the first place? Who others whom? In any process of othering, there has to be a posited self against which the other is measured and judged. Who determines the 'other'? What are the conditions of power by which this determination is made possible and hegemonized?

Once again, instead of succumbing to the platitudinous 'common sense' generated by global cultural theory on the over-reiterated discourse on the self and the other, it is necessary to inflect how notions of the self and the other are actually enforced – and performed – in specific political cultures. In India, for instance, by the late 1920s, it was made emphatically clear by extremist Hindu communal organizations like the Rashtriya Swayamsevak Sangh (RSS) that the 'self' – or, more precisely, the 'authentic Indian self' – had to be seen as intrinsically, and uncompromisingly, 'Hindu'.[72] The RSS defined the 'Hindu' as 'Indian' in explicitly exclusionary terms. Against this absolutism, all religious minorities – and not just Muslims, but Christians, Jains, Buddhists, Sikhs, Parsis and Jews as well – had no other option but to be othered. Significantly, they were othered in different ways, but 'the authentic Indian self' against which others were discriminated remained unequivocally 'Hindu'.

V.D. Savarkar, an early ideologue of the Hindu Right, for instance, defined the 'Hindu' in 1923 as 'a person who regards the land of Bharatvarsha from Indus to the Seas as his Fatherland [*pitribhumi*], as well as his Holy Land [*punyabhumi*] – that is the cradle land of his religion.'[73] Along with notions of belonging to a common territory, there was the more materialist association of owning – and not just sharing – a 'common blood': 'We are all Hindus and *own* a common blood.'[74] Once again, the reference to 'owning' takes us back to the idea of property, and, indirectly, to notions of verification, regulation and copyright. Blood, it would seem, is not just a primordial essence, but a vital component of proving one's proprietary rights in a larger territory. Inevitably, against the implacable belief in such a right that disingenuously brought brahmans and 'low' castes together under the rubric of 'Hindu', those non-Hindu communities which could not *own* this 'common blood' through birth or religion or, by implication, culture, were summarily regarded as 'foreigners'.

Some communities were more 'foreign' than others: while the Buddhists, Jains and Sikhs could claim India as the *janmabhumi* (land of birth) of their religious identities and traditions, this was not true for the Christians, Parsis and Jews, who were categorically linked to a different ancestry, culture and tradition lying outside of India. Yet these communities could be more tolerated than their Muslim counterparts because they had, in their own ways, accepted India as their country or contributed to its development, unlike Muslims, whose loyalties allegedly lay elsewhere in West Asia and, most ignominiously, in Pakistan. The very proximity to, if not equation of Muslims with Hindus before their conversion further contributed to their image as 'traitors'. It is not surprising, therefore, that through the struggle for independence and increasingly after independence, as many researchers have pointed out, Muslims have had to *prove* their patriotic credentials before they can be regarded as 'Indian', and not as 'open or closet Pakistanis'.[75]

Returning to the tropes of 'passing' and 'covering', one could say that within the ideological strictures of Hindutva Muslims continue to be accused of 'passing' as Indians while secretly holding on to their primordial identities as closet Pakistanis. 'Covering' their more overt signs of difference could be one way for them to be accepted, which would extend to their capacities of social accommodation and of being assimilated into the mainstream of Indian society. However, this covering is more often than not seen as opportunistic, if not incomplete, playing into the ferocious stereotype of Muslims as 'bad minorities' (those who refuse to subdue their assertions of difference or misplaced loyalties), as opposed to 'good minorities' (those who behave themselves and contribute to the growth of the nation).

If there is one trope that connects the Indian 'good minorities/bad minorities' discourse to the more global 'good Muslim/bad Muslim' discourse, first enunciated by conservative academics such as Bernard Lewis and then brazenly polemicized by George Bush in the immediate aftermath of 'September 11', it is necessary for both 'good minorities' and 'good Muslims' to *prove their credentials*.[76] Bush reiterated the point, chorused by Tony Blair, that it is 'bad Muslims' who are responsible for terrorism, while 'good Muslims', on the other hand, want to support 'us' in the 'war on terror' because they are innately decent, God-fearing folk. However, as Mahmood Mamdani points out, drawing on a well-known trope in legal discourse: 'unless proved to be "good", every Muslim was presumed to be "bad"'. Only by joining in the war against 'bad Muslims' could Muslims in general prove themselves to be 'good'.[77] While in the language of the law, it is assumed that a criminal suspect is innocent unless proven guilty, in the discourse of terrorism, all Muslim suspects are *ipso facto* guilty until they align themselves actively to the war on terror.

By pitting 'good Muslims' against 'bad Muslims' there was clearly an attempt to create an inner split among Muslims worldwide, in yet another variation of the old imperialist strategy of 'divide and rule'. However, the scale of today's Islamophobia is much larger than any colonial policy used by the state to coerce and divide Muslims within the boundaries of the nation-state. Extending beyond the troubled spots in Iraq, Iran, Palestine or Pakistan, the 'war on terror' has built its legitimacy through the positing of an 'axis of evil', yet another warmongering construction of the Bush administration that has attempted to propagate the good Muslim/bad Muslim divide. Against this absolutist dichotomy, there is the more paradoxical proposition put forward by Faisal Devji, that 'the only good Muslim is a dead Muslim'.[78] While we will deal with the reality of 'dead Muslims' (victims of the Gujarat genocide) in the next section, Devji's construction is contextualized specifically within the liberatory assumptions of suicide-bombing, where the 'goodness' of the suicide bomber is ensured through his or her state of martyrdom. Even as one may reject this extremist logic, it counters the norms affirmed by Bush and Blair in their self-righteous need to defend Islam against its internalized 'evil' others. Suicide bombers do not need their definitions of 'good Muslims' and 'bad Muslims' to affirm their supra-national sacrifice, which is made possible through acts of terror *on their own terms* and *through their own means*, notably their bodies which double as explosive devices.

## GENOCIDE IN GUJARAT

Against this background, I return to the widely circulated comment attributed to the Chief Minister of Gujarat, Narendra Modi, on Star News, shortly before he allegedly masterminded and legitimized what has been described as a 'genocide' in Gujarat: 'All Muslims are not terrorist, but all terrorists are Muslim.'[79] Significantly, this insidious language of communal equivocation is presented as an axiomatic truth that lies beyond questioning or critical dispute. Not only is Modi's communal logic devious, based on manufactured lies and a refusal to engage with the intransigence of defining a 'terrorist', in the first place, it erases the role of the state in perpetrating terror.

Widely condemned by citizens' committees and human rights groups in India, the genocide in Gujarat, which specifically targeted Muslims between 28 February and 3 March 2002, has been extensively analysed as an instance of state-sponsored ethnic cleansing. Shamefully marginalized by the 'international community', more preoccupied with the global magnitude of 'September 11' and the 'war on terror', the atrocities in Gujarat provide disturbing evidence of a growing Islamophobia among the leaders and supporters of the Hindu

Right.[80] The current reports indicate that more than 3,000 Muslims were killed in Gujarat and over 100,000 were displaced, of whom 21,000 continue to live more than ten years later in transit relief camps. For a state that prides itself on 'development', Gujarat shows no compassion for its most destitute and vulnerable citizens – or, more precisely, non-citizens – divested of their basic human and constitutional rights.

Using the argument of 'retaliation', the representatives of the Hindu Right have justified the killings in Gujarat on grounds of the Hindu masses reacting violently, yet unavoidably, to the burning of 59 *kar sevaks* or Hindu pilgrims returning from Ayodhya. In a terrifying incident, whose extremity needs to be acknowledged and condemned in its own right, these pilgrims were burned alive in a railway compartment of the Sabarmati Express in Godhra, on 27 February 2002. To this day, there are no clear indications as to how an entire train compartment was gutted, which clearly necessitated the use of a massive amount of fuel from within the compartment. In the immediate aftermath of the burning of the *kar sevaks*, without any state or judicial inquiry or attempt to calm communal tensions, Narendra Modi, the Chief Minister belonging to the BJP (Bharatiya Janata Party), capitalized on the volatile situation. Arguably, if the genocide against Muslims was allowed to ignite and spread, it is because the commander-in-chief of the state resolutely failed to call on the Army to prevent the situation from getting out of hand.

Still in power as the Chief Minister in 2014 with an aggressively nationalist profile as a promoter of 'development' and as the Hindu Right's top candidate for Prime Minister in the 2014 elections, Modi remains a deeply controversial figure in the larger context of the Gujarat genocide of 2002. A wide range of social organizations have questioned his role in engineering the genocide, notably the National Human Rights Commission, Human Rights Watch, Concerned Citizens Tribunal, and activist journals like *Communalism Combat*. In addition, the larger communal context of Gujarat has been documented in critical editions of essays and primary texts by Asghar Ali Engineer (2003), Siddharth Varadarajan (2002), scholarly studies by Martha Nussbaum (2007) and Christophe Jaffrelot (2010), supplemented by incisive analytical reports provided by historian Tanika Sarkar (2002) and legal activist Arvind Narrain (2004), in addition to Rakesh Sharma's documentary film *Final Solution* (2004). At a discursive level the evidence is massive even as it fails to fully capture the brutality of the genocide. As communal violence erupted in Gujarat hospitals turned away Muslim victims, while the police refused to intervene and check systematic attacks on Muslim neighbourhoods and slums. These attacks were led by frenzied mobs wielding *trishuls* (tridents) and hurling gas cylinders as explosives. *Dargahs* (Muslim shrines) were burned and replaced by Hanuman temples, while shops owned by Muslims in entire localities were systematically listed, marked and destroyed with the calculation of a masterminded pogrom.

All these facts indicate clearly that the events in Gujarat can be justifiably described as a 'genocide', in so far as a particular religious community was targeted with predetermined calculation and the intention to kill. A brief look at the genealogy of 'genocide' is appropriate in this context. Coined by Raphael Lemkin, a Polish lawyer, the word 'genocide' is derived 'from the Greek word *genos*, which means "race, nation or tribe" in ancient Greek and *caedere*, which means "to kill" in Latin.'[81] The word was first used in international law in 1948 when it was incorporated into the newly installed Convention on the Prevention and Punishment of the Crime of Genocide, which applied the law to the extermination of the Jews during the Second World War. Tellingly – and problematically – genocide has not been invoked to condemn the mass killings of homosexuals, communists or indigenous peoples (even though the annihilation of the Native American population in the United States can justifiably be regarded as a genocide on the basis of which the world's most powerful democracy has built its credentials).

As Arvind Narrain emphasizes in his valuable reflections on 'Truth Telling, Gujarat and the Law' (2004), the 'only groups deemed worthy of protection under the Genocide Convention, 1948, were national, religious, racial and ethnic groups.'[82] Using this official definition of 'genocide', one could argue that the Muslims of Gujarat as members of a specific religious community were victims of genocide; more critically, they were killed and their property destroyed not because of 'random violence that the state was unable to control', but because of the complicity of the state in the perpetration of the violence. As the reports of the Concerned Citizens Tribunal in addition to the National Human Rights Commission have confirmed, 'a willful and mediated State' abdicated 'responsibility of protecting the life of its citizens. The State stood by and watched murder, rape, destruction of property, and desecration of religious places, and in some cases even aided the process.'[83]

In this brazen display of violence, which was made possible through the larger communalization of civil society in Gujarat, it becomes difficult to seek solace in the academic discriminations of communalism by which the 'othering' of Muslims has been rationalized on cultural rather than on racial or eugenic grounds. No longer, I would emphasize, can the exclusion of the Muslim Other be so euphemistically explicated through a 'racism of domination' that leaves open the humiliating possibility for Muslims of 'integrating' themselves into Indian society at the level of subordinate, second-class citizenship.[84] Today, we are compelled to acknowledge the emergence of a 'racism of extermination' as it manifests itself through eruptions of rigorously monitored, barbaric violence. This drive towards extermination has been substantially marked in the documentation of violence surrounding the Gujarat riots.

All genocides are marked by their ruthless and, occasionally, sadistic demonstrations of senseless and excessive violence. Gujarat was no exception. If one accepts the truism that violence is not arbitrary, and follows specific cultural patterns and rituals of torture, killing and the mutilation of targeted victims,[85] *how one kills* is intrinsically related to *how one views the Other*, and, arguably, how one sees – or fails to see – one's self in the process. In this regard, one can acknowledge a performativity in the act of killing itself, in so far as it is linked to the production of a particular subject. And yet, this thesis built on intentionality and assumptions of differences across ethnic and religious groups cannot be made axiomatic; rather one needs to engage with the actual reality surrounding the act of violence whose intensity and virulence have the capacity to disrupt any neat academic thesis on subject formation.

To provide some examples: in Gujarat, the bodies of Muslim women in particular were subjected to terrible acts of violence, with foeticide featuring as part of the genocidal killings. From the evidence of the historian Tanika Sarkar, we learn that

> a majority of rape victims were burnt alive . . . Some were beaten up with rods and pipes for almost an hour. Before or after the killing, their vaginas would be sliced or would have iron rods pushed inside. Kausar Bano, a young girl from Naroda Patiya, was several months pregnant. Several eyewitnesses testified that she was raped, tortured, her womb was slit open with a sword to disgorge the foetus which was then hacked to pieces and roasted alive with the mother.[86]

Faced with such evidence, the predilection to explain genocide or ethnic cleansing within a global postmodern hermeneutics of an 'intimacy gone berserk',[87] as Arjun Appadurai has elaborated in a provocative essay, seems somewhat glib. We shall elaborate on the difficulties of Appadurai's position shortly, but if Kausar Bano is 'personalized' in the mutilated remains of her body, it should be remembered that her destroyed foetus remains unnamed, anonymous, ungendered and yet, irrevocably, marked as 'Muslim'.

With an activist's investment in documenting the actual psychopathological evidence of genocide, Sarkar has attempted to explain genocidal foeticide as 'a symbolic destruction of future generations, of the very future of Muslims themselves'.[88] Linking such foeticide, and the burning of men, women and children to the destruction of evidence itself, Sarkar stretches her otherwise grounded interpretation to suggest that the enforced Hindu 'cremation' upon the Muslims of Gujarat results in a 'macabre post-mortem forced conversion'.[89] I would argue that there is a hermeneutic excess, if not a misconstrued performative in this construction, which does not illuminate the violence in question. While conversion, as I have argued earlier in this chapter, has been one of the primary causes of the resentment directed against Indian Muslims in the subcontinent, it can no longer provide the *raison d'être* for the rage directed against them today.

If we have to address the performativity of conversion, it would be more accurate to address the coercive re-conversions of tribal communities and dalit Christians who have been forcibly brought back 'into the fold' by Hindutva zealots, even while their 'authentic' Hindu filiations remain forever tainted. These re-conversions can be described as the new performative rituals by which 'upper-caste racism' is reasserted. What happened in Gujarat was formidably different, in so far as the killing of Muslims was not linked to any attempt to 'restore' Muslims to their real, pre-converted, 'Hindu' selves. It was directed more ruthlessly to the fact that Muslims cannot be trusted; they are intrinsically violent and, therefore, should be exterminated. It would be desperately hopeful to assume that in their liquidation the story of communal terror ends, but, perhaps, another cycle of terror is already in the making.

## 'DEAD CERTAINTY': THE LIMITS OF PERFORMATIVITY

Against the critique of the Gujarat genocide substantiated within the communalizing tendencies of the Indian nation-state, it would be useful to juxtapose a more global perspective on ethnic violence, as provided by Arjun Appadurai in his essay, 'Dead Certainty: Ethnic Violence in the Era of Globalization' (1998).[90] A brief look at this essay would indicate not just the uncanny correspondences at work in the 'surplus of rage' (243) characterizing such violence across cultural contexts; it could also reveal the different theoretical modalities attempting to 'make sense of violence', to use Mahmood Mamdani's pertinent phrase.[91] While Appadurai does not specifically use the discourse of performativity to 'make sense' of violence, his essay is a virtuoso performance in its own right, encompassing an extraordinarily vast sweep of diverse brutalities and modes of torture inflicted on the body – or, more precisely, 'the ethnic body' – which is not just the 'site' of violence, but 'a *theater* for the engagement of uncertainty under the special circumstances of globalization' (226; my emphasis).

In 'Dead Certainty', globalization is made culpable for the 'radical social uncertainty' of our times, reinforced through 'weakened states, refugees, economic deregulation, and systematic new forms of pauperization and criminalization' (226). Porous borders, the speed and intensity of trade, the circulation of ideas through the internet and other global media, along with the sheer numbers of people migrating from one place to another: all these factors contribute towards a scenario of global *uncertainty* which is irreversible and, to a large extent, non negotiable. Alongside this scenario, which complicates his somewhat more euphoric affirmation of global 'flows' in his earlier book, *Modernity at Large* (1997), Appadurai posits the equally formidable intensification of ethnic violence, which he proceeds to map through intersecting anthropological, cultural and philosophical discourses.

In the process, he levels the killing fields of the world with rhetorical bravura and an encapsulation of several taxonomies of violence. What matters is the citational and discursive sweep of this violence at a global level rather than a close reading of any one particular genocide, atrocity or ethnic killing. While local contexts and manifestations of violence are masterfully extrapolated from the dense fieldwork and ethnography of major studies of violence set in Rwanda, Tanzania, India, Sri Lanka, Northern Ireland, Cameroon and China, Appadurai fails to problematize the fact that these countries are positioned in radically different ways in relation to the forces of globalization. Instead, he positions the uncertainties of our times in relation to the inexorable reality of ethnic violence within the same grid of globalization. In the process, I would argue, he essentializes the state of global uncertainty to posit his thesis of 'dead certainty', implying that the totalizing impact of 'uncertainty' is directly responsible for the 'dead certainty' of ethnic violence in our times.

Along with the 'uncertainties' of globalization, Appadurai emphasizes the aporias produced by mega-identities like the scheduled caste (SC), scheduled tribe (ST) and other backward class (OBC), which are the dominant reservation categories deployed by the postcolonial Indian state for millions of socially and economically disadvantaged people in order to provide them with economic and social opportunities. In highlighting the identitarian 'uncertainties' emerging from such governmental mechanisms, Appadurai fails to consider that they are of a different nature from those produced by global agencies and have considerably different impacts on local communities. For all the confusions and backlash of resentment generated through reservations, there are benefits by way of social and economic opportunities which are perceived and desired by large sections of the population, even if these opportunities do not necessarily materialize. Even if one had to argue that the politics of reservations ignites the identitarian uncertainties of Indian society, one should also keep in mind that not every form of identitarian uncertainty is necessarily prone to ethnic or communal violence.

Accumulating his evidence in a more performative register, Appadurai adds to his list of 'uncertainties' the 'instability of the signs of bodily difference', which makes it difficult to identify 'ethnic bodies' both of victims and killers. For example, with reference to the ethnic conflict in Rwanda, he claims: 'Not all Tutsis are tall; not all Hutu have red gums; not all noses help identify Tutsi, nor do all modes of walking help identify Hutu' (232). Playing on such physiological variables, along with other somatic and kinetic slippages, Appadurai affirms that 'the ethnic body . . . is itself potentially *deceptive*' (232). A sentence later, he reiterates that 'the ethnic body *turns out to be itself* unstable and deceptive' (232; my emphasis), the earlier reference to 'potentiality' replaced by hermeneutic certainty.

Ultimately, it is neither factuality nor historiography that motivates Appadurai's postmodern thinking on ethnic violence, which is presented through a reversal of rhetorical tropes revolving around vivisection and other forms of brutalization of the human body. Getting to the crux of his thesis, Appadurai posits 'ethnic labels' as 'abstract containers for the identities of thousands, often millions, of persons' whose 'large *numerical* abstractions' provoke 'grotesque forms of bodily violence' (240). Ostensibly, these forms of violence, which he specifically designates as vivisectionist, 'offer temporary ways to render these abstractions *graspable*, to make these larger numbers *sensuous*, to make labels that are potentially overwhelming, for a moment, *personal*' (240; my emphasis). Building on this rhetoric, Appadurai affirms his primary thesis that 'the most horrible forms of ethnocidal violence are mechanisms for producing persons out of what are otherwise diffuse, large-scale labels that have effects but no locations' (241). It is in this act of *producing persons through the act of killing* that Appadurai comes closest to affirming a performative, though not without opening a range of troubling questions relating to the agency, interpretation and the ethics of killing.

Attempting to circumvent these questions that his thesis so audaciously provokes, Appadurai acknowledges that his position 'modifies' the more established interpretation put forward by leading scholars of genocide and political violence in Rwanda and Northern Ireland, who suggest that 'ethnic violence produces abstract tokens of ethnicity out of the bodies of real persons' (242).[92] In contrast, Appadurai does not so much 'modify' this 'position'; he actually *reverses* it by saying that it is abstractions that produce violence, which in turn makes persons out of bodies. But to what extent does this reversal hold up to the brutal fact of violence itself? For *whom* is the 'person' attributed by Appadurai in his theoretical *coup d'état* a *person*, and not another dead body or victim? How is a 'person' to be regarded in the first place, dead or alive?[93] Uninterested in attempting any critical reflexivity or empathy towards the world of victims, who are reduced to 'bodies', or, worse still, mutilated bodies, Appadurai would seem to deny the possibility of 'personhood' to victims prior to the act of the violence inflicted on them. In this perverse logic, vivisection almost becomes a necessity to transform abstraction into personhood.

Reiterating the same point with incremental eloquence in different aphoristic modes, Appadurai adds that violence is not just about identifying the indeterminacy of the other; rather the act of killing becomes '*one means of satisfying one's sense of one's categorical self* (244; my emphasis). How this 'self' relates to its imbrications within the larger institutions and identifications of 'community', 'caste', 'tribe', 'race' and 'nation', under whose aegis the worst forms of sectarian violence are unleashed, is left unclear in Appadurai's oddly primordialist thesis.[94] Ironically, the problem with the thesis could be its own 'dead certainty', which, for all the provocation of its central conceit, does not take into account the volatility of ethnic violence in relation to the very precise institutionalization of ethnic identity.

As Mahmood Mamdani has attempted to make sense of the lethal phenomenon of 'victims becoming killers',[95] in an analysis that is more measured and yet inflected than Appadurai's theoretical bravura, it is not the 'uncertainty' of Hutu or Tutsi ethnic identities in the genocide of Rwanda that is strategized to account for the sheer *scale* of the mass killing. Rather, Mamdani elaborates on the long-standing accumulation of ethnic tensions by which the Hutu and the Tutsi have been marked and divided (since 1959) by the agencies of the colonial and postcolonial African state, through civilized/uncivilized, indigenous/immigrant, majority/minority categories. The reversal of 'victims becoming killers' cannot be separated from this larger political process embedded within intricately encoded statist, economic and social laws and sanctions, which may be 'abstract' at a discursive level, but which have very tangible and identifiable manifestations in everyday life.

While no direct causality can be made between these laws and sanctions, and the actual brutality of violence, they provide a necessary framework in which to ask the hard questions concerning the agency of the perpetrators of violence. As Mamdani articulates the problem with critical empathy, 'Who did the Hutu who killed think they were? And whom did they think they were killing in the persons of the Tutsi?'[96] The enigma of these killings is substantially different from Appadurai's assertion of 'dead certainty' in the act of violence itself. More critically, in acknowledging the 'persons' of the Tutsi, Mamdani also reinstates the dignity of the victims, which, in Appadurai's construction, is suspended till they are actually killed.

In seeking a rationale for violence within the parameters of his own 'ethnocidal imaginary',[97] Appadurai would seem to be more theoretically challenged by the *excess* of violence than by the realities of violence itself. Indeed, there is almost a performative relish in his sifting of global evidence relating to depravity and perversity. This relish becomes increasingly pronounced as perverse details of violence are decontextualized from larger ethnographies and, in the process, sensationalized – for instance, the removal of foetuses from pregnant women intact followed by forcing the mother to eat the foetus.[98] These details are steeped in the sexualization of the enemy through acts of penetration and cannibalism ('eating the liver or heart of the exposed "class enemy'"), compelling Appadurai to acknowledge with a far-too-easy eloquence that 'eating the enemy is one way of securing a macabre intimacy with the enemy who was so recently a friend' (239).

While the brutal intimacy of such acts of violence cannot be denied, the danger is that it can divert critical attention away from the more sober task of addressing the 'banality of evil', as addressed by Hannah Arendt in her unfailingly resonant reminder that evil gets normalized through the routine protocols of the state. Banality, far more than uncertainty, could be one of the most enduring tropes of violence in our times. Reinforced through different agencies of bureaucratization, it does not so much precipitate violence as it legitimizes it, compelling it to be normalized and even accepted as a fact of life. This is certainly the case in post-genocide Gujarat, whose chief perpetrators still remain at large, if not firmly empowered within the armature of the state, despite recent judgements that have been passed in 2012 against the perpetrators of the Naroda Patiya slaughter in 2002.

It should also be acknowledged that the communal violence legitimized by the Gujarat state and subsumed within the discourse of 'development' would not have been possible without the larger communalization of civil society at large. Godhra and Gujarat, one could argue, did not create communal violence; rather it is a particularly virulent outcome of what already existed and continues to be justified. Certainly, the violence did not erupt because Muslims and Hindus were 'uncertain' about where they stand in relation to each other. On the contrary, within the implementation of Hindutva's anti-minority agenda and ideology, large sections of Hindu and Muslim communities were only too 'certain' of their standing in relation to each other.

In short, I would submit that the 'dead certainty' of the Gujarat genocide cannot be separated from the terrifyingly banal truth that the perpetrators of this genocide were fully aware that they would get away with their crimes. Even if the law was not on their side, it could be suspended indefinitely to allow their barbarity to be systematically erased and forgotten. Against the 'dead certainty' of violence, therefore, one may also need to inscribe the *uncertainty* of justice, which could be, in the final analysis, one of the most deadly sanctions for the continuation of violence in our times.

Sadly, the narrative of violence does not end with the death of its victims, whose bodies are often so mutilated that they are almost 'unrecognizable'. Appadurai puts it effectively when he acknowledges that there are no lingering truths in the aftermath of 'dead certainty': '[T]he "theatre of the body" on which this violence is performed, is never truly cathartic, satisfying or terminal. It only leads to a deepening of social wounds, an epidemic of shame, a collusion of silence, and a violent need for forgetting' (244). Against this bleak scenario, the resources of hope for victims of genocide obtaining justice or being healed from their wounds would seem to be very limited. I will elaborate on this condition by examining alternative models of truth and reconciliation in chapter 3, followed by harder questions on the possibility of seeking justice outside the law towards the end of chapter 4.

For the moment, let us shift the scenario of this chapter from the magnitude of genocide to some surprising counters to the violence of our times in the cultures of everyday life. Ironically, yet significantly, these revelatory moments get illuminated through minor accidents, contradicting Virilio's more formidable understanding of environmental, global, nuclear and technological accidents manifesting themselves as disasters. In contrast, the accidents of everyday life through human encounters can illuminate alternative possibilities of self-definition and creative renewal.

## OUTING THE SELF

Against the ambivalences of what is 'certain' and 'uncertain' about violence, I end this chapter with an anecdote that marks what Walter Benjamin has so aptly described as 'the true method of making things present: to imagine them in our space (and not to imagine ourselves in their space).'[99] There is always a problem in sanitizing the terror of genocide 'out there' within the safe confines of any piece of writing: the onus to report and call attention to violence can give way to the comfort of self-righteous vindication. The trials of long-distance witnessing can even succumb to the discomfort of voyeurism. This discomfort, of course, should not be used to justify a moratorium on fact-finding, which could merely enhance the complicities of silence. Nor is it necessary to berate oneself for the obvious 'inadequacy' of one's representation: this can be a self-perpetuating gesture of a strategically nuanced 'failed' authorship. Perhaps one possibility of dealing with violence that has not been personally witnessed is to inscribe one's distance from its location. In this distance, there is both a profound sense of unease and the possibility of rethinking the ordinariness of life in one's own location in which violence ignites.

I began this chapter by sharing a conversation in which I passed as a Muslim, who was always already a terrorist. I went to the extent of saying that it is 'dangerous passing as a Muslim these days'. Perhaps what I did not sufficiently emphasize is the ethical dilemma of how to resist being 'passed' as a Muslim in coercive circumstances, while resisting in equal measure a total disidentification from the category of 'Muslim'. Disidentification, after all, can easily capitulate to the negative stereotypes of 'Muslims', which, as this essay has attempted to demonstrate, are steeped in the worst forms of demonization.

As I end this essay, let me share another story, not of disidentification but of mistaken identity, where being passed as a Muslim can also be a source of hope and self-renewal:

*The details are blurred in my mind. I am on a street in Calcutta, not far from my home. Suddenly, a rumour cuts through the street like a knife. There is an eruption of fear and panic, suggesting the imminence of a riot. Within seconds, the street is deserted, the corrugated iron shutters of shops descend in quick succession with a clanging sound, collapsible gates are bolted and there is ominous silence. I am left on the street confronting an uncertainty I cannot fathom, but wish to escape. A taxi is speeding and is about to take a sharp curve in the bend on the street. A split-second eye-contact with the driver is all I remember. He yells at me to get in. I sit in front, no questions asked.*

*Gradually, as the car speeds on this surreal journey to no particular destination, I find things returning to normal. The familiar is no longer unfamiliar. I turn to the driver and thank him for his help. Only after he mumbles that we're bound to help members of 'our own community' do I realize that he has mistaken me for a Muslim.*

*I can keep quiet about this and allow the moment to pass. However, something compels me to speak out: 'But I'm not a Muslim.' 'What are you?' he asks, taken aback. 'Parsi.' 'What's that?' Before I can answer, he says, 'Oh, I've got it, you're Bohra.' 'No.' 'Khoja?' 'No.' These are versions of Muslims. I am compelled to clarify the obvious: 'Parsi is something else. It's another community (*'Alag jaat hai'*).'*

*The driver looks at me quizzically, not entirely convinced, and shakes his head. We begin to laugh. It doesn't matter that he is Muslim and I am Parsi, even though his mistaking me for a Muslim was the accident that brought us closer together. My passing for a Muslim did not deny me my identity; it became the occasion for me to declare my 'self'.*

As I recall my conversation with the driver, my memory playing tricks with an event – or, perhaps, non-event – from the past, I realize the inadvertent possibilities of drawing an ethics of the self from the chimeras of colliding identities. Through these moments of recognition, mere glimmers of coexisting with the other in others and in ourselves, we can learn to imagine a future not with 'dead certainty', but rather with the living uncertainties of the present moment.

# 3

# COUNTERING TERROR?

## The Search for Justice in Truth and Reconciliation

## MAPPING THE TERRAIN

### MULTIPLE LOCATIONS, DIFFERENT STAKES

Following the focus on 'September 11' and Islamophobia in the first two chapters, this book now widens its exploration of terror by shifting its attention to Truth and Reconciliation in post-genocide Rwanda and post-apartheid South Africa. Arguably, the prefix of 'post-' in the context of massive tragedies like genocide and apartheid is deceptive in so far as it implies a clean break with the past, which, in actuality, continues to haunt the present through lingering legacies of violence, humiliation and injustice. One should acknowledge, therefore, that the 'post-' has, at best, an expedient significance that demarcates 'official' endings of national crises and states of emergency as determined by the agencies of the state. What continues to exist at ground levels in the hearts and minds of people is a different reality.

With this qualification in mind, let me specify the key question underlying the argument of this chapter in the larger context of transitional justice in Rwanda and South Africa: What are the performative dimensions underlying these states of transition, and how do they engage with truth and reconciliation in coming to terms with the terror and atrocities of the past? At one level these 'performative dimensions' are documented and assessed in this chapter through the testimonials provided by the victims and survivors of genocide and apartheid, whose evidence of the torture, pain and suffering inflicted on them provides a searing documentation of human cruelty. At another level, following Judith Butler's precise formulation of performativity as 'the power of discourse to produce what it names',[1] the conceptual thrust of this chapter is on the legal mechanisms and apparatus invented by the state to legislate and enforce new modes of 'forgiveness' and 'reconciliation'.

Performativity, I should emphasize, cannot be understood outside of these mechanisms, which provide the framework in which specific performances are rendered intelligible in the first place. This is not just a matter of providing a context of the performative circumstances that make truth and reconciliation possible; more specifically, one is dealing with an entire armature of laws, rules, protocols, time schedules and training processes that constitute the modalities of putting truth and reconciliation into practice. Without these modalities the performances would not exist in the first place. This point needs to be emphasized at the start of this chapter to prepare the reader for the heavy dose of factuality that dominates the opening sections, which will be followed by descriptions of actual performances and more philosophical speculations on truth and reconciliation.

To spell out some basic facts, while the discourse of Truth and Reconciliation was officially inaugurated in South Africa in 1996 in the form of a Commission (TRC), its model was substantially questioned, critiqued, adapted and indigenized in Rwanda following the genocide in 1994. Even as the goal of both these experiments was to enable survivors and perpetrators of violence to live together in reconstituted societies with new imaginaries of coexistence, they differ significantly in terms of their philosophical and methodological premises. First, while the post-genocide juridical process in Rwanda was structured around trials, the post-apartheid truth and reconciliation process in South Africa was built around a Truth Commission.[2] Second, while the Rwandan government rejected the principle of *impunity*, demanding prosecution for all perpetrators through different legal procedures, the transitional South African government allowed conditional *amnesty* for political crimes. Third, at a purely quantitative level, the scale of the Rwandan experiment far surpassed the TRC experiment in South Africa: while as many as 1,210,368 trials were conducted in Rwanda at local-level grassroots courts (*gacaca*) between 2005 to 2010,[3] the Human Rights Violations Committee of the TRC in South Africa accepted only 21,400 statements by the victims of apartheid, of which only one-tenth were actually heard by the Commission in testimonials made by the victims.[4]

In relation to the overwhelming diversity and scale of material addressed in this chapter, I have chosen to inflect the mega-discourse of Truth and Reconciliation through the missing link of *justice*, which would appear to be either short-circuited or absented (as in the case of South Africa), or else, reduced to the technicalities of juridical procedures with questionable accountability and expertise (as in the case of Rwanda). While my focus on Rwanda will engage with some fragments of evidence relating to how the law was reinvented at a performative level on a mass scale through grassroots trials (*gacaca*), my engagement with South Africa will draw on – and question – the actual construction and projection of the TRC *as a performance* in its own right.

Broadly, at a political level I would endorse the widely held view that the TRC failed to engage with the wider 'structural and everyday violence of apartheid',[5] in addition to the economic violence controlled by an oligarchy of elite families and corporations. In effect, the selective mandate of the TRC left 'thousands of apartheid functionaries unscathed', while 'the majority of those who benefited from apartheid – mainly, the broad white population – [were let] entirely off the hook.'[6] In contrast, I would acknowledge that the Rwandan experiment in truth and reconciliation attempted to provide justice to the widest possible representation of the genocide's victims at a scale that totally defies any such experiment in justice. To what extent this experiment 'worked' is another matter – there have been widespread allegations of corruption, intimidation and a travesty of justice by international standards – but the attempt on the part of the Rwandan government to confront the genocide at a multitudinous grassroots level needs to be acknowledged for its conceptual audacity and unprecedented execution.

## THE RIGHT TO INTERVENE

Given the complexity of the field, one could justifiably question my right to intervene in the truth and reconciliation processes in Rwanda and South Africa even at a purely discursive level. Neither a legal expert on transitional justice nor a political authority on either South Africa or Rwanda, I could also be accused of not having any direct 'experience' of the processes in question. I have not confronted any of the atrocities addressed in this chapter except through their reportage, critical analysis and representations in the media, which makes me, at best, a 'secondary witness',[7] as Catherine Cole designates the readers of her substantial study on *Performing South Africa's Truth Commission: Stages of Transition* (2010). Indeed, it would be accurate to identify my own position in this chapter as a critical reader whose engagement with Cole's research on post-apartheid South Africa, along with Ananda Breed's (2007, 2008, 2009, 2014) interventions on post-genocide Rwanda, enable me to foreground some key issues in which the interstices of performance and the law are played out in the Truth and Reconciliation discourse.

Confronting her own right to intervene in Rwanda even as she has spent many years researching post-genocide performances, Breed raises some searching questions:

> What right does any Western theatre practitioner have to engage with Rwandans in a discourse about human rights? In a country that has been destabilized, and that could erupt in violence again, is it a mistake to empower people to question the government's campaign to rewrite history? Could one possibly incite conflict by encouraging multiple narratives that challenge the government's simplistic

> version of the utopian precolonial past and a peaceful present and future? What is possible?[8]

To the urgent and ethical tenor of these questions, one could add that that it is not just the 'Western' theatre practitioner who needs to be on the alert in preaching the discourse of human rights. As Gayatri Spivak has alerted us, '[t]he work of righting wrongs is shared above a class line that to some extent and unevenly cuts across race and the North–South divide.'[9] The relationship of postcolonial intellectuals and activists in the global South to the lure and inherent traps of the human rights discourse is fraught with its own contradictions and deceptions.

Against Breed's cautious and reflexive 'right to intervene' at a micro level, there is little comparison with the more arrogant, if not imperialist position adopted by the 'Western powers', notably the United States, in its unquestioned and self-righteous 'right' to protect the people of the world against foreign aggressors and from sectarian factions operating within their own states. As Tzvetan Todorov (2003) has pointed out, such a unilateral 'right to intervene' comes with its own political agendas and electoral strategies at home. In effect, the United States did not intervene in Rwanda despite numerous warnings by the Canadian General Romeo Dallaire monitoring the UN observation mission in Rwanda that inter-ethnic hatred was brewing: 'American delaying tactics ensured that not a single extra soldier, not a single arm arrived in Rwanda before the genocide had run its course.'[10] In contrast, the haste in 'intervening' in Iraq on totally fabricated suspicions of 'weapons of mass destruction' reveals that the United States's 'right to intervene' is inextricably linked to its own geopolitical strategies masquerading as humanitarian concerns.

In contrast to the 'promotion of universal justice' underlying the right to intervene – a 'universal' that has a dubious ancestry in earlier vindications of colonialism and imperialism – Todorov (2003) offers the 'duty to assist' as a more modest and dialogic mode of action. This 'duty' prioritizes the ethical and practical dimensions of providing 'aid' within a framework of attentive witnessing, vigilance and care. Shifting the agency from those who are in power and in a position to intervene to those who need help in situations of distress, the primary value of such 'duty' is that 'it is offered and not imposed.'[11] In effect, this means that potential beneficiaries can always refuse humanitarian assistance given to them. The *right to reject* assistance, therefore, is one of the possible consequences of the duty to assist.

Admittedly, the exact fault lines between 'right' and 'duty', 'intervention' and 'assistance' are not as categorical as Todorov makes them out to be in his own, somewhat too self-absorbed moralizing. Can they not shift according to context and situation – the duty to intervene, the right to assist? Can rights be so peremptorily erased from the obligations of duty? How, indeed, are they imbricated in each other's priorities? While Todorov's theoretical discriminations may provide useful criteria to judge the ethics of military intervention in states of war and genocide, they become more complicated in assessing performative interventions where justice is at stake in the larger, state-determined performances around truth and reconciliation.

Returning to the risks of my own intervention in this chapter, which amount to nothing less than the *right to write*, I should acknowledge that one of the primary impulses for addressing truth and reconciliation in the first place is inextricably linked to the political uncertainties of my own location in India. Along with Rwanda and South Africa, India could be regarded as the 'third space' that facilitates my critical inquiry at subterranean and reflexive levels. One could justifiably ask: What are the critical links between these locations, and what are their stakes in the larger context of truth and reconciliation?

Unlike transitional governments in Rwanda and South Africa, the Indian state, it should be emphasized, has never embarked on a truth and reconciliation process following any of the numerous atrocities, genocides and communal riots in the post-independence period. At best, there have been citizens' hearings organized by activist and social action groups, but these harrowing expositions of pain and suffering through testimonials have not been given much legal weight; nor have they been mediatized to the nation at large on the lines of the daily radio broadcasts and television reportage of the Truth and Reconciliation process in South Africa. Whether one is dealing with the anti-Sikh riots in 1984, or the communal disturbances following the demolition of the Babri Masjid in Ayodhya in 1992, or the more recent Gujarat genocide in 2002, the vast majority of the victims and survivors of these outbreaks of violence continue to seek justice often without the most basic legal aid by which their grievances can be voiced to the public at large. Meanwhile, the perpetrators and instigators of these atrocities are not merely at large, but are entrenched in positions of power. Clearly, there is no 'transition' at work here for these legitimized criminals; it is 'business as usual'.

Despite the spate of disillusionments that obstruct and caricature the possibilities of justice, the dogged belief among the widest spectrum of Indian activists remains that 'the law needs to take its course'. By law is meant the process of criminal justice represented by the legal institutions of the state through all the protocols, modalities and procedures demanded by the courts, with all the inevitable delays, suspensions, blackmail and threats constituting a systematic denial or deferral of justice. Against this oppressive reality, the hopeless, yet tenacious faith in a justice-to-come, which fuels the struggle against communalism in India, is something I share, fully aware of its frustrations though not entirely convinced of its futility.

Far from seeing readymade alternatives in the performative reinventions of the legal system in Rwanda and South Africa, I am compelled to question the long-term efficacy of such processes even while recognizing their transformative potentiality. This questioning inevitably calls into question the *limits* of performing truth and reconciliation at purely symbolic, expressive, dramatic and rhetorical levels. Even while I am aware of the crude and unproductive instrumentalism involved in reducing any truth and reconciliation process to the bald question of 'was it "good" or "bad", effective or not?',[12] I do not believe that the issue of efficacy can be separated from almost any reading of performativity. Far from seeing an 'intellectual *cul de sac*'[13] in raising questions around 'good' and 'bad', or 'effective' and 'ineffective', I believe that it is necessary to engage with these binaries within the ambivalences of justice. This questioning of justice has to take place not just at the level of its technicalities, but in terms of how it actually gets performed through the energy and tangibility of its diverse gestures, declarations and speech acts. Efficacy, as will become clear in the argument of this chapter, is as much a performative concern as it is a legal issue.

With these preliminary remarks that frame the larger stakes of the chapter, let us focus now on the interplay of justice with truth and reconciliation in the contexts of Rwanda and South Africa, which will be interrogated in two separate sections. This will be followed by reflections in a more philosophical register on three specific motifs – silence, forgiveness, time – that run through the Truth and Reconciliation discourse both within the contexts of Rwanda and South Africa, and beyond.

## RWANDA

### THE TERROR OF STATISTICS

The tragedy of Rwanda's genocide has barely survived the numbing effect of its overwhelming statistics. In her compilation of facts on the hundred-day genocide in 1994, Ananda Breed indicates its Reign of Terror: 'Over 1 million Tutsis and moderate Hutus killed, 400,000 women widowed, and 500,000 children orphaned.'[14] Stretching the time frame, the Penal Reform International quotes an official government study confirming that '1,074, 017 people were killed' between 1 October 1990 and 31 December 2004, 'of whom 93.7% were Tutsis'.[15] Against the ruthless depersonalization of these statistics in the archive of genocide – and the implicit demonization of the killer Hutu community – we could juxtapose more personalized fragments of terror in narrating Rwanda's genocidal history and memory. A few examples:

> A 45-year-old Rwandan woman was raped by her 12-year-old son – with Interahamwe [genocidal militias] holding a hatchet to his throat – in front of her husband, while their five other young children were forced to hold open her thighs.[16]

> Some [victims] were penetrated with spears, gun barrels, bottles or the stamens of banana trees. Sexual organs were mutilated with machetes, boiling water and acid; women's breasts were cut off.[17]

> A Hutu mother described how she had beaten to death the children next door who looked at her with wide-eyed amazement because they had been friends and neighbors all their lives. . . . She justified the slaughter as doing 'a favor' to those children, who would have become helpless orphans given that their parents had been murdered.[18]

If the statistics of casualties tend to sanitize the actual brutality of extreme acts of violence, providing an escape route from the confrontation of pain and suffering, the snippets of terror quoted above, focusing on lurid and sadistic acts, risk becoming 'pornographic'.[19] Avoiding the reflex of playing into a 'desire to shock', I will not focus on actual enactments of terror in Rwanda, but on the ways in which the Rwandan government has attempted to deal with it through a grassroots judicial system involving the entire population of the country. Inevitably, this necessitates an engagement with official discourse, which plays an integral role in activating the performativity that goes into rebuilding lives in a post-genocide era. This official discourse in turn cannot be separated from its strategization of particular facts.

Against the widespread casualties of the genocide, one learns that the judicial system was 'shattered' in 1994 with five judges and fifty lawyers remaining alive in the entire country.[20] This diminution of numbers has a particularly unsettling effect when one reckons with the pragmatic reality that it would take 'over 150 years to try the over 120,000 prisoners accused of participating in the genocide'[21] – criminals occupying prison space designed to accommodate only 18,000 inmates.[22] The daunting *impossibility* of arriving at any sense of justice in this scenario where the logistics of the law and basic human norms have fallen apart is what compelled the Rwandan government to arrive at another method of prosecuting and punishing the perpetrators.

By default, then, it could be argued that the government prioritized alternative modes of justice, even as it would have been easier to abdicate the rule of law in a state of emergency and total collapse of civic services. Affirming – indeed, claiming – the genocide, instead of discrediting it as a monstrous aberration, the Secretary General of the Ministry of Justice, Busingye Johnson, tells Ananda Breed: 'We wanted to allow this genocide . . . [to] appear like it is a Rwandese problem created by us, and therefore should be solved by us.'[23] It is instructive how this owning up to moral responsibility also conceals a disguised form of national pride in so far as Johnson appears to claim categorically that 'we have solutions for our own problems'. It was out of this mindset that an indigenous and traditional form of conflict resolution – *gacaca* – was reinvented by government authorities to engage with the after-effects of the genocide.

## REALIZING THE UNTHINKABLE: THE PROVOCATION OF *GACACA*

What is *gacaca*? Literally 'grass' in the language of Kinyarawanda, also translated as 'a grassy place' or 'judgment on grass' at various points in Ananda Breed's writings, *gacaca* refers to a traditional, precolonial form of arbitrating disputes, with opposing families sitting on the grass opening themselves to the mediation of community elders. These elders are identified as the *inyangamugayo*, generally described as 'persons of integrity', but more literally translated as 'those who detest disgrace'.[24] Working within the values and logic of what could be described as 'traditional wisdom', *gacaca* exemplifies the eminently sound principle that 'to settle brotherly disputes, you must put aside your family ties'.[25] The disputes represented in earlier forms of *gacaca* involved problems relating to land, inheritance, property and marital relations, but not 'cattle theft, murder, or other serious crimes', as Lars Waldorf emphasizes.[26] Almost without exception, these disputes were local, domestic and strictly bound within the life practices and economies of local communities. If the verdict of the *inyangamugayo* was accepted by the opposing parties of a dispute, the case would be closed, but, if the conflict could not be resolved, the case would then be brought before a regular court.

At first glance, the model of *gacaca*, both at precolonial and postcolonial levels, does not seem to be significantly different from other such traditional structures of conflict resolution presiding over 'customary law' in the rural-based economies of the cultures of the South. The *panchayats* of India, for instance, originally constituted as councils of elders, continue to thrive in almost every village of the country even as their autonomy is increasingly circumscribed by the larger political culture of the state.[27] While the *panchayat* tradition has often been invoked as a grassroots model of 'Indian' democracy despite recent aberrations of patriarchal and sexist abuse, the possibility that it could be re-invented to sit in judgment on communal atrocities or genocide in a national context would be regarded as not just absurd, but somewhat unthinkable. It is in the context of the 'unthinkable', therefore, that I am compelled to reflect on how the traditional structure of *gacaca* has been radically transformed and mobilized for the dispensation of justice in post-genocide Rwanda.

For some critics, the 'reinvention' of *gacaca* is nothing short of a hoax, with transitional justice scholar Lars Waldorf categorically declaring that the post-genocide *gacaca* has 'no resemblance to customary dispute resolution other than the name'.[28] If the older tradition of *gacaca* worked within the framework of customary law for the arbitration of local disputes, the new *gacaca* had the onus and prerogative to *judge* 'serious crimes' within an intricate and highly bureaucratic assemblage and demarcation of different kinds of crimes legally defined by the state.[29] Second, as Waldorf has emphasized, while the former *inyangamugayo* (persons of integrity) were village elders, exclusively male and known to the community at large, the mass of 250,000 new *inyangamugayo* (both male and female) were elected by public vote and given a crash-course ranging from thirty-six hours to a week in arbitrating genocide, often with disastrous results and massive allegations of corruption.[30] Third, a key difference between the old and the new forms of *gacaca*, accord-

*Gacaca* (Photograph: Ananda Breed)

ing to Waldorf, had to do with the audience of the court proceedings. While the traditional *gacaca* was open for participation only to the opposing families in the presence of the *inyangamugayo* – in this sense, it was an oddly private affair even while being grounded in the life of a community – the new *gacaca* was played out in public spaces for the interrogation and live participation of citizens at large.

One could regard this mass participation of citizens in the collective act of judging perpetrators of violence as a highly performative democratic exercise. As Ananda Breed has emphasized, the sheer repetition of the *gacaca* sessions on a weekly basis for five years endowed it with an almost ritualistic quality of a *kugangahura*, or cleansing ritual.[31] Highlighting the intimacy of communitarian gestures in theatrical enactments of *gacaca*, like passing around and drinking banana beer shared by the entire community, Breed suggests that such gestures of solidarity have the potential to 'supersede the localness of terror', thereby creating new possibilities of 'remapping or restaging [social] cohesion' in localities that had been torn apart with ethnic violence during the genocide.

Against the hopeful tenor of this interpretation, one is also compelled to emphasize, as almost every critic of *gacaca* has pointed out, that attendance at the *gacaca* sessions was made *compulsory* by the state for all its adult citizens. It was not a 'free choice' or an affirmation of the collective unconscious of the community. Performing *gacaca* through regular attendance and participation in its sessions was the mandatory responsibility of all citizens living in the new Rwanda. Once again, invoking the 'unthinkable', my mind boggles as to how this responsibility could have been instituted and regulated in the most remote villages and towns with all the accompanying logistical problems. People had to travel long distances to attend a *gacaca* session, compromising or sacrificing on their available time or daily income. At times the sessions were interrupted or cancelled on account of the rain, or due to the lack of sufficient numbers to constitute a legal quorum. To counter the absence of attendance through such circumstantial factors, there was a surveillance system built into the operation of *gacaca* at local levels, with penalties, threats and blackmail inflicted on those who played truant from performing their national duty.

Beyond such oppressive constraints, which inevitably frame the ideological differences between the consensual model of the old *gacaca* and its more coercive, post-genocide 'reinvention', the most substantial difference concerns the cultural expression of ethnic identities. Earlier, the participants in *gacaca* identified themselves as Hutu, Tutsi or Twa. Today, however, in post-genocide Rwanda, these ethnic categories have been officially outlawed and criminalized, making it illegal as such for Rwandan citizens to affirm differences on the basis of their inherited racial identities. In effect, the affirmation of compliant citizenship is being sanctioned through a false resemblance to the earlier tradition of *gacaca*, which is assumed to have embodied an intrinsic social harmony divested of any ethnic tensions. The irony is that this constructed utopia of racial togetherness is premised on the assumption that different ethnic groups ostensibly *lived together* in the precolonial past, while the 'new Rwanda' is imagined to be 'unified' only through an *erasure* of ethnic filiations.

Once again, drawing on the communal context in India where violent clashes have taken place between, within and across communities and castes, I am compelled to ask: How would one begin to outlaw the identitarian categories of caste and community responsible for such clashes? How would one judge them as being intrinsically evil? More critically, how would one proscribe their use in the social interactions of everyday life? Once again, it is the 'unthinkable' that provokes one to question the assumed relationship between 'de-ethnicization' and the framing of a 'common' identity based on the norms of an ostensibly homogenized Rwandan citizenship.[32] The assumption that a 'common identity' can exist only through an elimination of differences plays into the most deeply entrenched statist affirmations of 'national integration' and 'communal harmony'.

## *GACACA* AS PERFORMANCE: A THEORETICAL TRAP?

Enough of a context has been provided in delineating the differences between the actual practice and philosophy of precolonial *gacaca* and its contemporary avatar for us to raise more direct questions in relation to its *performance* today. Keeping in mind that the new *gacaca* has been described by diverse commentators as 'hybrid', 'neo-traditional' and as an 'invention of tradition', it would be a mistake to conflate the *gacaca* of the past and the present in its precolonial/pre-genocide 'reality' and its postcolonial/post-genocide 'adaptation'. To look upon *gacaca* as a performance is not exactly the issue: what has *happened* to its performance over the years? And what is it *saying* and *doing* in opposition to its affirmed intentionality?

Circumventing the dense factuality of her own research, Breed draws somewhat too readily on Richard Schechner's concept of performance as 'twice-behaved behaviors', 'restored behaviors', and 'performed actions that people train to do, that they practice and rehearse', in order to explain how *gacaca* works.[33] Given the disjunction that exists between the traditional model of *gacaca* and the one 'restored' by the present Rwandan government for its nation-building exercise, we need to question more sharply what is meant by *behaviour* in the first place. In Schechner's formulation, there is an odd singularity in the use of the word, which gets replicated across the spectrum of theatre, ritual and public culture, with the adjectival prefixes of 'twice-behaved' and 'restored' almost normalizing the axiomatic repetition of any behaviour.

To what extent is 'behaviour' an appropriate category to represent genocide, both in its actuality and performative replication?

At a more general level, one could question whether the sociological resonance of the word 'behaviour' applies to all performances, particularly to those that are highly aestheticized and formalized. More specifically, in the realm of *gacaca*, it could be argued that the word is more resonant in so far as victims and perpetrators *perform themselves* by re-enacting or reconstructing genocidal violence through testimonies, accusations and confessions. But can these enactments of brutality and massacre be so unproblematically subsumed within the category of 'behaviour'? One is compelled to question whether the word is not appallingly euphemistic in calling attention to genocidal violence in all its sadistic virulence. The actual frenzy of violence, I would submit, challenges the normative underpinnings of what is understood by 'behaviour' in the first place.

A more critical question would relate to the modalities of 'restoration' itself. Restored to what? – one could ask. There is no pristine state of *gacaca* to fall back on, even as its imagined precolonial social harmony is essentialized by the Rwandan government in its deliberate attempt to arrive at a solution to deal with the genocide. However, in terms of the new *gacaca*'s political ideology and criminalization of racial identities, the post-genocide *gacaca* is emphatically *not* a performance based on some assumedly prior behaviour. On the contrary, its performative circumstances have been radically altered. In effect, this is what Busingye Johnson, the Secretary General of the Ministry of Justice, emphasizes when he affirms that *gacaca* is 'something new. Not only new in Rwanda, but new in the world.'[34] It is the 'newness' of *gacaca*, authored, stage-managed and orchestrated by the state, that legislates a 'new behaviour' from its citizens. In essence, the word *gacaca* is being used for something that is fundamentally different.

In invoking the construct of 'restoration of behavior' to explain how a pre-genocide tradition of *gacaca* is being 'restored' in its post-genocide simulation, one has to be careful in eliding the actual *politics of transformation* embedded in this process. In not acknowledging the conflictual dimensions underlying any act of 'restoration', and by leaving the options of 'restoration' far too open, Schechner's concept can lend itself to 'evasiveness', as W.B. Worthen has emphasized.[35] Not only does 'restoring', for Worthen, have 'a kind of ritual/religious tang to it that makes the ideological work of that evasiveness scarier', it 'doesn't quite get at the policing of the activity either: not everyone's restorative behavior counts as restorative; some count as idolatrous, some count as defamatory.'[36] And some 'restorations', I would add, as in the case of the new *gacaca*, are inextricably part of state propaganda – clearly, a far cry from the numerous studies that have emerged in the field of theatre and performance studies around 'twice behaved' behaviours represented in theme parks, heritage villages, Disneyland and diverse forms of theatrical reenactment.

Drawing on Worthen's useful intervention, I would argue that the basic problem with 'restoration of behavior' in the context of *gacaca* is that it would seem to soften the more virulent political dimensions of what would need to be regarded as state authoritarianism. The meaning of Schechner's concept, I would argue, lies in its specific uses *and misuses*, and not in its general theorization of how performance is always already in the state of being repeated – and transformed – through its ceaseless repetition and iterability. Probing the specific modalities of repetition, one would need to move beyond the somewhat formalist premise that 'restored behavior is living behavior treated as a film director treats a strip of film. These strips of behavior can be rearranged or reconstructed; they are independent of the causal systems (social, psychological, technological) that brought them into existence.'[37] While affirming that '[t]hey have a life of their own' wherein 'the original "truth" or "source" of the behavior may be lost, ignored, or contradicted – even while this truth or source is apparently being honored and observed', Schechner pushes his conceptual paradigm to acknowledge that 'how the strip of behavior was made, found, or developed may be unknown or concealed: elaborated; distorted by myth or tradition.'[38]

The distortion in the case of *gacaca*, I would argue, has serious political implications, in so far as the 'myth' and 'tradition' underlying post-genocide *gacaca* are being invented to produce a new apparatus of citizenship divested of ethnic differences, in favour of a common Rwandan identity. Within the mechanisms of such an apparatus, a concept like 'restoration of behavior' needs to be more rigorously problematized so that the very epistemology of 'restoration' can be called into question, if not rejected. Arguably, contexts of terror and genocide *decimate* the very idea of 'restoration' in the first place, compelling one to consider how 'new' concepts and practices are born out of the debris of massacres and the annihilation of normative structures of behaviour.

What is being 'restored' in Rwanda today is terrifyingly 'new', but it is not 'new' as Schechner's concept implies, in the sense of a 'living behavior' that has endured a process of training or rehearsal which the state is then in a position to 'edit', rather like a film director treating a strip of film. On the contrary, it could be argued that the Rwandan state is simultaneously producing, editing and distributing the film in question, and, in the process, demanding of all its citizens a new performance within the disciplinary procedures of the state, dislocated from earlier ethnic histories and memories. Therein lies the underlying terror of the state's performativity in enforcing truth and reconciliation through justice, which is propagated regardless of the differences which continue to afflict victims and perpetrators in an essentially coercive process of social transformation.

## DRAMATURGY OF *GACACA*

At this point, let me narrate some of the key dramaturgical components of a particular performance of *gacaca* witnessed by Ananda Breed, which she describes as 'the trial of Emmanuel in Gahini'.[39] All statements in italics below are drawn from Breed's original description and commentary.

> *The setting: a giant Umunyinya tree in the middle of an open dirt expanse. As a prelude to the* gacaca, *there is a dance performance by the association* Abiyunze *(United), comprising of 30 perpetrators, 40 survivors and 60 community members. To the beating of a drum, two lead dancers step into the centre, their arms stretched outwards. No ordinary dancers bound together by professional ties and training, we learn that 'the male dancer was a perpetrator, and the female dancer a survivor; he had killed the woman's uncle during the genocide.'*[40]

Already, before the performance of *gacaca* begins, there is a jolt in this narrative: who or what exactly is being seen? Dancers? A man and a woman? A perpetrator and survivor? Or all these multiple personae at the same time? In such a 'new' enactment of *gacaca*, what exactly is being 'restored'? And 'who' is being 'restored' to 'what'? And at 'which' point in time?

> *A single bench and table are placed in front of the seated audience.*[41]

This could be regarded as a scene change in 'full lights'. After the preliminaries of the dance, the real 'performance' begins.

> *Ceremoniously, nine judges wearing sashes of the Rwandan flag with the word* Inyangamugayo *imprinted on it walk in single-file across the dirt expanse to the desk.*[42]

This suggests the power of a chorus, as in Greek tragedy, making its entrance and observing the entire proceedings, leading to the final judgment.

> *The crowd stands for a moment of silence.*[43]

A civic ritual, a mourning for the dead. The space suddenly assumes the aura of what Breed describes as a 'commemoration space', in which silence is linked to an officially sanctified code. Linking the memory of national tragedy to the specific task of judging a perpetrator's actions, the act of *mourning* is embedded in the collective responsibility to *judge* the perpetrator.

> *Emmanuel, an accused perpetrator, testifies to the crimes committed. According*

*to the scripted narrative of testimony requested, he gives a full account of how he murdered seven individuals with the tools of grenades, arrows and machetes.*[44]

Clearly, Emmanuel is the protagonist of this drama as he holds forth on his crimes. It is significant that his ostensibly prepared but improvised account is in direct response to what Breed describes as a 'scripted narrative of testimony' that has been specifically 'requested' from him.

*The audience makes soft clicks in their mouth as they listen to the testimony.*[45]

These are pre-verbal, visceral responses to known, but not fully acknowledged narratives.

*After a more graphic description of actual violence, in which Emmanuel describes how the victim was hit on the head with a hammer, then struck on the legs with a machete, followed by his throat slit, the perpetrator breaks down and openly weeps.*[46]

This moment of grief is painful even as its resolution is left open. Emmanuel appears to break down under the pressure of his testimony. Or is the weeping a mandatory requirement of the script? Is Emmanuel likely to be pardoned if he doesn't weep?

*The resident trauma counselor makes her way through the audience to offer him tissues.*[47]

This somewhat surreal insertion of a totally unexpected 'character' opens up the role of trauma management by the state: is this counselling service made available out of compassion for the victims, or in response to the trauma industry endorsed by European humanitarian services?

Culminating her account without quite telling us how exactly Emmanuel was punished – did he land up in prison, or was he given the option to do community service? – Breed mentions how the 'grief counselor' elaborates on the larger aura of comfort provided by *gacaca* to local communities. Is this a temporary reassurance, or the beginnings of a long-term reconciliation? How does Emmanuel face the family of his victims in everyday life, and to what extent do they continue to 'forgive' him after the performance of *gacaca* is over? There can be no conclusive answers to these questions.

## THE EVIDENCE OF EXPERIENCE

Against the complexities of victims and perpetrators living together, a process seething with contradictions, how does one read the reconciliatory power of performing *gacaca*? I stress 'read', because words and images are all I have in my absence from any direct witnessing of *gacaca* as a performative event. Instead of regarding this loss in terms of an absence of experience, playing into a mystique of performance that rests entirely on the essentially ephemeral nature of its psychophysical presence, it is more useful to examine how performances like *gacaca* can have after-lives in the narratives that extend around them. Even if we had the opportunity to experience *gacaca* directly, we need to remind ourselves that the 'evidence of experience', in Joan Scott's (1993) powerful formulation, is discursive and political in its construction. It is not something that 'happens', and which we then need to recover and analyse in words; rather, 'experience is at once always already an interpretation *and* something that needs to be interpreted'.[48]

Keeping this in mind, how do I position myself in relation to the 'evidence' provided by Breed – evidence that pierces the mind with a collision of impossible realities? For example, the words of a woman breast-feeding a child: 'When I do theatre, I forget that this brother here killed my five children.'[49] My first response to this statement is one of total disbelief, which does not disappear even when Breed reminds us with due academic sobriety: 'During several observations . . . I witnessed the survivor holding her baby and laughing as she and the perpetrator conversed.'[50] The only other evidence provided for this woman's reconciliation is a long statement in which we learn about her relationship to art and theatre, and which is worth analysing in detail:

> At first I would be discouraged, I would be lonely; as I associate and interact with people, I begin feeling all right, I become happy. I can laugh. I can talk to people. I feel liberated.[51]

This feels like a highly subjective existential release of enormous pain, which is reinforced by the woman's admission that her 'fears' subside through the process of acting, performing and singing. By allowing herself to be absorbed in laughing, talking and being 'happy' with others, as the woman reminds us candidly, there is 'no time' to think about the fears of the past.

From this point onwards, the statement assumes a more formal register. The informality of singing and dancing becomes a 'mission'; it 'leads others to understand things which they didn't understand before'.[52] The sudden insertion of 'others' somewhat displaces the personal voice into a more generalized 'you':

> [T]here are things that were hidden from you which you get to know.[53]

And then, abruptly, there is a shift to 'we':

> The good news is that when we are invited to say something or perform somewhere, you find yourself participating in nation building.[54]

This 'good news', I have to acknowledge, sends a shiver up my spine, compelling me to ask: Who is speaking through this woman? How does the discourse of nation-building interpellate her voice? And to what extent is it a complicit voice, a voluntarily propagandized voice?

In answering these difficult questions, we would do well to remember Scott's advice that the task at hand is not 'the reproduction and transmission of knowledge said to be arrived at through experience, but the analysis of the production of that knowledge itself'.[55] While Scott is primarily concerned with the writing of history, particularly the history of the socially marginalized and excluded, drawn out of 'first-hand' exposures to their 'real' pain and suffering or to moments of empowerment, she offers performance theorists some valuable clues in terms of how 'experience' can be constructed at a theoretical level.

Cautioning against any attempt to 'naturalize' experience, or to render it 'neutral' through objective witnessing or recording, Scott reminds us that experience is not 'the origin of our explanation, but that which we want to explain'.[56] While this approach would seem to 'undercut politics by denying the existence of subjects' in all their flesh-and-blood corporeality, which is what tends to be prioritized in the limited ethnographies of the subaltern subject in performance studies, what is of critical importance is to realize *how subjects are brought into being*, along with the other social and political processes which are part of their 'creation'.[57] How, indeed, are presences *summoned* into existence through discourses that already exist, and which shape the transitory tangibility of the here and now? The evidence of experience demands close attention to the inscriptions of the past in the present, along with projections of the future over which one may have not control even as one may be compelled to articulate it. In short, the illusion of 'being there' on the part of the writer needs to be complicated by multiple temporalities and subject positions outside the imagined coherence of shared experience.

## PERFORMING RWANDANICITY

Keeping this theoretical perspective in mind, let us return to the woman who seems to have unequivocally forgiven the perpetrator who has killed her five children. It could be argued that her seemingly upfront and candid exchange with Breed cannot be separated from the larger discourse of 'Rwandanicity', which, in her succinct formulation, is described as 'the performativity of the new Rwandan identity'.[58] Inevitably, in confronting this performativity, it is not just what the woman says that is of primary concern, but the official discourse surrounding and consolidating her voice, which facilitates its performativity within the framework of a seemingly spontaneous, yet predetermined script. Only a closer examination of such a script, as I have attempted in the earlier section, would indicate the fissures at work in representing different 'persons' ('you', 'she', 'I', 'it', 'we'), as opposed to a single subjectivity ('I') in which the conflicting temporalities and tenses of a particular voice are emphatically stabilized in an illusory present.

And yet, alongside the discursivity that produces new identities and relationships, it is vital not to close the possibilities of reconciliation, however fragile, that are negotiated through interpersonal relations. In this regard, it is necessary to acknowledge, as Breed has shared with me in personal correspondence, that when she last returned to Rwanda in 2010, she found both the survivor and perpetrator at a commemorative event. The survivor told Breed that since they had last met her child had fractured her leg, and that the perpetrator had visited her in hospital and taken care of her field. For Breed, these gestures of concern indicate that the perpetrator's 'remorse' for killing the five children of the women was not some fleeting emotion, but rather a confirmation of his decision to 'live a life focused on repentance'.

This complex, yet heartening example indicates that repentance can lead to reconciliation through a personally negotiated ethical bond between a particular survivor and perpetrator. However, the dominant reality in Rwanda is that the language of the state has legislated a new behaviour from its citizens, which may not, in actuality, exist. In this schism between what is legislated and what is 'real', the discourse of Rwandanicity asserts its official prerogative to *produce* new Rwandan identities in the most peremptory of registers. To illustrate the almost parodic quality of this discourse, Breed quotes the statement of a Brigadier General in the Rwandan biweekly newspaper, *The New Times*, who provides an unintentionally ludic dimension to the discussion by declaring that *gacaca* can be considered a '*lubricant* for the ideology of Rwandanicity'.[59] While *gacaca*, according to the General, has '*ensured* unity and cohesion in the society since the pre-colonial times', Rwandanicity *is* an ideology of 'our times'.[60] This temporal disjunction is summarily confused by the General, who goes on to say that

> by definition, Rwandancity *was* an idea and philosophy that *guided* the people's conduct and perceptions. As an ideology, therefore, it *is* what the people of Rwanda understood themselves *to be*, what they *knew* about themselves, and how they *defined* and *related* to each other and their country as a united people.[61]

In such a formulation, the stimulus for an essentialized national–cultural identity would seem to have evolved from the people themselves, as if it were part of their self-knowledge and ontology of being. Far from being imposed, the 'ideology' of Rwandanicity, as interpreted in this performative statement, is that essence which grows – and has always been growing – from within, not only in each individual but collectively, to form a 'united' Rwanda. It could be argued that this language is disturbingly close to an organic homogenization and consolidation of 'the people' in fascist narratives, which conflates almost effortlessly with ultra-nationalist agendas. Extending beyond an 'ideology', which encapsulates the genealogy of a new 'identity', the General goes on to claim that Rwandanicity is also 'the *medium* in which Rwandans get their world view'.[62] In other words, the ideology of Rwandanicity is all-encompassing, extending from the innermost depths of 'Rwandan being' to its mediation in the larger field of globalization.

Building on the premise that all performances relating to guilt, confession, accusation and repentance in the *gacaca* courts need to be contextualized within the discourse of Rwandanicity, Breed highlights the normativity that gets performed by repentant *génocidaires* seeking forgiveness for their crimes: 'How *well* prisoners perform their act of contrition may win them freedom or subject them to further time in prison. Rwandans I spoke with acknowledged the risk that *less-than-sincere* performances of contrition in *gacaca* courts may hamper *true* reconciliation.'[63] The question to be probed would be: How do we measure a 'good' performance when a prisoner performs the act of contrition 'well'? And how does one assess 'sincerity'? What are its performative signs so that it becomes possible to judge 'a less-than-sincere performance' (with all its legal implications)?

In this regard, the Penal Reform International Report on *gacaca* would appear to be totally out of its depth in measuring the norm that 'for a confession to be valid . . . it had to be "complete and sincere"'.[64] Acknowledging that 'sincerity' is difficult to 'judge', the Report nonetheless attempts to describe it through 'a fulsome apology',[65] without specifying what makes an apology 'fulsome' in the first place at vocal, gestural and expressive levels. Likewise, the PRI Report declares that '[t]he judges' ability to motivate and hold their audience over a protracted period also played a vital part in the search for the truth'.[66] Adopting what could be one of the oldest clichés in the arsenal of an actor's skills – the ability to 'hold' an audience – the PRI is unable to elaborate on what goes into this 'holding' at a performative level.

In dealing with such dead ends of interpretation, it becomes necessary to engage with a more somatic vocabulary of performance, whose dimensions are briefly suggested by Breed at a conceptual level rather than through thick description:

> In terms of the performance of confession, I have observed an etiquette of repentance at the *gacaca*. Although not considered as legally binding, there is an assumed mode of delivery and behaviour for the defendant's confession for an apology to be 'truthful.' The defendant's demeanour, body language, tone of voice, and even a word choice become elements of the 'performance' of the confession.[67]

Even as there are some subtle clues here as to how performances in *gacaca* are individually rendered through a specific tone of voice and body language, the challenge lies in actually fleshing out these details. Is the voice, for instance, nasal, high-pitched, growing in intensity, speed and volume, or does it remain centred around a particular tone? How do the hands and eyes work as a perpetrator of violence seeks forgiveness? What are the silences and pauses in the conducting of a particular *gacaca* session? In the final analysis, such a microanalytical perspective on performance is challenging not merely because it could be almost infinitesimal in effect, but because the performance has to conform to a particular grammar of behaviour that Breed describes very precisely as 'etiquette'.

Any embodiment of etiquette, in whatever context or set of circumstances, is a manifestation of specific manners which are always already implied and suggested as *appropriate* for specific situations. The codes of etiquette, one could argue, precede any possible improvisation through performance. In this regard, one could justifiably ask: How do Rwandan prisoners seeking their freedom in *gacaca* sessions 'learn' this etiquette of repentance, and to what extent is this learning already imbibed from other structures of interaction in everyday life? How do the institutions of family, school, community and church prepare the ground for this 'etiquette'? This is where an enormous amount of research remains to be done in figuring out the actual *transference* of behavioural codes and norms in everyday life into new performative structures where the telling of one's story or confession of violence can, quite literally, result in freedom or imprisonment. In the tense interstices that exist between the habitual performances of everyday life and the modulation of these performances within the performativity of state discourse, we face one of the deepest analytical challenges in understanding how new nations like Rwanda get performed on command.

In the section that follows on the TRC process in South Africa, we will revisit many of the problems raised in this section on Rwanda, notably the interrelations between theatre, performance and performativity. The 'evidence of experience' in the TRC process comes with its own emotional dynamics and intensities, which are nonetheless circumscribed by the politics of a nation in transition from the state of apartheid to a new democratic state ostensibly inclusive of all its citizens. Like the use of *gacaca* in the post-genocide context of Rwanda, the TRC process in post-apartheid South Africa is best regarded as an 'experiment'. And, as in all such experiments, the possibilities of struggle, failure, compromise and betrayal cannot be ruled out. What matters is that the experiment takes place, and that its consequences are made accountable to the people involved in it and the world at large, providing critical insights on what can be learned in dealing with the terror of the past and on what needs to be avoided in perpetuating its legacies today.

# SOUTH AFRICA

## THE 'IMPOSSIBLE MACHINE'

Arguably, no reflection on truth and reconciliation today, in whatever context, can afford to ignore the spectral omnipresence of the TRC process in South Africa. Now hegemonized as a model for Truth Commissions at a global level, the post-apartheid TRC discourse serves as both an inspiration and a provocation for my own problematization of truth and reconciliation in this section. Unlike *gacaca*, which prioritized the implementation of justice at mass levels within a larger performative structure, the TRC generally tends to be read *as a performance* whose overall emotional *affect* tends to supersede, if not overwhelm, the actual *effects* of social transformation. In the course of this chapter, we will question this dominant assumption by examining how the backstage control of the juridical proceedings of the TRC monitored its high-voltage expositions of pain and suffering, along with chilling confessions of former perpetrators of heinous crimes. If, in the context of *gacaca*, justice was foregrounded albeit in rough and corrupt circumstances, justice in the TRC context tends to be invisibilized, even as it was monitored through the modalities of what Adam Sitze (2013) has so rigorously theorized as an 'impossible machine'.[68]

Highlighting the etymological root of the word 'machine' in the Greek word *mēkhanē*, Sitze calls attention to the theatrical apparatus of the *deus ex machina* ('the god from the machine'), which was often used in the staging of Greek tragedies in the fifth century either to resolve the endings of plays or to complicate them at ironic levels. Through an intricate system of a crane, pulleys and weights – one of the earliest instances in Western theatre history of 'technology' being put into practice – an actor was suspended in the air to create the illusion of a god levitating in celestial space. However, contrary to what Sitze assumes, this 'illusion' in the thoroughly non-illusionist dramaturgy of Greek theatre was made visible; in other words, there could have been no means by which the relatively open stage of the Greek amphitheatre could have disguised the artifice of the god suspended in the air.

Despite this slight inflection to Sitze's understanding of the *deus ex machina* as a miracle-making machine that 'works only to the extent it itself remains invisible and off-stage',[69] I am more in agreement with his political use of the metaphor of the *deus ex machina* in his reading of the TRC as an 'impossible machine'. *Impossible*, not least because the TRC facilitated the unimaginable confessions of perpetrators and the heartrending testimonials of victims, who were made to confront each other and negotiate the possibilities of forgiveness and reconciliation. *Machine* because, as Sitze reminds us, this miraculous facilitation of 'impossible' meetings and affects could not have been made possible without a politically determined legal apparatus with meticulous rules and regulations, which monitored the 'drama' of the TRC in the first place. For Sitze, this apparatus was not just 'inscrutable' but 'impractical'; it was a 'machine whose mandate was either too good to be true, too broad to be practical, or too constrained to be transformative – but that, in any case, did not deliver, and arguably could not have delivered on its great potential.'[70]

Before we begin to dismantle the components of this 'machine', it would be appropriate within the larger context of this chapter to assess the theatrical impact of the TRC – and I mean 'theatrical' as opposed to 'performative', drawing on the most fundamental associations of theatre as a 'place for seeing', where embodied performances by real-life actors in a particular space and time elicit strong emotional responses from an audience. Keeping theatricality in mind, then, let us begin with the most publicized and mediatized of the TRC's enactments by considering the hearings and testimonials of victims, which have been vividly foregrounded in Catherine Cole's research on *Performing South Africa's Truth Commission* (2010).

### THE THEATRICALITY OF HEARINGS

Returning to some of the early responses to the TRC, which were considerably less cynical than the somewhat burned-out reactions that one is likely to encounter in South Africa today, let us recall how the director and visual artist William Kentridge captured the TRC's theatricality:

> The Commission itself is theatre, or at any rate a kind of ur-theatre. Its hearings are open to the public, as well as televised and broadcast on the radio. Many of the hearings are presided over by Archbishop Tutu in full purple magnificence. The hearings move from town to town setting up in a church hall, a school auditorium. In each setting the same set is erected. A table for the witnesses (at least as high as that of the commissioners so the witnesses never have to look up to the commissioners). Two or three glass booths for the translators. A large banner hangs on the walls behind the commissioners, TRUTH THROUGH RECONCILIATION.[71]

As the performance theorist Ray Langenbach has pointed out, the missive 'Truth through Reconciliation' can be read as an emphatic performative that is almost flaunted in the faces of the audience and presented to the nation at large. However, I would argue that the 'counter-intuitive' and 'inverted' logic that Langenbach reads in the missive, as opposed to the more rational description of 'Reconciliation through Truth', is a performative that fails to be enforced. Subsumed within the larger theatricality of the event, it resonates like an empty slogan without being enacted in the public domain.[72]

At every conceivable level – the set, the props, the locations, the costume of the Archbishop, the *Lehrstücke* like banner Kentridge evokes the TRC's performance in the broader context of a travelling show produced by a stock theatre company. The show may be improvised through the topographical and architectural demands of different 'settings', but nonetheless it is held together by a basic dramaturgical and visual structure. Within this rudimentary but robust structure, Kentridge highlights the emotional dynamics that were played out in the *mise-en-scène* of the hearings:

> One by one witnesses come and have their half hour to tell their story, pause, weep, be comforted by professional comforters who sit at the table with them. The stories are harrowing, spellbinding. The audience sit at the edge of their seats listening to every word. This is exemplary civic theatre, a public hearing of private grief which is absorbed into the body politic . . . This theatre rekindles each day the questions of the moment.[73]

Here again, as in the context of *gacaca*, there is a choreography that is built into the rendering of cathartic emotion, supplemented by civic provisions for dealing with emotional excess. Like the trauma counsellor who hands out tissues to the perpetrator Emmanuel in the *gacaca* session discussed in the

South African Truth and Reconciliation Commission
(Photograph: courtesy, Gallo Images/Getty Images)

earlier section on Rwanda, here in the TRC we have professional 'comforters', earth-mother figures, who take care of the grief-stricken as they break down or become agitated.

Circumventing, if not transcending, the performative features of any regular court trial, the TRC catalysed the 'emotional truth' of victims at levels which made veterans in the field of the law, like the South African Constitutional Court judge Albie Sachs, marvel at the unprecedented intensity of the experience:

> [The TRC] was about the acting out of a story of revelation, discovery and human interaction . . . [T]here was that sense of something real, special, and dramatic happening all the time . . . It's seeing the people, the faces, hearing the voices, it's the tears, the actual tone of voice, the body language that's so recognizable – what people can identify with – that makes such an impact.[74]

While acknowledging that some interactions were also 'stiff' and 'disappointing',[75] Sachs, in the final analysis, is ultimately overwhelmed by the 'sense of real personalization' that was tangibly felt through the hearings.[76] Significantly, he makes a distinction in so far as this 'personalization' is not made possible through 'actors playing the parts of the different personae', but rather through the real-life experience of witnessing an actual victimized or tortured person tell his or her story.[77] Drawing uninhibitedly on the language of empathy, Sachs proclaims: '[T]he voices were our voices. The tears were our tears. The emotion – it was the emotion of everybody. And it had a register and resonance that you certainly don't get in court trials, which are very formalized and stylized – so this had a much more open quality.'[78] While one could question the ease with which Sachs is able to conflate the voices, tears and emotion of the victims as 'our' voices, tears and emotion – the personal and the national are almost entirely collapsed – there is a directness in his response which reinforces the theatrical thrust of Catherine Cole's reading of the TRC's hearings.

For Cole, some of the key motifs of this theatricality would include 'emotional expressiveness and volatility', 'communication through the dense registers of embodiment', and 'moments of direct conflict and confrontation between perpetrator and victims' with the live audience serving as 'a kind of Greek chorus'.[79] Witnesses broke down periodically in the TRC hearings, and unlike judges in court, Archbishop Desmond Tutu, the Chairperson of the Truth Commission, would be seen to weep openly at critical moments, apart from praying, lighting candles and bursting into song. Tellingly, these seemingly spontaneous histrionics went against the veracity of the TRC for a large number of critics and editors, who feared that the process of authenticating 'truth' could be discredited through emotional excess. Instead of accepting the tears, cries and sobs of the victims as 'non-verbal' signs of the destruction of language through pain, they became the very grounds on which the exposition of truth was distrusted. Archbishop Tutu was occasionally taken to task for reducing the hearings to 'tearful occasions', thereby undermining his own impartiality. As Claudia Braude has assessed the situation, the Commission's impartiality was undermined by 'truth that is *felt*'; tears 'raise[d] questions about the TRC's legitimacy'. Indeed, 'truth and tears counter[ed] each other'.[80]

Only a few independent interlocutors of the TRC process have been able to engage with the psychological complexity of emotional breakdowns during the hearings. Here is one such analysis of the archetypal moment of the TRC, which has been defined by Archbishop Tutu as 'the defining sound of the TRC',[81] and by Deputy Chairman Alex Boraine as a 'cry from the soul', a 'howl', which captured in its agonizing acoustics 'all the darkness and horror of the apartheid years':[82] the sound, the cry, the howl of Nomonde Calata in the TRC hearing in East London.

Seizing this moment with the intensity of a gifted poet and journalist, Antje Krog, in her masterful personal account of the TRC process, *Country of My Skull* (1999), gives Nomonde Calata's testimony a somewhat fictional frame by articulating it through the words of a 'Professor Kondlo, the Xhosa intellectual from Grahamstown',[83] who is Krog's invention. Even while one needs to pay attention to Cole's critical observation that Krog's use of testimony, passing as 'real' but severely edited, runs the risk of appropriation and distortion, it remains, for me, an enormously rich testimony in its own right – the testimony of a writer seeing and listening to the immediacies of the TRC's hearings. With this qualification in mind, let us listen now to an evocation of Calata's heart-wrenching wail in the words of Krog, as put into the mouth of the fictional Professor Kondlo:

> For me, the crying is the beginning of the Truth Commission – the signature tune, the definitive moment, the ultimate sound of what the process is about. She was wearing this vivid orange-red dress, and she threw herself backwards and that sound . . . that sound . . . it will haunt me for ever and ever . . . [T]o witness that cry was to witness the destruction of language . . . was to realize that to remember the past of this country is to be thrown back into a time before language. And to get that memory, to fix it in words, to capture it with the precise image, is to be present at the birth of language itself. But more practically, this particular memory, at last captured in words, can no longer haunt you, push you around, bewilder you, because you have taken control of it – you can move it wherever you want to. So maybe that is what the Commission is all about – finding words for that cry of Nomonde Calata.[84]

Countering this encapsulation of a heartrending moment of pain, it could be argued: 'What the Truth Commission is all about – *not* finding words for that cry of Nomonde Calata.'

In making this statement, I am already anticipating my critique of the TRC's limitations that follows later in the section. For the moment, let us accept that the evidence of the theatricality and emotional intensity animating the TRC's hearings is so palpable (even in its derivative discourses) that the case for reading the TRC as performance can be regarded as axiomatic – indeed, so axiomatic that it risks becoming illustrative rather than critical. Having made this point, one is compelled to ask: Does this focus on the emotionally charged, theatrical dynamics of the hearings of victims get to the heart of the TRC? Is this the entire story?

### AMNESTY IN PERFORMANCE

Let us proceed cautiously by shifting the focus from the theatrical dynamics of the hearings to the performative registers of the TRC, which were most apparent in the cross-examination of perpetrators seeking amnesty. Here, Cole makes the important theoretical point that the Amnesty Committee hearings had a performative capacity that 'far exceeded the Human Rights Violation Committee hearings', in so far as the decision-making power of the Amnesty Committee to grant or to reject amnesty had an immediate effect on the future life of the perpetrator.[85] In contrast, the Human Rights Violation Committee (HRVC) was restricted to selecting the testimonies to be heard, and to designating the witnesses as 'victims' who then had the right to receive reparations. Even as the Amnesty Committee had the capacity to 'act', and to *implement* its verdicts instead of merely *describing* them, Cole acknowledges that its hearings were not as 'theatrical as the HRVC hearings in terms of emotional expressiveness':

> Amnesty hearings were much more constrained by courtroom protocol, with lawyers and advocates making presentations to judges. There were 'objections', cross-examinations, and requests to approach the bench. Often the perpetrators who came forward were affectless and subdued in their testimony, reporting heinous, grotesque acts of inhumanity in unwavering, flat tones.[86]

This 'innate drama', as Cole puts it – 'drama' not because of its expression (or lack of it), but because of 'who was speaking and what they were saying' – receives a nuanced reflection by the writer Jane Taylor, Kentridge's collaborator on *Ubu and the Truth Commission*. Seeing through the flat, almost deceptively eerie non-performance of the perpetrators, Taylor says:

> Over the past eighteen months of listening to the disjuncture between the tes-

> timony of those looking for amnesty and those seeking reparation, it has been chilling to note the frequency with which an astonishing act of cruelty has been undertaken, as it were, negligently, with no sense of the impact of such actions on other human lives; when confronted with the families of victims or survivors, those perpetrators who seem to have some capacity for remorse, appear to be shocked at observing, as if from the outside, the effect of their behavior. Others simply show no remorse at all, so profound is the denial, or the failure of moral imagination.[87]

Drawing on the horror of the situation, Taylor suggests a gamut of barely visible emotions expressed by the perpetrators, which would appear to be far less harrowing – and, by default, more chilling – than the cries of the victims giving testimony. Here one is compelled to read the perpetrator's muted performances – or non-performances – with irony. One can almost read their devious and thoroughly disingenuous subtexts: Did I really perform this terrible crime? Could it have been so bad that it destroyed and actually killed people, apart from causing so much suffering? In such responses, there is at least the faint possibility of 'remorse', as opposed to the indifferent, stone-wall denial that a crime was done in the first place. It is this 'wall' of no remorse, no repentance, just a dogged affirmation of injured pride and privilege – the right to receive amnesty for a crime that has *not* been done in the perpetrator's mind – that strikes terror in my heart.

Significantly, perpetrators in the TRC's Amnesty Committee hearings were not required to 'express contrition or remorse'.[88] As Cole specifies, '[t] here was no incentive or encouragement for those who appeared before the Amnesty Committee to "perform" in the sense of projecting any particular demeanor, emotion, or attitude.'[89] In this regard, we confront here a totally different set of protocols from what one has examined in the earlier section of the *gacaca* court hearings, where there were expectations of 'sincere' performances driven by a particular 'etiquette'. This would not seem to have been the case for the TRC's Amnesty hearings, which were disciplined within a more formal juridical process.

Building on the premise that it was the law and not reconciliation that dominated the day-to-day work of the TRC, Fullard and Rousseau (2008) emphasize that the entire Amnesty Committee consisted of judges and lawyers whose 'performativity', however limited in terms of the actual execution of verdicts, was built on an anti-theatrical prejudice. Arguably, the Committee circumvented any possible disruption of legal protocols through theatrical distractions. The first Amnesty hearing, therefore, was delayed by hours because, as Catherine Cole puts it candidly, 'the judges worried about the symbolism of having perpetrators sit on the same raised platform as the judges'. They even 'fretted about where the victims should sit: Should they be on the stage or down among the audience? Should they face the commissioners or face outward toward spectators?'[90] Clearly, our 'learned friends' were not comfortable adapting their legal protocols to the topography of schools and town halls, which did not easily accommodate the hierarchical structure of power built into the architecture of a courtroom. Even as the organizational demands of the TRC in its freewheeling, multilocational, mobile structure clearly depended on an improvisatory impulse towards the kinetic and somatic adaptations of the legal machinery, it would seem that the Amnesty Committee was not open to such improvisations.

Instead of highlighting this disjunction between the 'formal' and 'informal' performativity of amnesty, Fullard and Rousseau adopt a brusque, almost technocratic tone as they undermine the muted 'drama' of the Amnesty hearings by saying, 'whether amnesty applicants expressed regret or not, or whether victims granted forgiveness or not, their statements in this regard generally passed unremarked upon by the Amnesty Committee as neither were *relevant* in determining whether amnesty should be granted.'[91] This uninflected endorsement of official norms indicates that there were clear cut-off points in determining what the Amnesty Committee included – or excluded – in relation to what they considered 'relevant' to their assessments. Post-performance encounters between perpetrators and victims, for instance, 'in the back corners of the hall as the TRC staff packed up the chairs', were 'not recorded in any way by the TRC, or accorded any official recognition'.[92] This was messy, personal stuff involving the actual negotiations of pain and forgiveness, accusation and bitterness between victims and perpetrators.

Instead of endorsing the summary denial of such 'off-stage' performances, I would claim that these peripheral interactions are very much part of the TRC's history. Only, this history of what gets *excluded* in scenarios of transitional justice is more likely to be written by journalists and subaltern historians than by the writers of the TRC Report because, as Fullard and Rousseau put it somewhat too defensively, the task of the Report was not to write history in the first place. Still less was the TRC Report obliged to represent a unified and consensual national history; instead, it set itself the task of presenting an overview of the event within the grammar and protocols of earlier Truth Commission Reports from Argentina, Chile and El Salvador, which served as models for the TRC in South Africa.

In reality, as stated bluntly by Catherine Cole, the TRC Report is one of the most underread and overpriced documents of its kind,[93] indicating that the larger phenomenon of the TRC cannot be adequately addressed through its officially sanctioned reportage. Instead, it could be justifiably argued that the multitudinous performances of the TRC, supplemented by the massively popular, 87 television episodes of the *TRC Special Report* and daily radio bulletins, constitute an epic narrative in their own right, which is larger and more vivid than the Report. Tellingly, this narrative has yet to be seriously confronted by academic historians who have not fully accepted that the TRC's performativity, both at histrionic and discursive levels, is a vital component of its multivalent 'truth'. Far from being the source of 'misrepresentation' or 'distraction', performance is what makes the TRC intelligible. But, to return to my earlier question: Is this the entire story?

## BETWEEN PERFORMANCE AND JUSTICE: AN ETHICAL IMPASSE

While amnesty for the perpetrators of political violence was the *condition* on the basis of which the TRC Commission was set up in the first place, the legal and moral right of the victims to obtain reparations was *postponed* until after the hearings could be adequately assessed and discriminated. When these reparations were eventually sanctioned by the Rehabilitation and Reparations Committee – a meagre one-time payment of 30,000 rand (US$3,900 in 2003)[94] – it revealed the bitter truth that 'justice delayed is justice denied'. Clearly, there are ruptures in the time-continuum of this truth and reconciliation process, which compels one to question the ethical impasse between performance and justice.

The irony is staggering: even as the victims waited for years to receive their minimal compensation from the state, most of the perpetrators of violence have merely consolidated their old roles as the beneficiaries of the South African global economy or security system. Instead of using this irony to puncture the efficacy of 'telling the truth', the TRC's supporters continue to uphold the reconciliatory power of sharing 'the pain of South Africa's past' through storytelling. Even the TRC Report, for all its attempt to foreground a measured objectivity of facts grounded in legalities rather than emotion, implies that what is important is 'not so much *what* is told (which has to be verified, and is thus suspect), but rather *that* telling occurs'.[95] Likewise, sceptical as he is that 'truth' can be regarded as 'a road to reconciliation', the philosopher Avishai Margalit is hopeful because even if retributive justice for the victims is not available – it can be 'too costly, or a political impossibility' – the positive outcome of the TRC was that the suffering of apartheid's victims was duly 'recognized' through the telling and sharing of their stories.[96] This *recognition*, I would argue, has been too readily inscribed in the history of the TRC, leaving out the difficult questions of what happens *after* recognition.

Here is a diary extract from one of the Commissioners of the TRC, Piet Meiring, who approaches an old Xhosa woman shortly after she has narrated the brutal torture and subsequent killing of her fourteen-year-old son:

> 'Please, tell me: was it worth it?'
>
> The tear marks were still on her cheeks. But when she raised her head and smiled, it was like the dawn breaking: 'Oh yes, sir, absolutely! It was difficult to talk about these things. But tonight for the first time in sixteen years, I think that I will be able to sleep through the night.'[97]

One wonders if this was the case, or whether the old woman was able to get on with her life. Was she summarily forgotten after sharing her heart-breaking evidence? Did she receive any medical or material help while waiting to hear from the Reparation and Rehabilitation Committee, if indeed she qualified for any compensation in the first place? Reconciliation without reparation, it would seem, is, at best, a wish-fulfilment; at worst, a perpetuation of injustice for apartheid's victims. First the victim tells her story, she is ostensibly 'healed' through the process, she 'touches the hearts' of her listeners, the Truth Commission is duly 'enriched' by the process, but ultimately she is subject to the legalities of the TRC discourse over which she has no control. In addition, it is assumed that she endorses the official point of view being articulated in her name, when, in actuality, the possibility of her dissent, or sense of betrayal or anger with the TRC process, is not even acknowledged.

This travesty of truth and reconciliation in the absence of justice and basic human concern is movingly substantiated by Catherine Cole in the account of her visit to Nomonde Calata's home in July 2007 in the farming centre of Cradock in East London. When asked how she feels about her legendary cry being used over and over again on the media, and in the larger discourse of the TRC, Calata confesses: 'I feel sad. I feel sad. Because I still feel that I'm still crying.'[98] While acknowledging that the act of expressing her pain during her hearing made her feel 'a little better', Calata promptly goes on to say, 'What came out of me, it's still there, and I have no one to talk to at home.'[99] These harrowing words compel one to question what was achieved by Calata's testimony at a performative level. What has it *done* for her if she continues to feel the same pain, and if she has no one to talk to? Indeed, this is not just Calata's predicament; it would seem to be representative of a large body of apartheid's victims. This is confirmed by one of TRC's former Commissioners, Yasmin Sookia, who has the honesty to acknowledge that most victims are not living in peace, but rather 'in the twilight zone, never being allowed to forget their pain and not being able to heal or put closure to their memories.'[100]

Keeping this terrible impasse in mind, the utopian hope of reconciliation built into the voicing of victims' stories becomes increasingly more difficult to sustain, both at human and ideological levels. It would be better to acknowledge the *limits* of storytelling in the South African 'experiment', whose premises were not intrinsically flawed; the problem is that the experiment did not go far enough in terms of its faith in the cathartic role of storytelling for the nation at large. Instead, it allowed this process to be far too circumscribed within other bureaucratic, juridical and political protocols and strictures that not merely compromised the moral authority of the Commission, but may even have perpetuated the trauma of the victims themselves.

### THE 'TRUTH' OF STORYTELLING

In a statement by one of the TRC's Commissioners, Mary Burton, which opposes the possibility or desirability of 'publicly sanctioned history', she says: 'there can never be one truth, and certainly not a single truth, as defined and decreed by the majority.'[101] Arguably, she could be speaking at an axiomatic level not only for Truth Commissions, but for other practices of 'truth' as well. For instance, there can be few illusions about truth in the practice of theatre: it is neither an 'absolute' nor a 'given'. Indeed, there is no one Truth in the theatre. Rather there are many possible truths – mutable, fluid and, above all, deviant – that have to be constantly *produced* from the guts, the bodies, the voices and imaginations of actors.

Earlier in the book, I had engaged briefly with Jean Genet's dramaturgy, which exemplifies the absolute denial of Truth in a metaphysical sense. Given the phenomenology of performance in theatre, truths are constantly breaking down; given its repetition, truths have to be reconstructed, relived, 'restored'. The paradox of truth-making in theatre, therefore, increases when one acknowledges that theatre could be one of the most illusory places in the world, where it is legitimate to lie knowingly.[102] And yet, paradoxically, truth matters; it is that chimerical, constantly disappearing, constantly reappearing element which keeps the process of 'lying' meaningful and alive.

Like theatre, stories matter in any exposition of 'truth' not only because they enable us to illuminate particularly elusive realities, but because they help us to deal with the aporias of pain. The writer Isak Dinesen once said, 'All sorrows can be borne if you put them into a story or tell a story about them.'[103] The word 'borne' is equivocal: within the context of Dinesen's statement it means 'endured', but it also suggests that pain is actually 'born' (created, stimulated, embodied) through the telling of the story itself. Endorsing Dinesen's statement, Hannah Arendt extends it in her reflections on *Between Past and Future*: 'To the extent that the teller of factual truth is also a story-teller, he brings about that "reconciliation with reality" which Hegel . . . understood as the ultimate goal of all philosophical thought, and which, indeed, has been the secret motor of all historiography that transcends mere learnedness.'[104] Perhaps this is a magisterial assumption on Arendt's part, even though it is generous in its qualification ('*To the extent* that the teller of factual truth is also a story-teller'). There is no such qualification in the TRC Report, which suggests that the teller of factual truth is not a storyteller, or, more emphatically, that the storyteller is no teller of facts.

In fact, the Report differentiates very sharply between 'factual or forensic truth' and 'personal or narrative truth', among other truths. Predictably, 'factual truth' is defined as a form of scientifically 'corroborated evidence', drawn on 'accurate information through reliable (impartial, objective) procedures', framed within a social-scientist methodology of research.[105] This truth has been unequivocally prioritized in the Report. In contrast, 'personal or narrative truth' conveyed through the medium of storytelling is granted, at best, some kind of 'healing potential' for the victims in particular.[106] And yet, it would be disingenuous to deny that these stories provided the primary evidence of the Truth Commission; indeed, the most terrifying truths of the violence of apartheid were voiced through personal stories. But to what end? Ultimately, it would seem that the 'truth' of storytelling was too 'subjective' to hold up as accurate evidence for punishing the perpetrators. Within the rigours of the written word, as opposed to the volatility of the spoken, the 'veracity' of stories was called into question even as 'they provided unique insights into the pain of South Africa's past'.[107] With such a patronizing attitude, it is hard to imagine that apartheid's storytellers could be 'reconciled with reality', still less with their fractured selves, even though this lapse would be emphatically denied by the TRC's advocates.

Having acknowledged this lapse, I would also emphasize that there is a privilege in telling a story, even a sense of empowerment. Some stories have an epic ring to them, as is evident in Antjie Krog's quasi-fictional documentation of evidence in *Country of My Skull* (1999). Sadly, many thousands of truths that were never submitted to the TRC Commission are not likely to be part of this master narrative. Apart from the politics of exclusion, there is the problem of authorship. In this regard, one could argue: it is one thing for a woman to tell her own story, if there is anyone to listen to it in the first place; it is quite another matter when the story is told for her. While one cannot assume that the first narration is necessarily more 'true' or more 'authentic' than the other, the exploitative potential of another writer's story of her life cannot be ruled out. It all depends on *how* the story is told, and with *whom* it is being shared in the first place, and *why*.

At one point in the multilayered narrative of *Country of My Skull*, which is as much an experiment in storytelling as it is an agonized reflection on telling the truth of the TRC in South Africa, Antjie Krog recalls a conversation with playwright Ariel Dorfman. Known for his stories dealing with the Truth Commission in Chile, which, unlike the TRC in South Africa, was held 'behind closed doors', and therefore not open – or verifiable – to public scrutiny, Dorfman acknowledges that his writing is a hybrid of 'what he's heard' and of 'what he makes up'.[108] Krog questions him: '[I]sn't that a sacrilege – to use someone else's story, a story that has cost him his life?' To which Dorfman responds candidly: 'Do you want the awful truth? How else would it get out? How else would the story be told?'[109]

This stark revelation is given a reflexive turn as Krog incorporates this conversation into another, more intimate conversation that she is having with an unnamed male companion.[110] While she agonizes about the fact that writers in South Africa should 'shut up for a while' since they have no right to 'appropriate a story paid for with a lifetime of pain and destruction', her companion criticizes her '*over*-respectfulness' for the victims' suffering with allusions to German cultural history.[111] More specifically, he calls attention to the taboos relating to Auschwitz's representation, which, in the immediate aftermath of the Holocaust, almost assumed a 'holy character' that could not be 'trivialized' through fictional narration. Encapsulating the anti-representational argument and then arguing against it, Krog's companion says:

> It's all well and good to listen to victims in court cases . . . but artists should keep their grubby hands off the stories. German artists could not find a *form* in which to deal with Auschwitz. They refused to take possession of their own history. So the inevitable happened. Hollywood took it away from them. A soap opera laid claim to the statistic, the metaphor, the abstraction that was Auschwitz.[112]

To complicate this argument, one is reminded of the philosopher Theodor Adorno's paradigmatic statement in 1951 that 'to write poetry after Auschwitz is barbaric', which is often juxtaposed with his later acknowledgment in 1966 that '[p]erennial suffering has as much right to expression as one who is tortured has to scream; thus it may have been wrong [to have claimed] that after Auschwitz no more poems may be written.'[113] However, it is rash to juxtapose these two statements and read in the latter a 'retraction' by Adorno, which is how his position is generally read: a coming to terms with the necessity of poetry in a state of barbarism. Rejecting the idea of 'retraction', the cultural critic Gene Ray, in his reflections on terror and the sublime, calls our attention to the 'perennial suffering' invoked by Adorno, which continues to afflict those 'survivors' and 'latecomers' who 'must live under continuing conditions of social barbarism with the knowledge of culture's failure'.[114] This barbarism confirms the axiomatic truth that 'the objective social conditions that engendered fascism still continue to exist'.[115]

In this post-Auschwitz predicament of a continuing barbarism, there is no other option, as Ray argues, but to engage with the difficult aporia that even as 'the excess of real suffering *permits* no forgetting', this very suffering 'also *demands* the continued existence of the very art it forbids'.[116] Thinking through this aporia, Adorno turns to Samuel Beckett, the ultimate visionary of negative dialectics in the theatre, for artistic solutions to the problem of living and producing art after Auschwitz. But, as Ray emphasizes, there are no easy solutions: in Adorno's posthumous writings, art's 'right to exist' continues to be called into question, its aporetic condition echoing Beckett's famous maxim 'I can't go on, I'll go on.' While, for Adorno, going on is 'a form of complicity with barbarism', the failure to go on is 'even more barbarous'.[117] While agreeing with this reading of Adorno via Beckett, I would nonetheless add a caveat that Adorno never quite grasped the mordant humour underlying Beckett's robust embrace of failure as he urged his readers to 'fail, and fail again, but fail better'.[118] In Adorno's oeuvre one finds no such humour, however dark and bleak. As a performative strategy humour, I would argue, is less likely to be found in philosophy than in the practice of theatre, which is destined to 'fail' over and over again, its ceaseless repetition surviving multiple 'deaths'.

Moving beyond the angst-ridden problem of how Auschwitz should be represented artistically, the more demanding questions concern existence itself: Can one assume the *right to exist*, post-Auschwitz? One is reminded here of Hannah Arendt's profound acknowledgement, in the aftermath of the Second World War, that the 'shame of being German' is far exceeded by the 'shame of being human'.[119] This 'elemental shame' cutting across nationalities, which is ultimately what remains of 'our international solidarity', has not yet found a political expression, as Arendt puts it candidly. For her, the shame of being human is the 'purely individual' and 'non-political' expression of the critical insight that 'men must assume responsibility for all crimes committed by men and that all nations share the onus of evil committed by all others.'[120] In both Adorno and Arendt, survivors of the barbarism of the Second World War, there is an expansion of the concept of suffering beyond the pain of exile, towards the larger task of defining human responsibility. At one level this suffering is inexpressible, but, at the same time, it is embedded in a deep obligation to *articulate* the aporias of living, both within the nation and beyond. The comforting oblivion of silence is not an option.

## KEY MOTIFS OF TRUTH AND RECONCILIATION

### PERFORMING SILENCE

At this point I would like to shift the discursive register of this chapter by moving beyond the specificities of the Truth and Reconciliation process in Rwanda and South Africa, to question the political valences and resonances of silence. More often than not, silence in the context of transitional justice is equated in monolithic terms with repression, cowardice, fear or self-censorship. Indeed, if there is any element in the discourse of Truth and

Reconciliation that is consistently rejected, it is silence. Silence is unacceptable in dealing with any tragedy or atrocity, even as the absence of justice is tolerated. The survivor or victim is obliged to speak out.

In the Rwandan context, confessions in the *gacaca* process were often endorsed by survivors because they 'encouraged those who had opted for *Ceceka* (to stay silent) to own up'.[121] This 'breaking' of silence suggests not just an implicit act of violence, but the recognition of silence itself as a concrete, yet fragile *substance* endowed with its own materiality, which can be *broken*. Tellingly, silence is broken through articulation, more specifically, an act of vocalization, which is the underlying imperative of almost any exposure of violence, whether it concerns apartheid or the genocide in Rwanda, or, for that matter, the partition of India, which resulted in the barbaric killings of thousands of Hindus, Muslims and Sikhs across the Punjab border in 1947.

While it is ethically and morally questionable to endorse silence, especially when the truth of a particular crime needs to be acknowledged and condemned, it could also be argued that 'breaking silence' should not be made into a dictum. Silence, it could be argued, can be a political or cultural choice. As 'the other side of silence'[122] gets articulated with significant effect – the oral histories of the partition of India, for instance, have radically altered our knowledge of the inner dynamics of communal violence – we should not forget the worlds *within* silence, for which it is much harder to find an adequate language in words. Perhaps we should acknowledge that silence can be, in certain cases, for particular individuals, the only means of 'reconciling with reality'. As Veena Das has cautioned, drawing on her memorable studies on the partition and communal violence over the years, 'when we use such imagery as breaking the silence, we may end up using our capacity to "unearth" hidden facts as a weapon'.[123] Emphasizing the intimate linkage between silence, and the matrix of pain, language and the body in which silence resides, Das makes a strong case for honouring the social dynamics of pain in which we as interrogators of pain are implicated. In a memorable encapsulation of the complexity involved in reading silence through pain, Das asserts: '[D]enial of the other's pain is not about the failings of the intellect but the failings of the spirit.'[124]

Nonetheless, from another critical perspective, the belief that silence could be a courageous way to survive and reconstitute the self can be categorically opposed on ethical grounds, in so far as it challenges the fundamental premises of what it means to be 'human'. The anthropologist E. Valentine Daniel speaks powerfully against silence, even as one would imagine that his exposure to pain and suffering in the ethnic civil war of Sri Lanka would appear to have immunized him to the significance of words. And yet, the perpetuation of silence is precisely what Daniel opposes: while acknowledging the 'enormous difficulty', if not feeling of 'impotency' in 'mediating or communicating' the 'brutal immediacy' of violence, he nonetheless remains committed to sharing these stories of harrowing pain with the wider world through his writings.[125] It is less easy to figure out whether the telling of these stories has a therapeutic effect for the victims themselves, many of whom would appear to be re-traumatized by the actual re-telling of their stories, not unlike some of the victims of Rwanda and South Africa who have acknowledged their fear of being further tormented by re-living the past in public forums.

Even while the price of re-traumatization is hard to measure, Daniel warns against any submission to silence in the widest possible philosophical register:

> [Silence can] indicate the withdrawal from all anthroposemeiosis, *as much refusing to be fully human as rejecting others' humanity*. Being human is being part of the process of reception, transformation, and production of meanings, shared and sharable by an indefinitely open community. Silence could spell the cessation of that process. And that would be tragic.[126] (Emphasis added.)

Tragic: for whom? In whose definition of the 'human', and through whose abdication of the onus to participate in 'reception, transformation, and production of meanings', can the 'tragic' be so clearly affirmed? Perhaps, this withdrawal into silence from an ostensibly 'open community', which may have participated in the violence of genocide and ethnic conflict, could be one way to survive. Silence could also be the path of the renouncer or the seer or the drop-out. Alternatively, it could also assume a performative stance against the normalization of 'community'. Daniel's discomfort that the 'breach' between 'sign and object, words and their customary referents and interpretants', can *force* and even *shock* 'the "world" into taking notice',[127] may be entirely misplaced. This very capacity to call the attention of the world to one's predicament through silence could be regarded as a form of resistance and empowerment.

To demonstrate this point, I will now call attention to how victims of violence can choose to *perform* silence in order to emphasize not their victimhood, but rather the crimes inflicted on them. I draw on a fragment from Veena Das's research on the anti-Sikh riots in New Delhi in 1984, which had erupted following the assassination of Indira Gandhi by two Sikh security guards. While I have inscribed this fragment in my earlier writings on communalism,[128] it continues to haunt, demanding to be told and re-interpreted one more time.

This fragment, I should emphasize, is not a literal demonstration of silence – there is a strong gestural and somatic dimension attached to it – but it is indicative of how victims of communal violence can choose to present themselves to the world outside the protocols of storytelling. From their behaviour we learn that there are other ways of providing testimony, as the following example reveals with searing intensity. Surveying the post-riot relief camps and settlements of New Delhi, Das describes a group of Sikh women whose men have been slaughtered in the riots:

> As long as their suffering was not acknowledged and addressed, [the women] insisted on sitting outside their ruined houses, refusing to comb their hair, clean their bodies, or return to other signs of normality. Here the somatic practice drew deeply from the Hindu tradition of mourning and death pollution . . . I am not claiming that this discourse was explicit – it functioned rather as an unconscious grammar, but fragments of it were evoked when the women insisted that the deaths of their men should not go unavenged. I remember one instance in which there were rumours that Mother Teresa would visit the colony. X [a politician from the Congress Party] . . . implored the women to go back to their houses, to clean up the dirt and to return to some normality. They simply refused, saying he could himself sweep the remains of the disaster if that offended him.[129]

Anger and revenge, so emphatically silenced in the proceedings of *gacaca* in Rwanda and the TRC in South Africa, are the two motifs that surface in this fragment. What matters to these women is not reconciliation, but the recognition of the truth of violence *on their own terms*. On the one hand, there is the collective display of bodies in a state of 'pollution', which, as Das reminds us, recalls at a mythic level the violated figure of Draupadi from the *Mahabharata*: Draupadi, who is shared by the five Pandava brothers, gambled over and lost in a game of dice, and, subsequently, humiliated. On being violated, Draupadi refuses to remove the 'signs of pollution from her body', notably her dishevelled hair that is invariably used as a sign of her anger. In Kathakali performance, the actor playing Draupadi invariably tugs 'her' hair as a reminder of what has been done to her. In their Draupadi-like mythic personae, the women described by Das are not grieving widows and victims; they are not doing what we expect them to do as demonstrated in documentary reportage and television news, which capitalize on the grief of victims. They are witnesses to their own suffering; indeed, they are sentinels of their own suffering.

Along with this witnessing, there is also a decision-making process at work here, which relates specifically to how the women wish to be seen in the eyes of the law, which in turn would prefer *not* to see them in that state. In this process, Das emphasizes that the 'passive display of pollution' is so 'terrible' that 'it could not even be gazed at'.[130] However, this very difficulty (if not assault on the eyes) converts the 'female body into a political subject that forcibly [gives] birth to a counter-truth of the official truth about the riots'.[131] The body, therefore, is not just a source of pollution; it becomes a site of political evidence.

Against the idea of closure, which is more often than not facilitated through palliative pseudo-peacemaking measures, the Sikh women represented in Das's ethnography deliberately work against any tidy solutions provided by interventions of the law and 'concerned' civic authorities. Most striking in their spectacle of suffering – a very different, corporeal spectacle from the sensational victimization readily available on the media – is the affirmation of anger. This compels one to place on the agenda of truth and reconciliation that component of human suffering which is so often ruthlessly excised from transformative agendas: *anger*. What would it be like if, instead of Truth and Reconciliation, one could offer the redemptive possibilities of Anger and Reconciliation?

Even as this would appear to play into the ultimate anathema of revenge, we also need to acknowledge that there is a necessary space for anger in any reconciliatory process. Perhaps, one needs to push the normative premises of the Truth and Reconciliation discourse even further by questioning why revenge has to be summarily dismissed as an unthinkable aberration, if not perpetuation of violence. At one level the profoundly Christian underpinnings of the Truth and Reconciliation processes in South Africa and Rwanda, with the focus on 'forgiveness' and 'loving thy enemy' – constructions which I will discuss in the next section – reduce revenge to the primordial exactitude of 'an eye for an eye, and a tooth for a tooth'. Within the strictures of such a formidably literal logic, it could be argued that there can be no hope for the transformation of any society, but merely a means of 'settling scores', with every possibility of intensified resentment and counter-revenge. On the other hand, if one had to shift the logic of revenge to the popular sentiments animating, say, the blockbuster narratives of Hindi cinema – I am thinking in particular of the superstar phenomenon of Amitabh Bachchan in the 1970s, who incarnated the fantasies of millions of 'angry young men' fighting 'the system' in India – it would be hard to deny that revenge is not just irresistible but eminently desirable, and linked to the urgency and moral legitimacy of implementing justice outside the law.

While I cannot enter into the intricacies of this debate here, which would require a detailed analysis of the ethical and social values built into popular cinema, it would be useful to ask if there is a possibility of a vicarious or surrogate revenge being *performed* by those who have been directly affected by an atrocity or act of injustice. Here, the focus would not be on the ruthless logic of killing or eliminating the Enemy, but on giving vent to one's own frustration and sense of righteous anger in order to reconstitute the self and restore a sense of balance. In this regard, there is a startling insight from Ananda Breed's research on pre-genocide performances of earlier practices of *gacaca* in Rwanda. Breed informs us that 'on rare occasions of homicide in traditional courts, the affected family seeking retaliation would act out their vengeance upon the trunk of a banana tree with a machete'.[132] This might seem like a primitivist mode of unleashing rage, but it offers a prototype, affirming how revenge can be processed in a situation of intolerable violence and injustice through an enactment of anger. To assume that reconciliation can be achieved through 'truth' alone, with generous doses of pain and suffering, does not quite engage with the cathartic efficacy of revenge released – and transformed – through improvised anger.

## FORGIVENESS, OR 'LIVING WITH EVIL'?

Underlying the rationales for truth and reconciliation in Rwanda and South Africa is the crucial role of *forgiveness* in the transitional processes of re-inventing the nation. Here, it becomes almost impossible to separate the trope of 'forgiveness' from the regal figure and performative presence of Archbishop Desmond Tutu, who presided over the entire TRC process in South Africa, endowing it with considerable moral weight and an aura of Christian magnanimity. Despite the redemptionist role played by the Church in Rwanda at grassroot levels, there is no ready parallel or substitute for Tutu in the Rwandan context of Truth, Reconciliation and Justice, no charismatic figure-head dominating the thousands of trials in the *gacaca* process. This absence of a dominant personality need not necessarily be seen as a disadvantage in the implementation of justice at ground levels.

Significantly, there are divergent views on the Christian religiosity embodying Tutu's performative use of forgiveness. Fullard and Rousseau, for instance, would argue that reconciliation in the TRC was not 'conceived in a single, Christian frame', and that the TRC Report actually highlighted the 'dangerous confusion' between a Christian idea of reconciliation and 'the more limited, political notion of reconciliation applicable to a democratic society'.[133] However, the larger aura of the TRC's global significance, I would argue, cannot be easily divested of Tutu's eminently media-savvy, man-of-God personality, which has in effect made him a global ambassador for truth and reconciliation in conflict zones worldwide.

Responding with his characteristic wit to those advisors in the early stages of the TRC who did not want Tutu to wear his purple robes, the Archbishop countered their objections by saying, 'But the people want it.' In contrast, in a crucial meeting with Rwandan President Paul Kagame, where Tutu specifically urged the use of 'restorative' as opposed to 'retributive' justice in order to break the cycle of violence and move towards forgiveness, it seems that Kagame responded to the Archbishop's 'sermon' by saying: '[The Rwandans] were ready to forgive . . . but even Jesus had declared that the Devil could not be forgiven.'[134] This gets to the most complex philosophical, if not spiritual layer in understanding any process of transitional justice, where the ubiquity or the lingering ghosts of evil continue to haunt and impede the possibilities of victims sharing the same space as perpetrators.

How, indeed, does one 'live with evil', as Mahmood Mamdani puts it in his forthright manner.[135] In what remains for me one of the most chilling formulations of the TRC, I am reminded of his provocation that the pursuit of reconciliation could be an 'embrace of evil'.[136] Taking on one of the most radical statements in the Bible where Jesus Christ exhorts his followers, 'Love thy enemies and pray for those who persecute you' (Matthew 5:44), Mamdani pushes the premises of this statement: 'Before you *love* thy enemy, must you not recognize the *enemy*?'[137] Identifying 'the enemy' not as an external agency, but as the 'potential for evil [which] could exist in Self', Mamdani stretches the discursive limits of his political theory and its predilection for pragmatic rationality by raising deeply moral questions. He asks, for instance, whether the 'potential of evil in oneself necessarily leads one to a recognition of evil in the Other.'[138] In other words, is there the possibility of a meeting of minds through evil, and, in this crucial sense, a reconciliation of differences through compatible evils? Or can the recognition of evil in oneself not lead to 'a struggle against evil on all fronts, neither to demonize the Other, nor to sanctify oneself'?[139]

In response to the gravity of these questions, let us insert into the discussion two concepts aligned to 'forgiveness' – *kubabarira* and *ubuntu* – that were specifically invoked in the truth and reconciliation processes in Rwanda and South Africa, respectively. In the context of Rwanda, which specifically rejected the path of 'restorative justice' in favour of 'retributive justice', forgiveness nonetheless played an important role through the Rwandan concept of *kubabarira*. This word would seem to affirm a different epistemological significance from what 'forgiveness' connotes in English-language civic contexts. Explicating its significance to Ananda Breed, Simon Gasibirege, Professor Emeritus of Psychology at the National University of Rwanda, emphasizes that *kubabarira* does not mean the same thing as 'pardon' in English; rather it connotes 'suffering', and, more specifically, the sharing of this 'suffering' with others.[140] According to Gasibirege, the law of *gacaca* demands that after the perpetrator has confessed his or her crimes, the victim does not merely pardon the perpetrator; instead, the process of forgiving is shared. Gasibirege further emphasizes that *kubabarira* is possible not because it is a legal construct, but because it is a deeply embedded Rwandan cultural principle which facilitates 'the process of healing focused on bereavement'.[141]

Even as this statement is insightful, it is unclear whether Gasibirege's idea of forgiveness as 'shared suffering' resonates unequivocally in the context of the *evidence* provided by a large number of post-genocide/post-*gacaca* survivors. These individuals have gone on record acknowledging their complicity in a narrative of *coercive forgiveness*, where victims forgave their perpetrators under conditions of fear, intimidation, expediency and an absence of options. As one survivor acknowledged to an interviewer from the Penal Reform International team, 'The government has forgiven you and me, I cannot refuse it to you.'[142] This double negative – 'cannot refuse' – captures succinctly the coercive circumstances in which forgiveness had to be performed: there was no option in this regard. Against such chilling evidence, post-genocide *kubabarira* could be less of an organic, traditional and essentialized reflex, as Gasibirege makes it out to be, than a strategic way to survive. Indeed, as he engages today with a surfeit of trauma-related crimes and domestic violence in the post-*gacaca* period of Rwanda's reconstruction, Gasibirege is only too keenly aware of the schisms that have emerged *within* the families of survivors, perpetrators and former prisoners.[143] Now, the trials of forgiveness have extended to the inner recesses of family structures, which have been disrupted and traumatized through the after-effects of state-determined forgiveness.

Arguably, 'real' forgiveness – an unconditional forgiveness of the heart, in Derrida's sense, divested of calculation or strategic determination – has yet to evolve. At a more philosophical level, which embraces the 'impossible', Derrida affirms the 'aporia' in all its 'dry and implacable formality' that 'forgiveness forgives only the unforgivable'.[144] Given the ubiquity of the 'unforgivable' in terms of the monstrous crimes that human beings inflict on each other in the world – the genocide in Rwanda would seem to exemplify these crimes in their most extreme manifestations – 'the call to forgiveness', far from being numbed, finds itself 'reactivated, remotivated, accelerated' by the 'unforgivable itself'.[145] And yet, with due deference to Derrida's exacting premise of the 'impossible', one would have to say that at ground levels this does not necessarily mean that all victims are in a position to actually *forgive* their perpetrators, bound as they are in a vortex of simmering resentment and new forms of violence.

Countering the experiment in Rwanda, one could argue that in the context of truth and reconciliation in South Africa, where 'restorative' justice was privileged through the principle of 'conditional amnesty', forgiveness is almost built into the larger ethos of the TRC's quest for justice. Here the overriding concept of *ubuntu*, masterfully rhetoricized and strategized by Archbishop Desmond Tutu, provokes the same ambivalence that I had indicated in my reading of *kubabarira*. A 'traditional' African concept ostensibly pitted against the mechanisms and innate violence of European 'retributive justice', resonating compassion and love at deeply interpersonal and communitarian levels, *ubuntu* can also be read as a camouflage for perpetuating some of the worst principles of apartheid jurisprudence. This radical position has been argued forcefully by Adam Sitze, who focuses on Tutu's assumption that *ubuntu* sanctions the principle of 'conditional amnesty', which can be better read, in Sitze's view, as an 'empty vessel that contains, among other things, the criteria and principles specific to the juridical power that apartheid jurists once called "indemnity".'[146]

While 'amnesty' is generally defined as a general pardon or act of forgiveness for past offences, 'indemnity' is a form of protection or security or compensation against damage or loss. Drawing on the Ciceronian maxim underlying one of the foundations of apartheid law – *salus publica suprema lex* ('the safety of the state is the supreme law') – Sitze argues how the principle of indemnity could be used by apartheid jurisprudence to 'legalize illegalities that were committed in good faith to protect the *salus publica,* whether or not those illegalities were at all necessary.'[147] With this maxim in mind, Sitze deconstructs Tutu's rapturous reading of *ubuntu* while acknowledging the generosity of its foundational principle that 'a person is a person through other people.'[148] Countering the rationally bound Eurocentric philosophical premise affirming 'I think therefore I am', *ubuntu* suggests another paradigm of living in coexistence: 'I am human because I belong.'[149] Against these magnanimous assumptions of a shared humanity, Sitze seizes on Tutu's less generous argument that 'social harmony is for us the *summum bonum* – the greatest good. Anything that subverts or undermines this sought-after good is to be avoided like the plague.'[150] In this reading, *ubuntu* ceases to be 'altruistic'; rather it becomes, in Tutu's candid words, 'the best form of self-interest'.[151]

For Sitze, it is this elevation of 'social harmony' to the level of Cicero's *salus publica* that provides a shifty ground for 'the expulsion or suppression of precisely the sort of dissent that Tutu himself so fully personifies.'[152] While *ubuntu* can provide the basis for an inventive 'egalitarian politics', it can also serve as 'the premise for the most repressive actions of police forces whose main task is simply to "keep the peace".'[153] Therein lies the ambivalence of *ubuntu* and its potential to be politically misused. While Sitze's argument could be countered at more nuanced cross-cultural levels, it is a chastening reminder of how even the most resonant of traditional categories, like *ubuntu*, can be used to justify 'conditional amnesty' for criminals within the framework of the TRC. At a broader social level of sanctifying an ostensibly 'new' South Africa, it can also provide a total *carte blanche* for those leading politicians of apartheid who did not even appear before the TRC, but were nonetheless 'forgiven'.

## TIME AND RECONCILIATION

Along with the motifs of 'silence' and 'forgiveness', we need to open the dimension of time in the context of transitional justice. It is commonly assumed that time heals, and with the passing of time, the scars are supposed to fade away. Certainly, we know that this cannot be so easily assumed when there is a *time-frame* on particular processes of truth and reconciliation, as in Rwanda and South Africa, where there were specific schedules for hearings, consultations, meetings and submissions of reports. This bureaucratic pressure of time seems almost ludicrous when one confronts the truism that 'centuries of oppression cannot be removed overnight'. And yet, as the veteran of the Chilean Truth Commission, José Zalaquett, has affirmed: 'The process [of Truth and Reconciliation] must stop! Just as a patient undergoing a critical operation should not stay in the theatre too long, a truth commission should know when to call it a day.'[154] Hopefully, one assumes that the unacknowledged doctor in Zalaquett's metaphor will not prematurely stitch up the patient before fully attending to his or her problem, or, worse still, after dismissing the patient as a 'hopeless case'. Whether or not the operation is successful in the 'theatre' – the word acquires a peculiarly sinister resonance, as much a place for healing as a possible site of death – the point is that while the process of reconciliation may begin with the deliberations of a Truth Commission, it certainly does not end there.

Perhaps we should not presume to imagine that new societies can be born in the aftermath of even the most time-conscious and efficient of Commissions. This would be a kind of hubris that would place an act of social engineering over and above the capacities of human beings to understand and live together through the residues of violence at institutional and symbolic levels. In her epilogue to *Country of My Skull*, Antjie Krog acknowledges that few people believe that the TRC process achieved reconciliation, and, indeed, surveys indicate that 'people are further apart than before'.[155] This does not mean that the process of reconciliation is not going on, but to realize its outcome, we need a larger envisioning of time. As Krog sees it, 'Reconciliation is not a process. It is a cycle that will be repeated many times.'[156] The unspoken assumption is that if reconciliation is destined to repeat itself, so will the memories of violence that refuse to die.

Confronting this reality, Krog opts less for a submission to the larger poetics and metaphysics of time than for more time-bound secular solutions to human coexistence, which compels her to speak the unlikely language of a social scientist rather than a poet. Pragmatically, and in a tone that is totally at odds with the reflexive nature of her book, Krog falls back in the closing paragraphs of her epilogue on the most banal truisms of conflict resolution. She reduces reconciliation to 'one of the most basic skills applied in order to survive conflict'; its 'essence' is 'survival', its 'key' the art of 'negotiation' – less negotiation than an almost biological need to get on with life.[157] This resilience is determined less by civility or good faith than by 'our genetic make-up',[158] as Krog puts it all too emphatically, in a vocabulary that is clearly not her own.

A somewhat more pragmatic source for implementing reconciliation comes from the post-apartheid refashioning of identities, which Krog views as a 'fundamental step' towards reconciliation.[159] It is hard to fully share this optimism, particularly as she views 'blacks' as redefining themselves within the 'African renaissance'. One is compelled to ask: Which minuscule sections of the blacks are in the process of 'redefining' themselves in this mode? Can this so-called renaissance (replicating the 'Asian renaissance' of East Asian global capitalism) not be seen as another form of neo-colonialism in the new South Africa? Even as the beneficiaries of global capital among the black elite may be ready to assert a new cosmopolitan, neo-liberal, 'renaissance' identity for themselves, the reality is that they are not prepared to share the economic benefits of this 'renaissance' with their less privileged brothers and sisters, whose economic misery in the new South Africa is one of the continuing sources of rage and social unrest.

For that matter, even as Achille Mbembe posits the hopelessly optimistic possibility of South Africa creating 'the first credible nonracial society on the planet', he is also compelled to acknowledge grim home truths: 'Pervasive material inequality between whites and blacks coexists with formal legal equality'; 'Black South Africans still command less than 5 percent of the national economy'; the attempts to 'empower' them through the politics of transformation have led to accusations by the ruling corporate elite of playing into incompetence, corruption and crime.[160] This is a familiar story to any observer of a democratizing process, as in contemporary India, where systemic changes by the government through the implementation of reservations have been made to facilitate social and economic opportunities for the underprivileged and 'low'-caste marginalized sectors of society. However, the South African story has a different gravity. Here, in the name of 'transformation', as the political economist Moeletsi Mbeki has put it, a 'historical compromise' was worked out between the 'white economic oligarchy owning and controlling the mineral–energy complex' of South Africa's resources, and 'the politically dominant black upper middle class'.[161] In this collusion of interests constituting a new regime of strategic compromise, the backstage politics that had made Truth and Reconciliation possible in the first place have now been more pragmatically 'outed'. In the process, the performative aura of the TRC's ostensibly cathartic, beneficent and healing rhetoric and discursive practices has increasingly been called into question.

Once again, as in the rest of this book, I am interested in the aftermath, in speculating on what happens when a particular process *ends*. Is there a new beginning in any end, or is it more of the same, or worse, a concealment of the crimes of the past? As time passes, these crimes in South Africa would seem to loom larger, even as they are legitimized and freed from any critical or juridical scrutiny. In Mbembe's unsparing critique, we are provided with a context in which the impasse of transformation is located:

> In a country where very few apartheid-era atrocities have been prosecuted, where key political figures refused to testify to the Truth and Reconciliation Commission, where there have been hardly any acts of public contrition from former executioners, where most killers and torturers have escaped jail time, the persistent denial of white privilege partly explains the acrimonious nature of the controversy.[162]

Instead of countering and privileging 'black victimhood' against 'white denialism', Mbembe, wisely and deftly, reads a collision *and collusion* in the ways that both victimhood and denialism 'foster a culture of mutual *ressentiment*'.[163] Likewise, by affirming the *ethical* necessity of transformation, and not just its quantitative and technical implementation, Mbembe acknowledges the fundamental contradiction underlying any process of 'transformation', namely, the insertion of 'a degree of inequality in the very process by which it aims at reaching the goal of equality', or, in plainer terms, 'when two individuals possess the same qualifications, preference should be given to the "formerly disadvantaged" individual'.[164] Suffice it to say that there is no 'cross-racial ethical consensus'[165] around transformation in South Africa, not least because the in-built contradictions of the concept have yet to be adequately grasped in the public domain.

In this impasse, I sense deep affinities with the most pressing political problems underlying the processes of democratization in India through reservations for 'low'-caste communities, where one faces the same distrust, the same incomprehension and, above all, the same backlash of resentment from the economic elite or the upper-caste hegemony. It would seem that in addition to retributive justice or restorative justice, which were the models practised in Rwanda and South Africa, respectively, what is urgently needed is a more economically grounded *social justice* model that has the potential to transform the everyday lives of people. This process has to begin by engaging with their means of livelihood, control over resources, and, above all, their capacity to mobilize dignity and self-respect for a better life.

For any process of social transformation to be meaningfully 'performed' – in other words, put into action, realized, concretized, *in*, *through* and *beyond* the utterance of words – education plays a vital mediating role, as Amartya Sen has pointed out in his numerous writings on activating 'capability' through social and economic opportunities.[166] While the role of education in relation to transformative performance lies beyond the framework of this book, it is worth pondering that if agendas of social justice flounder or backfire, it is because the fundamental premises animating their contradictory agendas fail to be understood in the public sphere. Much more debate and dialogue, with the capacity to listen on multiple sides, is urgently needed to grasp a difficult, yet necessary point: the privileging of the formerly underprivileged, not as a form of quantitative tokenism but through a recognition of past injustices, is an *ethical* responsibility for society at large. Only by working through this process of recognition and redistribution of resources does reconciliation become possible in a substantial sense; or else, it remains an empty word, still waiting to be fully 'performed'.

## CODA

Against the enormity of the task of social transformation, we have no other option but to complicate the exigencies of 'time frames' for the implementation of Truth Commissions alongside the 'cycles of time' in which reconciliation is destined to play itself out. For this we need another vocabulary and perspective on time, for which I would like to turn, somewhat elliptically, at the end of this chapter, to the insights offered by one of the greatest seers of our time, Jiddu Krishnamurti. Unlike the architects of Truth Commissions, Krishnamurti would question, I believe, the very assumption that there *can* be a positive outcome in negotiating a path from truth to reconciliation, or from violence to non-violence. In his barely veiled critique of Gandhi, for instance, he emphasizes that the evolution from 'violence' to 'non-violence' implies that one needs time to become non-violent. In working towards this 'ideal', which Krishnamurti equates with an 'escaping process', all that emerges is a 'division' in the mind, which can only perpetuate 'conflict'.[167] Indeed, 'the very resistance to conflict is itself a form of conflict'.[168]

If this is not a language that one associates with activism of any kind, I should qualify that Krishnamurti is not addressing political time, but what he describes as 'psychological time', which is determined by the interval, the division, the gap between 'this' and 'that', between 'one action and another', between 'one understanding and another', between 'seeing something, thinking about it, and acting'.[169] This very *movement* embodied in time, carrying the conceptual baggage of our thoughts, memories, desires and motives which are the cause of our suffering, compels Krishnamurti to posit 'a time of non-movement', which is without momentum, direction or continuity.[170] Calling attention to the state of 'passive awareness' in which the dissolution of psychological time becomes possible, he advocates nothing less than 'the ending of time'.[171] This is not an apocalyptic premise, but a very tentatively posited 'new beginning' by which we can begin to re-invent and sustain our inner selves on a different 'ground' of being.

If I choose to inscribe 'the ending of time' at the end of this chapter, it is not because I see it as some kind of solution. Indeed, Krishnamurti would not want us to believe in solutions because that would imply a progression in time, which is the very source of our pain. Rather he would be sceptical of our attempts to articulate this 'ending', as indeed he was frustrated by his own attempts to put vision into words: 'We are using words to measure the immeasurable, and our words have become time.'[172] I use Krishnamurti as a provocation because, in a sense, he works against the argumentative premises of this chapter on truth, reconciliation and justice; he complicates the agenda and compels us to rethink our words. Most decisively, he infiltrates the conjunction 'and' separating and linking 'truth' *and* 'reconciliation' to 'justice'. He breaks the in-built causality, temporality and assumed correspondences between these words, and in that sense, he fills us with profound unease.

To articulate this unease, we need to ask: Does justice materialize through the process of truth and reconciliation, or is its suspension a means of getting on with life in the continuation of terror? Can justice, however flawed and incomplete in its execution, be regarded as a means of countering terror? In this chapter, I have juxtaposed the performative dimensions of two models of transitional justice, in which the experiments of *gacaca* in Rwanda attempted to reach out to the widest cross-section of society by rejecting the principle of impunity, while the Truth and Reconciliation process in South Africa premised its operation on the principle of amnesty for select political crimes. Both experiments have proved to be deeply flawed and compromised by the juridical mechanisms of transitional states, affirming democracy and equality across – and beyond – ethnic and racial differences, even as the unresolved hierarchies, inequalities and injustices of the past continue to be embedded in the present.

Despite these limitations, which in a more optimistic register could be regarded as illuminations of positive failure, I would emphasize that there is much to learn from both these experiments. To my mind, they are most productively read not as antithetical forces, but as contrapuntal exercises in the actual making of democracy in very fragile, and as yet emergent, public spheres. It is one thing to formulate democracy at a constitutional level, but it is quite another matter for people across diverse class and social groups to actually perform its negotiations of difference through critical debate and dialogue. All too often the eruptions of violence and simmering hatred result in acute breakdowns of trust, compelling one to acknowledge that the struggle involved in performing citizenship in post-apartheid and post-genocide societies cannot be underestimated.

This is particularly true if by 'performing' we mean not just a deferential response to the rhetorical commands of the state, but the actual questioning by citizens of state-determined rights and norms. More often than not, this questioning takes the form of activism and public protest, which can be regarded as 'performances' in their own right. In the next chapter, I will focus on such acts of cultural resistance to deepen the critical inquiry of the ambivalent relationships between justice and law. More specifically, I will address these relationships not by documenting yet another experiment in truth and reconciliation, but by examining the practice of *non-violence*, at discursive, performative and political levels. From the failed experiments in truth and reconciliation, what other performances might we consider to engage with the possibilities of justice? This question takes us to the final chapter of this book, which is less a conclusion than a reflection on the ways in which the terror of our times can be countered – and hopefully, transformed – through a conscious engagement with the philosophy and praxis of non-violence.

# 4

# PERFORMING NON-VIOLENCE IN THE AGE OF TERROR

## ENTER GANDHI

Unexpectedly, as this book reaches its final act, there is a knock on the door not unlike the *Verfremdungseffekt* described by Walter Benjamin in his evocation of Brecht's epic theatre. Highlighting this theatre's tendency to 'reveal' rather than to 'reproduce' reality through processes which are interrupted, Benjamin provides the 'crude' example of a 'family row': 'The mother is just about to pick up a pillow to hurl at the daughter, the father is opening a window to call a policeman. At this moment a stranger appears at the door.'[1] The stranger featured in this chapter is not the man on the street, but one of the world's most obstinate and visionary of radicals, who invariably had the last word in any argument: Mahatma Gandhi. Against my will – or perhaps with no predetermined strategy on my part – he will have, if not the last word on terror, then the strongest questions and provocations as to how we can go about countering it in the immediacies of the here and now. In this epilogue, Gandhi is more of a catalyst than the repository of solutions, the initiator of questions that stretch the limits of this book beyond its discursive framework into the domain of possible action.

In response to Jiddu Krishnamurti's passing riposte in the concluding pages of the last chapter, that the prospect of moving from violence to non-violence can only intensify conflict, Gandhi would agree: how could it be otherwise? Conflict as such is not to be feared; it is violence that needs to be rejected. Unlike Krishnamurti, who was able to divide time into 'physical time', 'historical time' and 'psychological time', there are no such demarcations in Gandhi's embrace of multiple temporalities: the personal, the political and the spiritual are deeply embedded in his larger search for truth, which has all the vulnerability of a ceaseless 'experiment' that is constantly failing, and yet surviving.

At a more thematic level, Gandhi interrupts the narrative of this book in specific response to the truth and reconciliation process in South Africa, a country where he spent twenty-one years of his life and which provided him with the basic training ground for the activation of *satyagraha* (literally, the 'insistence of truth', more commonly understood in terms of 'soul-force' or 'truth-force'). While the 'experiment' of the TRC, to my mind, would have moved Gandhi deeply, I also see him disagreeing with Nelson Mandela and Archbishop Desmond Tutu, firmly yet affectionately. Perhaps, this agonistic confrontation between Mandela, Tutu and Gandhi could be the subject of a massive play or opera set against the killing fields of the world, but for the moment, let it suffice that the spectral presence of Gandhi in this epilogue offers critical dissent not only in relation to the outcome of the TRC process in South Africa, but also to its very premises. Needless to say, we have entered an area of hypothesis here, which is better explored through reasoned speculation than through overconfident assertion. I approach my own process of thinking through Gandhi, therefore, with some caution, but also by working against the grain of his exceptionalism, the oppressive mahatmahood which has been thrust on him, numbing his own uncertainties and censoring our own need to question his often prescriptive opinions.

## GANDHI AS TRUTH COMMISSION

Arguably – and problematically – Gandhi could be described as a one-man truth commission, which is how he functioned in the aftermath of communal riots and atrocities in the Indian subcontinent. Significantly, he functioned like a truth commission even as the Indian state to this date has denied the relevance of such commissions in interrogating and resolving communal violence and genocide. Keeping in mind the legal status of such commissions, it can never be forgotten that Gandhi was trained as a lawyer, who, in all probability, would have been deeply concerned not only with the symbolic or healing dimensions of the TRC in countries like South Africa, but with its actual legalities and their implications. In this regard, it is not likely that he would have supported the principles of amnesty or forgiveness without real evidence of *repentance* on the part of the perpetrators. It would not be sufficient, in this regard, to assess the 'sincerity' or 'genuine' nature of the perpetrators' acknowledgement of their crimes. Mere 'regret' or an 'apology' would be inadequate for Gandhi's rigorous understanding of justice. Instead, what he would require of perpetrators of violence would be nothing less than an act of repentance by which they could actually demonstrate their willingness to rebuild the shattered lives of their victims.

In this context, it is likely that Gandhi would have responded positively to the practice of community service, which was the option given to many thousands of perpetrators in post-genocide Rwanda in lieu of imprisonment.

There were two such forms of community service – one centred within the neighbourhood or district where the crime took place, thereby compelling perpetrators and victims to recognize each other's existence; the other was more institutionalized within the framework of prison-like camps situated far away from the perpetrators' homes.[2] In all likelihood, Gandhi would have prioritized the first form of community service, because of the face-to-face encounter of victims and perpetrators working together in the process of rebuilding trust and shared responsibilities. While, for Gandhi, *seva* (service) was one way of demonstrating genuine remorse in the aftermath of violence – rebuilding the house of one's enemy, destroyed or burned in a communal riot, could be one gesture of reconciliation – this material consideration needed to be supplemented by a religious commitment to the larger process of healing pain.

Perhaps, this commitment is epitomized by Gandhi after the 1946 Calcutta killings in that paradigmatic moment when he is confronted by a Hindu man who has lost his son in the riots. Gandhi's words of consolation to the man are well worth remembering:

> If you really wish to overcome your pain, find a young (Muslim) boy, just as young as your son . . . whose parents have been killed by Hindu mobs. Bring up that boy like you would bring up your own son, but bring him up in the Muslim faith to which he was born. Only then will you find that you can heal your pain, your anger, and your longing for retribution.[3]

What is striking about Gandhi's insistence that the Hindu father should bring up a Muslim orphan as his own son, but in the Muslim faith, is that it totally challenges the notion that cultural and religious identities are interchangeable. Tellingly, for Gandhi, despite the terrifying evidence of Hindu–Muslim hatred in the Calcutta killings of 1946, the categories – and, more important, the cultural and religious foundations underlying the categories of 'Hindu' and 'Muslim' – remain intact; they are not blurred by postmodern hybridity or subsumed under a nebulous 'human' identity. The idea of non-religious, non-caste, non-racial community identifications would not make sense to Gandhi. For him, humanity needed to be asserted in and through the recognition and respect for identitarian differences. The Hindu father invoked by Gandhi in the incident mentioned above does not become less human for bringing up the Muslim orphan as a Muslim; on the contrary, both his humanity and that of the child are enhanced in the process.

Countering the theoretical babel that identities can be affirmed only in a state of plurality and infinite flux, or, more blatantly, that the very idea of identity should be de-linked from the fetishization of difference, Gandhi, in my reading, would urge us to hold on to differences which enable the recognition of, and possibility of living with, the other. Without denying the value of larger universals like liberty, equality and fraternity, even while affirming the need to redefine these terms on specifically religious grounds outside the logic of modernity, Gandhi invariably worked through the contradictory processes of diverse and conflicting religious particularities in order to arrive at a highly personal, contingent and complex articulation of Truth.[4] The danger, I would submit, in today's theoretical climate, is that the cult of sameness is being too rashly substituted – or coercively affirmed – in the name of integration, substituting the uneasy and fractious coexistence of differences, particularly those differences associated with religious communities.

Engaging with incommensurable identities in an age of terror, Gayatri Spivak emphasizes the crucial importance of being 'trained into imagining the other', which she identifies as 'a necessary, impossible and interminable task'.[5] Without a submission to this task, Spivak makes the sober prediction that 'nothing we do through politico-legal calculations will last'.[6] It is not sufficient, in this context, to 'know' the other through a form of anthropological information retrieval, or by upholding an essentialized knowledge of one's own culture; one has to be 'trained' to *imagine* the other (and, implicitly, oneself). Clearly, this is a different agenda from what Gandhi has in mind; for him, the categories of 'Muslim' and 'Hindu' are perhaps too readily 'known' for any particular 'training' to be required.

Spivak troubles this 'knowing' by engaging with the Gandhi story mentioned above, in which he recommends that a Hindu father should adopt a Muslim orphan. However, instead of deconstructing the religious moorings of Gandhi's assumptions, she turns the binaries of 'Muslim' and 'Hindu' on to herself:

> What is offered as the identity of the subject must be accessed in the imagination when every impulse is to repudiate it. It is no use saying, with the reverse fundamentalists, true Hinduism is not like this; or to exclaim, with the secularists, I am a secularist, I do not vote with these people. The toughest task is to *imagine myself a Hindu*, when everything in me resists, to understand what in us can respond so bestially . . .[7]

Spivak goes on to make the more difficult point that the only way to counter the imposition of 'rules that will break' is to arrive at a 'sustained and uncoercive rearrangement of desires with moves learned from the offending culture'.[8] While she sees this pedagogy of an 'uncoercive rearrangement of desires' being 'prepared' in the domain of her own academic discipline in the humanities – it might be somewhat too utopian to imagine how this kind of training could counter the more coercive training of suicide bombers and other assailants – what is pertinent to the discussion here is her emphasis that this pedagogy will need to be learned in collaboration with 'moves learned from the offending culture'. While she does not spell out the exact nature of these 'moves', it is significant that any attempt to break the Hindu–Muslim divide conclusively has to work through such a mutually embedded pedagogical process of 'imagining the other'.

## PERFORMING THE TRUTH COMMISSION: GANDHI IN ACTION

Returning to the motif of Gandhi as a one-man truth commission, one needs to ask: how did it function? Or, more precisely: how did *he* function? Gandhi, it could be argued, facilitated the commission with the performative weight of his statements, accompanied by strategies, threats, warnings and solutions. Invariably, he took it on himself to *stop* communal violence through a personal act of penance and extreme self-discipline, which was often centred around a fast unto death. Underlying this fast was a clearly articulated decision and ultimatum: *I will not break this fast until all violence has ended.* Or, in another slight variant: *This fast will not end until Hindus and Muslims live together like brothers and sisters.* There is a performative assertion in such statements in so far as their utterance more often than not *produced* the desired result. The violence would end, and only then would Gandhi be persuaded to break the fast.

At one level much can be made of the fact that the ritual practice of fasting was socially imbibed by Gandhi, particularly from his close observation of his mother's regular fasts in a predominantly Vaishnavite religious context. At a later stage he actively encouraged the ethics of fasting among the inmates of Tolstoy Farm. But, in order to highlight the phenomenon of *fast as performance*, one needs to move beyond the fast as a habit and everyday life practice, and situate it in a more public context wherein a specific political objective is clearly annexed, mobilized and played out *in the eyes of the world* for as long as the fast lasts. The fast as performance has to be assessed as a political phenomenon, and not just as a personal and spiritual discipline.

Needless to say, in the absence of Gandhi in our world today, such Gandhian solutions for truth and reconciliation processes in India or elsewhere cannot be readily recommended. Indeed, one could justifiably reject the messianic quality of Gandhi's interventions, which would seem to override the role of social, political and cultural *institutions* in facilitating any process of change from 'barbarism' to 'reconciliation'.[9] One could further argue that there is something unreal and even 'magical' in the fact that a single individual can stop genocide. In less 'magical' circumstances, as, for instance, during the bloodbath of the partition, where Gandhi was not around to stop the violence – indeed, he is often blamed by his critics for contributing to the partition – it could be argued that a *collective* expression of grievance and responsibility is necessary before forgiveness and reconciliation can materialize.[10] Only then is there a possibility of implementing peace in a context where one-man truth commissions do not suffice.

Despite this disclaimer on the limitations of truth commissions, one should acknowledge that the actual performance of Gandhi's fasts did succeed on many occasions in bringing peace to warring communities. This was made possible not just by his charismatic presence, but rather through a larger context and structure of emotions by which his fast and its implications became tangible and palpable to millions of people. There is an *intelligibility* in Gandhi's performance of the fast, regardless of the controversies surrounding its politics and occasional blackmailing tactics. If Gandhi's 'fast unto death' resonated at a mass level, it cannot be separated from the fact that fasting as a religio-cultural practice has multiple resonances and associations with penance and sacrifice; it is sanctioned by a plethora of religious and social norms, although, arguably, it carries a specific resonance within the *habitus* of an upper-caste Hindu way of being.

In understanding Gandhi's performance of the fast, therefore, it is necessary not to overly personalize its interpretation even as it is anchored in his own singular presence; rather, we need to link Gandhi's fasts to the dominant *affect* of a larger religio-cultural context, which was predominantly Hindu in practice and spirit despite Gandhi's ceaseless affirmation of a 'religion under-

Gandhi's Salt March (Photographs: courtesy, Sabarmati Ashram)

lying all religions'.[11] It is this understanding of 'religion' to which the practice of his politics is inextricably linked, functioning alongside his contradictory assertion that 'religion' is a 'personal affair' and 'the State has nothing to do with it'.[12] He had also argued in specific contexts that the government does not 'belong to any particular religion', nor should it be held responsible for 'religious education'.[13] Against this apparently robust assertion of a 'secular' politics, Gandhi emphasizes with equal fervour that there can be 'no politics without religion',[14] a statement which, in my reading of Gandhi, carries more resonance, even as his understanding of 'religion' in the widest spectrum of its contradictions is highly personalized, if not idiosyncratic. Arguably, Gandhi pushed the norms of upper-caste Hinduism while remaining doggedly loyal to the framework of *varnashrama dharma*, the fundamental tenets and duties legitimizing the four *varnas* (literally, 'colour', referring to the four basic social divisions of ancient Indian society). To deny or to evade the contradictions of religion in Gandhi's politics is to undermine the complexity of his performative practice.

### THE PERFORMATIVITY OF SALT

Let me focus now on how Gandhi's politics gets activated with specific reference to the events surrounding the famous Dandi March or Salt March. Through the widespread performance of this march in the Indian public sphere, he succeeded in attacking the economic hegemony of colonial rule

by specifically targeting the Salt Tax, the most onerous of taxes imposed on the poorest of the poor. For Gandhi, salt was one of the basic necessities of life along with air and water. As is well known, Gandhi's denunciation of the Salt Tax was achieved by literally picking up a fistful of salt from the banks of the River Dandi in Gujarat on 6 April 1930, following a twenty-three-day, 240-kilometre march, which had begun on 12 March 1930. In that gesture of picking up – and, in the process, making – salt, Gandhi affirmed the fundamental Indian right not only to produce salt, but to use it, buy it, sell it and claim it as an indigenous resource, all these fundamental rights contributing towards the affirmation of *swaraj* or 'self-rule'.

In this scenario, the performative gesture is what stands out, claiming the attention of the world: *with this fistful of sand, I repeal the Salt Tax*. Even without an image, the sheer force of the gesture at a discursive level cannot be separated from its political and economic significance. However, I would emphasize that Gandhi's performativity cannot be restricted to the gesture alone – indeed, one could argue that the gesture was over even before it could be fully made. In a phenomenological sense, it can be said to evoke bathos rather than a rousing, climactic, histrionic effect; its affect is humbling rather than stirring. Far removed from the activist performances of our times, with wannabe 'Gandhis' pathetically mimicking his archetypal gestures on prime-time TV, the performativity of this most unobtrusive of gestures needs to be aligned less to Gandhi's personality than to those political circumstances that made it possible in the first place. This is what tends to be forgotten in almost any encapsulation of Gandhi's politics: the enormously hard work, labour, strategy, networking and backstage *organization* that went into the performance of his gestures.

Before he could lift the salt from the banks of the Dandi, thereby unleashing a multitude of similar gestures across the country – 'Law-breaker' is how Gandhi's colleague Sarojini Naidu had hailed his gesture[15] – the Dandi March had been prepared for months. Drawing on Rajmohan Gandhi's (2006) biography of the Mahatma, in which facts are sifted rigorously without succumbing to the traps of hagiography, we learn that the idea of the Salt March was first envisioned by Gandhi, who gradually shared its radical possibilities with a few of his colleagues. As discussions around the politics of salt became more concrete, the march began to take concrete shape as its route was meticulously mapped across a network of diverse constituencies of Gandhi's supporters. Keeping in mind that the process of learning through activism was as important as the larger objective of any campaign, Gandhi prioritized the possibilities of grassroots research by a special team whose task was to collect information on the economy, caste and class configurations of the villages visited during the course of the march. More emphatically, the preparation for the march came with an entire set of ethical codes expected of those participating in it – codes of conduct relating to sexual abstinence, rejection of greed, embrace of frugality and gratitude to villagers for their hospitality. More strikingly, these protocols of behaviour were supplemented by rules of non-violence towards the British in the eventuality of arrest and intimidation – rules that were internalized and rigidly enforced by the relatively small group of 78 *satyagrahis* who had committed themselves to performing the abolition of the Salt Tax.

All these preparations, I would argue, in their individual and cumulative impact, made Gandhi's gesture of making salt on the banks of the Dandi politically resonant. Its performativity, therefore, does not lie in the discreteness of the gesture, or in its literality or understated corporeality, or even in its symbolic power; rather it is its embeddedness in a much larger *movement* of non-violent political resistance that contributes towards the overall performance of the event. If there is an image that represents this event, it is not the fistful of salt held by Gandhi but his energetic *walk*, the stride and momentum with which he led his fellow-activists towards Dandi.

Following the Dandi March and Gandhi's arrest, the *satyagraha* movement gravitated in the direction of the Dharasana Salt Works, where salt heaps were guarded in barbed-wire enclosures by twenty-six rifle-holding soldiers and about 400 policemen.[16] As they attempted to break the barricades, Gandhi's followers were beaten mercilessly. With dignity and fortitude they received the blows inflicted on them, offering no resistance. This moment is perhaps best captured in the words of the American journalist Webb Miller of the United Press, whose report did much to disseminate the atrocity to the world at large:

> Not one of the marchers raised an arm to fend off the blows. They went down like nine-pins. From where I stood I heard the sickening whacks of the clubs on unprotected skulls . . . Then another column formed . . . They marched steadily with heads up . . . The police rushed out and methodically and mechanically beat down the second column . . . The blankets used as stretchers were sodden with blood . . . Finally the police became enraged by the non-resistance . . . They commenced savagely kicking the seated men in the abdomen and testicles.[17]

Clearly, we are being made to witness here the brutality of how violence is performed in a scenario that almost seems staged: the *satyagrahis* marching forwards, row by row, with their heads up, the police smashing their skulls and kicking their testicles. The violence in this *mise-en-scène* of collective resistance is only too evident, overwhelming the more crucial question: How is non-violence performed? Not through action, but inaction. Not through blows, but passive reflexes: a resolute non-resistance to the violence inflicted on the body.

## NON-VIOLENCE: SACRIFICE OR SUICIDE?

Non-violence provides the central trope for the intervention of this chapter, which draws its inspiration beyond Gandhi from one of the many sane reflections made by Susan Buck-Morss in her *Thinking Past Terror* (2003), where she makes the important point: 'Terrorism will disappear because non-violent ways of communication and debate are possible'.[18] This seemingly simple, perhaps overly hopeful statement raises some critical questions: How do we imagine violence 'disappearing' in an age of terror through the resurgence of non-violence? How do we practise non-violence in everyday life? And, at what point does this practice assume a performative register and immediacy of effect?

Working against the grain of an implicit 'good' embedded in the act of non-violence, one could argue that non-violence in the age of terror is another form of suicide. Faisal Devji, for instance, has provocatively attempted to link the sacrificial instinct underlying Gandhi's non-violence with that of the Al-Qaeda suicide bombers. There are a number of complex concepts at work here in this disturbing conflation – sacrifice, suicide and martyrdom – which figure prominently in Devji's analysis, but at the expense of any serious engagement with the religious content of non-violence (*ahimsa*), which cannot be separated from the multiple dynamics of *satya* (truth) and *daya* (compassion).[19] While acknowledging that his linkage between Gandhi and the Al-Qaeda – and even, more provocatively, Gandhi and Osama bin Laden – is 'grotesque',[20] given the antithetical nature of their personalities and politics, Devji nonetheless pursues the analogy in his attempt to come up with a new hermeneutic framework for understanding terrorism outside the dominant narratives determined by Euro–American security specialists and think-tanks.

Against an over-hyped backdrop of changing perceptions of war in an age of globalization, seething with all kinds of mobility, transfers of media and capital, and cultural idiosyncrasies like 'jihad tourism', Devji draws his rationale for Gandhi's sacrificial instinct from the philosopher Karl Jaspers. Setting up Gandhi somewhat too unequivocally as 'the chief and indeed only global example of modernity's sacrificial logic',[21] Devji highlights the global implications of Gandhi's 'sacrificial logic' in the context of the 'suprapolitical', a crucial term adopted by Jaspers in terms of 'its purposeful withdrawal from institutional politics and so in a sense from political rationality itself'.[22] To the 'suprapolitical' Devji adds his own inscription of the 'subpolitical',[23] in so far as Gandhi's sacrificial actions did not transcend everyday life, but were embedded in the ordinary and the everyday. Tellingly, Devji fails to read the dimensions of the ordinary and the everyday in the actual practice of Gandhi's politics, surrendering instead to an overly valorized reading of global politics in which his interpretation of Gandhi's sacrifice is ultimately located. To supplement and complicate this interpretation, it becomes necessary to juxtapose more local and nuanced readings of Gandhi's concept of sacrifice, which cannot be separated from its religious – and, more specifically, Hindu – implications.

I turn to Tridip Suhrud, one of India's leading scholars of Gandhi, who has emphasized that sacrifice (*yajna*) is most precisely read within Gandhi's ceaseless quest for 'self-purification'.[24] Troubled by the impurities of the embodied self even as he was ruefully aware that one cannot exist without the body, Gandhi embarked on a notion of 'training the body' so that it could become the appropriate 'source' of sacrifice. Arguably, the practice of 'training the body' is startlingly performative, as demonstrated in that turbulent moment following the 1946 Calcutta killings when Gandhi began to operate as a one-man truth commission. By this time, in the very thick of the worst communal violence, he prepared himself to 'cleanse' the body through sacrifice. While negotiating the most sensitive political differences across warring parties and communities, he doggedly renewed his commitment to his ongoing 'life-experiment', which involved nothing less than a form of spiritualized celibacy, or *brahmacharya* (literally, *charya* or 'conduct', that leads one to *brahma* or 'truth').[25] It was through such experiments on the body, beginning with the disciplining of his sexuality but moving towards a 'control of all the senses', that he believed that the violence surrounding him could be removed. Preposterous at one level to his critics, both in his own time and ours, this 'sacrifice' is what made sense to Gandhi in his ceaseless engagement with violence and increasingly fervent attempt to assume spiritual responsibility for the actions of others.

In a less corporeal register, Suhrud interprets Gandhi's concept of sacrifice as 'an offering of the Self as the oblation in the *yajna* [sacrifice]'.[26] This surrender or dissolution of the Self into the Reality of sacrifice is what gave Gandhi the strength to hear his 'inner voice' and to arrive at 'self-knowledge', which are antithetical principles to the act of physically killing one's self through the act of suicide and martyrdom. Contradicting the conflation made in Devji's reading between terror and martyrdom, mediated by the sacrificial figure of the *shahid* (martyr), which in turn is summarily equated with the phenomenon of Al-Qaeda suicide bombers, Gandhi's idea of sacrifice functions with a radically different ethos: the closer the proximity to destruction and killing the other, the greater the distance from the Self and the Truth of one's sacrificial action.

Perhaps it is best to turn to Gandhi himself to highlight the complexities of the symbiotic relationship between *ahimsa* (non-violence) and *satya* (truth):

> This much everybody should know: without *ahimsa* the search for *satya* is

> impossible. *Ahimsa* and *satya* are as inseparable as two sides of a coin . . . Who can say which is the obverse and which the reverse? Nevertheless, *ahimsa* may be considered the means and *satya* may be considered the end. The means is what is within our reach, and this is why *ahimsa* is the supreme *dharma* [*paramdharma*, 'supreme duty']. *Satya* becomes God. If we keep attending to the means, we will someday behold *satya*.[27]

Complicating the logic of means and ends, Ajay Skaria cautions that even while '*ahimsa* is a means to realize *satya*, it is not a means in the sense of being an instrument that leads to *satya*; rather, *ahimsa* is itself the being of *satya*'.[28] More critically, Skaria points out that even as *satya* and *ahimsa* are almost 'indistinguishable', the paradox is that 'they are not the same – *satya* and *ahimsa* remain constantly outside each other, each oriented to and necessitating the other without passing over into the other'.[29] Referring to the closing lines of Gandhi in the passage quoted above, where the possibility of 'beholding' *satya* evokes the act of *darshan*, Skaria argues provocatively that 'devotion does not and indeed must not overcome the gap between the devotee and *satya*. Rather, the devotee must practise *ahimsa* in order to properly sustain the gap; devotion will provincialize its own truth.'[30]

While this explanation may sound somewhat abstruse, there is a complexity in Skaria's deconstructionist approach towards reading *ahimsa*, which is drawn partially from one of Gandhi's deep influences in the '*neti neti*' (not this, not that) construction of Advaita philosophy. It is precisely because *ahimsa* involves a 'notness of being', as Skaria argues, that Gandhi is compelled to think of it as 'self-sacrifice'. In a more robust explanation provided in 'Doctrine of the Sword', Gandhi offers yet another perspective on sacrifice by emphatically rejecting the use of arms to kill, invoking instead the 'power of the soul' that reveals an inner strength. 'He is the true warrior', as Gandhi emphasizes, 'who does not die killing but who has mastered the *mantra* of living by dying.'[31] Apart from the sages of the past who actually embodied and put into practice the non-violence of 'living by dying', Gandhi associates the 'true warrior', in a totally unexpected analogy, with Socrates from Plato's *Apology*, which he had rendered into Gujarati in 1908 under the title *Ek Satyavirni Katha* (Story of a Warrior for Truth). What made Socrates a *satyagrahi* in Gandhi's eyes was his absolute fearlessness of death. Along with this absence of fear, a true warrior for Gandhi is one who does not surrender his life for a 'larger or transcendent cause'; rather, at a paradoxical level, the giving up of his life needs to be seen as a 'gift' to the one he battles against. This 'worthy opponent' is perceived not so much as an enemy who is unequivocally othered or demonized, but one who provides an 'immeasurable equality', in Skaria's formulation, to the 'truth' of the warrior himself.

Needless to say, in this enormous respect for one's 'worthy opponent' – the legal resonance of this category can scarcely be overlooked – we are dealing with a different kind of 'true warrior' from the 'holy warrior' discourse to which Faisal Devji links Gandhi's sacrificial logic in a predominantly liberal and global discursive context. It follows that any rash equation between Gandhi's concept of sacrifice and a militant-Islamist reading of *jihad* is totally off the mark. Even as one may acknowledge Devji's strategic discourse in linking Gandhi to 'the modernization and the globalization of South Asian Islam', without which, as he emphasizes, 'the Al-Qaeda could never have been founded in the region',[32] the logic is warped: surely, the 'suprapolitical deployment of sacrifice' that Devji reads in Al-Qaeda's militants is hardly a Gandhian legacy, with or without Gandhi's alleged contribution to the Al-Qaeda's global modern status. This logic simply fails to confront the obvious point that the Al-Qaeda idea of 'sacrifice' has been built on the basis of its own distortion and fabrication of Islam, intensified by hatred of 'the enemy'. *In the name of Islam*, then, rather than through any sustained devotion to its religious tenets, suicide-bombing as practised by the Al-Qaeda is best contextualized within its own pathology and self-inflated notion of martyrdom, rather than linked to Gandhi and his faith in non-violence.

Perhaps, the methodological problem with Devji's reading of terror could lie in its forced interpretations. Just as he overreads the rhetoric of humanism and humanitarianism in the global missives of Osama bin Laden, failing to unearth the subversive ghost-writing of these proclamations,[33] he mistakes Gandhi's exhortations of collective dying for actual performatives resulting in action. Therefore, in his attempt to suggest that Gandhi, like bin Laden, used the word *shahadat* for martyrdom 'very regularly', and 'as frequently expressed the desire that a million innocent lives be willingly surrendered to achieve India's freedom',[34] one would have to emphasize that this is a far too literal and reductive reading of Gandhi's apparent thirst for collective martyrdom. Moreover, while Devji is correct in associating *shahadat* with the act of 'witnessing', he overstretches the point by emphasizing that it

> involves not only the person whose life is voluntarily sacrificed for the cause of God, but everyone annihilated in this cause whether willingly or not. Not only people, but animals, buildings, and other inanimate objects as well may participate in the rites of martyrdom, including even those who witness the martyrdom of others without themselves being killed.[35]

This martyrdom by proxy and multiple witnesses, including non-human ones, is less a theological truth than a hermeneutic strategy by which Devji stretches his idea of martyrdom to encompass a global canvas of witnessing through acts of 'seeing' made available by the media and news reportage.

Through these collective modes of seeing, at once virtual and dispersed, the 'landscape of the jihad', according to Devji, becomes a 'site of sociability'.[36] Not only are such shifts in Devji's hermeneutics somewhat too quick, as martyrdom melds into sociability via the global media, but the veracity of his theological references for martyrdom becomes even more suspect in the absence of any critical engagement with relevant passages from the Quran or Hadith literature. Surely, it is not enough to 'see' to become a martyr, either within an actual site of suicide bombing or through its transference in the media. The norms of spectatorship, I would argue, cannot be so easily conflated with modes of collective witnessing, which have their own psychophysical and political dynamics and compulsions. To what extent and in which circumstances can spectators become witnesses? And can this transformation of roles be so readily assumed on a 'collective' basis? In a more explicit theological context, the Indian Islamic scholar and social reformer Asghar Ali Engineer has emphasized that *shahadat* involves a voluntary, embodied and conscious act of commitment; it cannot be vicariously assumed on the basis of an accidental witnessing of a person who voluntarily sacrifices his or her life for God.[37]

Building on his rash equations between terror and non-violence, Devji invokes the pivotal passage from Gandhi's *Hind Swaraj* (1909) where, in the form of a strategic dialogue between the Editor and the Reader, there is an explicit exchange on the subject of terror. Upholding the need for armed struggle to gain freedom, the Reader says:

> At first, we will assassinate a few Englishmen and strike terror; then, a few men who will have been armed will fight openly. We may have to lose a quarter of a million men, more or less, but we will regain our land. We will undertake guerrilla warfare, and defeat the English.[38]

To this anarchist affirmation, Gandhi in his surrogate role as Editor says:

> That is to say, you want to make the holy land of India unholy. Do you not tremble to think of freeing India by assassination? What we need to do is to kill ourselves. It is a cowardly thought, that of killing others.[39]

The point to be made is that even if Gandhi urged his followers to subject themselves to death, this admittedly explosive statement is best read against the 'cowardly thought' of 'killing others' rather than as an unequivocal advocacy of collective suicide. Once again, Devji is somewhat too literal in affirming that '[t]owards the end of his life Gandhi longed for as many such Hindu and Muslim deaths as possible, so that these rival communities might cement their unity in blood.'[40] Without undermining the volatility of such rhetoric, it is necessary to reiterate that the prospect of killing 'ourselves', for Gandhi, could never be used to justify the act of 'killing others'. Unlike the Al-Qaeda, Gandhi could never have justified the deaths of others for any particular cause, however transcendent and absolute: this would have been morally unacceptable to him.

Contrary, therefore, to the ethos of the Al-Qaeda militants, notably Khalid Sheikh Mohammed who categorically asserts, 'You have to kill', not least because this is the only way of answering the United States in their own 'language',[41] Gandhi would reject this imperative. Nor would he accept that only a 'balance of terror'[42] on Osama bin Laden's terms ('just as they are killing us, we have to kill them') could result in a restoration of humanity. This 'balance of terror' would be as unacceptable to him as the logic of nuclear deterrence (which Gandhi had totally rejected in response to Hiroshima), seeing through the bogus logic of warmongers affirming 'peace' in an allegedly equal contestation of nuclear power. Such 'balance' for Gandhi was another way of continuing the logic of destruction.

Only non-violence could suggest a way out of the impasse of warring factions through its own paradoxical logic: *ready to die, but not prepared to kill.* If Agamben's *homo sacer* can be defined as one 'who can be killed and not sacrificed',[43] and the martyr in Islamic global militancy can be described as one 'who can be sacrificed but not killed',[44] Gandhi's *satyagrahi* can be upheld as 'one who is prepared to die but not kill'. The distinctions are crucial and need to be kept in mind before any rash analogy between Gandhi and militancy (of any denomination or constituency) can be upheld as a new paradigm for the political imaginary of terror in our times.

## SUICIDE-BOMBING: ACTS OF PERFORMANCE

Let us now use this discussion on 'sacrifice' to focus briefly on the most lurid and yet familiar figure in the discourse of terror – the suicide bomber – whose actions have far extended the political premises of an earlier history of assassinations. Gandhi was familiar with the phenomenon of assassinations: in *Hind Swaraj*, he had condemned the assassination of Sir William Curzon-Wyllie by Madanlal Dhingra at the Imperial Institute in South Kensington, London, shortly before *Hind Swaraj* was published in 1909. In response to the 'morality' of such assassinations, this is how Gandhi categorically summed it up: 'Those who believe that India has gained by Dhingra's act, and other such acts in India, make a serious mistake. Dhingra was a patriot, but his love was blind. He gave his body in a wrong way [*kumarga*, 'wrong or evil path']; its ultimate result can only be mischievous.'[45]

Not only is it 'mischievous', Dhingra's act needed to be condemned on other grounds as well, which Gandhi had categorically spelt out in the *Indian Opinion* shortly after the assassination.[46] In his view, Dhingra had violated the basic codes of hospitality and equality by killing his opponent within his own home territory. In addition, by refusing to regard his opponent as an equal, Dhingra had merely succumbed to a state of intoxication (*nasha*), instead of pondering his act through a process of suffering and reflection. Clearly, in these unorthodox objections to the patriotic defence of 'killing the enemy', Gandhi was rejecting the late nineteenth-century phenomenon of 'propaganda by the deed', whereby specific individuals from upper classes or government authorities were duly targeted and killed after activists had calculated the risks of the assassination and its possible gains for the movement at large.

Rejecting the moral legitimacy of assassinations, Gandhi is not likely to have endorsed the more recent and arbitrary phenomenon of suicide-bombing, which is inextricably linked to the random killing of innocent people in terrorist attacks. For a phenomenon that appears to be at once ubiquitous and omnipresent, reinforced through incessant television reportage and 'live' replays of action in several electronic media, it is telling to learn from a comprehensive database covering 'every suicide bombing and attack around the globe from 1980 to 2011', that they number 188 in all.[47] This exceptionally modest figure in relation to the enormous attention suicide-bombing has received in the discourse of terrorism is subjected to sceptical and rigorous theoretical reflection by Talal Asad (2007), one of the most mature voices on the moral and ethical vacuity in the discourse of terrorism, particularly its interpretation and condemnation by Euro–American liberal thinkers.

Asad is compelled to ask: What is it that makes suicide-bombing so specifically and viscerally horrifying to Western sensibilities? Acts of war result in far larger numbers of deaths, often disguised by the pernicious logic of 'collateral damage'. War also legitimizes torture and dehumanization in all kinds of devious ways, and yet it is suicide-bombing that elicits the sharpest condemnation not only of violence, but also of some kind of *evil* as Asad emphasizes, more often than not marked as 'Muslim' or 'Islamic'. In reality, the relationship between suicide-bombing and religion is at best tenuous, if non-existent: the database mentioned above specifies that of the 188 suicide bombings recorded, 75 were committed by the LTTE in Sri Lanka, a predominantly secular organization, prompting the question whether there is anything specifically 'Islamic' or, for that matter, 'religious' about suicide-bombing.[48]

If war, as Asad theorizes the problem succinctly, is not, in principle, 'immoral', even though there can be unjust wars (as even the most vehement theorist of 'just war' theory, Michael Walzer, is compelled to admit), terrorism, in its most virulent and seemingly irrational manifestation of suicide-bombing, is 'always, and in principle, evil'.[49] Why is this the case? In an authoritative reading of several interpretations of 'terrorism' (of which I will focus only on one interpretation followed by a critical reading of Walzer's 'just war' theory), Asad refuses to be overawed by the unspeakable 'horror' of terrorism's inherent 'evil'. Instead, he sifts through the words of how this 'evil' is constructed by diverse critics, the most perceptive of whom are capable of reading the phenomenon with a sense of the macabre without succumbing to quick moral judgments. Such is the perceptive formulation provided by Jacqueline Rose, who clearly situates her response within the affect of terrorism:

> The horror [of suicide-bombing] would appear to be associated with the fact that the attacker also dies . . . Why dying with your victim should be seen as a greater sin than saving yourself is unclear. Perhaps, then, the revulsion stems partly from the unbearable intimacy shared in their final moments by the suicide bomber and her or his victims. Suicide bombing is an act of passionate identification – you can take the enemy with you in a deadly embrace.[50]

In a differently inflected, yet similar register, Gayatri Spivak identifies not the 'erotics' of the final 'embrace' but the 'autoeroticism' of suicide-bombing, in so far as 'the destruction of others' is 'indistinguishable' from 'the destruction of the self'.[51] The 'others' in this extreme act of self-annihilation also include one's own 'self', which is seen as an 'object, capable of destruction, in a world of objects'.[52]

For Asad, Rose's focus on 'the reaction of horror' (as revealed in the fact that the 'attacker also dies') melds far too swiftly into a larger 'puzzlement' about 'the perpetrator's moral status'.[53] In a more pragmatic register, one could question whether the fact that the suicide bomber *dies* registers at all for the viewers of his or her action. Is it not more likely that the bomber becomes expendable, after precipitating a lot of damage in the process of his or her self-detonation? This position would link neatly with Achille Mbembe's reading that '[t]he body [of a suicide bomber] does not simply conceal a weapon. The body is transformed into a weapon, not in a metaphorical sense but in the truly ballistic sense.'[54] In this 'necropolitics', where 'resistance and self-destruction are synonymous', the target is not so much other 'persons' but *bodies*, in all their multiplicity, corporeality and presentness. Death in the act of suicide-bombing jettisons the dignified constructions of the 'self' and 'the other' into a scattering of 'pieces of inert flesh', which need to be 'assembled with difficulty before the burial'.[55]

This loathsome detail compels one to emphasize that if there is something specifically 'horrifying' about suicide-bombing, it is not so much its action or effect or purpose, but its visceral *affect*, as one attempts to assimilate the image of human beings reduced to spare parts and shreds of flesh – not just in distant battlefields, but within the everyday familiarity of a bus stop or shopping mall. Today, we live in a world where the hypothetical construct of 'the body without organs' posited by Antonin Artaud has been replaced by the more chilling ubiquity of 'organs without bodies' – fragments of erstwhile life reduced to body parts.[56] Even as one confronts such grotesque details of dismemberment in the banalities of the here and now, one realizes how the eschatologies of horror in our times can be replicated by a new technologization and mediatization of the body which make available its destruction for ceaseless prime-time viewing. In the process of this replication and endless seriality of flesh transformed into image, the horror could lie in the fact that we cease to be shocked by what flashes on our television screens. The residues of suicide-bombing become part of the routine horror of our daily visual culture.

Far too much has been written and staged about suicide-bombing for me to attempt a comprehensive summary of its diverse representations. Suffice it for me to elaborate on one particular condition which is pertinent to the context of this book: the death of the suicide bomber is often prefigured by a 'performance' in which a testimony is made in front of the camera before the bomber has committed the act and killed herself/himself. This pre-recorded testimonial is a calculated premonition of the future, which is played back shortly after the event takes place, more often than not on the television evening news of 'that very day' on which the bombing takes place. In this collision of times, we realize the complex temporality of any suicide-bombing, as it operates almost simultaneously in the past, present and future. Without the playback of what has already been recorded and authenticated by the suicide bomber, the event is not fully commemorated and the martyrdom of the bomber remains suspect or incomplete.

This contextualization of suicide-bombing, however, is culturally grounded in so far as it applies to, say, the phenomenon in Lebanon, but not to the context in Sri Lanka, where the practice of providing suicidal testimonials on camera does not exist as part of the country's relentless ritual of suicide-bombings during the ethnic conflict. In Lebanon, however, the performance artist Rabih Mroué recalls watching testimonials of suicide bombers on television with such frequency that it assumed the quality of a genre, a kind of 'performance art' in its own right, perhaps the first of its kind in Lebanon. Later, this experience of 'witnessing' testimonials of suicide bombers provided the stimulus for Mroué's outstandingly reflexive performance piece entitled *Three Posters* (2006), co-authored with writer Elias Khoury.

Briefly, this performance was sparked by the discovery of unprecedented evidence: the 'uncut rushes' of a suicide bomber's video-tape, a 'found object' lying in the office of the Lebanese Communist Party fourteen years after the bomber's death in 1985.[57] In these rushes, the suicide bomber (Jamal Sati) repeats his testimonial three times with minimal differences, his reiteration of the same text voiced with an uncanny matter-of-factness before he *decides* on 'the best version to be presented to the public'.[58] Drawing on this repetitive structure, Mroué builds the dramaturgical structure of *Three Posters* by juxtaposing the suicide bomber's video in all three takes with his own performative renditions and variations of the same text. These renditions and variations are played out with minimal, yet significant histrionic differences, with Mroué re-enacting the dead bomber's three-part testimonial on a recorded video in the fictional persona of a Lebanese militant (Khaled Ahmad Rahhal). These three 'takes' by the fictitious Rahhal are juxtaposed, in turn, with Mroué presenting his own autobiographical background as a political activist, which he reads out to the audience. Following this self-inscription, Mroué then presents the video-rushes of the 'real' suicide bomber (Jamal Sati) as a homage to the memory of all martyrs of the Lebanese National Resistance Front. From enacting a fictional Lebanese militant on video followed by his own matter-of-fact self-documentation as a former member of the Lebanese Communist Party, Mroué then becomes a spectator of the original video by Jamal Sati, whose 'performance' had sparked his decision to re-enact it in the first place.

Inevitably, yet chillingly, the meta-commentary facilitated by these multiple performances teases out a number of enigmas – 'what is real' and 'what is staged'; the infinitesimal differences between 'actor' and 'character', 'improvisation' and 'text'. Most intriguing of all the enigmas is the juxtaposition of multiple 'deaths': the suicide bomber's death in real life, his imminent death recorded on camera, and the actor's metaphorical and phenomenological 'death' in the theatre. Dramaturgically, these juxtapositions concretize the infinitesimal *limits* of different kinds of representations as one performance follows another, repeating more or less the same script: a powerful demonstration of different kinds of 'restoration of behavior' in actual performance practice.

While I cannot go into the details of *Three Posters* here, I would like to highlight two salient facts emphasized by Mroué himself: one, the political identity of the 'real' suicide bomber (Jamal Sati), who was not affiliated to the Al-Qaeda or to any other Islamist militant group in a post-September 11 context, but who was a combatant of the National Resistance Front affiliated to the pro-Moscow Lebanese Communist Party in the 1980s. This fact compels Mroué and Khoury to end *Three Posters* somewhat ironically with a recorded interview featuring a contemporary politician from the Lebanese Communist Party, who provides a guarded critique of the role of the Party in relation to the resistance movement – a critique that could be read in the larger context of the failure of the Left. As Mroué puts it bluntly, *Three Posters* makes 'a critical and autocritical assessment of the Left's absence today in the Lebanese political arena – and in a way, declares our defeat.'[59]

The second, even more startling fact that needs to be highlighted about *Three Posters* is that once the production became a 'hit' on the international festival circuit, Mroué and Khoury had the political intelligence and responsibility to stop performing it for post-9/11 audiences who refused (or were unable) to accept the radically different political context of the piece. I respect the fact that *Three Posters* was not allowed to become an alibi for 9/11 fantasies and trauma relating to the figure of the 'Islamic terrorist'. Ironically, Mroué recalls in his incisive post-mortem accounts of the production how audience members would congratulate him for delivering a 'better' performance than his real-life counterpart, Jamal Sati. With such irony, what hope can there be for truth (at least in the Gandhian sense of the word); this irony is closer to Genet in its strategic embrace of the subtle falsehood of theatre in which a provisional truth is found and then disappears, only to reappear in a fabricated state.

Clearly, this is not a territory for which we can turn to Gandhi for direction. It is far too embedded in the performativity of our times, caught within the embodied simulacra of diverse reconstructions of the 'same' performance, which in turn call attention to the shifting *ethics* of representation in a predominantly secular framework of reference. In examining Gandhi's performativity, on the other hand, particularly against the background of war, armed militancy or terrorism, it becomes almost impossible to avoid a discussion of *morality* in a larger religious context. With this premise in mind, let us turn briefly to the 'just war' discourse, enunciated and reiterated by Michael Walzer (2000, 2004) over the years, which is specifically cast within the framework of 'moral argument'. Focusing on the dogmatic assumptions of this far-too-prescriptive and non-reflexive 'morality', I turn once again to Talal Asad who has provided one of the most comprehensive critiques that the 'just war' discourse has received to date. This critique in turn will provide a viable entry-point for incorporating Gandhi later into the discussion.

## 'JUST WAR': AMBIVALENCES AND DUPLICITIES

Far too dignified to exaggerate Walzer's double standards, Asad nonetheless monitors his critique by articulating the obvious political ambivalence of Walzer's position at the level of his understated affiliations to the *realpolitik*. More bluntly, while Walzer in his numerous writings unequivocally upholds the moral legitimacy of the state of Israel, he refuses to grant a similar legitimacy or 'just-ness' to the Palestinian struggle. If Israel attacks Palestine and usurps vast territories on the West Bank and kills civilians, it is 'self-defense' and a necessary 'retaliation' for the protection of its citizens; on the other hand, when Palestine attacks Israel, it is seen as 'terrorism'. The crudity of this position, and the subterranean accusations of anti-Semitism that are often brought against those who question it, are tedious and counterproductive. We cannot think critically and responsibly within the binaries and bigotry of such arguments.

Wisely, Asad works through Walzer's eminently lucid liberal rhetoric, which embodies the quintessence of 'reasonableness'. In the process, he points out Walzer's blind spots and curiously dogmatic positions. While war, for Walzer, can be regarded as a 'legal activity' so long as it fulfils conditions of 'self-defense' or 'a treaty obligation toward a state that is attacked', terrorism is 'not only illegal and therefore morally worse than killing in war; it is worse even than the crime of murder'.[60] The 'peculiar evil' of terrorism, for Walzer, lies not just in 'the killing of innocent people', but in 'the intrusion of fear into everyday life, the violation of private purposes, the insecurity of public spaces, and the endless coerciveness of precaution.'[61] One wonders to what extent any of these aberrations – 'fear', 'violation of private purposes', 'insecurity' and 'coerciveness' – can be minimized in states of war divested of terrorist violence.

Drawing on Walzer's key constructs for the justification of war, like 'emergency ethics' or 'the last resort' – these are euphemisms that have been used for the killing of thousands of civilians, as in the Second World War in Germany when the Allied forces resorted to 'terror bombing' – Asad counters the duplicities of such 'justified' killing. More astutely, he highlights the hypocrisy underlying the qualms of conscience and unrest which appear to torment 'good' warmongers before they commit their unavoidable, last-resort acts of murder. In this regard, Walzer's rhetoric speaks for itself:

> A morally strong leader is someone who understands why it is wrong to kill the innocent and refuses to do so, refuses again and again, until the heavens are about to fall. And then he becomes a moral criminal (like Albert Camus's 'just assassin') who knows that he can't do what he has to do – and finally does.[62]

To this liberal angst, Asad's response is appropriately terse: 'If he [the moral criminal] killed the innocent without a flicker of conscience, he would simply be an immoral criminal.'[63] It is almost as if anguish exonerates the crime.

Inevitably, this juxtaposition of 'moral' and 'immoral' criminals opens up the double standards of liberal thought that underlie the justification of war and other atrocities by well-meaning, liberal democratic governments. Aligning his critique with that of the historian Richard Tuck (1999), Asad emphasizes that:

> Violence is . . . embedded in the very concept of liberty that lies at the heart of liberal doctrine. That concept presupposes – so Tuck maintains – that the morally independent individual's natural right to violent self-defense is yielded to the state and that the state becomes the sole protector of individual liberties.[64]

The complicity between the 'liberal autonomous individual' and the state is further consolidated by the civilizational assumptions underlying the right to kill: 'The right to kill is the right to behave in violent ways toward other people – especially toward citizens of foreign states at war and toward the uncivilized, *whose very existence is a threat to civilized order*.'[65]

This position reaffirms how old colonial perspectives on civilization, on the basis of which entire native populations under colonial rule were demeaned and exploited for a larger civilizational purpose, continue to provide the basic rationales for war. These rationales are perpetuated even as the languages of democracy, justice, social and economic restructuring, and a return to normalcy are used to camouflage the legitimization of violence by an implicit civilizational superiority.

Uncannily, even as Gandhi had a healthy respect for many aspects of liberal thinking, notably the right to free speech, equity and civility – it is one of his many strokes of political genius to see public protest in the context of '*civil* disobedience' – he had no illusions about the violence underlying the 'civilizing' mission of imperialist powers. If the British colonizers met their match in him, it is because he was able to see through the duplicities of their apparently liberal, non-coercive governance, apart from their more blatant demonstrations of economic loot and mass murder as in Jallianwala Bagh and elsewhere. To Gandhi's credit, however, he did not restrict this duplicity of violence to colonial rule; he was able to extend it to other forms of justified violence like assassinations and terrorism. As we have examined earlier in this chapter, Gandhi totally rejected the terrorist path in favour of *swaraj*, or 'self-rule', whose foundations are centred on an alternative civilizational base which has yet to be realized through a ceaseless quest for truth.

If, with Gandhi, we are compelled to open up dimensions of religion, faith and spirituality which lie outside the secular boundaries of the 'just war' discourse as articulated by Michael Walzer, there is a significant complication in the argument if we insert alongside Gandhi the voice of another seer, Sri Aurobindo. His perspective on 'just war', specifically in the struggle against fascism, reveals a different perspective from that of Gandhi. It is worth quoting at length the relevant passage from Sri Aurobindo's vast corpus of writings, which begins with a rhetorical question:

> We will use only soul-force and never destroy by war or any even defensive employment of physical violence? Good, though until soul force is effective, the Asuric force, in men and nations tramples down, breaks, slaughters, burns, pollutes, as we see it doing today . . .[66]

In invoking the 'Asuric force' in his orotund, yet forceful Victorian prose, Sri Aurobindo is referring specifically to the threat posed by fascism during the Second World War, which he believed could result only in the worst form of 'barbarism' if it was allowed to materialize. Against this threat,

> . . . you have perhaps caused as much destruction of life by your abstinence as others by resort to violence; still you have set up an ideal which may someday and at any rate ought to lead up to better things. But even soul force, when it is effective, destroys.[67]

Echoing the familiar logic that we may need to dirty our hands to root out evil, Sri Aurobindo then clinches the argument with some startlingly 'realist' thinking:

> It is not enough that our own hands should remain clean and our souls unstained for the law of strife and destruction to die out of the world; that which is its root must first disappear out of humanity.[68]

I have deliberately inserted these unequivocal words of an erstwhile revolutionary Aurobindo Ghose, whose abandoning of extremist politics during the Swadeshi period in the first decade of the twentieth century and retreat into the most rigorous discipline of 'soul-force' resulted in his transformation as Sri Aurobindo at his ashram in Pondicherry. And yet, as this passage reveals, the lessons of the revolutionary are not so easily forgotten, as Sri Aurobindo questions the 'effectiveness' of soul-force against fascism. It is not that he rejects soul-force as the source of catalysing 'better things', but he is sceptical that it can work against the onslaught of 'barbarism'.

While this position would seem to link Sri Aurobindo to the primacy of the 'just war' theory, the significant difference is his inclusion of 'soul-force' as the primary agency of transformation: a transformation that cannot be restricted to the political domain, but which involves the potential evolutionary consciousness of men and women at intellectual, social, moral and planetary levels. It is this heightened consciousness out of which 'soul-force' can manifest itself in a different state of being that Sri Aurobindo posits against Gandhi's use of 'soul-force', which he criticizes as a 'rigid mental belief'.[69] Somewhat more generously, he acknowledges that for Gandhi, soul-force resembles a 'strong vital will which has taken a religious turn', with the potential for 'a tremendous force for action'.[70] Against this reduction of soul-force to a political principle, and in favour of his own more exacting definition of soul-force as 'another law of being', Sri Aurobindo inserts a sceptical note by doubting the *viability* of this force in countering states of war.

In contrast, Gandhi, I would argue, doggedly believed in the effectiveness of 'soul-force' as a religious and political principle in fighting the most 'Asuric' of calamities. Against the impossibility of its realization, he unfailingly believed that it could be invoked and put into practice, not just by himself, but by all who were capable of submitting to a particular discipline of the body and spirit. In this concrete sense, we are compelled to acknowledge a radical utopianism in Gandhi's embrace of struggle, which counters the realities of doubt and possible failure through a ceaseless ferment of faith and resolution. The seer Sri Aurobindo would appear to be far more circumspect in accounting for the accessibility of soul-force to counter fascist violence.

## TRAINING TO DIE? THE VIABILITY OF NON-VIOLENCE

Returning the discussion to the practice of theatre and performance while drawing on the philosophical registers of the discourse generated around 'just war' and 'suicide-bombing', we need to ask ourselves: What does non-violence mean in the context of theatre and performance practice? What, in particular, does it mean in contexts of war in cities like Ramallah and Jenin in Palestine, where theatres have been regularly targeted, if not destroyed, along with other civic institutions like hospitals and schools? In such battlefields, we are compelled to engage with the horror of actual sites and buildings of theatre being reduced to rubble. How can theatre be sustained in such conditions? And how can theatre activists presume to adopt a Gandhian path of non-violence when they could be under attack for the innocent reason of performing a play for their embattled communities?

Faced with these questions, I am compelled to return to some key references in my introduction, where I had teased out the censoring devices of *protecting* the civility of theatre through the security devices of apparently impregnable playhouses. The fact that theatres can be subject to aerial bombing totally destroys the illusions of any particular sanctification of theatre practice. Indeed, the recent phenomenon of drone attacks almost makes the entire apparatus of protecting buildings at ground levels redundant. Despite an investment in its own cultural and artistic capital, the Israeli state has not stopped its armed forces from targeting civil and social institutions, including theatres, in Palestine, whose destruction is grudgingly acknowledged as constituting the 'collateral damage' of war in the inevitable defence of its own citizens. In Palestine today – and let us not forget Iraq and Afghanistan (of whose performance cultures we know much less) – theatres would seem to be almost expendable, their annihilation or erasure not even worth an outcry in the global media.

Against this bleak reality, one could present a different argument by focusing critically on the exceptionalism of theatre in states of war. What makes theatre so special that it should be spared the bombardment of the enemy? If hospitals and schools can be razed to the ground, why should theatres be an exception to the rule of rampant destruction? Without playing into the meritocracy of theatre over the basic needs provided by education and health, one could argue that civilian activity in *any* social or cultural institution should be declared out of bounds for enemy attack. And yet, this basic protocol has been repeatedly abused in Palestine, making a mockery of Jean Genet's somewhat too precious assertion that theatre is best performed once within the confines of a cemetery.[71] This assertion, I would argue, could be made at a time when theatres and cemeteries were distinct sites, but today, when theatres are in the process of becoming cemeteries, one is compelled to reject Genet's iconoclastic option. No longer can we take refuge in the metaphor of the 'cemetery' as the ideal site for the death-in-life of theatre; today, the actual linkage of death to the practice of theatre has become terrifyingly real.

The most moving tribute to the endurance of theatre lies in the fact that performances continue to take place in the most extreme and dangerous circumstances, as, for instance, in the refugee camps of Palestine. In the eye of terror, theatre persists in extraordinarily rough and vulnerable conditions, through workshops, improvisations and productions. This practice compels one to ask not just what is produced 'in place of war',[72] as an anthology on performance in the state of war documents in meticulous detail, but also to probe how actors are trained in such circumstances and what they are trained for. What are the moral and ethical implications of doing theatre in conditions where one runs the risk of being killed?

With this question in mind, let us focus briefly on the Freedom Theatre based in Jenin, Palestine, which was built out of the rubble of the Care and Learning Project, set up in 1989 during the first Intifada by the intrepid Arna Mer, an Israeli Jew and Communist Party member. When the theatre building was destroyed during the second Intifada in 2002, Arna's son, Juliano Mer Khamis, of mixed Palestinian–Israeli and Jewish–Arab parentage, returned to Jenin and tried to trace the children who had been part of the Care and Learning Project. Many of them had since died in the freedom struggle, and it was out of the memories of the survivors, and the continuing siege and daily terror in Palestine, that Mer Khamis created his memorable film *Arna's Children* (2003), which could be described as a performative requiem for the dead. In 2006, Mer Khamis was inspired to form the Freedom Theatre, which has grown in international recognition following his tragic and senseless killing on 4 April 2011 by a Palestinian fundamentalist and former Al-Aqsa Brigades militant.

In his critically empathetic account of these facts, Indian street theatre activist Sudhanva Deshpande (2011) correctly places the death of Juliano Mer Khamis in a larger archive of 'living martyrs' in the theatre, including the Indian communist theatre-activist Safdar Hashmi. As is well known in Left theatre circles, Hashmi's brutal killing on 1 January 1989 during the performance of a street play, *Halla Bol* (Attack!), in the urban village of Jhandapur outside Sahibabad, Delhi, catalysed the debate around 'the right to perform'.[73] Without attempting a detailed description of the Freedom Theatre, let me highlight a key passage quoted by Deshpande in which Juliano Mer Khamis clarifies the kind of 'training' given to the young actors there. His words offer a stirring challenge to the ethos of non-violence, which is the central trope of investigation in this chapter:

> You don't have to heal the children in Jenin. We didn't try to heal their violence. We tried to challenge it in productive ways. And more productive ways are not an alternative to resistance. What we were doing in the theatre is not trying to be a replacement or an alternative to the resistance of the Palestinians in the struggle for liberation. Just the opposite. This must be clear. I know it's not good for fundraising, because I'm not a social worker, I'm not a good Jew going to help the Arabs, and I'm not a philanthropic Palestinian who comes to feed the poor. We are joining, by all means, the struggle for liberation of the Palestinian people which is our liberation struggle . . . We're not healers. We're not good Christians. We are freedom fighters.[74]

This rousing, no-holds-barred affirmation of training actors to be freedom fighters highlights at least two positions: on the one hand, following Mer Khamis's barely concealed scorn, if not contempt, for the path of 'healing' children from the violence that permeates their lives, we are made to confront the defeatist cop-out of a therapeutic form of theatre practice playing on humanitarianism and victimhood, greatly favoured by foreign foundations and other institutions espousing a neo-liberal agenda. Here one needs to be careful about dismissing this 'soft', palliative approach to theatre in a state of war by emphasizing that there are ways, as Maurya Wickstrom (2012) has persuasively argued, in which foreign-funded theatre groups in Palestine working on developmental and educational agendas can subvert, ever so subtly, their strategies of survival. It would be wrong to totally dismiss their efforts to work from within power structures and funding constraints as a mere capitulation to neo-liberal ideology.

However, there is another path that is less fraught with compromise and conciliation, where there is no equivocation about the fact that theatre is not a counter to the risks and dangers of the freedom struggle. Rather theatre is intrinsically a part of the freedom struggle, as Juliano Mer Khamis affirms, drawing its adrenaline from the actual engagement with the specificities of this struggle, along with the larger archetypes, symbols, dreams and visions of freedom. There can be no compromise on the demand for this freedom – it is not a freedom-in-waiting, but a freedom which is embodied and lived every single time in the here and now of performance practice.

Perhaps, these words are somewhat too rhapsodic in the context of the real risks faced by young actors performing the role of freedom fighters both on stage and off. A hard question in this context would need to be answered: If one trains actors to be freedom fighters, is one not training them to die? Here, within the larger narrative of this book, I am reminded of Genet's *Prisoner of Love* (1989), his posthumously published book on the joy he received in the last years of his life while sharing his life with the *fedayeen* in Palestine. In passage after passage in the book, while describing the *fedayeen* discussing politics, strategizing attacks and defences, holding singing contests, cleaning their guns, washing themselves, breaking up into clandestine groups and transporting coffins, the young freedom fighters are driven by an inexplicable, yet implacable *jouissance*. If they have to die, they will do so willingly, compulsively. Very few of them survive, and the ones that do, disappear into what appear to be less joyous lives in the hidden corners of the European metropolis, surviving on menial jobs, or suffering the loneliness and isolation of reluctant exiles.

Like the *fedayeen* but, perhaps, more starkly, the heartbreakingly young and energetic actors among *Arna's Children* die one after the other. At the end of the film there are none alive, compelling one to ask: can this be justified? It could be argued that there is no way out; the logic of survival in any freedom struggle is tough and not meant for those who are not prepared to die. But, to repeat the question: can these relentless deaths of actors be justified as theatre becomes a training ground for the imminent dead? Indeed, is this possibility of death factored into the training process of actors, or is it taken for granted? These questions compel one to interrogate the intimate complicity between the practice of theatre in conditions of war and the prospects of involuntary suicide. To what extent is this complicity a basis for political commitment, and can it be so readily extended to the lives of children?

## THE VIOLENCE OF NON-VIOLENCE

These hard questions challenge the earliest incarnation of this book in my essay 'Genet in Manila: Reclaiming the Chaos of Our Times' (2003b), which I had ended on a euphoric note by affirming the need to counter terror by countering counterterror. In the course of researching this book, I have learned that counterterror can be more lethal than terror because its invariably excessive violence is driven by a sense of justice and right. I continue to believe that countering counterterror is as necessary a task as countering terror, but I am also compelled to acknowledge that if we restrict our options to terror and counterterror, we are caught in a terrifying bind. Today, I see both agendas feeding on each other, playing into each other's narratives of revenge and grotesque one-upmanship. Too many innocent people and children have to die to cater to the egos of leaders obsessed by their death-driven visions. We desperately need a way of breaking out of this cycle of violence through new imaginaries of non-violence. But how is this to be achieved in our relatively frail and small attempts to face terror through theatre and performance?

To answer this question, however tentatively, we would do well to spare ourselves some illusions. For a start, let us stop thinking that theatre is intrinsically 'non-violent', and open ourselves instead to the ways in which we are complicit in larger scenarios of terror, which would appear to be distant from the protected confines of theatre. More often than not this complicity deepens without our knowledge as we continue to do 'what we believe in', either by remaining oblivious to the violence that surrounds us or by making a virtue of the fact that 'the show must go on'. It is also questionable to what extent one can justify doing 'theatre in a time of terror' within the 'permitted spaces' allotted by the state.[75] While there are all kinds of theatrical devices like allegory and symbolism that can be used to suggest the actual political state of affairs in these 'permitted spaces', these devices also run the risk of formalizing camouflaged dissent. More often than not theatre in a permitted space is an activity that is complicit with the state's agenda of terror, whose endorsement becomes possible through the failure to acknowledge other forms of underground theatre practice that may be struggling to survive in more volatile parts of the same country.[76]

Countering conventional theatre practice, one strategy could be to invent diverse modes of 'invisible theatre', that incendiary form of performance practice first articulated by Augusto Boal (1979) in his attempt to infiltrate public spaces 'invisibly', and stir up trouble and debate from within their boundaries. The aesthetics of invisibility would seem to be a necessary strategy to provoke the protocols of terror, even while surviving its explosive potentiality; it could also be regarded as a courageous way of fighting, and not just surviving, censorship in state-determined 'permitted spaces'. How theatre goes underground in times of terror, how it organizes itself through clandestine networking, and how it finds new spaces for survival in the privacy of apartments or through new modes of 'silent acting' in conditions of extreme censorship – these are testaments of theatre's extraordinary capacity to mutate and take on new manifestations when its basic 'right to perform' is summarily denied. Through all these experiments there is no denial of the omnipresence of violence; rather there is a transformation of violence into subversive languages of underground theatre, which emerge through the imagination and cunning of its creators in response to new codes of censorship and surveillance.

Against these viable, yet risky options, what would be the consequence of highlighting not just the transformation of violence into creative acts, but also the actual insertion of *non-violence* into the imaginary of theatre and performance practice? Perhaps, at this point, one needs to highlight the paradox that is written into the concept of non-violence: on the one hand, it can be read as an outright negation of any form of violence; on the other hand, keeping in mind that any negation calls attention to what is being negated, non-violence can only begin to resonate in a larger context of violence which has to be implicitly acknowledged in any act of non-violence.

These paradoxes of non-violence came alive for me in an encounter with the legendary Brazilian activist Herbert de Souza, better known as 'Betinho' or the 'Gandhi of Rio', whose pioneering role in the Third Sector movement around citizenship and civil society in Brazil I have briefly addressed in an earlier book.[77] At some point in a meeting with Indian activists, while Betinho was holding forth in an eminently genial way on the need for 'partnerships' and 'dialogue' and 'short-term alliances' – secular shibboleths of an arguably neo-liberal mode of creative resistance – I couldn't help playing the devil's advocate by asking a somewhat provocative question: 'Does that mean we no longer have to fight?' Almost instantly I remember that question touching a nerve, as Betinho's Left–liberal persona assumed an anarchist dimension. With blazing eyes he looked directly at me and almost spat out the words: 'Of course we have to fight.' And then, driving his point home while addressing my own location in India, he added: 'Think of Gandhi. *What could be more violent than non-violence?*'

But what is this 'violence'? Clearly, as my argument in the earlier discussion on suicide bombing has demonstrated, the violence of non-violence cannot involve killing or even abusing the other; rather it necessitates the courage of standing up to the other, receiving the blow and being prepared to die, not for some ideal of heroism or transcendent ideal, but for the affirmation of truth. The preparation to die in the Gandhian context, as I have argued earlier, should not be read as an endorsement of suicide. In a more somatic and corporeal register, one could also argue that the spiritual rigour of non-violence can be inherently 'violent' in terms of an extreme disciplining of the body and self through a form of *tapasya* or penance. Rejecting an overly ethereal process of sublimating non-violence, Gandhi had candidly acknowledged in his commentary on the *Bhagavad Gita* that 'the idea of a human being having no body at all exists only in our imagination'. Building on the notion of self-purification forged through a relentless trial and testing of the body's limits and capacities of endurance, Gandhi added: 'Mortification of the body, therefore, is the only means of self-realization and the only *yajna* (sacrifice) for everyone in the world.'[78]

Keeping this injunction in mind, I will demonstrate in the next section how particular acts of political activism embrace self-mutilation as the only means of asserting human dignity and freedom. Clearly, we need to engage with different epistemologies and imaginaries of 'violence', even while being extremely vigilant that the violence of non-violence in the Gandhian sense should not degenerate into brute force or the actual dehumanization of others. As I unravel these thoughts I realize how difficult, if not impossible, it is to 'fix' non-violence as a particular creed or set of practices. Perhaps, like Gandhi's primary concept of *swaraj* (self-rule), it is best subjected to relentless scrutiny and reflexivity in a constant search for the deepening of political struggle through a transformation of the self.

## LIP-SEWING AND BLOOD GRAFFITI: THE WEAPONS OF THE WEAK

As I end this book, I find myself functioning like a dramaturge engaged in the necessary task of what Brecht would describe as 'crude thinking'. How can thinking against terror get translated into practice? Perhaps, we need to find the courage not to be intimidated by the scale of violence and begin our creative struggles with small interventions. In addition, even as we alert ourselves to the agency and potentiality of our own 'small actions', we need to remind ourselves that these actions already exist in a multitude of ways by the most marginalized and desperate of communities. I am thinking here of the condition of refugees, not in some 'Third World' terror-ridden country, but in the 'First World' of detention camps in countries like Australia where civilized brutality has assumed new dimensions of official legitimization, catalysing an altogether unprecedented corporeal activism among the non-citizens of the world.

In the deeply stirring and relentless exposures of the dehumanization of refugees and asylum seekers in such detention camps, Joseph Pugliese, in his numerous essays on the 'necroethics of terrorism' (2010), 'the incommensurability of law to justice' (2004a), and 'the civil modalities of refugee trauma, death, and necrological transport' (2009), has called attention to some painful 'performances' by refugees and asylum seekers – so painful, indeed, that one can scarcely imagine their actual practice. 'Lip-sewing' is one such practice by which the practitioners use their only resource available – their own bodies, or, more precisely, the folds of flesh sealing their mouths – to call attention to the barbarity of the state which denies them 'the possibility of ethical dialogue', as Pugliese puts it. Needless to say, such 'performances' have enraged the ministers of the Australian state, who have self-righteously denounced the barbarity of the prisoners without recognizing their own brutality which provokes the act of lip-sewing in the first place. Countering the outrage of politicians who are unable to see how the 'literal and metaphorical fuse' in the 'violent intextuation' of lip-sewing, Pugliese emphasizes: 'Contrary to what [they] claim, lip sewing is a product of "our" culture: we produce it legislatively, juridically and penally.'[79]

Another such 'performance' in the detention camps of Australia involves the use of a detainee's blood to paint slogans which would otherwise not be heard or seen. A description of this 'blood graffiti' is well worth quoting in Pugliese's description of an event that took place in the Woomera detention camp:

> [A] Sabean Mandean refugee fleeing persecution in Iran, cuts open a vein and draws a large quantity of blood. This blood, collected in a tin can, will be his paint. On a wall of the prison, he inscribes the word 'FREEDOM', in both English and Farsi. The words tower high over the compound . . . The words on the wall shimmer; they mark the contours of a desire that exceeds the perimeter fence of the prison. Two languages bleed into each other. This blood on the wall, with its tremulous drips and escape lines, blurs the borders between his body and the physical fabric of the prison – the blood, the wall become coextensive with his body: the body of his prison. One is binding on the other: a double bind that defies reason.[80]

What is striking about the visceral power of the language quoted above is how it captures the corporeality of the self-tortured body within the larger lethal environs of the prison. This specific corporeality mediated by blood is ultimately concentrated in language that is strategically essentialized to one critical word, 'FREEDOM' (both in English and Persian). When one encounters such words as images, one is not dealing with the theatre of cruelty in the Artaudian sense, as Pugliese implies. Perhaps, one is closer to the extremity of body art and its numerous derivations in performance art,[81] where the performer's body is a self-conscious site of injury and mutilation, resulting in lurid displays of blood, wounds and severed limbs.

Moving beyond the location of detention centres, one should acknowledge that the practice of painting slogans with one's own blood has been strategically adopted by activist groups like ACT UP in protest against the ruthless indifference of state authorities to the AIDS epidemic in the United States.[82] Likewise, at least two legendary performance artists have specifically used the act of lip-sewing to call attention to their own rage against political systems that 'silence' minorities. David Wojnarowicz had sewed his lips during the AIDS crisis in New York in protest against the deafening silence of the state in acknowledging the epidemic.[83] More explicitly, in relation to the Australian context of asylum seekers, Mike Parr had staged *Close the Concentration Camps* in 2002, where over a period of six hours his lips, eyes and ears were sewn together, and the skin on his thigh was branded with the word 'ALIEN'.[84]

While Parr's performance can be seen as a visceral and empathetic response to the violence inflicted on the bodies of refugees and asylum seekers, it cannot be equated, to my mind, with the lip-sewing of those marginalized figures stigmatized by inhospitable nation-states. While both sets of 'performances' shock with their individual intensities – Parr's performance is perhaps a lot more virtuoso and mediatized, countering the relative 'invisibility' of the lip-sewing by asylum seekers – the intentionality enforcing their actions is of a different order and urgency. If Parr calls attention to the dehumanizing absence of citizenship for 'aliens' in his own country, he is in a position to enact his rage *as a citizen*. In contrast, the refugees and asylum seekers are using their only means available to call attention to their *statelessness*. Not only are they being denied citizenship through a process of law, they are also divested of the fundamental rights to live like human beings.[85]

At a biopolitical level, the gesture of protest through lip-sewing can be seen as a form of 'non-violent' political assertion. Non-violent? The word may seem odd when blood is involved, but it is not the blood of others. It is the blood of the detainees themselves that is voluntarily instrumentalized to make a statement by which they can call attention to their oppressive and unacceptable condition. In this self-injurious performative act, I would assert, there is both vulnerability and strength that cry out to be recognized and upheld through an altered notion of hospitality, which is denied to refugees and asylum seekers by the Australian state. As the former Prime Minister John Howard had once categorically affirmed: '*We* decide who comes to this country and the circumstances in which they come.'[86] Clearly, this 'declaration of war against the refugee', as Pugliese puts it, is the most blatant affirmation of national sovereignty in a territorial sense – the very sovereignty which is deeply entrenched, as Jacques Derrida (2000) has emphasized, in the 'exercise' of 'filtering', 'choosing', 'excluding' and 'doing' violence to those strangers who would like to enter our home.[87]

Against the dominant notion of hospitality which cannot exist 'without finitude', Derrida reiterates and extends Levinas's notion of 'unconditional hospitality' which, while appearing to be 'an apolitical and irreceivable proposition', is nonetheless a necessary condition for justice. Derrida emphasizes that 'a politics that does not maintain a reference to this principle of unconditional hospitality is a politics that loses its reference to justice.'[88] While the magnanimity underlying the affirmation of justice through unconditional hospitality is the radical antithesis of what has been described as the 'paranoid nationalism'[89] of John Howard, among other conservative Australian politicians, it can be more closely aligned to Aboriginal perspectives on the ethical imperative 'to embrace other people in their need'.[90] This is not so much a 'civil' gesture, but a 'duty' by which the basic tenets of humanity are defined and affirmed in a broader universal perspective that transcends the narrow interests – and paranoia – of national sovereignty.

Returning to the performativity of extreme acts like lip-sewing and blood graffiti, which are directly positioned against the denial of hospitality by the state, we need new methods of seeing and researching such acts. Clearly, these methods cannot duplicate the methodology involved in deconstructing grand spectacles performed on global festival circuits like Ariane Mnouchkine's *Le dernier caravansérail*, a highly aestheticized and epic encapsulation of the lives of refugees from diverse parts of the world, which, not surprisingly, was hailed by the political elite of Australia. In contrast to this 'tasteful' reminder of the human condition, which almost made the actual politics of displacement negligible, the 'performances' of refugees and asylum seekers in detention camps operate with *desperation*. In their self-projection of misery and brutality, they challenge the possibilities of artistic representation by affirming – and claiming – their own rights to performance through embodiments of resistance. Not only is a new sensitivity needed by researchers and activists to *see* such acts, we need new strategies as to how we can *access* them in the first place, given the fact that they are performed in distant locations with almost no access to public communication.

Here I join Susan Buck-Morss in her cautious but optimistic endorsement of the new media. Acknowledging that 'the new [global] counter-culture cannot be envisioned outside the media', Buck-Morss adds that 'we do not know as yet how successful such a movement may be', even as we have reason to be 'cautiously optimistic'.[91] Without new possibilities of infiltrating security zones with innovative visual technologies, we are not in a position to know what is going on in these 'black sites' and clandestine prisons. In this regard, the infinitesimal subterfuges of the new media are vital for opening the secrets of nation-states that have hitherto been far too securely protected for the alleged benefits of national security. If the acts of lip-sewing and blood graffiti by refugees and asylum seekers have circulated beyond the boundaries of isolated detention camps, this is because the media has made such acts visible, either inadvertently or through their own craving for sensationalized 'human rights' stories.

Even so, an enormous amount of vigilance and stamina is needed by researchers to actually track the movements of those who are denied visibility and a voice. This is what scholar–activist Joseph Pugliese exemplifies as he takes note on television of those blurred, static-ridden figures of refugees and asylum seekers being 'deported out of Australia, or being shunted from one prison facility to another'.[92] His words capture the pain of seeing:

> I have seen faces of anguish mouthing silently to the reporters as they film a van or bus whisking the deportees to the nearest immigration prison or airport. Some can be seen gesticulating frantically while others appear fatalistically resigned. In the space of a few seconds these images vanish off the screen.[93]

I am humbled by this effort to capture the 'few seconds' of a disappearing person's life, and to give it some space in academic reflection. Likewise, I am moved by Pugliese's attempt to see what remains *unseen* – not the spectral presence of the phantom terrorist, the bogey figure that the political producers of terrorism have created for their own purposes – but, instead, those wretched of the earth who are on the run, seeking any way to survive. 'One looks at a departing truck but cannot see the body embedded in the axle; one looks at the plane flying overhead but cannot perceive the body frozen solid to the wheels.'[94]

With a combination of rage and compassion, Pugliese infiltrates the comfort zones of academia as to how terror should be written about by calling attention to human residues of another kind of terror that do not quite enter the discourse of 'major events' like 'September 11'. These residues would include 'decomposing bodies of Ghanaians found in a shipping container on arrival at the port of Hull; the electrocuted body of an Afghan refugee on the train tracks of Channel Tunnel; the shattered body of a Cuban found on Gatwick's airport runway after being dropped from a plane's wheelbay'.[95] The details are brutal, calling attention to the fact that the terror of our times is not limited to what has been designated as 'terrorism'. As I have emphasized in the introduction to this book, terror extends far beyond the official discourse and stipulations as to what qualifies as being worthy of 'terrorism'. By acknowledging the deaths of refugees and asylum seekers in terrifying circumstances, one is compelled to engage with unimaginable acts of risk-taking which result in involuntary suicide: underreported, if not erased, not worthy of global reportage or the most basic human concern. Inevitably, this indifference to brutality compels one to open the crucial issue of justice, to which I turn my attention now in the concluding reflections of this book.

## TOWARDS JUSTICE?

If there is one particularly disheartening leitmotif that underlies the expositions of terror in this book, it is the sobering and banal fact that justice never seems to materialize for the victims of terror, whether they are targets of terrorism, communal riots, genocides, torture or detention. Almost consistently, the perpetrators of terror (and counterterror) facilitate a distortion and evasion of justice. In India, many of the worst perpetrators of communal violence and genocide are not just free; in positions of power, they almost mock any attempt to bring them to trial or to acknowledge their crimes. In my reading of this intolerable situation, there can be no truth and reconciliation for the world at large if the existing legal systems at national and international levels are not adequately mobilized to redress this omnipresence of injustice.

While the International Criminal Court offers some hope for limited juridical interventions on genocide and ethnic cleansing at an international level, many countries in the world, as Talal Asad has pointed out, have not ratified its statute.[96] More critically, the United States, the world's most powerful democracy, has 'deliberately tried to circumvent it', out of concern that its 'soldiers or officials' – one could add ex-Presidents and their cohorts in the Security Department – could be 'subject to prosecution for war crimes in the court'.[97] Asad adds that the United States has negotiated 'over ninety bilateral treaties ensuring that other countries do not surrender US nationals to the ICC.'[98] In this affirmation of unilateral power which makes a mockery of the end of the Cold War, there is little hope for justice at an international level. Instead, what appears to be intensifying is the disequilibrium of justice in the world, which no 'balance of terror' can hope to correct. The 'balance of terror', as I have argued earlier, can only make the world a more violent place than it already is. We need new modalities and institutions, new imaginaries of activating justice at local, national and international levels.

While I realize the difficulty of engaging with a subject as vast and complex as justice towards the end of this book, suffice it to say that I am not attempting anything like an overview on the philosophy of justice in relation to terror. My purpose in inscribing justice on the borders of this book is to link it, however obliquely, to the larger performance of the law, which I have attempted to contextualize within the search for truth and reconciliation in South Africa and Rwanda in chapter 3. In the concluding pages of this book, I am more concerned with the grassroots efforts by activists to engage with the protocols of the law even as the law tends to perpetuate *injustice* through its endless postponements of trials. The law also has notoriously devious ways of reading evidence within the letter of the law, as opposed to recognizing the actual pain of victims and survivors who may have no legal aid to fall back on.

Despite this cruel mockery of justice, the law continues to be a relentless and, in some contexts, the only source of hope for thousands and, at times, millions of victims and survivors of genocides, ethnic cleansings and communal riots. Within my own location in India, it is useful in this regard to be reminded of some of the voices of the victims of the Gujarat genocide in 2002, who continue to live more than ten years after the genocide in abject conditions, in so-called transit camps festering with mounds of garbage and a total absence of basic amenities. Heartrendingly, in the most dehumanizing of conditions, where their capacities to assert the basic rights of citizenship are systematically undermined, the survivors of Gujarat continue to seek justice.

In a moving testimony entitled 'In Search of Justice' (2012), the journal *Communalism Combat* has collated and reflected on a spectrum of views which capture the myriad dimensions of justice as envisioned by people who have been denied its possibilities. Rejecting the impulse of rage to 'sentence one man [the Chief Minister of Gujarat, Narendra Modi]' as an adequate 'atonement' for the evils of genocide, and dismissing the validity of equating justice with seeking a 'balance' or following 'procedure', the collective voices animating the search for justice affirm their loss of faith in civic and juridical codes.[99] This loss of faith is made palpable by the bureaucratic nightmare for women (particularly for those who cannot read or write) of filing affidavits relating to rape in two languages. There is also the more visceral humiliation of women watching their rapists joking with the policemen sent to 'protect' them.[100] From the voices of these survivors, one is alerted to the partial truth that 'justice delayed is justice denied'; what is 'truer' is that 'justice waylaid is justice denied'.[101] Waiting is 'liveable', but 'watching justice being mimicked cynically is painful'.[102]

In contrast to the despair that underlies these statements, it is heartening, indeed, to acknowledge that some justice has finally materialized for the victims of the Gujarat genocide. On 29 August 2012, as many as thirty-two persons who had been charged for their participation in the Naroda Patiya mass murder, including a former BJP minister of the Gujarat government, were sentenced to life imprisonment. The role of the courageous eyewitnesses, who had testified to the crimes despite relentless threats to their lives, finally paid off. But does this mean that justice has been affirmed in the larger context of the Gujarat genocide? Hardly. There are many killers and silent perpetrators of violence who still remain free.

In its zeal and uncompromising commitment to pursue justice through the agency of state law, it could be argued that the *Communalism Combat* team has inadvertently failed to posit imagined structures of justice outside the law. Perhaps this is not an appropriate strategy for any activist-driven juridical process. But to pose a challenge: Instead of merely invoking the law, only to be disillusioned repeatedly by the arbitrary judgments of Special Investigation Teams or transfers of cases from one court to the next, among other manipulations of the juridical machinery, what other forms of justice can one facilitate to keep the hopes of victims alive? Here one needs to mention the public hearings of victims' testimonies, which, as I have mentioned earlier, have not been adequately mediatized or given much juridical weight in India. Unlike the daily radio reports and television documentation of the TRC in South Africa, which affected the national consciousness of an entire people, the hearings of victims' testimonies in India have not become a vital component of national public discourse and culture in India. In effect, their potential power has not been realized at a performative level.

Arguably, social networking has proved to be more effective, even as the dissemination of information via the internet tends to work within tight or overly random circuits. One runs the risk here of either preaching to the converted, or else, of getting the message lost in the anonymity of 'activist fatigue' of virtual communication. Countering this trend, the actual sentences passed against perpetrators, as in the case of the Naroda Patiya case, have contributed more substantially to the sustenance of the struggle against communalism. At a less euphoric level, however, one needs to acknowledge that for every positive verdict of the law in favour of the victims, there are hundreds of other verdicts (or non-verdicts) that merely perpetuate the worst forms of injustice.

If justice is a form of waiting, it could be argued that terror is always already imminent, in the near future, even as it strikes with deadly immediacy. Our vigilance, therefore, can never be compromised by a false complacency that the world we live in is less terrifying than before. Who knows what lies in store for us as we wait against our will for the next terror attack to strike? In contrast, justice is not something for which we can wait indefinitely, rather like Estragon and Vladimir waiting for Godot. The new modalities of justice to stop terror have to be initiated in the here and now, and not, as Derrida would enigmatically appear to suggest, indefinitely postponed: 'Justice remains to come, it remains by coming (*la justice reste à venir*), it has to come (*elle à venir*), it is to-come (*avenir*).'[103] If this is not a language that most activists would readily comprehend, one should hasten to point out the aporetic nature of Derrida's thinking, which has this extraordinary capacity of embracing the necessity of the impossible while never divesting itself of political urgency. Admittedly, this urgency is subsumed in the complexity of his deconstructive thought process, which refuses to submit to the crudities of quick-fix, short-term solutions to the most pressing problems of our times.

Therefore, in his dense reading of the 'Force of Law' (1989), which in many ways is a pivotal text on the basis of which his later reflections on hospitality and forgiveness are formulated, he positions justice (or '*the* law') as something that situates itself beyond the realm of actually existing 'law' (or 'the laws').[104] While laws are always 'deconstructible', embedded as they are in the norms, codes and discourses of specific historical and cultural contexts, justice is more akin to the act of deconstruction itself in so far as it destabilizes foundational certitudes. Lying outside 'the logic of exchange', which would include the components of 'reciprocity, debt, proportion, calculation, compensation, distribution', justice, in the Derridean sense, works on grounds which are 'unconditional, absolute, infinite, gracious, antieconomic'.[105] In short, justice borders on a kind of 'madness', as Derrida puts it, with his inimitable gift to push the normativity of words – a madness that does not merely arise out of the 'impossible demand of justice', but is inextricably linked to a 'responsibility without limits'.[106]

Even as it would appear that this justice is 'undecidable', this does not mean that it refuses to decide and make a choice; rather, as Gene Ray works through Derrida's aporias painstakingly, undecidability is better read as a 'moment of deferral, not a refusal'.[107] Even as justice is nothing short of an 'ordeal' in terms of its realization, as opposed to 'the programmable application or unfolding of a calculable process', which could qualify as 'legal' but not 'just', it is significant how Derrida complicates the undecidability of justice within the urgencies of the real.[108] Therefore, instead of waiting for justice to materialize through an acquisition of the most comprehensive knowledge of diverse legalities of a particular situation or predicament, justice in the Derridean sense demands a different temporality of intervention:

> To be direct, simple and brief, let us say this: a just decision is always required *immediately*, 'right away'. It cannot furnish itself with infinite information and the unlimited knowledge of conditions, rules or hypothetical imperatives that could justify it. And even if it did have all that at its disposal, even if it did give itself the time, all the time and the necessary facts about the matter, the moment of *decision, as such*, always remains a finite moment of urgency and precipitation.[109] (Emphases in original.)

This 'direct, simple, and brief' qualification on the part of Derrida compels one to rethink what would appear to be his apolitical stance in relation to the actual manifestation of justice. It is not as if he is denying the possibility or necessity of justice being passed by the courts of law. Rather he is compelling his readers to face the harsh reality that there can be no ready acceptance of the law being translated into justice, and that justice has to be re-invented over and over again through a submission to the ordeal, the rigour, the test of fire that it demands. Not only can there be no complacency in assuming that justice will materialize on the basis of applying the law, it is even more fatuous to assume that once it materializes in a particular case it will necessarily set a precedent of just practice for the future.

Returning to the crucial issue of temporality in the manifestation of justice, I would emphasize that if justice is not realized in the imminent present, the spectres of terror can only become more monstrous through new forms of legitimization and illusions of normalcy. Moreover, if justice cannot be implemented by the existing legal institutions, we may need to find new ways of imagining how justice can be envisioned outside the law through new modes of non-violent critical thinking and dialogue. Here one needs to inscribe the courageous and vastly underreported struggle of peace activists across the world, working against the most formidable odds as they sustain their sporadic and vulnerable movements against the force of state power and counterterror vigilance.

In the most concentrated nucleus of terror in the world, we find peace activists working across the borders of Israel and Palestine in interstitial spaces secreted in the nooks and corners of walled security zones, guarded by the Israeli army and territorialized by settlers resorting to violent attacks on displaced Palestinians. Some of these attacks have included the poisoning of soil in the fields owned by Palestinians. Clearly, for all their religious zeal, these settlers have no difficulty in desecrating the Holy Land in their attempt to exterminate not just the alleged intruders, but their agricultural produce and animals as well. Facing hate-driven abuse and the imminence of arrest by the Israeli army, a scattering of a few hundred peace activists congregate to show solidarity with the displaced. They express this solidarity not just through lectures, slogans and songs, but by digging the fields of the Palestinians, rebuilding their broken roads and houses, providing medical help and sharing food. In this restrained, yet joyous defiance of the arbitrary rule of the state, and in the readiness to die without killing, we encounter an unprecedented manifestation of Gandhi's non-violence.

In the words of David Shulman, best known as one of the foremost Sanskritists in the world but relatively unknown as a long-term peace activist, we are compelled to engage with a new, robust affirmation of *ahimsa*:

> We will meet our foe at every point – every house he demolishes, every olive tree he uproots, every rock field he is intent on stealing. We will engage him over and over, without violence. We will watch and record and bear witness, and, from time to time, we will stop him. He has guns; we have each other, determination, and some dogged convictions about what it means to be human. That, and a certain dark hope.[110]

This 'dark hope', as Shulman puts it powerfully, without false sentimentality or an illusory optimism divested of any real struggle, is what we need to build on for the realization of peace.

Non-violence, I would submit, is not an abdication of struggle; it is the readiness to open one's innermost self to struggle, not necessarily through the force of Law or the legitimacy of a Constitution, or even the potential efficacy of a clearly worked out Political Agenda. Rather this is a struggle which is consolidated through a fellowship with the 'lonely few', as Shulman puts it, 'on both sides' – one could add, on all sides of existing divides – who 'refuse to be enemies', and 'who will take any risk for the other's sake and for the sake of peace'.[111] We have to affirm peace not because it is comforting, but because it could provide, more surely than any other option available in a world of disintegrating justice, new possibilities of imagining how our world can become somewhat more sane and civil through the affirmation of non-violence. By activating non-violence in the terror of everyday life, at home and in the world at large, we may be in a better position to sustain the ceaseless and turbulent quest for peace.

# POSTSCRIPT

To end a book on terror is somewhat illusory, if not hopelessly optimistic, as I suggested in the preface to this book. Not only does the global phenomenon of terror continue to mutate and acquire new forms and manifestations, our attempts to comprehend it are constantly frustrated as insights into its existing modalities and assemblages yield to terrifying revelations of its emergent modes of operation and inexplicable rationales. In this regard, almost any book on terror risks coming across as slightly dated, as the phenomenon of terror far surpasses our capacities to understand its metastasis.

The problem is not just a matter of catching up with new technologies: if long-distance drone missiles are the most deadly performers of death and destruction today, one should also keep in mind the coexistence of low-tech explosive devices like pressure-cooker bombs, which were used in the Boston Marathon terrorist attack of 15 April 2013. Such strategic amateurism almost mocks the hubris of those weapons experts who would like to believe that high-tech weapons are in a position to annihilate all existing forms of opposition with maximum efficiency and minimal loss. This dubious ethos is not likely to stop terror from surfacing in even more deviant and quotidian ways.

If the act of writing about terror cannot be reduced to its multiple technicalities, it would be more accurate to view its complexities in relation to colliding temporalities: even as terror strikes at unprecedented levels in the instantaneous present, it is at once the outcome of a *longue durée* of clandestine time in which it is nurtured in virtual secrecy; simultaneously, it also presents the deferral or postponement of a more virulent terror to come, as this book has argued, drawing on Derrida's theory of the 'new temporalization' of terror.[1] Within such devious slippages of past, present and future, any attempt to 'fix' terror *in* time – and thereby to 'explain' it or to 'end' it, if only within the discursive confines of a book – remains a grand illusion.

Acknowledging that the deadly temporalities of terror make it a massively elusive phenomenon, what I offer here is not a conclusion or even a coda, in the tradition of the minor key giving way to the major in the conventional *Tierce de Picardie* which ended many of Bach's fugues. To 'resolve' terror in this manner would be a baroque indulgence. Instead, I opt for a postscript – something more cryptic, a concatenation of fragments, left-over thoughts, *aides-mémoire* for future narratives and last-minute insertions of what did not get adequately addressed in the book.

If terror is a mutant phenomenon today, far removed from the more ideologically driven assassination attempts and master plots of the past to eliminate demagogues, feudal landlords, class enemies, guerrillas and enemies of the state, this can be related to its increasingly virtual and privatized processes of incubation. In this concealed state, rehearsals of terror-in-the-making, targeting entire sections of the population, are strategized through combinations of hatred, rage and unacknowledged trauma.

Of late, the lethal secrecy of this phenomenon has been explained in the context of 'self-radicalization', one of those neologisms entering the vocabulary of terror for which there are both supporters (like President Obama, who described the Boston terrorists as 'self-radicalized') and detractors (those ideologues who dismiss 'self-radicalization' as 'chic', the 'preposterous theory *du jour*').[2] Perhaps the truth lies somewhere in between these binaries, as die-hard condemnations of all terrorists being 'converted' and 'recruited' to already existing extremist and fundamentalist groups have yet to acknowledge the enigmas of more infinitesimal processes of indoctrination. In these processes, the 'self' becomes an integral element of an ideological construct of terror, at once driven by a traumatic personal biography and inextricably linked to the intimacies of an electronic 'community'.

Such a 'self' is evident in the example of Anders Behring Breivik, who bombed government buildings in Oslo on 22 July 2011, resulting in eight casualties, followed by a systematic shooting of as many as 77 victims, mostly young teenagers attending a summer camp of the Workers' Youth League of the Labour Party on the island of Utøya. Arguably, Behring can be regarded as the prototype of a self-radicalized 'new terrorist'. No Boston Strangler or Son of Sam, it would be a mistake to categorize him as a 'mass murderer' on the lines of deranged killers caught in a vortex of obsessive murders, rapes and perverse crimes. Rather the targeting of 'his own people' was premised ideologically on his unequivocal hatred of Islam, cultural Marxism and multiculturalism – hatred which was, to a large extent, fed by his voracious appetite to engage with virulent right-wing xenophobic propaganda available on the internet. In terms of his actual terrorist practice, the formidable professionalism of Behring's shooting expertise needs to be linked to his systematic use of video-games like *World of Warcraft* and *Call of Duty: Modern Warfare 2.*

It is through the split-second reflexes of multiple killings in the make-believe scenarios of these games that he trained himself as a terrorist, building his expertise towards that predestined act of terror.

To what extent do the performative circumstances of Breivik's 'training' and 'rehearsals' as a terrorist qualify as 'self-radical'? Breivik may have acted alone, but the imaginary of his crime was fed at a prodigious global level through stimuli received from right-wing networks and websites across the world, which enabled him to forge the most unlikely liaisons – even with extremist Hindu organizations like the Rashtriya Swayamsevak Sangh.[3] To emphasize a crucial point, the process of his 'radicalization' cannot be separated from 'mediatization', which far surpasses any earlier forms of indoctrination through face-to-face interactions with ideologues in terrorist cells or camps.

In this surrender to a rampant, yet palpable virtuality, we have come a long way from earlier epistemologies of 'radical' and 'radicalization', as delineated so precisely in Raymond Williams's *Keywords* (1985), where we encounter the word vacillating between its renegade and liberal manifestations over centuries. However, the keyword today, as I see it, in the problematic of 'self-radicalization' is not so much the 'radical' or 'radicalization', but the 'self'. How do we see the 'self' in the age of terror? Both the American supporters and critics of 'self-radicalization' seem to invoke a liberal understanding of the 'self' as an autonomous free agent, however circumscribed by the trials of immigration and a disturbed family life. These extenuating circumstances are almost destined to produce 'losers', the quintessentially American word by which the Boston bombers were branded by some members of their family and the media. Perhaps we need to arrive at a more globalized understanding of the 'self', which is less autonomous and more wired into an interactive network of indices and permutations stimulating interventions of potential terror. The liberal construction of the 'self' *as freethinking individual* – 'free' to either act independently as a radical/terrorist or to voluntarily join an already existing terrorist organization – would seem to be somewhat obsolete in the age of terror.

Writing this book has made me aware about the trials of research that lie ahead in the fundamental acts of reading and seeing terror. The future of researching terror, I would submit, is as challenging as trying to predict how one can begin to assess its material opacity. In this regard, Joseph Pugliese correctly characterizes all research on terror, particularly in its technocratic dimensions, as 'inscribed by a *constitutively incomplete* scholarship'.[4] Much of what is happening in the secret prisons of Afghanistan, for instance, like the Salt Pit, the Hangar, the Dark Prison and Panjshir, remains unseen and, therefore, unknown, isolated from the eyes of the world. All that exists of such black holes, among other sites, are official documents where, if the zealous researcher is lucky, the name of a victim can appear in a footnote, after being systematically 'redacted' in the rest of the document. A redaction is not just another erasure in which traces and palimpsests of earlier words can be traced. It is more of a dark blot, a brutal scoring-out of controversial facts relating to torture and the victim's identity. However, on rare occasions, a name can be inadvertently revealed through 'redaction fatigue', as Pugliese puts it succinctly: such was the case with Gul Rahman, who lies 'buried in footnote 28 of the Classified Response to the US Department of Justice Office of Professional Responsibility Classified Report, July 29, 2009.'[5] What's in a name, one could ask. I would say *life* in all its vulnerability and corporeality, even if that life has been terminated.

If the act of 'seeing' is put under severe duress through the censorship of official documents, it becomes almost more complicated to figure out how to read the proliferation of images around those rogue snapshots that have been generated around the Abu Ghraib prison. Needless to say, for the hundreds of images available of sadistic torture inflicted on the bodies of male Iraqi prisoners, there are as many images, if not more, which remain undisclosed of the violence inflicted on the bodies of Iraqi women. In this systematic censorship, the complete evidence of dehumanization in Abu Ghraib, masquerading as 'fun and games', has not yet been available for critical scrutiny and justice. On the contrary, some of the most loathsome images from the Abu Ghraib archive have been used as legal justification for *freeing* the torturers who participated in these games, ostensibly on grounds of their courageous and subversive decision to reveal the US military's atrocities.

Such is the position offered by whistleblower US Army Specialist Sabrina Harman, who is shown in a series of images smiling into the camera with a triumphant thumbs-up gesture, her relaxed demeanour radiating cheer, while alongside her lies the battered corpse of Manadel al-Jamadi on the ground. Better known as 'the Ice Man', one among a series of insulting pseudonyms whereby the names of Iraqi prisoners have been erased and substituted by categories like 'the Shit Boy' and 'the Man on a Leash', Manadel al-Jamadi was 'battered, suffocated to death, and iced away'.[6] After his body was preserved in the shower room, it was then taken out on a stretcher the following day as if he were seriously ill, but alive. It is hard not to read in this perverse deceit by the US military a crime, if not against 'humanity' at large, then against another human being: Manadel al-Jamadi.

How do we read Sabrina Harman's 'performance', as she smiles and makes a thumbs-up gesture, against the official verdict that her 'later actions' need to be seen in the context of 'resistance' and 'civil disobedience'?[7] This last category has a particularly ugly resonance in the context of the political philosophy and practice of Gandhi, for whom 'civil disobedience' never involved the strategic embrace of evil, which is the primary ground on which Harman managed to gain her freedom in the world at large. Tellingly, it is not terror experts or visual theorists who have been able to see through Harman's 'heroic' performance, but a literary theorist, Alex Danchev (2011), who offers the cogent thesis that Harman's multiple images and performances are perhaps not so different as she (or her defendants in court) would like us to believe.

Danchev elaborates on the deceptions at work in the juridical decision to free Harman by calling attention to her first image, where she had photographed a naked, handcuffed detainee with underwear covering his head. Even as she claims to have seen an uncanny resemblance to Jesus Christ in the detainee's tortured body, which made her laugh, the point is that this reflex then compels her to acknowledge, more critically, that the tortured Iraqi prisoner is being subjected to 'molestation'. This insight, in turn, leads to some kind of epiphanic self-realization on Harman's part, which compels her to play the role of an undercover agent driven by the mission 'to get the pictures and prove that the US is not what they think'.[8]

However, the 'awkward fact', as Danchev points out, is that

> the later, sentient Sabrina continued to act very like the earlier, insensate Sabrina, complete with smile, thumb and camera, in the thick of the worst abuse, and to *take exactly the same sort of photographs on demand*. There is also the question of *what precisely she understood her 'proof' to demonstrate*.[9] (Emphases in original.)

It is in such close readings of images, working through their minutiae and repetitions of the same performance, that one can begin to unsettle the ways in which torture and sadistic cruelty can be exonerated and even justified.

Harman's acts may belong to the seemingly normative category of 'performance', but, to reiterate Genet's categories discussed earlier in this book, they are fraught with manifestations of brutality, as opposed to violence. Regardless of the legal opinions by which her posing for cheerful photographs alongside a corpse has been hailed as the daring action of a true (and patriotic) American whistleblower, one is left with the chilling thought that Sabrina Harman is an exceptionally good performer. Even as her conscience is disturbed by her own admission in her act of posing with a corpse, she continues to smile as if she were enjoying the crimes surrounding her. What I read here is not subversive heroism, but the smiling face of complicity in evil.

This interpretation, I should acknowledge, could be countered by other readings of Harman's smile – readings which indicate the new challenges involved in reading images surrounding the hermeneutics of terror. To extend the dilemmas of interpretation, one could argue that if Harman is hailed unequivocally as a good American, why should another kind of whistleblower, notably Edward Snowden, be branded so categorically as an enemy of the state? The war on terror would seem to be entering a new phase as the war on information becomes increasingly more visible and played out with intensified aggression in the global political arena. What are the stakes here?

While both Harman and Snowden are exposing 'state secrets' – one relating to torture in an actual prison, the other to covert acts of spying of the United States on other nations and its own people – the former is hailed for her action, while the latter's citizenship is revoked with no possibility of legal appeal. A new form of terror: a stateless Snowden, imprisoned for a month in the transit area of Moscow airport, desperately seeking the right to travel. Far from being a new terrorist, as right-wing hawks in the US establishment are likely to believe, it is possible to see here a new form of resistance to 'information imperialism', whose implications have yet to be adequately assessed.

In the interim, it is useful to remember that at least one senior and highly respected civil rights leader and elder statesman of the United States, John Lewis, has responded to Snowden's alleged 'civil disobedience' with carefully considered words:

> In keeping with the philosophy and the discipline of non-violence, in keeping with the teaching of Henry David Thoreau and people like Gandhi and others, if you believe that something is not right, something is unjust, and you are willing to defy customs, traditions, bad laws, then you have a conscience. You have a right to defy those laws and be willing to pay the price.[10]

A day later, Lewis was compelled to clarify that he was neither 'comparing' Snowden to Gandhi, nor was he 'praising' Snowden's actions: 'I cannot say and I did not say that what Mr Snowden did is right. Others will be the judge of that.' All he was calling attention to was the fact that there is a price to be paid for any act driven by the dictates of conscience, claimed by Snowden and tacitly endorsed by Lewis himself.

Moving beyond the excessive media attention around individuals like Snowden, which runs the risk of depoliticizing a larger movement around the right to information, we need to pay attention to Noam Chomsky's cryptic statement: 'Everybody's worried about stopping terrorism. Well, there's a really easy way: stop participating in it.'[11] One assumes that this participation applies as much to 'spectators' as it does to 'actors', those who actually perpetrate acts of terror. While supporting Chomsky's matter-of-fact and sound advice, I would argue that the demand to 'stop participating' in terror is easier said than put into practice for millions of people across the globe who consume terror on a daily basis through the prodigious manufacturing of images and thought-bytes on television and social media. To circumvent, if not to oppose, today's 'manufacture of consent' requires a lot more than critical vigilance and reflexivity; it necessitates a new apparatus of survival, new forms of protection and civic education that do not merely feed the dominant cultures of surveillance.

But how is this apparatus to be formed from the residues of civil society in post-communal and post-genocidal states, where the police and other guardians of the law could be the most virulent perpetrators of terror in our times? Do people have to fall back on other forms of vigilante justice outside the law, which may lead to intensified violence? At no point has the need for justice and peace activism at grassroot levels of public culture and community interaction been more urgent. While I have no 'good news' to offer the reader at the end of this book, no light at the end of the tunnel, I would place my faith in ongoing non-violent struggle, whose imaginaries and strategies need new structures of performances to counter terror in body and spirit. *A luta continua.*

# NOTES

## PREFACE

[1] Abhimanyu's identification as a child-soldier became clear to me on seeing an original play, *Shadows* (in English), collectively created by the senior students and apprentices of the Kattaikkuttu Gurukulam, Tamil Nadu, directed by Craig Jenkins, in December 2011.

[2] Said, 'The Essential Terrorist', 150–51.

[3] Statement by Andrew Silke, director of Terrorism Studies at the University of East London; quoted in Laurent Bonelli, 'The secret lives of terrorists', 12.

[4] Ibid.

[5] Even at a quantitative level Pinker's thesis is questionable, in the light of the most recent statistics provided by *The Global Terrorism Index*, December 2012, which clearly indicate that while terrorist activity may have decreased after 'September 11' to pre-2000 levels, it has since intensified. While in 2002 there were 982 terrorist incidents causing 3,823 deaths, there were as many as 4,564 terrorist incidents in 2011, resulting in 7,473 deaths. Significantly, these figures do not take into account 'government-backed action' such as aerial bombing or other killings. Drone attacks, in particular, have yet to be adequately factored into the intensification of terrorism in our times. For a fuller context on *The Global Terrorism Index*, read the Reuters report by Peter Apps, 'Terrorist attacks soar, India among most affected nations', *Yahoo News*, 4 December 2012.

[6] McKenzie, *Perform or Else*, 13.

## INTRODUCTION

[1] By placing 'September 11' within inverted commas, I call attention to its construction as an event, which, as Jacques Derrida (2003) has reminded us, has always already been 'cited' and affirmed in a hegemonic way as a '*major* event' in the global public sphere (87–88). Highlighting this act of naming as a 'menacing injunction', or worse, as a 'terrorizing if not terrorist imperative', Derrida links the 'Anglo–American' idiom of 'September 11' to 'the political discourse that dominates the world stage' (88). In contrast, 11 September 2001 is the actual date around which the events of 'September 11' or '9/11' have been constructed.

[2] 'To invent the sailing ship or the steamer is to invent the shipwreck. To invent the train is to invent the rail accident', as Paul Virilio elaborates in *The Original*

*Accident*, 10. The possibility of catastrophe, therefore, is built into every technology – not just the lethal technology of nuclear power, but something as ordinary as electricity, whose invention also makes possible the threat of electrocution.

[3] Virilio, *Unknown Quantity*, 26.

[4] Derrida, 'Autoimmunity', 87–136.

[5] Asad, *On Suicide Bombing*, 7.

[6] Quoted in Whitaker, 'The definition of terrorism'.

[7] Ibid., 2.

[8] Todorov, *Torture and the War on Terror*, 32. Page references included in text for the next three paragraphs.

[9] Todorov's primary source of information is drawn from the 'Torture Memo' submitted by the US Department of Justice's office of Legal Counsel on 1 August 2002. This memorandum cites 'legal reasons according to which the acts committed are deemed lawful and do not fall into the category of prohibited acts of torture as defined by international conventions and the US Code (2340–2340A).' See ibid., 26.

[10] In *The Lucifer Effect*, Zimbardo quotes Ron Nordland, *Newsweek*'s Baghdad bureau chief, saying, 'There is no evidence that all the mistreatment and humiliation saved a single American life or led to the capture of any major terrorist, despite claims by the military that the [Abu Ghraib] prison produced "actionable intelligence"' (379).

[11] Danchev, *On Art and War and Terror*, 176.

[12] Ibid., 220.

[13] Ibid.

[14] Drawing on a report by Andrew Buncombe on 'Prisoner 345', Danchev identifies Sami Al-Haj as 'a Sudanese journalist detained without charge in Guantánamo Bay since December 2001' (ibid., 232). He was released on 1 May 2008.

[15] Ibid., 219.

[16] Derrida, *Rogues*, 106.

[17] Ibid., 97.

[18] Derian, 'The terrorist discourse', 69, 71.

[19] For a succinct mapping of eight formations of terror, read ibid., 73–87. Briefly, Derian identifies *mythoterrorism* with millennarianistic insurrections like the Crusades; *anarchoterrorism* with Tsar Alexander II's assassination by the Narodnaya Volya (The People's Will) in 1881; *socioterrorism* with the 'systematic social violence' of Robespierre, Saint-Just and other Jacobins during the French Revolution; *ethnoterrorism* with the Kurds pursuing their struggle for statehood; *narcoterrorism* with the Sendero Luminoso (Shining Path) in Peru; *state terrorism* with Hitlerite Germany and Stalinist Russia; *antiterrorism* with the Israeli Sayeret Matkal and the German Grenzschutzgruppe 9 (Border Protection Group 9); and *pure terrorism*, which Derian links to nuclear power, and more broadly to Paul Virilio's interpretation of 'pure war', as 'The art of deterrence, prohibiting political war, [and favouring] the upsurge not of conflicts, but of *acts of war without war*' (86).

[20] Gene Ray, 'Listening with the Third Ear: Echoes from Ground Zero', *Terror and the Sublime in Art and Critical Theory*, 137–38.

[21] Ibid.

[22] For a comprehensive survey of the events leading to the demolition of the Babri Masjid in Ayodhya on 6 December 1992, and its political implications within the larger context of secularism in India, read Gopal, ed., *Anatomy of a Confrontation*.

[23] Tilly, 'Terror, Terrorism, Terrorists', 5.

[24] Ibid., 9.

[25] Ibid., 12.

[26] See the comprehensive entry on 'terrorism' in the *Stanford Encyclopedia of Philosophy*, first published 22 October 2007, substantive revision 8 August 2011, available at http://plato.stanford.edu/entries/terrorism

[27] Eagleton, *Holy Terror*, 1.

[28] See entry on 'terror' in the *Oxford English Dictionary*.

[29] Walzer, *Just and Unjust Wars*, 259–60.

[30] Ibid., 253–54.

[31] Spivak, 'Terror', 91.

[32] Ibid., 92.

[33] Ibid.

[34] Ibid.

[35] Eagleton, *Holy Terror*. Pagination included for all references to this text in the following section on 'Holy Terror'.

[36] Unable to provide a detailed ethnography of Theyyam within the confines of this introduction, I nonetheless find it necessary to give the reader some description of its terrifying affect. Let me quote at length from a vivid eyewitness account of Pepita Seth, a photographer who has been engaged in the process of 'seeing' Theyyam in remote villages of Kerala, India, over several years:

> There is a lot of very real terror in Theyyam, the nature of so many deities is to be frightening. Certain Theyyams have a license to kill even if someone stands before them. One of the most dangerous moments is when a deity's 'performance' begins and the *karmi* 'sends' the deity to the performer. One wrong move and it's over.
>
> There is an island in the river where the deity, a Bhagavathi, goes in the evening to a shrine in the deep forest, her way lit by a man holding a lamp. Then, after the deity's make-up is completed, the man leaves. All you can hear, all night long, is her terrible roaring. People only go to make their offering after daylight when her mood has changed. Even during the rest of the year it is a dangerous place to approach as her presence remains.
>
> Just the look of another deity will freeze your blood. I know, I've experienced it. I think it's terror, not horror: terror being an apprehension that something nasty may happen; horror is seeing it happen. While most deities are associated with terror, they are still 'mothers' capable of showing another side of themselves. Kali is one such deity, but those of a really frightening aura – Karim Chamundi, Puthiya Bhagavathi, Karoth Naga Bhagavathi, and so on – are all deities who protect their devotees and are the 'same' deity. I have seen what shape-shifters they all are, how their identities are concealed, how who they actually are is generally unknown.
>
> The reaction of Nharambil Bhagavathi, a forest deity, to the husband of a devotee who killed his wife because she was late giving him lunch, was to spontaneously burst into flames, seize and kill him. No messing about!

I am grateful to Pepita Seth for sharing this visceral first-person account of Theyyam which was written on my request. For glimpses of Seth's powerful photography of different Theyyams, along with lucid commentary, read her *Reflections of the Spirit*.

[37] Thanks to Sundar Sarukkai for providing the philosophical clues on '*neti, neti*'.

[38] See, for instance, Ray's eloquent *Terror and the Sublime in Art and Critical Theory*.

[39] Nair, *Poetry in a Time of Terror*, 7.

[40] Read Mukhopadhyay's ethnographic analysis, '"Dream Kitsch?" Folk Art, Indigenous Media and "9/11": The Work of *Pat* in the Era of Electronic Transmission', in *The Rumor of Globalization*, 105–26. For a more measured account of the *pat* tradition's engagement with modernity *vis-à-vis* the global event of 'September 11', read Roma Chatterji, *Speaking with Pictures*, chapter 2.

[41] Nair, *Poetry in a Time of Terror*, 7.

[42] Ibid., 12.

[43] Ibid., 8.

[44] Ibid.

[45] In her description of the terrorist attacks in Mumbai on 26 November 2009, which is almost entirely mediated by television reportage, monitored 'over seventy-two hours by a tireless Greek chorus of television anchors' (xix), Nair, in her *Poetry in a Time of Terror*, tends to over-read the primary elements of Aristotelian Greek tragedy into the event, drawing on familiar tropes like catharsis, suspense, conflict, identification. In the process, she fails to highlight the devious and intricate mediatization of the spectacle whereby Indian television channels in their 'real time' broadcasts were inadvertently providing actual clues to the terrorists as to how they could re-strategize their tactics and kill innocent people with more deadly accuracy. Far from being a simulacrum of the chorus in Greek tragedy, the Indian television networks, it could be argued, were complicit in the actual production of terror in 'real time'.

Likewise, I would argue that the Mumbai terror attacks had fewer affinities to the poetics of spectacle in fifth-century Athens than to the glittering, action-packed, tacky, seductive 'reel-life' of Bollywood. Strangely, this most massive of image industries in the Indian subcontinent never enters Nair's imaginary except for a passing reference to the one terrorist who survived the attacks, the cheeky and deceptively casual Ajmal Kasab (sentenced to death in India in November 2012), who had no difficulty in delivering his line – 'I did right, I have no regrets' (xxiii) – with all the panache of a cool, New Age, Hindi film villain.

[46] Mitchell's talk was held on 18 May 2011 at the Hebbel am Ufer Theater (HAU 1) in Berlin.

[47] Bial, Introduction to 'What is Performance?', *The Performance Studies Reader*, 59. Among the broader understandings of 'performance', which have now assumed an axiomatic resonance in performance studies, Carlson, in 'What is Performance?', specifies 'the display of skills', 'a recognized and culturally coded pattern of behavior', and the measure of 'success' by which a particular activity is assessed in relation to 'some standard of achievement that may not itself be precisely articulated' (as, for instance, sexual or linguistic performance, or a child's performance in school) (72).

More precisely, performance has been linked to its innate *reflexivity*. As ethnolinguist Richard Bauman elaborates in the entry on 'performance' in the *International Encyclopedia of Communications*, 'All performance involves a consciousness of doubleness, through which the actual execution of an action is placed in mental comparison with a potential, an ideal, or a remembered original model of that action' (73). Building on this formulation, Carlson emphasizes that, 'We may do actions unthinkingly, but when we think about them, this introduces a consciousness that gives them the quality of performance' (72).

48 McKenzie, *Perform or Else*, 208. This exceptionally thorough reading of the theoretical principles of J.L. Austin and Judith Butler in relation to notions of the 'performative' and 'performativity' remains a valuable attempt to bridge the discourses of performance studies and critical theory.

49 Butler, 'Critically Queer', 17.

50 Quoted in Devji, *The Terrorist in Search of Humanity*, 95.

51 Butler, 'Critically Queer', 17.

52 Devji, *The Terrorist in Search of Humanity*, 93.

53 Quoted in ibid., 95; my emphasis.

54 Butler, 'Critically Queer', 24; entire passage in italics in the original. Quoted in McKenzie, 'Genre Trouble', 58.

55 Quoted in McKenzie, 'Genre Trouble', 227.

56 Ibid.

57 Ibid., 229.

58 Ibid.

59 Taylor, 'Translating Performance', 383. Highlighting the fundamental 'untranslatability' of 'performance', particularly in the Latin American context, Taylor suggests that in order to re-inscribe the non-discursivity of the word 'performative', it would be useful to borrow a word from 'the contemporary Spanish usage of performance – *performático*, or "performatic" in English' (383). Sadly, the translation of conceptual categories from 'other' languages continues to be highly marginalized in the arguably 'imperialist' use of English in performance studies worldwide.

60 Agamben, 'What Is the Contemporary?', 50.

61 Ibid., 51.

62 Ibid., 41; my emphasis.

63 Bell, 'Performance Studies in an Age of Terror', 57–58.

64 Worthen, 'Disciplines of the Text', 17.

65 Ibid., 19–20.

66 Ibid., 20; my emphasis.

67 Jackson, 'Professing Performances'.

68 Richard Schechner's concept of 'restoration of behavior' can be read in diverse versions: see Schechner, 'Restoration of Behavior'; *Between Theater and Anthropology*; and *Performance Studies*.

69 Derian, *Virtuous War*, 144.

70 Read Esposito on the Dubrovska event in the introduction to *Bios*, 5.

### CHAPTER 1

1 *The Maids* was produced by the Philippine Educational Theater Association (PETA) at the Republic of Malate, a popular music and dance club in Manila,

between 16–24 November 2001. I am deeply indebted to the translator of the play, Rody Vera, for his insights into the performative dynamics of Filipino public culture.

[2] Derian, *Virtuous War*, 258. Since we cannot 'reverse history', as Derian argues, we nonetheless need to 'get beyond 9/11' by articulating a 'counter-factual experiment by reversing dates' (257). One such reversal of dates is 11/9, the date that marks the demolition of the Berlin Wall. In order to 'reclaim the dream of 11/9', Derian emphasizes that 'we must use counter-factuals to awake from the nightmare of 9/11 and to imagine plausible alternatives to the dominant narrative of terror' (258).

[3] Lavery, 'An Interview with Richard Schechner', 213–14. Recalling his production, Schechner relishes his terror tactics as a director by getting his actors to switch roles during the rehearsal process: 'The actress who thought she was playing Claire ended up playing Solange. The actress who thought she was playing Solange played Madame. Everybody was mad at me. They'd given up their time, learnt their lines and developed their characters, and now they were told to do something else. They didn't know who they were anymore. I thought that was very Genet' (217).

[4] Finburgh, 'An Interview with Jean-Baptiste Sastre', 195.

[5] Ibid., 194.

[6] Roces, '"The Maids" in Manila', 251.

[7] 'The Rights of Passage' was mounted in the interstitial space of the Republic of Malate's cavernous lobby through which audiences had to pass and encounter a deconstruction of the mythology of 'the maid' in the Filipino context. The first provocation of this installation was a large blow-up of a page from the *Oxford English Dictionary* which had defined 'maid' as 'Filipina' and 'domestic helper' in one of its early editions. Other signs of the maid's mythology included a double-decker bed with pornographic images of 'the maid' drawn from comics and pulp fiction. While representing the site of rape and sexuality, the bed also served as a shrine with candles and a phallus-like statue of the Virgin Mary. Other abstractions of 'the maid' were fetishized through intricate clusters of iconic objects – hair clips, combs, Vicks bottles, pins, needles – enclosed in vitrines. Dominating the installation were the two actors playing the maids (Melvin Lee and Phil Noble), silhouetted behind sickly-yellow nylon mosquito nets with Madame (Bart Guingona) positioned in between, playing the role of a security guard.

[8] Bersani, *Homos*, 160–61.

[9] Brygo, 'Always be punctual and don't count the work you are doing'.

[10] Valerie Chew, investigative report on 'Flor Contemplacion', *Singapore Infopedia*, National Library Board Singapore, 27 July 2009.

[11] Genet, 'Violence and Brutality', 172. In his superb notes, Dichy points out that Genet's 'affinities' to the Red Army Faction were less clearly spelled out than his political affiliations to the Black Panthers and the Palestinians. Dichy makes the important point that, 'More than the political thought [of the Red Army Faction], it was the terrorists' status as "indefensible" that inspired Genet to defend them' (348).

[12] Ibid., 172.

[13] Ibid., 171.

[14] Taussig, 'NYPD Blues', 176. Taussig draws on Benjamin's 'Critique of Violence'. In this dense essay, where the keyword '*Gewalt*' denotes both 'violence' and 'force', the power of the police is peculiarly double-edged in so far as it conflates 'violence for legal ends' and, simultaneously, the 'authority to decide these ends itself within wide limits' (286). In its denial of 'the separation of lawmaking and law-preserving', the police intervene arbitrarily in the lives of ordinary citizens 'for security reasons', even reducing the state to 'impotence' (286–87).

[15] Ibid., 178.

[16] Ibid., 177.

[17] Bello, 'The May 1st Riot'. While Bello is right in suggesting that the EDSA 3 movement demands a new explanation of 'the political', outside the rationales provided for 'people's power' in 'orthodox Leninist and western-oriented Social Democratic' discourses, it is unlikely that 'the core values of equality, democracy, liberty and decency' can be retained in the search for a 'populist' language of politics. A far more cogent theorization of movements like EDSA 3 is more likely to be found in Partha Chatterjee's reading of 'political society', which exists outside the norms of civil society, citizenship and the state, affirming a new ethics of illegality and communitarian rights. For Chatterjee's most recent study of political society, read *Lineages of Political Society*.

[18] Quoted in programme of *The Maids*, produced by PETA, Republic of Malate, Manila, November 2001.

[19] Read the arresting passage in *The Thief's Journal* where a formal delegation of Carolinas ('faggots', 'Daughters of Shame') walk in a procession through the streets of Barcelona, in 'shawls, mantillas, silk dresses and fitted jackets', towards the site of a 'demolished street urinal' on which they place a bunch of red roses (52–53).

[20] Benjamin, 'Eduard Fuchs', 27.

[21] Quoted in Adrian Kear's lucid exposition of Badiou's philosophy, 'Thinking out of Time', 99.

[22] Badiou, *Manifesto for Philosophy*, 127.

[23] Kear, 'Thinking out of Time', 100.

[24] Wickstrom, *Performance in the Blockades of Neoliberalism*, 16. All references to Badiou in the following two paragraphs are drawn from Wickstrom's text with the appropriate page numbers.

[25] Hallward, *Badiou*, 228; quoted in Lavery, *The Politics of Jean Genet's Late Theatre*, 183.

[26] As Lavery (ibid.) has examined in meticulous detail, Genet's realization of the 'equal worth of human beings' first gets illuminated not in relation to a political event of the magnitude that Badiou affirms, but through a more personal, strangely erotic and almost mystical experience, as he 'catches the eye of a decrepit old man sitting opposite him in a third-class railway carriage' (71). In this split-second encounter, Genet experiences a transference of bodies that connotes an equality of being.

[27] Betrayal, for Genet, begins with language itself: 'The moment I begin to speak, I am betrayed by the situation. I am betrayed by whoever listens to me, simply because of communication itself. I am betrayed by my choice of words.' Genet, Interview with Rüdiger Wischenbart and Layla Shahid Barrada, 244.

[28] On the refusal to acknowledge a 'solidarity with criminals', Genet says, 'if there

was such a thing as solidarity, that would be the beginning of morality, and thus the return to goodness . . . I had to betray the thief that I was in order to be the poet I hope to have become'. Genet, Interview with Madeleine Gobeil, 450–51.

[29] Genet's penchant to make a virtue out of betraying his closest friends is attributed by Bersani, in *Homos*, to the dynamics of 'anti-relationality', which is 'inherent in all homo-ness'. Even as the inherent anti-relationality of 'homo-ness' can be rejected as an essentialism, the betrayal of friendship in Genet's oeuvre contributes at an intensely paradoxical level to an intensification of love.

[30] Said, 'On Jean Genet's Late Works', 4.

[31] Ibid.

[32] Genet, Interview with Madeleine Gobeil, 457.

[33] Said, 'On Jean Genet's Late Works', 3.

[34] Ibid.

[35] Ibid.

[36] Genet, Interview with Rüdiger Wischenbart and Layla Shahid Barrada, 244.

[37] Quoted in Lavery, *The Politics of Jean Genet's Late Theatre*, 28.

[38] Ibid.

[39] Genet's production of *The Screens* created a furore in April and May 1966 at the Odéon-Théâtre de France, when '*ex-parachutistes* and *ancien combatants*, associated with the extreme right-wing movement Occident, threw smoke bombs and bottles onto the stage before proceeding to attack the cast.' While Carl Lavery provides a brilliant reconstruction of the event in his book, I would choose to work against the grain of his somewhat too rapturous interpretation of the incident as a political event with direct 'revolutionary' connection to Genet's later phase as a journalist and activist. Lavery, *The Politics of Jean Genet's Late Theatre*, 168–69.

On the contrary, in his caustic recollections of the event, Genet categorically says: 'What are referred to as poetic or artistic revolutions are not exactly revolutions. I don't believe they change the order of the world. Nor do they change the vision we have of the world. They refine vision, they complete it, they make it more complex, but they don't entirely transform it, the way a social or political revolution does . . . [P]olitical revolutions rarely, I might say never, correspond to artistic revolutions'. Genet, Interview with Hubert Fichte, 128. Later, in 1985, Genet specifically invoked – and undermined – the occupation of the Odéon-Théâtre de France by radical students in May 1968: 'If they had been real revolutionaries, they wouldn't have occupied a theatre, especially not the National Theatre. They would have occupied the law courts, the prisons, the radio. They would have acted as revolutionaries do, the way Lenin did'. Genet, 'Interview with Nigel Williams', 263.

[40] Derrida, 'Autoimmunity', 88.

[41] *Theatre Journal*, 54.1, 95–138. All references to the *TJ* forum in the remainder of the chapter will be indicated with the appropriate page numbers.

[42] Derrida, 'Autoimmunity', 90–91.

[43] In '9/11: Before, After, and In Between', Derian documents media responses to the World Trade Centre attacks in 1993 (179).

[44] Derrida, 'Autoimmunity', 89.

[45] In *Terrorist Assemblages*, Jasbir K. Puar elaborates at length on RAWA's strong protest against the appropriation of their struggle by the Feminist Majority

Foundation in the US, which assumes that it had 'single-handedly freed the women of Afghanistan from an oppression that started and ended with the Taliban' (6). Equating the Foundation with 'hegemonic, U.S.-centric, ego driven, corporate feminism', RAWA also accused the Foundation of omitting any reference to the 'abuse of women by the Northern Alliance', whose crimes were in no way less brutal than those of the Taliban. While highlighting this debate between two contexts of feminism, Puar also calls attention to Gayatri Chakravorty Spivak's timely reminder that RAWA itself is fundamentally aligned to middle-class prerogatives, 'altogether distant from the subaltern classes "in their own culture," whose possibilities of entering the "global feminist stage" are remote' (7).

46 Mamdani, *Good Muslim, Bad Muslim*, 10.

47 Significantly, there is just one reference to melodrama in the *TJ* forum in a specifically American socio-cultural context, where Marvin Carlson acknowledges that 'our [American] melodramatic construction of the events of September 11' has camouflaged the possibilities of 'tragic insight' (134). Without questioning this anti-melodramatic prejudice, so pervasive in theatre academia, Carlson affiliates his understanding of melodrama to what Peter Brooks, in his canonical study on *The Melodramatic Imagination* (1976), has defined as an 'intense emotional and ethical drama based on the manichaeistic struggle of good and evil'. Astutely, Carlson points out 'the easy reversibility' of the 'Manichean structures' informing the black-and-white, good-and-evil oppositional modalities of melodrama, whereby 'many in the world see the US as the powerful Darth Vader and Osama bin Laden as a kind of defiant Luke Skywalker' (134). While this reversal of roles is politically pertinent, one would need to question the assumptions underlying melodrama's seemingly innate and inflexible Manichaeism.

Instead of reducing melodrama to Manichaeism, it would be more productive to see its performative dynamics in a more affective register, as a structure of emotions, almost musical in effect, drawing on a visceral, sensory and larger-than-life amplification of the 'real'. The critical notion that melodrama can be regarded as the 'real' of our times has been investigated in depth in film studies, where the concept of melodrama has been stretched beyond its formal and structural antecedents in mid-nineteenth-century European stage melodrama, in which most contemporary theatre scholars are still entrapped. See, for instance, perspectives from film studies in Madhava Prasad, 'Melodramatic Polities?' and Ravi Vasudevan, *The Melodramatic Public*.

48 The historical and biographical material on Artaud in the following paragraphs is drawn from Stephen Barber's formative research on the Artaud archives, which has been deftly collated in his triad of books entitled *Anatomy of Cruelty*.

49 Correspondence with author, 28 June 2013.

50 Barber, 'Genet and Artaud'.

51 Richard Schechner's influential concept of the 'restoration of behavior' has received many theoretical reiterations, from his early essay entitled 'Restoration of Behavior' to later versions included in *Between Theater and Anthropology* and *Performance Studies*.

52 Phelan, 'Introduction', *The Ends of Performance*, 10.

53 Artaud, 'No More Masterpieces', 75.

54 Derrida, 'The Theater of Cruelty and the Closure of Representation', 14; emphasis in original.

[55] Artaud, 'The Theatre and the Plague', 27–28.
[56] Derrida, 'The Theater of Cruelty and the Closure of Representation', 7.
[57] Ibid., 17.
[58] Ibid., 16.
[59] Ibid.
[60] Ibid., 17.
[61] Virilio, *Unknown Quantity*, 63. Drawing on Hannah Arendt's thesis that 'Progress and catastrophe are the opposite faces of the same coin', Virilio emphasizes speed as the crucial factor behind 'man-made accidents', 'ecological accidents' and 'eschatological tragedies', which are linked to the 'computing of the genome and biotechnology' (24).
[62] Artaud, 'The Theater and the Plague', 17–18.
[63] Derrida, 'Autoimmunity', 97.
[64] Drawing on Cathy Caruth's *Unclaimed Experience*, Mick Wallis and Patrick Duggan, in their jointly edited issue 'On Trauma' for *Performance Research* (2011), suggest that 'there is a performative bent in traumatic suffering itself – the trauma symptom is a rehearsal, re-presentation, re-performance of the experience of the trauma-event, which irrupts unbidden into the sufferer's daily life' (2).
[65] Derrida, 'Autoimmunity', 97.
[66] Ibid.; emphasis in original.
[67] Kirshenblatt-Gimblett, 'Kodak Moments, Flashbulb Memories', 11.
[68] Ibid., 19.
[69] Ibid., 11.
[70] Ibid., 23.
[71] Ibid., 17–18.
[72] Ibid., 12.
[73] Among the censored creative expressions in the wake of 'September 11', one of the most arbitrary was the overnight censorship (and, in effect, liquidation) of a collective effort to build The International Freedom Center (IFC) on the World Trade Center site. Admittedly, the focus on freedom was a radical choice on the part of the IFC team. Ambitious in its panoramic global view encompassing the visions of Locke, Montesquieu, Jefferson, Gandhi, Martin Luther King, Sakharov and Nelson Mandela, among many other unknown freedom fighters of the world, the IFC blueprint was also committed to asking hard questions relating to racism, slavery, bonded labour and poverty. Can one be free if one is starving and without the basic right to food? Can one afford to ignore that Jefferson's ownership of slaves contradicted his vision of universal freedom? Can there be a balance between freedom and national security? Such troubling questions, which I was privileged to read in an unpublished document on the vision statement of IFC, were obviously unpalatable to the city authorities, who censored the museum on grounds of insensitivity to the dead and a lack of American patriotism.
[74] For hypothetical manifestos on these two museums and their political urgency, read Virilio's *Unknown Quantity*.
[75] Derrida, 'Autoimmunity', 94; emphasis in original.
[76] Campbell, 'Interview with Roberto Esposito', 53.
[77] Ibid., 51.

78 Ibid.

79 Ibid., 50. Esposito further elaborates that both '*immunitas*' and '*communitas*' originally derive from *munus*, which in Latin signifies 'gift', 'office' and 'obligation'. However, if *communitas* has 'positive connotations', *immunitas* has a 'negative' relationship to gift-giving. As Esposito explains, 'the members of a community are characterized by an obligation of gift-giving thanks to the law of the gift and of the care to be exercised toward the other'. 'Immunity', on the other hand, 'implies the exemption from or the derogation of such a condition of gift-giving' (50).

80 Ibid., 54.

81 The concept of autoimmunity is prefigured in Jacques Derrida's text on 'Faith and Knowledge'. According to Campbell, this reading of immunity ignites in reaction to the convergence of religion and tele-technoscience, which are fundamentally incompatible forces. Campbell, Interview with Roberto Esposito.

82 Derrida, 'Autoimmunity', 187–88, note 7.

83 Ibid., 95.

84 Ibid., 116.

85 Bell, 'Performance Studies in an Age of Terror', 56–58.

86 Ibid., 57. The 'Lucifer' connection in 'terror studies' is most prominently marked in Philip Zimbardo's *The Lucifer Effect*, which is an exhaustive study of torture and violence in Abu Ghraib *vis-à-vis* the Stanford Prison Experiment of 1971.

87 Quoted in Christopher Balme's contribution to the *TJ* forum, 115. All further references to the *TJ* forum in this chapter will be given in the text itself.

88 Artaud, *The Theatre and its Double*, 27–28.

89 Nandy, *Traditions, Tyranny, and Utopias*, 1.

90 Dolan, *Utopia in Performance*.

91 For an elegant and rigorous exposition of empathy, read Foster, *Choreographing Empathy*, where she maps the history of the concept in relation to interrelated genealogies of choreography and kinaesthesia.

92 Ibid., 129.

93 Ibid., 154.

94 Quoted in Nyers, 'The accidental citizen', 23.

95 Ibid.

96 Savarese, 'The Arabian Phoenix Goes to the Theatre', 40. The two ballerinas who died of burns were Clara Webster at London's Drury Lane Theatre in 1844, and Emma Livry at the Paris Opéra on 15 November 1862.

97 Read Saverese's erudite historiography on the fires in Naples and Buenos Aires, in 'The Arabian Phoenix Goes to the Theatre', 45–47 and 53–55. The reference to the 1856 fire in Covent Garden is mentioned in Alan Read's section on 'Combustion: Fire and safety', in *Theatre and Everyday Life*, 214.

98 Ibid., 217.

99 Saverese, 'The Arabian Phoenix Goes to the Theatre', 48. The European legislation of the 1881 fire prevention measures followed four major fires at the Franz Josef Theatre in Timisoara (30 April 1880), the Nice Opera (23 March 1881), the National Theatre of Prague (12 August 1881) and the Ring Theatre in Vienna (30 December 1881).

100 Artaud, Preface to *The Theatre and Its Double*, 13.

101 Badiou, *Ethics*, 42.

[102] Quoted in Reinelt's 'Theatre and Politics', 90.

## CHAPTER 2

[1] Benjamin, *The Arcades Project*, quoted in Sieburth, 'Benjamin the Scrivener', 23.

[2] For an elaboration on the dynamics of authentic identity *vis-à-vis* the masquerade of an assumed impostor, read Partha Chatterjee's ethnographic blockbuster, *A Princely Impostor?*. While teasing out the enigmas of identity by providing conflicting evidence as to how 'persons' are identified at once through juridical processes, and the more physical and psychological modes of identification in everyday life, Chatterjee focuses his argument around the key principle: 'If the reformed criminal law of our time is proceeded by the presumption that a person is innocent until proven guilty, then the modern governmental regimes must presume every individual to be an impostor until he or she is able to prove the contrary' (361–62).

[3] Goffman, *Stigma*, 11.

[4] Ibid.

[5] Quoted in Yoshino, 'The Pressure to Cover', 2.

[6] Ibid., 4.

[7] Ibid., 6.

[8] Ibid.

[9] Ibid.

[10] Ibid., 7.

[11] Ibid.

[12] Ibid., 8.

[13] For a comprehensive perspective on how secularism in India engages at a constitutional level with diverse religious practices in the public domain, along with a negotiation of tensions relating to the 'majority-minority syndrome', read Bhargava, *The Promise of India's Secular Democracy*.

[14] These provocative constructions have been sharply conceptualized and documented by Katrin Bromber and Benjamin Zachariah in their essay '"Muslims," "Islam," and the Ordering of the World'. Among the many colourful examples used to buttress their argument, the authors call attention to South Asian propagandists in the German POW camps of the First World War, like Bhupendranath Datta, the brother of Swami Vivekananda, who were *not* Muslims, but who "used Muslim aliases to act with Muslim prisoners . . . as well as for other political missions"' (1).

Bromber and Zachariah also call attention to the multiple identities of 'real' Muslims, notably the two brothers, Abdus Sattar Kheiri and Abdul Jabbar Kheiri, who were accused of 'fomenting *jihad* in India during the First World War in collusion with the Turkish and German governments' (10). Even as they self-identified as 'Muslims by faith' and were clearly marked as 'Indians by geographical origin', they were also known as 'Boy Scout instructors in Beirut, pro-Central Powers propagandists in Germany and Turkey, revolutionaries sent to the Soviet Union', among other avatars. Why, as Bromber and Zachariah argue, should one 'expect consistency and continuity in the biographical details of individuals' (10)?

The obvious answer is that in the larger context of how cultural and political identities get constructed in the Indian subcontinent, the category of 'individuals' cannot be valorized outside a broader matrix of communitarian considerations relating to family, caste and religion. Along with global cosmopolitan identities favoured by Bromber and Zachariah, non-liberal options in defining 'Muslim' identity also need to be placed on the agenda, along the lines of Talal Asad's *Formations of the Secular* and Saba Mahmood's *The Politics of Piety*.

[15] Appadurai, 'Dead Certainty', 226.

[16] These facts relating to the construction of 'Muslims' in colonial Indian census reports are cogently represented in Viswanathan, *Outside the Fold*, 153–63.

[17] For more background on Risley's 'pseudo-scientific' racism, read Crispin Bates, 'Race, Caste, and Tribe in Central India: The Early Origins of Indian Anthropometry', in *The Concept of Race in South Asia*, 1999, 241–49.

[18] Viswanathan, *Outside the Fold*, 156.

[19] Khan, 'Trespasses of the State', 180.

[20] Ibid., 181.

[21] Ibid.

[22] Ibid., 185.

[23] Mamdani, 'Making Sense of Political Violence in Postcolonial Africa', 31.

[24] Ibid.

[25] McKenzie, 'The Liminal Norm'.

[26] Mamdani, 'Making Sense of Political Violence in Postcolonial Africa'.

[27] Paul Rae, correspondence with author, 23 September 2010. Many thanks to him and Frederick Hertz for their insightful inputs on 'passing', a correspondence initiated by Ray Langenbach.

[28] Paul Rae, correspondence with author.

[29] Pugliese, 'Biotypologies of terrorism', 53.

[30] Ibid.

[31] Ibid., 56.

[32] Fanon, *Black Skin, White Masks*, 170. The vicious equation of 'the penis' with black men still continues to dominate the racial imaginary, most recently in South African painter Brett Murray's controversial painting, *The Spear* (2012), which showed South African President Jacob Zuma in a Lenin-like pose with his genitals exposed. What was meant to be a liberal and satirical critique of Zuma's sexism within a larger political disenchantment with the post-apartheid politics of the African National Congress landed up re-inscribing one of the worst racist stereotypes of black African men.

[33] Quoted in Puar, *Terrorist Assemblages*, 257.

[34] Ibid., xxiii.

[35] Ibid.

[36] Devji, *The Terrorist in Search of Humanity*. Devji makes a convincing case for the 'ordinariness' of the London bombers, none of whom attended mosques on a regular basis and who, unlike the September 11 bombers, made no attempt to 'dignify their last moments with some ritual or prayer' (72). Most of them attempted to 'rejoin mainstream British society prior to attacking it', some of them revelling in 'hitherto illicit pleasures of the flesh' (70). Their training did not take place in 'any secret hideout or religious lair, but in public spaces like gyms, youth clubs and rafting expeditions' (76).

[37] Puar, *Terrorist Assemblages*, 46.

[38] Ibid., 37.

[39] Ibid., 38.
[40] Ibid., 257.
[41] Quoted in Ahmed, 'Omar Saeed Sheikh the *sohna*, the *haseen*, the *jameel*, the beautiful', 9.

I am grateful to Shad Naved for contextualizing the words of appreciation for physical beauty – *haseen, jameel* (Urdu) and *sohna, mohna* (Hindi) – which draw on 'stock poetic descriptions of the beloved in the Persianate *ghazal* tradition and panegyric poetry. Such words are also used in devotional poetry addressed to the various Imams. The conceit of the cypress tree (*sarv* in Persian) and the various tropes for the beloved's complexion come from the stock repertoire of describing the beloved (often gendered male) in the *ghazal* tradition. The Indic epithets contrast with the classical Persianate allusions because of their folk tonality.' Communication with author, 9 January 2014.

[42] Lévy, *Who killed Daniel Pearl?*, 82.
[43] Ibid., 140.
[44] Ibid., 141–42.
[45] Ibid., 142.
[46] Ibid.
[47] Ibid., 83.
[48] Ibid., 151. The former hostage who provides Bernard-Henri Lévy with this information is Rhys Partridge.
[49] Ibid.
[50] Ibid.
[51] Quoted in Puar, *Terrorist Assemblages*, 38.
[52] Ibid.
[53] Geronimo's 'double death' is analysed by Joseph Pugliese in *State Violence and the Execution of the Law*, 52.
[54] Puar, *Terrorist Assemblages*, 166.
[55] Ibid., 179.
[56] Ibid.
[57] Ibid., 187.
[58] Ibid.
[59] Ibid., 189. Puar draws inspiration from Brian Massumi's insistence, expressed in *Parables for the Virtual*, on the 'ties to affective processes that mediate cognitive and epistemic knowing' (189). For Massumi, the body's 'visceral sensibility' *anticipates* 'the translation of the sight or sound or touch perception into something recognizable associated with an identifiable object' (189). More graphically, he provides the example of how the 'lungs spasm even before the senses cognate the presence of a shadow in a "dark street at night in a dangerous part of town"' (189).
[60] Ibid., 194.
[61] Ibid., 211. The keyword 'assemblage' in Puar's construction of 'terrorist assemblages' is inspired by Deleuze and Guattari's use of the word as a 'collection of multiplicities', which has 'neither subject nor object, only determinations, magnitudes, and dimensions that cannot increase in number without the multiplicity changing in nature' (211).

On the critical category of 'queerness', I would call attention to the risks in neutralizing the politics of naming diverse – and conflicting – queer identities in favor of an ubiquitous 'queerness', which could, in effect, diffuse actual political movements around sexuality. I am thinking in particular of the Indian subcontinent where emergent sexual cultures based around 'gay', 'lesbian', 'transgender' and 'MSM' (men who have sex with men) identities, among other indigenous sexual categories in Indian languages, are getting systematically subsumed under the global pressure of 'queer' as a politically correct, hegemonic category favoured by foreign funding agencies.

[62] Ibid., 212.

[63] Ibid.

[64] Ibid.

[65] Ibid., 215.

[66] Ibid., 212.

[67] Ibid., 220.

[68] Ibid.; my emphasis.

[69] Ibid., 222.

[70] Viswanathan, *Outside the Fold*, 163.

[71] Banerji, 'Legal Invention of an Artefact', 4153.

[72] For a succinct overview on the role of the RSS in relation to other parties and organizations affiliated to the Sangh Parivar of the Hindu Right, read Basu *et al.*, *Khaki Shorts, Saffron Flags.*

[73] Quoted in ibid., 8.

[74] For an inflected contextualization of this statement drawn from Savarkar's *Hindutva – Who is a Hindu?*, read Jaffrelot, 'The Idea of the Hindu Race in the Writings of Hindu Nationalist Ideologues in the 1920s and 1930s', 333–36.

[75] For background on the communalization of Muslim identity in the Indian context, read Pandey, 'Can a Muslim be an Indian?', and his edited collection of essays, *Hindus and Others.*

[76] The most comprehensive discussion on this subject is Mamdani's *Good Muslim, Bad Muslim.*

[77] Ibid., 15.

[78] This provocative statement by Faisal Devji in *The Terrorist in Search of Humanity* (70) is made in the context of suicide-bombing, and, more specifically, in the context of the London bombers' performativity in appearing 'normal', by participating in the social practices of mainstream British society, before blowing themselves up as 'good Muslims'.

[79] I am grateful to Siddharth Varadarajan, former editor of *The Hindu*, for confirming that Narendra Modi made this statement in his presence on *The Big Fight* show, anchored by Rajdeep Sardesai for Star News (NDTV), a week after 11 September 2001 and shortly before Modi became Chief Minister of Gujarat.

[80] For a detailed report on 'Genocide: Gujarat 2002', read the special issue of *Communalism Combat.* The facts presented in this issue are interrelated with two subsequent issues of *Communalism Combat*: 'The Gujarat Genocide: Ten Years Later' and 'Prosecute Modi'. I am grateful to Teesta Setalvad, co-editor of *Communalism Combat*, for her patient and detailed clarifications of a struggle in which she has increasingly become one of the most courageous and vocal critics of the Modi regime.

[81] This genealogy is mentioned in Arvind Narrain's useful legal perspective, 'Truth Telling, Gujarat and the Law', 222. All facts in this paragraph are drawn from Narrain's essay.

[82] Ibid., 223.

[83] Ibid., 220.

[84] Christophe Jaffrelot argues this position in his essay, 'The Idea of the Hindu Race in the Writings of Hindu Nationalist Ideologues in the 1920s and 1930s'. While Jaffrelot interprets the politics of the Hindu Right from the 1920s as a 'racism of domination' rather than a 'racism of extermination', the recent events in Gujarat suggest that a more virulent form of racism is in the making.

[85] Appadurai, 'Dead Certainty', 229.

[86] Sarkar, 'Semiotics of Terror', 2875.

[87] Appadurai, 'Dead Certainty', 240.

[88] Sarkar, 'Semiotics of Terror', 2876.

[89] Ibid.

[90] Appadurai, 'Dead Certainty'. All quotations from this essay will be marked in the main text with the appropriate page numbers.

[91] Mamdani, 'Making Sense of Political Violence in Postcolonial Africa'.

[92] In 'Dead Certainty', Appadurai refers to two major studies of violence: Allen Feldman's *Formations of Violence* and Liisa H. Malkki's *Purity and Exile*.

[93] While Appadurai claims in a footnote to his essay that his preferred use of 'person' over 'subject' does not foreclose references to 'the Hegelian idea of subjectivity, as well as its Foucauldian version in respect to violence and agency' (241), he does not provide any theoretical discrimination of 'person' from 'subject'. Such a discursive analysis could have complicated his reading of violence. Is a 'person', for instance, to be equated with the victim (now stripped of the abstraction of his or her ethnic label), and is the assailant a 'subject'? Or is the assailant a 'person' in his or her own right? When is a 'person' not a 'subject', and what are the conditions that catalyse this shift in identity?

[94] 'Oddly' primordialist, because I am aware of Appadurai's trenchant critique of primordialist readings of community in *Modernity at Large* with which I am in substantial agreement. However, in his reading of ethnic violence and the narrowing of its focus to the frenzied intimacy of killers and victims, locked as it were in an embrace of death, there are subtextual strains of primordialism to which Appadurai submits with no critical reservations.

[95] Mamdani, *When Victims Become Killers*.

[96] Mamdani, 'Making Sense of Political Violence in Postcolonial Africa', 34.

[97] 'Ethnocidal imaginary' is Dipesh Chakrabarty's phrase, which Appadurai acknowledges in a footnote to his essay along with a note of thanks to Chakrabarty for alerting him to 'the dangers of moving from global questions to globalizing answers'. Appadurai, 'Dead Certainty', 243.

[98] This horrifying detail is drawn from Liisa Malkki's (1995) research on Hutu refugees in Tanzania. It is duplicated with an almost eerie sense of retaliation in the violence inflicted on Tutsis by Hutus in the genocide of Rwanda in 1994. Victims become killers, in Mahmood Mamdani's unsparing construction, with the inevitable corollary of killers becoming victims in a relentless cycle of violence.

[99] Quoted in Sieburth, 'Benjamin the Scrivener', 23.

## CHAPTER 3

[1] Butler, 'Critically Queer', 17.

[2] According to Michael Humphrey, in his *The Politics of Atrocity and Reconcialiation*, 'Truth commissions, focusing on the suffering of individual victims, employ the language of psychology. The legacy of violence is supposed to be expelled from the individual through the cathartic experience of revealing and sharing it' (127). In contrast to this individually grounded, catharsis-driven revelation of the 'truth' of a particular suffering, which is witnessed and shared with the public in what appears to be a collective healing process, trials operate within a more legal framework.

[3] Unless otherwise indicated, I draw all statistics and facts relating to the genocide in Rwanda from Ananda Breed's rigorous research, which sets a model for performance theorists in her engagement with the social sciences. Apart from her numerous articles ('Performing *Gacaca* in Rwanda'; 'Performing the Nation'; 'Participation for Liberation or Incrimination?'), I am grateful to Breed for allowing me to draw on the manuscript of her book *Performing the Nation* before it is published in 2014, and for providing a helpful response to my chapter. In addition to Breed's research, I draw on the comprehensive reports by Penal Reform International, which has monitored the *gacaca* process with vigilance and critical accountability. Thanks to Mark Cumming and Tom Crowley of Trocaire for perspectives on the ground.

[4] My primary sources of information for the TRC in South Africa are Cole, *Performing South Africa's Truth Commission*; Krog, *Country of My Skull*; and Mamdani's seminal interventions ('From Justice to Reconciliation'; 'A diminished truth'; 'Making Sense of Political Violence in Postcolonial Africa'; *When Victims Become Killers*), among other publications indicated in the chapter. I am grateful to Premesh Lalu for his guidance over the years, and for his introduction to Adam Sitze's legal analysis of the TRC in *The Impossible Machine*, which has been particularly valuable in framing my analysis.

[5] Fullard and Rousseau, 'Uncertain borders', 225.

[6] Ibid. Fullard and Rousseau draw on Mahmood Mamdani's critique of the Truth and Reconciliation process ('A diminished truth'), which was one of the first to expose the double standards of the TRC's selectivity in highlighting a few political crimes at the expense of addressing apartheid's systemic violence.

[7] Cole, *Performing South Africa's Truth Commission*, 162.

[8] Breed, 'Performing the Nation', 49.

[9] Spivak, 'Righting Wrongs', 171.

[10] Todorov, 'Right to Intervene or Duty to Assist?', 37.

[11] Ibid., 47.

[12] Cole, *Performing South Africa's Truth Commission*, xvii.

[13] Ibid.

[14] Breed, 'Performing *Gacaca* in Rwanda', 306.

[15] Penal Reform International, *Eight Years On . . . A Record of* Gacaca *Monitoring in Rwanda*, 20.

[16] UN report quoted by Philip Zimbardo in *The Lucifer Effect*, 14.

[17] Ibid.

[18] Ibid., 13.

[19] E. Valentine Daniel, in his book *Charred Lullabies*, calls attention to 'the pornography of violence' in dealing with the ethnography of ethnic conflict (4).

[20] Daly, 'Between Punitive and Reconstructive Justice', 34. Quoted in Breed, 'Performing *Gacaca* in Rwanda', 307.

[21] Stockman, 'The People's Court', 22. Quoted in Breed, 'Performing *Gacaca* in Rwanda', 307.

[22] Penal Reform International, *Eight Years On . . . A Record of* Gacaca *Monitoring in Rwanda*, 13.

[23] Breed, *Performing the Nation*, 99.

[24] Lars Waldorf provides this translation in '"Like Jews Waiting for Jesus"', 186.

[25] This proverb in Kinyarawanda – '*Ukiza abavandimwe arararama*' – indicating the need for an open mind to settle disputes, is inserted in the official definition of *gacaca* offered by the National Service of Gacaca Courts. Quoted in Breed, 'Performing the Nation', 34.

[26] Waldorf, '"Like Jews Waiting for Jesus"', 186.

[27] Today's *Panchayati Raj* cannot be separated from the larger electoral politics of the Indian state, dominated by rival political parties, caste politics, reservations, and 'democratic' protocols like the mandatory 50 per cent reservation of seats for women in panchayats – protocols which have been adopted by some states, even as they are opportunistically exploited and blatantly abused by local patriarchies.

[28] Waldorf, '"Like Jews Waiting for Jesus"', 188.

[29] See Penal Reform International, *Eight Years On . . . A Record of* Gacaca *Monitoring in Rwanda*, 24–25, for a categorization of different crimes in post-genocide Rwanda. Not every crime, it should be emphasized, could be judged in a *gacaca* court. For instance, all crimes committed by the predominantly Tutsi-dominated Rwandan Patriotic Front could be tried only in the state courts, thereby predetermining, as Ananda Breed puts it succinctly, 'who is a victim and who is a perpetrator'. While the crimes committed by Hutus against Tutsi were summarily categorized as 'genocidal', similar crimes inflicted on the Hutus by the Tutsi were deemed as 'acts of war'.

[30] Ibid., 29. From this report, we learn that the voter turnout for the appointment of 2,50,000 judges in 2001 was as high as 87 per cent. Clearly, this mega-operation of appointing a grassroots judiciary far exceeds the more modest appointments of respected 'persons of integrity' by local communities in the earlier practice of *gacaca*.

[31] Correspondence with author, 22 January 2013. All facts in this paragraph are drawn from this correspondence.

[32] Citizenship in the reconstituted public sphere of Rwanda has been reinforced by a new national anthem, flag and slogan ('Tell what we have seen, admit what has been done, and move forward to healing').

[33] Schechner, *Performance Studies*, 22; quoted by Ananda Breed in *Performing the Nation*, 88.

[34] Interview with Ananda Breed, 11 January 2005, quoted in *Performing the Nation*, 98.

[35] Correspondence with author, 11 April 2012. I am grateful to Bill Worthen for enabling me to think through some of the political assumptions underlying 'restoration of behavior' in the context of genocide.

[36] Ibid.
[37] Schechner, 'Between Theater and Anthropology', 35.
[38] Ibid.
[39] Breed, 'Performing *Gacaca* in Rwanda', 308–09.
[40] Ibid., 308.
[41] Ibid.
[42] Ibid.
[43] Ibid.
[44] Ibid.
[45] Ibid.
[46] Ibid.
[47] Ibid., 309.
[48] Scott, 'The Evidence of Experience', 412.
[49] Breed, 'Performing the Nation', 33.
[50] Ibid., 41.
[51] Ibid.
[52] Ibid.
[53] Ibid.
[54] Ibid.
[55] Scott, 'The Evidence of Experience', 412.
[56] Ibid.
[57] Ibid.
[58] Breed, *Performing the Nation*, 7.
[59] Brigadier General Frank K. Rusagara, 'Gacaca: Rwanda's truth and reconciliation authority', *The New Times*, 16 May 2005; quoted by Ananda Breed in *Performing the Nation*, 88; emphasis added.
[60] Ibid.; emphasis added.
[61] Ibid.; emphasis added.
[62] Ibid.; emphasis added.
[63] Ibid., 98; emphasis added.
[64] Penal Reform International, *Eight Years On . . . A Record of* Gacaca *Monitoring in Rwanda*, 35.
[65] Ibid.
[66] Ibid., 31.
[67] Breed, *Performing the Nation*, 127, note 22.
[68] Sitze, *The Impossible Machine*. I am grateful to Premesh Lalu for calling my attention to this valuable analysis of the TRC process, and to Adam Sitze for allowing me to quote from his manuscript as the book was in the process of being published.
[69] Ibid., 19.
[70] Ibid., 20.
[71] Kentridge, 'Director's Note', viii–ix.
[72] Correspondence with author, 10 February 2013.
[73] Kentridge, 'Director's Note', ix.
[74] Interview with Albie Sachs; quoted in Cole, *Performing South Africa's Truth Commission*, 77.
[75] Ibid. In *Performing South Africa's Truth Commission*, Catherine Cole quotes from a critique by the journalist Mark Gevisser who points out that 'the hundreds

of hours of testimony [in the TRC] have been, almost by definition, banal and routine rather than heightened and dramatic. The halls are drafty and echoing; neon-light flattens all contours; amplified sound deadens voices and simultaneous translation renders testimony affectless' (12). A rare critique, I would have to say, that highlights the anti-theatricality of the TRC as a performative event.

[76] Interview with Albie Sachs; quoted in Cole, *Performing South Africa's Truth Commission*, 92.

[77] Ibid.

[78] Ibid.

[79] Ibid., 13.

[80] Braude, 'The Archbishop, the Private Detective, and the Angel of History', 61.

[81] Tutu, *No Future without Forgiveness*, 148; quoted in Cole, *Performing South Africa's Truth Commission*, 79.

[82] Quoted in ibid.

[83] Krog, *Country of My Skull*, 56.

[84] Ibid., 64.

[85] Cole, *Performing South Africa's Truth Commission*, 14.

[86] Ibid.

[87] Taylor, 'Writer's Note', iv.

[88] Cole, *Performing South Africa's Truth Commission*, 14.

[89] Ibid.

[90] Ibid., 16.

[91] Fullard and Rousseau, 'The TRC and the (un)making of public myths', 223; my emphasis.

[92] Ibid.

[93] In *Performing South Africa's Truth Commission*, Cole emphasizes that unlike the TRC Report, which was priced at 1500 rand, way beyond the economic reach of most South African citizens, Argentina's National Commission on the Disappeared published a best-selling book, *Nunca Más*, a 'report from Hell' (7). This abridged version of the 50,000-page original report had as many as thirteen editions between November 1984 and May 1986.

[94] Ibid., 123.

[95] Sanders, 'Truth, Telling, Questioning', 75.

[96] Margalit, 'Is Truth the Road to Reconciliation?', 64.

[97] Meiring, 'Truth before Justice and Reconciliation', 5–6.

[98] Cole, *Performing South Africa's Truth Commission*, 79.

[99] Ibid., 80.

[100] Yasmin Sooka, quoted in David Yutar, '"Prosecute Apartheid Politicians"', *Cape Argus*, 21 April 2006, inserted by Cole in *Performing South Africa's Truth Commission*, 123.

[101] Mary Burton, cited by H. Giliomee, *Cape Times*, 9 October 1997; quoted by Fullard and Rousseau, 'Uncertain borders', 225.

[102] Arendt, 'Truth and Politics'. In this essay, Arendt designates the act of 'lying' in the political realm as the unconscious prerogative of politicians, their 'second nature'. While the professional truth-teller is out of place in the world of politics, the liar is 'already in the midst of it' (250). An 'actor by nature', he refuses 'to say what is' (the truth-teller's responsibility); rather he 'says what is not so because he wants things to be different from what they are' (250). In short, he is a 'man

of action', which the truth-teller is not (250). The question is: How do we view the *actor* in theatre who is neither a professional truth-teller nor a politically motivated liar? It would seem that the actor's position is more liminal, as s/he is committed to conveying the truth of 'what is', while recognizing the illusion of what 'is not'.

103 Quoted by Arendt in 'Truth and Politics', 262.

104 Ibid.

105 Highlighting 'the social scientist's approach' of the TRC Report, Mark Sanders makes the cogent point that while the Report does not oppose 'narrative' (or 'personal') truth to 'falsehood', it nonetheless 'distances' itself from it 'by treating it as if it were something one could oppose to falsehood; or worse, by treating it provisionally, in effect, *as* falsehood.' See Sanders, 'Truth, Telling, Questioning', 74.

106 The Truth and Reconciliation Commission of South Africa Report, vol. 1, 112.

107 Ibid.

108 Krog, *Country of My Skull*, 361.

109 Ibid.

110 The intimacy of the conversation is framed – and distanced – by Krog's prefatory note that she is drawing on at least four texts: *Het Loon van de Schuld*, by Ian Buruma; *Guilt and Shame*, edited by Herbert Morris; *Imagination, Fiction, Myth*, by Johan Dagenaar; and *After the Catastrophe*, by Carl Jung (Krog, *Country of My Skull*, 359). These citations contribute to the meta-critical dimensions of Krog's conversation, which can also be read as an unacknowledged love story. For a Derridean reading of how Krog invents the figure of the beloved to complicate her mode of storytelling, read Sanders, 'Truth, Telling, Questioning', 80–83.

111 Krog, *Country of My Skull*, 360.

112 Ibid.

113 Gene Ray quotes Adorno's statements in revised translation in *Terror and the Sublime in Art and Critical Theory*, 66. Apart from *Negative Dialectics*, Ray draws extensively on Adorno's 1962 radio talk, 'Commitment' [Engagement], which was incorporated into *Notes to Literature* (1965), a critical response to Sartre's advocacy of *littérature engagée* in *What is Literature*? (1949).

114 Ibid.

115 Ibid.

116 Ibid., 65; emphasis added.

117 Ibid., 67.

118 In my essay, 'On failing failure', I have attempted to engage with 'positive failure' *vis-à-vis* Beckett's exhortation to 'fail better'.

119 Hannah Arendt's memorable statement from 'Organized Guilt and Universal Responsibility' (*Essays in Understanding*, 131) is quoted by Faisal Devji in *The Terrorist in Search of Humanity*, 35–36.

120 Ibid.

121 Penal Reform International, *Eight Years On . . . A Record of* Gacaca *Monitoring in Rwanda*, 64.

122 Butalia, *The Other Side of Silence*.

123 Das, *Life and Words*, 57.

124 Ibid.

125 Daniel, *Charred Lullabies*, 6.

[126] Ibid., 122.
[127] Ibid.
[128] See, for instance, my essay, 'Phantoms of the Other'.
[129] Das, 'The Spatialization of Violence', 201.
[130] Ibid.
[131] Ibid.
[132] Breed, 'Performing *Gacaca* in Rwanda', 311.
[133] Fullard and Rousseau, 'Uncertain Borders', 222.
[134] Tutu, *No Future without Forgiveness*, 209.
[135] Mamdani, 'From Justice to Reconciliation', 24.
[136] Ibid.
[137] Ibid.
[138] Ibid.
[139] Ibid.
[140] Quoted by Breed in *Performing the Nation*, 86.
[141] Ibid.
[142] Penal Reform International, *Eight Years On . . . A Record of* Gacaca *Monitoring in Rwanda*, 50.
[143] As the Director of the psychotherapeutic clinic, Centre de Guerison des Blessures de la Vie, Gasibirege is actively involved in the post-genocide/post-*gacaca* reconciliation process in Rwanda with a particular focus on domestic, sexual and intra-family violence within the larger context of the militarization of society in Rwanda today.
[144] Derrida, 'On Cosmopolitanism and Forgiveness', 32.
[145] Ibid., 33.
[146] Sitze, *The Impossible Machine*, 45.
[147] Ibid., 108.
[148] Tutu, *No Future without Forgiveness*, 34.
[149] Ibid.
[150] Quoted in Sitze, *The Impossible Machine*, 244.
[151] Ibid.
[152] Ibid., 245–46.
[153] Ibid.
[154] Quoted in Piet Meiring's address, 'Truth before Justice and Reconciliation', 9.
[155] Krog, *Country of My Skull*, 448.
[156] Ibid., 449.
[157] Ibid., 448.
[158] Ibid.
[159] Ibid. In 'Passages to Freedom', Achille Mbembe appears to endorse Krog's position relating to the re-fashioning of identities in South Africa by emphasizing: 'The categories "black", "Afrikaner", "white", "colored", and "Asian" are no longer pre-fixed' (6). While affirming that racism 'seems to be migrating into the realm of privately held beliefs' (6), Mbembe also acknowledges hard facts relating to the economic discrimination faced by the overwhelming majority of blacks in contemporary South Africa – a discrimination which indicates that residual racism is still very much alive.
[160] Ibid., 5.
[161] Ibid., 11. Mbembe questions the normative understanding of 'transformation'

as a 'set of policies designed by the government and the private sector to redress past racial discriminations and to redistribute wealth and income to previously disadvantaged groups' (7). On the contrary, he endorses the political economist Moeletsi Mbeki's position that transformation is less a 'policy' than a 'method perfected by the oligarchy to placate the political elites and to buy protection' (11).

162 Ibid., 7.

163 Ibid.

164 Ibid., 16.

165 Ibid.

166 Apart from classic texts by Amartya Sen like *Development as Freedom* (1999) and *India: Economic Development and Social Opportunity* (1995, co-authored with Jean Drèze), I would recommend more specific essays relating to Sen's capability theory and education, namely, Madoko Saito, 'Amartya Sen's Capacity Approach to Education: A critical exploration', *Journal of Philosophy of Education*, Vol. 17, Issue 1, 17–33, 2003; and Hans-Uwe Otto and Holger Ziegler, 'Capabilities and Education', *Social Work and Society: International Online Journal*, Vol. 4, No. 2, 2006.

167 Krishnamurti, 'On Time', 87.

168 Krishnamurti, 'Time and Transformation', 134.

169 Jayakar, 'Is there a Time of Non-Movement?', 250.

170 Ibid., 250–51.

171 *The Ending of Time* (1966) is a series of thirteen dialogues between Krishnamurti and the quantum physicist David Bohm. The keyword here is 'dialogue', the practice of which is rarely found in political and social forums, even as it is prioritized as a catchword by NGOs, Truth Commissions and social action groups advocating participatory democracy. Countering the apocalyptic resonance of its title, *The Ending of Time* is an extremely tentative, yet rigorous process of questioning that moves from abstract subjects like 'Ground of Being, Mind of Man', 'Mutation of the Brain Cells?' and 'Ending of "Psychological" Knowledge', towards a very fundamental question: 'Can Personal Problems be Solved and Fragmentation End?' The attention paid to the 'personal' calls attention to other possibilities of a 'reconciliation with the self', which are not readily found in the existing languages of the social sciences relating to transformation.

172 Jayakar, 'Is there a Time of Non-movement?', 254.

## CHAPTER 4

1 Benjamin, 'What is Epic Theatre? [First Version]', 5.

2 For more background on the role of community service in post-genocide Rwanda, read *Penal Reform International, Eight Years On ... A Record of* Gacaca *Monitoring in Rwanda*, 60–61.

3 Mander, 'Cry, the Beloved Country: Reflections on the Gujarat Massacre', available at http://www.sabrang.com/gujarat/statement/nv2.htm; quoted in Spivak, 'Terror', 98. Mander was an IAS (Indian Administrative Service) officer who resigned his job after the Gujarat genocide, acknowledging that he felt 'great shame at the abdication of duty of my peers in the civil and police administration' (98).

4 For a perceptive reading on the inscription of religion in Gandhi's political

thinking, read Ajay Skaria's dense and theoretically inflected essay, '"No Politics without Religion"'. Drawing on the key construction attributed to Gandhi – *sarva dharma sama bhava* ('equality of all religions') – Skaria makes the pertinent point that the 'equality' being advocated by Gandhi is 'neither formal nor substantive'; rather it is 'constituted by *dharma* rather than in a break with it' (183). At one level, this understanding of 'equality' works against the modern secularist (Nehruvian) appropriation of the equality of all religions, which the state assumes as an Archimedean position in which it is 'formally equidistant from all religions' (183). At a deeper level, however, Gandhi's belief in the equality of all religions is not merely a plea for the 'tolerance' of all religions. It demands nothing less than 'fighting religiously *for the other's religion*', which necessitates 'the giving of oneself . . . to *the other who remain[s] absolutely other*' (206; my emphasis).

5 Spivak, 'Terror', 83.

6 Ibid.

7 Ibid., 98.

8 Ibid.

9 This point has been finely enunciated by Rajeev Bhargava in his essay 'Between Revenge and Reconciliation', which frames the TRC process in South Africa *vis-á-vis* Gandhi's more personalized intervention as a one-man truth commission in the wake of the 1946 communal riots in Bengal.

10 In a normative register, Bhargava (ibid.) specifies trajectories of action that are needed before 'barbarism' can be tamed and transformed into 'reconciliation'. These necessary stages of action include 'restoration of peace – expression of grievances – their truthful assessment', leading to 'the acceptance of a *collective responsibility* for evil', which alone can produce 'the state of *forgiveness*, leading to *reconciliation*.' Arguably, in actual practice, the causalities written into these different stages are more disjunctive, if not likely to be disrupted.

11 Ajay Skaria, in '"No Politics without Religion"', captures the contradictions of Gandhi's multiple readings of 'religion'. On the one hand, there is a 'secularist' in Gandhi who declares that 'religion and State' should be 'separate', with religion being regarded as a 'personal affair' (174). On the other hand, Gandhi also affirms that 'there can be no politics without religion' (173). However, as he goes on to clarify in his general lament on the abandoning of *dharma*, 'I am not thinking of the Hindu or the Mahomedan or the Zoroastrian religion but of *that religion which underlies all religions*' (176; my emphasis). Gandhi, it could be said, is not arguing on ecumenical lines here, but on a different understanding of religion as *dharma*, which is opposed to the institutionalization of religion in our times.

12 Mahatma Gandhi, *Harijan*, 22 September 1946; quoted by Ajay Skaria in '"No Politics Without Religion"', 174.

13 Ibid.

14 Ibid., 173.

15 Gandhi, *Mohandas*, 334.

16 Ibid., 339–40.

17 Ibid., 339.

18 Buck-Morss, *Thinking Past Terror*, 15.

19 The religious component of *ahimsa* (non-violence) is undermined by Faisal Devji in his recent book, *The Impossible Indian: Gandhi and the Temptation of*

*Violence*, where the focus is on the almost indistinguishable affinities between violence and non-violence, the resistance of non-violence to being incorporated into history, and its refusal to regard life as an absolute value by seeking validation in the state of war. While I welcome the unsentimental and robust thrust of Devji's reading of non-violence, which is more precise and suggestive than his earlier attempt to link Gandhi with the Al-Qaeda, the basic problem has to do with his temptation to make good and evil so compatible that they almost fuse into each other. While one can agree with the proposition that evil requires goodness to sustain itself – indeed, Gandhi himself had emphasized this paradox in his reading of the Kauravas in the *Mahabharata* – it does not follow that 'evil itself, or rather the violence it [gives] rise to, [is] also a product of goodness and inextricable from it' (99).

For a more contextually grounded sifting of the contradictions in Gandhi's understanding of religion, I am grateful to Ajay Skaria for sharing sections of his forthcoming book, *Immeasurable Equality*, where he analyses in great depth the embeddedness of *ahimsa* (non-violence) in the larger epistemologies of *satya* (truth) and *daya* (compassion), drawing on Advaita philosophy and the Jain teachings of the seer Raychandbhai, respectively. From Skaria's reading, it becomes clear that the equation of *ahimsa* with sacrifice demands a complex engagement with multiple religious principles constituting – and complicating – Gandhi's renunciation of violence. Far from equating non-violence with sacrifice, it would be more accurate to acknowledge that sacrifice, for Gandhi, is merely one component in the larger philosophy of non-violence.

20 Devji, *Landscapes of the Jihad*, 132.

21 Devji, *The Terrorist in Search of Humanity*, 18.

22 Ibid.

23 Ibid.

24 All the views expressed in this paragraph are drawn from my correspondence with Tridip Suhrud, 25 April 2012. I am grateful to him for his insights, which are specifically grounded in traditional Hindu notions of self and being.

25 Read Rajmohan Gandhi's riveting account of the Great Calcutta Killings of 16–20 August 1946 and their turbulent aftermath, to get a fuller sense of Gandhi's *brahmacharya* as a radical action. Gandhi, *Mohandas*, 572–78.

26 Tridip Suhrud, correspondence with author, 25 April 2012. I extrapolate from this correspondence to highlight some of the points raised in this paragraph.

27 Letter to Narandas Gandhi, 28–31 July 1930, in *Complete Works of Mahatma Gandhi*, Vol. 49, 407; quoted by Ajay Skaria (7 July 2012) in the manuscript of his forthcoming book, *Immeasurable Equality*, part II, chapter 4, 13. I am grateful to Skaria for allowing me to draw on his formative research.

28 Ibid., 15.

29 Ibid.

30 Ibid.

31 Gandhi, 'Doctrine of the Sword', 15 August 1920, included in *The Collected Works of Mahatma Gandhi*, vol. 21, 160; quoted as an epigraph in Ajay Skaria, 'Living by Dying', 211. All references to Gandhi in the rest of this paragraph are drawn from Skaria's essay.

32 Devji, *The Terrorist in Search of Humanity*, 21.

33 In *Landscapes of the Jihad*, Devji quotes Osama bin Laden's 'Letter to America'

(November 2002) at length: 'You are a nation that exploits women like consumer products or advertising tools calling upon customers to purchase them . . . You then rant that you support the liberation of women . . . You have destroyed nature with your industrial waste and gases more than any other nation in history. Despite this, you refuse to sign the Kyoto agreement so that you can secure the profit of your greedy companies and industries . . . What happens in Guantánamo is a historical embarrassment to America and its values, and it screams into your faces – you hypocrites, "what is the value of your signature on any agreement or treaty?"' (128–29).

The challenge in reading any such text, I would submit, is not to take it too literally as a subversive form of liberal rhetoric, but to reveal the astuteness of its propaganda, which *mimics* the languages of humanism and global cosmopolitanism while *doing* something radically different. Devji is inaccurate, to my mind, when he affirms that bin Laden's call for 'universal justice puts al-Qaeda squarely in the ranks of global movements like environmentalism' (141). It would be more useful to interrogate the different – and conflicting – universalisms that are at stake in the age of terror.

34 Devji, *The Terrorist in Search of Humanity*, 19.

35 Devji, *Landscapes of the Jihad*, 94-95.

36 Ibid., 95.

37 Asghar Ali Engineer, communication with author, 24 April 2012. Even as Asghar-ji has passed on while my book was in the process of being completed, I remain grateful to him for providing so much clarity on the issues of martyrdom and suicide in the Islamic context. As a courageous social reformer of the Bohra community, he will be remembered as one of those rare Indian secularists committed to a critical inquiry of religious doctrine and practice.

38 Sharma and Suhrud, eds, *M.K. Gandhi's Hind Swaraj*, 63–64.

39 Ibid., 64.

40 Devji, *The Terrorist in Search of Humanity*, 48.

41 Ibid., 96.

42 Devji, *Landscapes of the Jihad*, 142.

43 May Jayussi, 'Subjectivity and Public Witness: An Analysis of Islamic Militance in Palestine', unpublished paper, 2004; quoted in Talal Asad, *On Suicide Bombing*, 48.

44 Ibid.

45 Sharma and Suhrud, eds, *M.K. Gandhi's Hind Swaraj*.

46 Gandhi's critique of Dhingra's act was first expressed in 'London', which was published in *Indian Opinion* on 14 August 1909. See Skaria, 'Living by Dying', 223, for a fuller elaboration.

47 These statistics are provided by Robert Pape, a political scientist, whose evidence is highlighted by Talal Asad in *On Suicide Bombing*, 54.

48 Ibid.

49 Ibid., 22.

50 Rose, 'Deadly Embrace'; quoted in ibid., *On Suicide Bombing*, 65–66.

51 Spivak, 'Terror', 95.

52 Ibid.

53 Asad, *On Suicide Bombing*, 66.

54 Mbembe, 'Necropolitics', 36.

[55] Ibid., 36–37.

[56] The construction of 'organs without bodies' is forcefully articulated in the conclusion to Gregory Whitehead's remarkable essay, 'The Forensic Theater Memory Plays for the Postmortem Condition', in Massumi, ed., *The Politics of Everyday Life*. Tellingly, the 'organs' documented in Whitehead's essay – 'the freeze-dried and plastinated lung of a crashed World War 1 aviator', 'the head of a defeated Parisian Communard, a single bullet hole staring bluntly from his cranium', and 'the hand of an anonymous Vietnam vet, blown off by a booby trap' (231–32) – are exhibited in the Armed Forces Medical Museum in Washington DC: a truly macabre post-mortem theatre. This museumization of 'horror' contrasts with Asad's reading in *On Suicide Bombing* of a macabre description of a suicide-bombing in Jerusalem, where the 'severed, bloody head of the suicide bomber, [sits] upright in the middle of the street like a Halloween fright mask' (70). Like Whitehead, Asad calls attention to the grotesque fragmentation of body parts while highlighting the 'construction' of the suicide-bombing event, whose narrative is intended to '[make] readers *feel* the horror of a suicide bombing' in the act of re-living its violence (70).

[57] All facts relating to *Three Posters* in this chapter are drawn from Rabih Mroué's introduction and the full text of the performance/video co-authored by him and Elias Khoury, published in *The Drama Review*, 182–91. A 'hit' on the international festival circuit between 2001–2002, *Three Posters* received its premiere at the Ayloul Festival in Beirut in September 2000.

[58] Ibid., 183.

[59] Ibid., 185.

[60] Asad, *On Suicide Bombing*, 16.

[61] Walzer, *Arguing About War*, 51; quoted in ibid.

[62] Walzer, *Arguing About War*, 45; quoted in ibid., 17–18.

[63] Ibid., 18.

[64] Ibid., 59.

[65] Ibid.; emphasis in original. One needs to add a caveat to Asad's trenchant critique of the 'right to kill', endorsed by Euro–American liberal thought, in so far as he is tacitly silent about other justifications of 'the right to kill' as demonstrated by terrorist organizations like the Al-Qaeda. Even as it is necessary to expose the violence of Western liberal democracies, and to create a critical space for 'non-liberal' assertions of freedom within religious and communitarian value systems in the Arab world and elsewhere, it is equally necessary to critique the aggressively anti-liberal ethos fuelling the performatives of extremist groups justifying violence for their own sectarian ends. This critique is tacitly missing in Asad's otherwise valuable contribution towards understanding the multiple epistemologies of terror.

[66] Aurobindo, 'Kurukshetra', 39.

[67] Ibid.

[68] Ibid., 40.

[69] Aurobindo, *The Complete Works of Sri Aurobindo*, vol. 35, 184.

[70] Ibid.

[71] The theatre/cemetery correlation is found in Jean Genet's notes to Roger Blin, the director of the French premiere of *The Screens*. In one of these references, included in the Gallimard publication of *Les Paravents*, Genet specifies: 'The

reader of these notes must not forget that the theatre where this work will be staged is constructed in a cemetery, that at this moment it's dark there and, somewhere, a dead body is being dug up to be reinterred elsewhere' (93). I am grateful to Stephen Barber for identifying and translating this reference.

72 Read the comprehensive and locally inflected reportage of an anthology entitled *Performance in Place of War*, edited by James Thompson, Jenny Hughes and Michael Balfour.

73 Hashmi, *The Right to Perform*. For a detailed account of how Hashmi was killed while protecting his actors from being attacked by a crowd of hoodlums in the Communist CITU (Centre of Indian Trade Unions) office in Jhandapur, read Sudhanva Deshpande's description of the attack culminating in Safdar Hashmi's death. This account was written on my request, and has been included in my essay 'Reclaiming the Right to Performance', 9.

74 Deshpande, 'The Killing of Juliano Mer Khamis', 2.

75 See, for instance, Ranjini Obeyesekere's study of *Sri Lankan Theater in a Time of Terror*.

76 Even while acknowledging the difficulties involved in covering theatre and performance practices in a state of war, it is hard to accept Obeyesekere's (ibid.) overly emphatic defence in focusing exclusively on Sinhala theatre. As she says, 'I make no reference in the book to Tamil theater in Sri Lanka. I do so partly because it is extraneous to my central theme of Sinhala theater and its "permitted space" which I see as a feature strongly influenced by Sinhala Buddhist culture; but also because by the 1980s the civil war in the North and the East and the tensions and disruptions it caused had made Tamil theater almost non-existent other than in small pockets in the North and the East' (15). It is difficult not to read an implicit nationalist bias in rejecting the fragmentary condition of Tamil theatre in its 'small', but, as Obeyesekere later acknowledges,'well-defined spaces' – spaces which were 'public' in their own right, as opposed to the 'permitted' national public sphere in which the Sinhala theatre was allowed to perform (15).

77 Read the section on the Third Sector movement in Brazil in the first chapter of my book, *In the Name of the Secular*.

78 Devji, *The Impossible India: Gandhi and the Temptation of Violence*, 109.

79 Pugliese, 'Penal Asylum', 7.

80 Pugliese, 'Subcutaneous Law', 29.

81 I am grateful to Ray Langenbach for calling my attention to the primacy of body art, as exemplified by the Viennese Actionists, Rudolph Schwarzkogler, Valie Export, Marina Abramović, Chris Burden and Stelarc, among others, who experiment 'responsibly', as he puts it, on 'the limits of body endurance, pain horizons, and death'.

82 Communication with Ray Langenbach, February 2013.

83 David Wojnarowicz's position on AIDS is sharply articulated in Rosa von Praunheim's documentary, *Silence=Death*, 1990.

84 More details on Mike Parr's 2002 performance on *Close the Concentration Camps* are available on http://www.themonthly.com.au/mike-parr-close-concentration-camps-2002-performance-art-masterpiece-anne-marsh.

85 Even as there is a widespread lineage of lip-sewing in demonstrations held across the world, including the United States, Bolivia, China and Australia, as Ray

Langenbach has indicated to me in personal correspondence, there is still a lot more research to be done on the significant differences of these actions within and across diverse political cultures. Besides, even as the cross-overs between 'life' and 'art' appear to be almost undifferentiated across cultural contexts, the political registers of lip-sewing as performed by artists for specific avant-garde audiences in the performance art circuit, and the protests of asylum seekers and refugees in 'real life' circumstances of borderline death, need to be more sharply differentiated.

86 Quoted by Pugliese in 'The Incommensurability of Law to Justice', 288.

87 Ibid., 291. Drawing on Derrida, *Of Hospitality*, 55, Pugliese highlights Levinas's concept of 'unconditional hospitality', which Derrida positions against the sovereignty of the state and in support of his own advocacy of 'sovereignty of oneself over one's home' (291).

88 Ibid., 292.

89 See Hage, *Against Paranoid Nationalism.*

90 In their book on *Performance and Cosmopolitics*, Helen Gilbert and Jacqueline Lo call attention to Aboriginal perspectives on hospitality that challenge 'the white establishment's claim to sovereignty by insisting on prior rights of custodianship' (207). In this regard they draw on a profound statement by Wadjularbinna, a Gungalidda elder from the Gulf of Carpentaria, who categorically claims: '[T]his is not John Howard's country, it has been stolen . . . taken over by the first fleet of illegal boat people' (207). Calling attention to the fact that all human beings share the same kinship system, Wadjularbinna insists that, 'Our religion and cultural beliefs teach us that everyone is a part of us and we should care about them . . . it's a duty' (208). The word 'duty' here has a strong resonance of *dharma* (righteous conduct) in the Indian context. However, unlike the caste determinants of *dharma*, Wadjularbinna draws on the kinship system shared by all 'humans', which provides the fundamental ground for hospitality.

91 Buck-Morss, *Thinking Past Terror*, 133.

92 Pugliese, 'Civil Modalities of Refugee Trauma, Death, and Necrological Transport', 158.

93 Ibid.

94 Ibid., 162.

95 Ibid.

96 Asad, *On Suicide Bombing*, 101.

97 Ibid.

98 Ibid.

99 'In Search of Justice', *Communalism Combat*, 6.

100 Ibid., 7.

101 Ibid., 8.

102 Ibid.

103 Derrida, 'Force of Law'; quoted by Pugliese in 'The Incommensurability of Law to Justice', 306.

104 I draw my understanding of Derrida's complex text on the 'Force of Law' from Gene Ray's lucid exposition in *Terror and the Sublime in Art and Critical Theory*, 109–15.

105 Ibid., 112.

106 Ibid., 114.

[107] Ibid., 113.
[108] Ibid., 112–13.
[109] Ibid., 114.
[110] Shulman, *Dark Hope*, 212.
[111] Ibid., 220.

## POSTSCRIPT

[1] See section on 'trauma' in 'Deconstructing terror', chapter 1.

[2] For a critique of 'self-radicalization', read Leeden, 'Self-Radicalization Chic'.

[3] From Praveen Swami's report on 'Norwegian mass killer's manifesto hails Hindutva' (2011), we learn how India figures in Breivik's 1,518-page manifesto through his deep regard for right-wing and Hindu nationalist organizations and parties. Not only does Breivik pledge 'military support' for 'the deportation of all Muslims from India', he even proposes that a 'Liberation of India Service Medal' should be awarded to those who assist India in this task. Significantly, despite his support for Hindu nationalism, there is no place for patriotic non-Muslim Asians in Breivik's vision of post-revolutionary Europe. At best, they will constitute a new 'servant class' living in 'segregated communities in pre-defined areas of each [European] city', working for twelve hours a day for a duration of six to twelve months, and then promptly flown back to their homelands. There are no equal rights for minorities in this brazen justification of racist apartheid.

[4] Pugliese, *State Violence and the Execution of the Law*, 27.

[5] Ibid., 161.

[6] These facts from Jane Mayer's 'A Dead Interrogation' in *The New Yorker*, 14 November 2005, are included in Zimbardo, *The Lucifer Effect*, 409–11.

[7] See Alex Danchev's chapter, 'It's All Fucked Up, or The Non-Fiction Horror Movie: The Cinema and the War on Terror', in *On Art and War and Terror*, 212. Harman's 'resistance' and 'civil disobedience' are explicitly suggested in Errol Morris's documentary film, *Standard Operating Procedure*, 2008.

[8] Danchev, *On Art and War and Terror*, 212.

[9] Ibid.

[10] Paul Lewis, 'Veteran Civil Rights Leader: Snowden acted in tradition of civil disobedience', *The Guardian*, 7 August 2013, available at http://theguardian.com, accessed on 18 August 2013. Subsequent clarifications in John Lewis's position are discussed in Andrew Beaujon's 'What exactly did John Lewis tell *The Guardian* about Edward Snowden?', *Poynter*, 12 August 2013, available at http://www.poynter.org; and Jim Galloway's 'Daily Jolt: John Lewis backs off comparison of Edward Snowden to Gandhi', *Political Insider*, 8 August 2013, available at http://www.ajc.com. Both articles accessed on 18 August 2013.

[11] This statement is included in John Junkerman's documentary, *Power and Terror: Noam Chomsky in Our Times*, 2002.

# BIBLIOGRAPHY


Adorno, Theodor, *Negative Dialectics*, London: Routledge, 1990.

Agamben, Giorgio, 'What Is the Contemporary?', in *What is an Apparatus? and Other Essays*, translated by David Kishik and Stefan Pedatella, Stanford: Stanford University Press, 2009.

Ahmed, Khaled, 'Omar Saeed Sheikh the *sohna*, the *haseen*, the *jameel*, the beautiful', *Indian Express*, 2 August 2002, 9.

Appadurai, Arjun, *Modernity at Large: Cultural Dimensions of Globalization*, New Delhi: Oxford University Press, 1997.

_____, 'Dead Certainty: Ethnic Violence in the Era of Globalization', *Public Culture*, Vol. 10, No. 2, 1998, 225–47.

Arendt, Hannah, 'Truth and Politics', in *Between Past and Future: Eight Exercises in Political Thought*, Harmondsworth: Penguin Books, 1993a.

_____, 'Organized Guilt and Universal Responsibility', in *Essays in Understanding, 1930–1954*, New York: Harcourt Brace & Co., 1993b.

Artaud, Antonin, 'The Theatre and the Plague', in *The Theatre and its Double*, translated by Mary Caroline Richards, New York: Grove Press, 1958, 15–32.

_____, 'No More Masterpieces', in *The Theatre and its Double*, translated by Mary Caroline Richards, New York: Grove Press, 1958, 74–83.

Asad, Talal, *Formations of the Secular: Christianity, Islam, Modernity*, Stanford: Stanford University Press, 2003.

_____, *On Suicide Bombing*, New York: Columbia University Press, 2007.

Aurobindo, Sri, 'Kurukshetra', in *Essays on the Gita*, Sri Aurobindo Birth Centenary Library, Vol. 13, Pondicherry: Sri Aurobindo Ashram Press, 1970.

_____, 'Remarks on Public Figures in India', in *The Complete Works of Sri Aurobindo*, Vol. 35, Pondicherry: Sri Aurobindo Ashram Press, 2006.

Austin, J.L., *How to do things with words*, edited by J.O. Urmson and Marina Sbisà, second edition, Cambridge: Harvard University Press, 1975.

Badiou, Alain, *Manifesto for Philosophy*, Albany: State University of New York Press, 1999.

_____, *Ethics: An Essay on the Understanding of Evil*, London: Verso, 2001.

Banerji, Anurima, 'Legal Invention of an Artefact: Birth of Identity in Asian America', *Economic and Political Weekly*, 5 October 2002.

Barber, Stephen, 'Genet and Artaud: The Crematorium and the Slaughterhouse', in *Genet: Flowers and Revolution*, London: Middlesex University Press, 1994.

_____, *Anatomy of Cruelty: Antonin Artaud, Life and Works*, Los Angeles: Sun Vision Press, 2013.

Basu, Tapan *et al.*, *Khaki Shorts, Saffron Flags*, New Delhi: Orient Longman, 1993.

Bates, Crispin, 'Race, Caste, and Tribe in Central India: The Early Origins of Indian Anthropometry', in Peter Robb, ed., *The Concept of Race in South Asia*, New Delhi: Oxford University Press, 1999.

Bell, John, 'Performance Studies in an Age of Terror', in Henry Bial, ed., *The Performance Studies Reader*, second edition, London: Routledge, 2007.

Bello, Walden, 'The May 1st Riot: Birth of Peronism Philippine-Style?', *Focus on the Philippines*, an electronic newsletter, Issue 20, 7 May 2001.

Benjamin, Walter, 'Critique of Violence', in *Reflections: Essays, Aphorisms, Autobiographical Writings*, translated by Edmund Jephcott and edited by Peter Demetz, New York: Harcourt Brace Jovanovich, 1978.

_____, 'Eduard Fuchs: Collector and Historian', in Andrew Arato and Eike Gebhardt, eds, *The Essential Frankfurt School Reader*, New York: Continuum Books, 1982.

_____, 'What is Epic Theatre? [First Version]', in *Understanding Brecht*, translating Anna Bostock, London: Verso, 1983, 1–13.

Bersani, Leo, *Homos*, Cambridge: Harvard University Press, 1995.

Bhargava, Rajeev, 'Between Revenge and Reconciliation: Gandhi and Truth Commissions', in *The Promise of India's Secular Democracy*, New Delhi: Oxford University Press, 2010.

Bharucha, Rustom, *The Question of Faith*, Hyderabad: Orient Longman, 1993.

_____, *In the Name of the Secular: Contemporary Cultural Activism in India*, New Delhi: Oxford University Press, 1998.

_____, 'Phantoms of the Other: Fragments of the Communal Unconscious', in *The Politics of Cultural Practice: Thinking Through Theatre in an Age of Globalization*, New Delhi: Oxford University Press, 2000.

_____, 'Muslims and Others: Anecdotes, Fragments, and Uncertainties of Evidence', *Economic and Political Weekly*, Vol. XXXVIII, No. 40, 4 October 2003a.

_____, 'Genet in Manila: Reclaiming the Chaos of Our Times', *Third Text*, Vol. 17, Issue 1, 2003b.

_____, 'Reclaiming the Right to Performance: Axioms and Evidence in Search of the New International', *On Civility*, *Performance Research*, Vol. 9, Issue 4, 3–17.

_____, 'On failing failure: A letter to Margaret', *Performance Research*, Vol. 17, No. 1, 2012, 101–04.

Bial, Henry, 'Introduction' to 'What is Performance?', *The Performance Studies Reader*, second edition, London: Routledge, 2007, 59–60.

Boal, Augusto, *The Theatre of the Oppressed*, London: Pluto, 1979.

Bonelli, Laurent, 'The Secret Lives of Terrorists', *Le Monde diplomatique*, October 2011, 12–13.

Braude, Claudia, 'The Archbishop, the Private Detective and the Angel of History: The Production of South African Public Memory and the Truth and Reconciliation Commission', *Current Writing*, Vol. 8, No. 2, 1996, 39–65.

Breed, Ananda, 'Performing *Gacaca* in Rwanda: Local Culture for Justice and Reconciliation', in Helmut Anheier and Yudhisthir Raj Isar, eds, *The Cultures and Globalization Series*, Vol. 1, London: Sage Publications, 2007, 306–12.

_____, 'Performing the Nation: Theatre in Post-Genocide Rwanda', *The Drama Review*, Vol. 52, No. 1, T 197, Spring 2008, 33–49.

_____, 'Participation for Liberation or Incrimination?', in T. Prentki and S. Preston, eds, *The Applied Theatre Reader*, London and New York: Routledge, 2009, 148–54.

_____, *Performing the Nation: Genocide, Justice, Reconciliation*, Kolkata, London and New York: Seagull Books, 2014.

Bromber, Katrin and Benjamin Zachariah, '"Muslims", "Islam", and the Ordering of the World', unpublished paper, ZMO, Berlin, 2011.

Brygo, Julien, 'Always be punctual and don't count the work you are doing: Filipino maids for export', *Le Monde diplomatique*, 8 October 2011.

Buck-Morss, Susan, *Thinking Past Terror: Islamism and Critical Theory on the Left*, London: Verso, 2003.

Butalia, Urvashi, *The Other Side of Silence: Voices from the Partition of India*, New Delhi: Penguin Books, 1998.

Butler, Judith, 'Critically Queer', *GLQ: A Journal of Lesbian and Queer Studies*, Vol. 1, No. 1, November 1993, 17–32.

_____, *Antigone's Claim: Kinship between Life and Death*, New York: Columbia University Press, 2000.

Campbell, Timothy, 'Interview with Roberto Esposito', *diacritics*, Vol. 36, No. 2, Summer 2006, 49–56.

Carlson, Marvin, 'What is Performance?', in Henry Bial, ed., *The Performance Studies Reader*, second edition, London: Routledge, 2007, 70–75.

Caruth, Cathy, *Unclaimed Experience: Trauma, Narrative and History*, Baltimore: Johns Hopkins University Press, 1996.

Chatterjee, Partha, *A Princely Impostor? The Kumar of Bhawal and the Secret History of Indian Nationalism*, New Delhi: Permanent Black, 2002.

_____, *Lineages of Political Society: Studies in Postcolonial Democracy*, New York: Columbia University Press, 2011.

Chatterji, Roma, *Speaking with Pictures: Folk Art and the Narrative Tradition in India*, New Delhi: Routledge, 2012.

Cole, Catherine M., *Performing South Africa's Truth Commission: Stages of Transition*, Bloomington: Indiana University Press, 2010.

*Communalism Combat*, 'Genocide: Gujarat 2002', March–April 2002.

_____, 'The Gujarat Genocide: Ten Years Later', February–March 2012.

_____, 'In Search of Justice', February–March 2012.

_____, 'Prosecute Modi', April–May 2012.

Daly, Erin, 'Between Punitive and Reconstructive Justice: The Gacaca Courts in Rwanda', *NYU Journal of International Law and Politics*, Vol. 34, 2002, 355–96.

Danchev, Alex, *On Art and War and Terror*, Edinburgh: Edinburgh University Press, 2011.

Daniel, E. Valentine, *Charred Lullabies: Chapters in an Anthopography of Violence*, Princeton: Princeton University Press, 1996.

Das, Veena, 'The Spatialization of Violence: Case Study of a "Communal Riot"', in Kaushik Basu and Sanjay Subrahmanyam, eds, *Unravelling the Nation: Sectarian Conflict and India's Secular Identity*, New Delhi: Penguin Books, 1996.

_____, *Life and Words: Violence and the Descent into the Ordinary*, Berkeley: University of California Press, 2007.

Derian, James Der, '9/11: before, after, and in between', in Craig Calhoun, Paul Price and Ashley Timmer, eds, *Understanding September 11*, New York: New Press, 2002.

_____, *Virtuous War: Mapping the Military–Industrial–Media–Entertainment Network*, second edition, New York: Routledge, 2009a.

_____, 'The Terrorist Discourse: Signs, states, and systems of global political violence', in *Critical Practices in International Theory: Selected Essays*, London: Routledge, 2009b, 68–96.

Derrida, Jacques, 'The Theatre of Cruelty and the Closure of Representation', *Theater*, Vol. 9, No. 3., Summer 1978, 7–19.

_____, 'Force of Law: The Mystical Foundation of Authority', *Cardozo Law Review*, Vol. 11, 1990, 920–1045.

_____, 'Faith and Knowledge: The Two Sources of "Religion" at the Limits of Reason Alone', in Jacques Derrida and Gianni Vattimo, eds, *Religion*, Cambridge: Polity Press, 1998.

_____, *Of Hospitality*, translated by Rachel Bowlby, Stanford: Stanford University Press, 2000.

_____, *On Cosmopolitanism and Forgiveness*, translated by Mark Dooley and Michael Hughes, London: Routledge, 2001.

_____, 'Autoimmunity: Real and Symbolic Suicides', in Giovanna Borradori, ed., *Philosophy in a Time of Terror: Dialogues with Jürgen Habermas and Jacques Derrida*, Chicago: University of Chicago Press, 2003.

_____, *Rogues: Two Essays on Reason*, translated by Pascale-Anne Brault and Michael Naas, Stanford: Stanford University Press, 2005.

Deshpande, Sudhanva, 'The Killing of Juliano Mer Khamis', *Newsclick*, New Delhi, 4 May 2011.

Devji, Faisal, *Landscapes of the Jihad: Militancy, Morality, Modernity*, London: Hurst & Company, 2005.

_____, *The Terrorist in Search of Humanity: Militant Islam and Global Politics*, New York: Columbia University Press, 2009.

_____, *The Impossible Indian: Gandhi and the Temptation of Violence*, Cambridge: Harvard University Press, 2012.

Dolan, Jill, *Utopia in Performance: Finding Hope at the Theatre*, Ann Arbor: University of Michigan Press, 2005.

Drèze, Jean and Amartya Sen, *India: Economic Development and Social Opportunity*, New Delhi: Oxford University Press, 1995.

Eagleton, Terry, *Holy Terror*, Oxford: Oxford University Press, 2005.

Engineer, Asghar Ali, *The Gujarat Carnage*, Hyderabad: Orient Blackswan, 2003.

Esposito, Roberto, *Bios: Biopolitics and Philosophy*, Minneapolis: University of Minnesota Press, 2008.

Fanon, Frantz, *Black Skin, White Masks*, translated by Charles Lam Markmann, New York: Grove Press, 1967.

Feldman, Allen, *Formations of Violence: The Narrative of the Body and Political Terror in Northern Ireland*, Chicago: University of Chicago Press, 1991.

Finburgh, Clare, 'An Interview with Jean-Baptiste Sastre', in Clare Finburgh, Carl

Lavery and Mari Shevtsova, eds, *Jean Genet: Performance and Politics*, London: Palgrave Macmillan, 2006, 193–98.

Foster, Susan Leigh, *Choreographing Empathy: Kinesthesia in Performance*, London: Routledge, 2011.

Fullard, Madeleine and Nicky Rousseau, 'Uncertain Borders: The TRC and the (un) making of public myths', *Kronos*, Vol. 34, Issue 1, November 2008, 215–39.

Gandhi, M.K., *The Collected Works of Mahatma Gandhi*, Vols 21 and 49, New Delhi: Publications Division, Government of India, 1958–1994.

Gandhi, Rajmohan, *Mohandas: A True Story of a Man, his People, and an Empire*, New Delhi: Penguin Books, 2006.

Genet, Jean, *The Thief's Journal*, translated by Bernard Frechtman, Harmondsworth: Penguin Books, 1965.

_____, *Prisoner of Love*, translated by Barbara Bray, New York: Picador, 1989.

_____, Interview with Madeleine Gobeil, recorded in Paris for *Playboy* magazine, in Edmund White, ed., *Selected Writings of Jean Genet*, Boston: Ecco Press, 1993, 447–60.

_____, 'America is Afraid', article written in August 1971 and published in *Le Nouvel Observateur*, included in Albert Dichy, ed., *The Declared Enemy: Texts and Interviews*, translated by Jeff Fort, Stanford: Stanford University Press, 2004, 89–90.

_____, Interview with Hubert Fichte, conducted on 19–21 December 1975 in Paris for the German daily *Die Zeit*, included in Albert Dichy, ed., *The Declared Enemy: Texts and Interviews*, translated by Jeff Fort, Stanford: Stanford University Press, 2004, 118–51.

_____, 'Violence and Brutality', first published in *Le Monde* on 2 September 1977, included in Albert Dichy, ed., *The Declared Enemy: Texts and Interviews*, translated by Jeff Fort, Stanford: Stanford University Press, 2004, 171–77.

_____, Interview with Rüdiger Wischenbart and Layla Shahid Barrada, recorded on 6–7 December 1983 in Vienna for Austrian Radio and the German daily *Der Zeit*, included in Albert Dichy, ed., *The Declared Enemy: Texts and Interviews*, translated by Jeff Fort, Stanford: Stanford University Press, 2004, 232–56.

_____, Interview with Nigel Williams, filmed in London in 1985 for BBC2, included in Albert Dichy, ed., *The Declared Enemy: Texts and Interviews*, translated by Jeff Fort, Stanford: Stanford University Press, 2004, 257–65.

Gilbert, Helen and Jacqueline Lo, *Performance and Cosmopolitics: Cross-Cultural Transactions in Australasia*, London: Palgrave Macmillan, 2007.

Goffman, Erving, *Stigma: Notes on the Management of Spoiled Identity*, London: Penguin, 1963.

Gopal, S., ed., *Anatomy of a Confrontation: The Babri Masjid–Ram Janmabhumi Issue*, New Delhi: Penguin, 1991.

Hage, Ghassan, *Against Paranoid Nationalism: Searching for Hope in a Shrinking Society*, Sydney: Pluto Press, 2003.

Hallward, Peter, *Badiou: A Subject to Truth*, Minneapolis: University of Minnesota Press, 2003.

Hashmi, Safdar, *The Right to Perform: Selected Writings of Safdar Hashmi*, New Delhi: SAHMAT, 1989.

Hughes, Jenny, *Performance in a Time of Terror: Critical Mimesis and the Age of Uncertainty*, Manchester: Manchester University Press, 2011.

Humphrey, Michael, *The Politics of Atrocity and Reconciliation: From Terror to Trauma*, London: Routledge, 2002.

Jackson, Shannon, 'Professing Performances: Disciplinary Genealogies', in Henry Bial, ed., *The Performance Studies Reader*, second edition, London: Routledge, 2007.

Jaffrelot, Christophe, 'The Idea of the Hindu Race in the Writings of Hindu Nationalist Ideologues in the 1920s and 1930s: A concept between two cultures', in Peter Robb, ed., *The Concept of Race in South Asia*, New Delhi: Oxford University Press, 1999.

_____, *Religion, Caste, and Politics in India*, New Delhi: Primus Books, 2010.

Jayakar, Pupul, 'Is there a Time of Non-Movement?', in *Fire in the Mind: Dialogues with J. Krishnamurti*, New Delhi: Penguin Books, 1995.

Kear, Adrian, 'Thinking Out of Time: Theatre and the Ethic of Interruption', *Performance Research*, Vol. 9, No. 4, 2004.

Kentridge, William, 'Director's Note: The Crocodile's Mouth', in Jane Taylor, *Ubu and the Truth Commission*, Cape Town: University of Cape Town Press, 1998.

Kirshenblatt-Gimblett, Barbara, 'Kodak Moments, Flashbulb Memories: Reflections on 9/11', *The Drama Review*, Vol. 47, No. 1, T 177, Spring 2003, 11–48.

Khan, Naveeda, 'Trespasses of the State: Ministering to Theological Dilemmas through the Copyright/Trademark', *Sarai Reader: Bare Acts*, New Delhi: Centre for the Study of Developing Societies, 2005.

Krishnamurti, Jiddu, 'On Time', in *Mind without Measure*, Madras: Krishnamurti Foundation India, 1983.

_____, 'Time and Transformation', *The First and Last Freedom*, London: Victor Gollancz, 1986.

Krishnamurti, Jiddu and David Bohm, *The Ending of Time*, Chennai: Krishnamurti Foundation India, 1996.

Krog, Antjie, *Country of My Skull*, London: Vintage Books, 1999.

Lavery, Carl, 'An Interview with Richard Schechner', in Claire Finburgh, Carl Lavery and Maria Shevtsova, eds, *Jean Genet: Jean Genet: Performance and Politics*, London: Palgrave Macmillan, 2006, 213–20.

_____, *The Politics of Jean Genet's Late Theatre: Spaces of Revolution*, Manchester: Manchester University Press, 2010.

Leeden, Michael, 'Self-Radicalization Chic: The Preposterous Theory du jour', *The Weekly Standard*, 20 May 2013; available at http://www.weeklystandard.com, accessed on 23 June 2013.

Lévy, Bernard-Henri, *Who killed Daniel Pearl?*, translated by James X. Mitchell, London: Duckworth, 2004.

Mahmood, Saba, *The Politics of Piety: The Islamic Revival and the Feminist Subject*, Princeton: Princeton University Press, 2004.

Malkki, Liisa H., *Purity and Exile: Violence, Memory, and National Cosmology among Hutu Refugees in Tanzania*, Chicago: University of Chicago Press, 1995.

Mamdani, Mahmood, 'From Justice to Reconciliation: Making Sense of the African Experience', *Crises and Reconstruction – African Perspectives: Two Lectures*, Nordiska Afrikainstitutet, 1997, 17–25.

_____, 'A diminished truth', *Siyaya*, No. 3, Spring 1998.

_____, 'Making Sense of Political Violence in Postcolonial Africa', in Okwui Enwezor *et al.*, eds, *Experiments in Truth*, Ostfildern-Ruit, Germany: Hatje Kantz Publishers, 2002a, 21–42.

_____, *When Victims Become Killers: Colonialism, Nativism, and the Genocide in Rwanda*, Princeton: Princeton University Press, 2002b.

_____, *Good Muslim, Bad Muslim: America, the Cold War, and the Roots of Terror*, New York: Pantheon Books, 2004.

Margalit, Avishai, 'Is Truth the Road to Reconciliation?', in Okwui Enwezor *et al.*, eds, *Experiments in Truth*, Ostfildern-Ruit, Germany: Hatje Kantz Publishers, 2002, 61–64.

Massumi, Brian, ed., *The Politics of Everyday Fear*, Minneapolis: University of Minnesota Press, 1993.

_____, *Parables for the Virtual: Movement, Affect, Sensation*, Durham: Duke University Press, 2002.

Mbembe, Achille, 'Necropolitics', translated by Libby Meintjes, *Public Culture*, Vol. 15, No. 1, Winter, 2003, 11–40.

_____, 'Passages to Freedom: The Politics of Political Reconciliation in South Africa', *Public Culture*, Vol. 20, No. 1, 2008, 5–18.

McKenzie, Jon, 'Genre Trouble: (The) Butler Did It', in Peggy Phelan and Jill Lane, eds, *The Ends of Performance*, New York: New York University, 1998.

_____, *Perform or Else: From Discipline to Performance*, London: Routledge, 2001.

_____, 'The Liminal Norm', in Henry Bial, ed., *The Performance Studies Reader*, second edition, London: Routledge, 2007.

Meiring, Piet, 'Truth before Justice and Reconciliation: The South African Experience', address at Centre for Dialogue and Reconciliation, New Delhi, 2 December 2000.

Mitchell, W.J.T., *Cloning Terror: The War of Images: 9/11 to the Present*, Chicago: University of Chicago Press, 2011.

Mroué, Rabih and Elias Khoury, 'Three Posters: A performance/video, introduction by Rabih Mroué', *The Drama Review*, Vol. 50, No. 3, T 191, Fall 2006, 182–91.

Mukhopadhyay, Bhaskar, *The Rumor of Globalization: Desecrating the Global from Vernacular Margins*, London: Hurst & Company, 2012.

Nair, Rukmini Bhaya, *Poetry in a Time of Terror: Essays in the Postcolonial Preternatural*, New Delhi: Oxford University Press, 2009.

Nandy, Ashis, *Traditions, Tyranny, and Utopias: Essays in the Politics of Awareness*, New Delhi: Oxford University Press, 1987.

Narrain, Arvind, 'Truth Telling, Gujarat and the Law', *Sarai Reader: Crisis/Media*, Delhi: Centre for the Study of Developing Societies, 2004.

Netanyahu, Benjamin, *Terrorism: How the West Can Win*, New York: Farrar, Straus and Giroux, 1986.

Nussbaum, Martha, *The Clash Within: Democracy, Religious Violence, and India's Future*, Cambridge: Harvard University Press, 2007.

Nyers, Peter, 'The Accidental Citizen: Acts of Sovereignty and (Un)making Citizenship', *Economy and Society*, Vol. 35, No.1, February, 2006, 22–41.

Obeyesekere, Ranjini, *Sri Lankan Theater in a Time of Terror: Political Satire in a Permitted Space*, New Delhi: Sage Publications, 1999.

*Oxford English Dictionary*, entry on 'terror'; available at http://www.oed.com, accessed on 14 September 2011.

_____, entry on 'performance'; available at http://www.oed.com, accessed on 20 November 2011.

Pandey, Gyanendra, 'Which of us are Hindus?', in *Hindus and Others: The Question of Identity in India Today*, New Delhi: Viking Books, 1993.

_____, 'Can a Muslim be an Indian?', *Comparative Studies in Society and History*, Vol. 41, No. 4, October 1999, 608–29.

Penal Reform International, *The Contribution of the* Gacaca *Jurisdictions to Resolving Cases Arising from the Genocide: Contributions, Limitations and Expectations of the Post-*Gacaca *Phase*, Final monitoring and research report on the *Gacaca* process by Penal Reform International, 2010a; available at http://www.penalreform.org, 1–56.

_____, *Eight Years On . . . A Record of* Gacaca *Monitoring in Rwanda*, 2010b; available at http://www.penalreform.org, 1–79.

Phelan, Peggy, 'Introduction', *The Ends of Performance*, New York: New York University, 1998.

Pinker, Steven, *The Better Angels of Our Nature: The Decline of Violence in History and Its Causes*, London: Allen Lane, 2011.

Prasad, M. Madhava, 'Melodramatic polities?', *Inter-Asia Cultural Studies*, Vol. 2, No. 3, 2001, 459–66.

Pugliese, Joseph, 'Penal Asylum: Refugees, Ethics, Hospitality', *Borderlands* e-journal, Vol. 1, No. 1, 2002.

_____, 'The Incommensurability of Law to Justice: Refugees and Australia's Temporary Protection Visa', *Law & Literature*, Vol. 16, Issue 3, Fall 2004, 285–311.

_____, 'Subcutaneous Law: Embodying the *Migration Amendment Act* 1992', *The Australian Feminist Law Journal*, Vol. 21, 2004.

_____, 'Biotypologies of Terrorism', *Cultural Studies Review*, Vol. 14, No. 2, September 2008, 49–66.

_____, 'Civil Modalities of Refugee Trauma, Death and Necrological Transport', *Social Identities*, Vol. 15, No. 1, January 2009, 149–65.

_____, 'Necroethics of Terrorism', *Law Critique*, Vol. 21, 2010, 213–31.

_____, *State Violence and the Execution of the Law: Biopolitical Caesurae of Torture, Black Sites, Drones*, London: Routledge, 2013.

Puar, Jasbir K., *Terrorist Assemblages: Homonationalism in Queer Times*, Durham: Duke University Press, 2007.

Ray, Gene, *Terror and the Sublime in Art and Critical Theory: From Auschwitz to Hiroshima to September 11 and Beyond*, New York: Palgrave Macmillan, 2005.

Read, Alan, *Theatre and Everyday Life: An Ethics of Performance*, London: Routledge, 1993.

Reinelt, Janelle, 'Theatre and Politics: Encountering Badiou', *Performance Research*, Vol. 9, No. 4, 2004.

Roces, Marian Pastor, '"*The Maids*" in Manila: A Thick Description', *FOCAS, Forum on Contemporary Art and Society*, Vol. 3, Singapore, 2002, 250–71.

Rose, Jacqueline, 'Deadly Embrace', *London Review of Books*, Vol. 26, No. 21, 4 November 2004, 21–24.

Said, Edward W., 'The Essential Terrorist', in Edward Said and Christopher Hitchens, eds, *Blaming the Victims: Spurious Scholarship and the Palestinian Question*, London: Verso, 1988, 149–58.

_____, 'On Jean Genet's Late Works', *Grand Street*, 1–7; available at http://www.grandstreet.com/gsissues/gs36/gs36c.html, accessed on 20 September 2010.

Sanders, Mark, 'Truth, Telling, Questioning: The Truth and Reconciliation Commission, Antjie Krog's *Country of My Skull*, and Literature after Apartheid', *Transformation*, No. 42, 2000, 73–91.

Sarkar, Tanika, 'Semiotics of Terror: Muslim Children and Women in Hindu Rashtra', *Economic and Political Weekly*, 13 July 2002.

Savarese, Nicola, 'The Arabian Phoenix Goes to the Theatre', *Performance Research*, Vol. 18, No. 1, 2013.

Schechner, Richard, 'Restoration of Behavior', *Performative Circumstances: From the Avant-Garde to the Ramlila*, Calcutta: Seagull Books, 1983, 164–237.

_____, *Between Theater and Anthropology*, Philadelphia: University of Pennsylvania Press, 1985.

_____, *Performance Studies: An Introduction*, London: Routledge, 2002.

Scott, Joan W., 'The Evidence of Experience', in Henry Abelove, Michele Aina Barale and David M. Halperin, eds, *The Gay and Lesbian Studies Reader*, London: Routledge, 1993, 397–415.

Sen, Amartya, *Development as Freedom*, New Delhi: Oxford University Press, 1999.

Seth, Pepita, *Reflections of the Spirit: The Theyyams of Malabar*, Ahmedabad: Mapin, 2006.

Sharma, Suresh and Tridip Suhrud, eds, *M.K. Gandhi's Hind Swaraj: A Critical Edition*, Hyderabad: Orient Blackswan, 2010.

Shulman, David, *Dark Hope: Working for Peace in Israel and Palestine*, Chicago: University of Chicago Press, 2007.

Sieburth, Richard, 'Benjamin the Scrivener', in Gary Smith, ed., *Benjamin: Philosophy, History, Aesthetics*, Chicago: University of Chicago Press, 1989.

Sitze, Adam, *The Impossible Machine: A Genealogy of South Africa's Truth and Reconciliation Commission*, Ann Arbor: University of Michigan Press, 2013.

Skaria, Ajay, '"No Politics without Religion": Of Secularism and Gandhi', in Vinay Lal, ed., *Political Hinduism: The Religious Imagination in Public Spheres*, New Delhi: Oxford University Press, 2009, 173–210.

_____, 'Living by Dying: Gandhi, Satyagraha and the Warrior', in Anand Pandian and Daud Ali, eds, *Ethical Life in South Asia*, Bloomington: Indiana University Press, 2010, 211– 31.

Sontag, Susan, 'Introduction', in *Antonin Artaud: Selected Writings*, translated by Helen Weaver, New York: Farrar, Straus and Giroux, 1976.

Spivak, Gayatri Chakravorty, 'Righting Wrongs', in Nicholas Owen, ed., *Human Rights, Human Wrongs*, Oxford: Oxford University Press, 2003, 168–227.

_____, 'Terror: A Speech After 9-11', *boundary 2*, Vol. 31, No. 2, Summer 2004, 81–111.

*Stanford Encyclopedia of Philosophy*, 'Terrorism', first published 22 October 2007, substantive revision 8 August 2011; available at http://plato.stanford.edu/entries/terrorism, accessed on 27 August 2011.

Stockman, Farah, 'The People's Court: Crime and Punishment in Rwanda', *Transition*, Vol. 9, No. 4, Issue 84, 2000, 20–41.

Swami, Praveen, 'Norwegian Mass Killer's Manifesto Hails Hindutva', *The Hindu*, 26 July 2011; available at http://www.thehindu.com, accessed on 23 June 2013.

Taussig, Michael, 'NYPD Blues', in *Walter Benjamin's Grave*, Chicago: University of Chicago Press, 2006, 175–87.

Taylor, Diana, 'Translating Performance', in Henry Bial, ed., *The Performance Studies Reader*, second edition, London: Routledge, 2007.

Taylor, Jane, 'Writer's Note', *Ubu and the Truth Commission*, Cape Town: University of Cape Town Press, 1998.

*Theatre Journal*, 'A Forum on Theatre and Tragedy in the Wake of September 11, 2001', edited by David Roman, Issue 54.1, 2002, 95–138.

Thompson, James, Jenny Hughes and Michael Balfour, eds, *Performance in Place of War*, London: Seagull Books, 2009.

Tilly, Charles, 'Terror, Terrorism, Terrorists', *Sociological Theory*, Vol. 22, No. 1, March 2004, 5–12.

Todorov, Tzvetan, 'Right to Intervene or Duty to Assist?', in Nicholas Owen, ed., *Human Rights, Human Wrongs*, Oxford: Oxford University Press, 2003, 28–48.

_____, *Torture and the War on Terror*, London: Seagull Books, 2009.

*Truth and Reconciliation Commission of South Africa Report*, 5 vols, Cape Town: Truth and Reconciliation Commission, 1998.

Tuck, Richard, *The Rights of War and Peace: Political Thought and International Order from Grotius to Kant*, Oxford: Oxford University Press, 1999.

Tutu, Desmond, *No Future without Forgiveness*, first edition, New York: Doubleday, 1999.

Varadarajan, Siddharth, *Gujarat: The Making of a Tragedy*, New Delhi: Penguin Books, 2002.

Vasudevan, Ravi, *The Melodramatic Public: Film Form and Spectatorship in Indian Cinema*, New Delhi: Permanent Black, 2010.

Virilio, Paul, *Unknown Quantity*, New York: Thames & Hudson, 2003.

_____, *The Original Accident*, Cambridge: Polity Press, 2007.

Viswanathan, Gauri, *Outside the Fold: Conversion, Modernity, and Belief*, New Delhi: Oxford University Press, 2001.

Waldorf, Lars, '"Like Jews Waiting for Jesus": Posthumous Justice in Post-Genocide Rwanda', in *Localizing Transitional Justice: Interventions and Priorities after Mass Violence*, Stanford: Stanford University Press, 2010, 183–202.

Wallis, Mick and Patrick Duggan, 'Editorial: On Trauma', *Performance Research*, Vol. 16, No. 1, 1–3.

Walzer, Michael, *Just and Unjust Wars: A Moral Argument With Historical Illustrations*, third edition, New York: Basic Books, 2000.

_____, *Arguing Against War*, New Haven and London: Yale University Press, 2004.

Whitaker, Brian, 'The Definition of Terrorism', *The Guardian*, 7 May 2001; available at http://www.guardian.co.uk, accessed on15 September 2010.

Whitehead, Gregory, 'The Forensic Theatre: Memory Plays for the Postmortem Condition', in Brian Massumi, ed., *The Politics of Everyday Fear*, Minneapolis: University of Minnesota Press, 1993, 229–44.

Wickstrom, Maurya, *Performance in the Blockades of Neoliberalism: Thinking the Political Anew*, London: Palgrave Macmillan, 2012.

Williams, Raymond, *Keywords: A Vocabulary of Culture and Society*, London: Fontana, 1985.

Worthen, W.B., 'Disciplines of the Text: Sites of Performance', in Henry Bial, ed., *The Performance Studies Reader*, second edition, London: Routledge, 2007.

Yoshino, Kenji, 'The Pressure to Cover', *The New York Times* magazine, 15 January 2006; available at www.nytimes.com, accessed on 1 January 2011.

Zimbardo, Philip, *The Lucifer Effect: Understanding How Good People Turn Evil*, New York: Random House, 2007.

Zück, Christina, 'The Captured Image', *frieze* magazine, Issue 3, Winter 2011–12.

# INDEX